FORCE

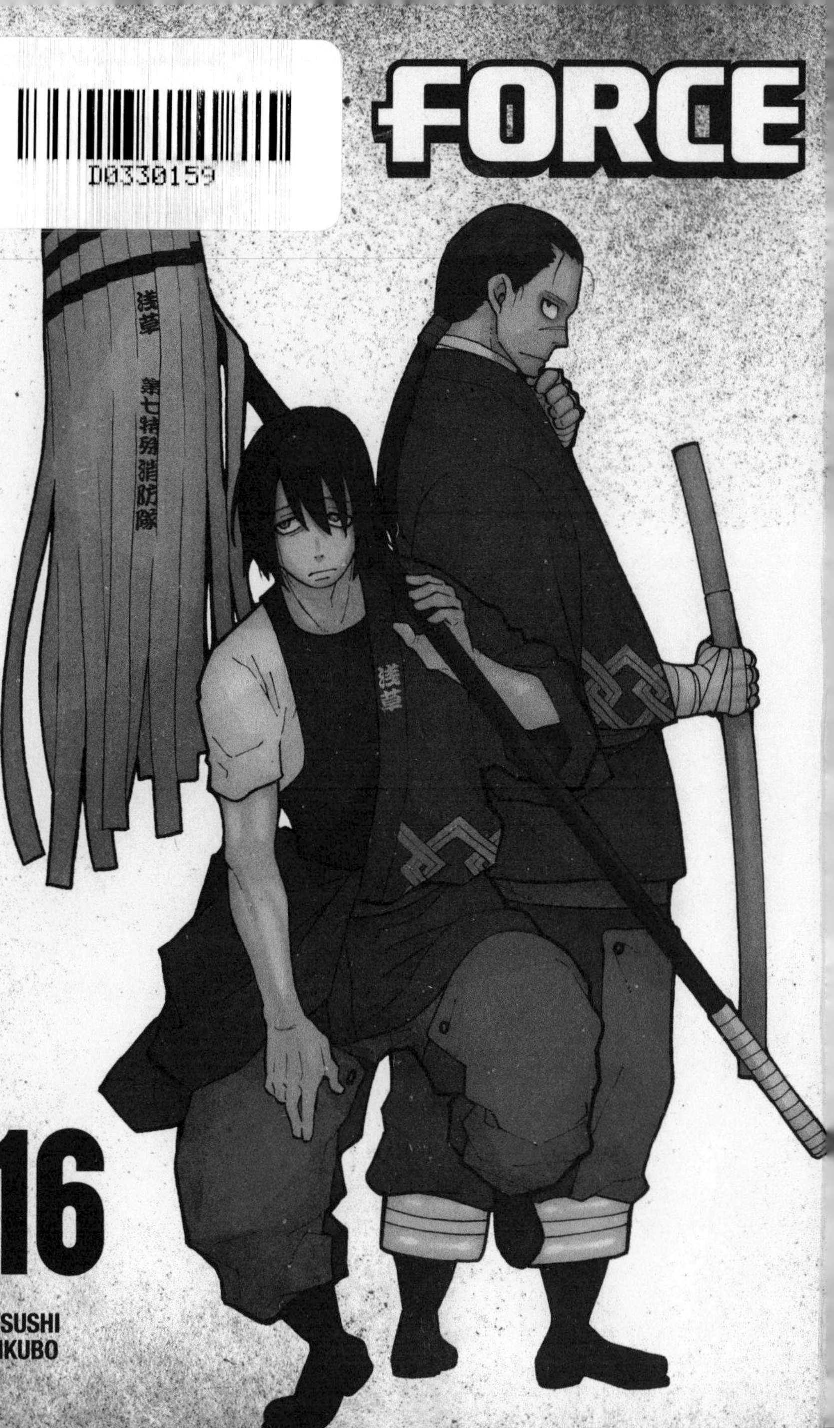
浅草
第七特殊消防隊
浅草

16

ATSUSHI
OHKUBO

Gray.

dominate
battle of
flame?

VOL.16

ATSUSHI OHKUBO

Blue.
White.

Who will
in the
crimson

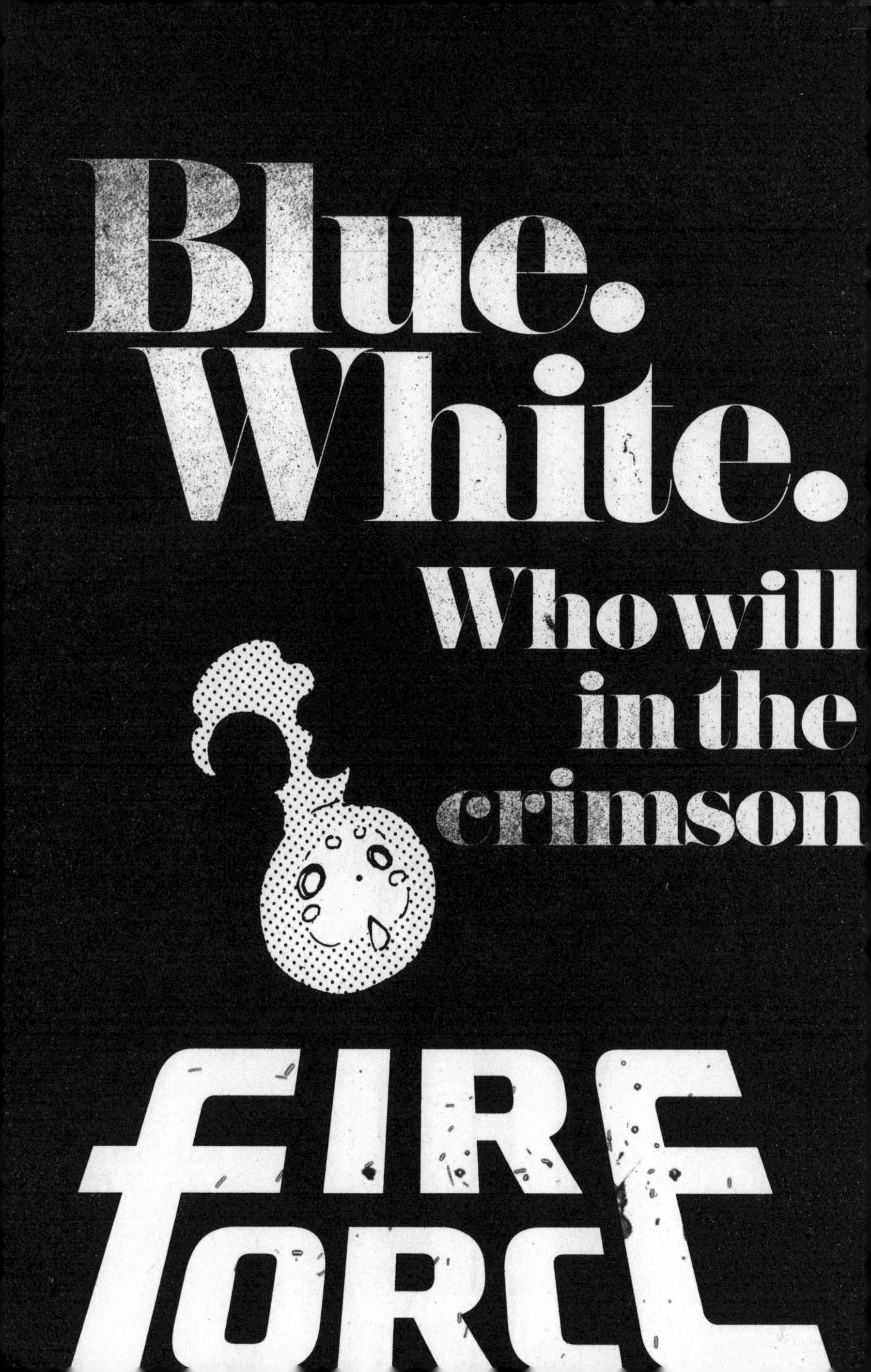

FIRE FORCE

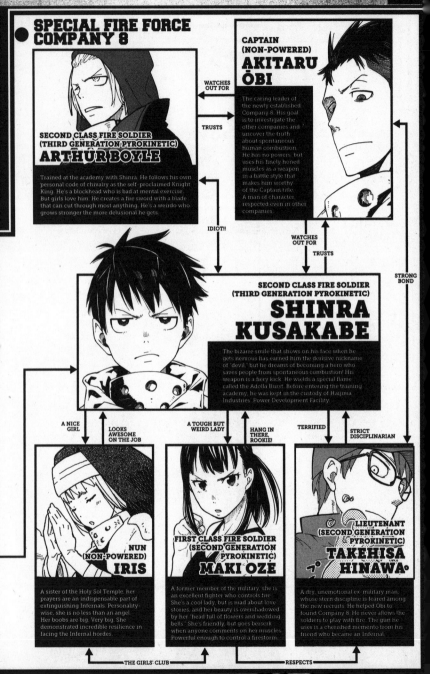

SPECIAL FIRE FORCE COMPANY 8

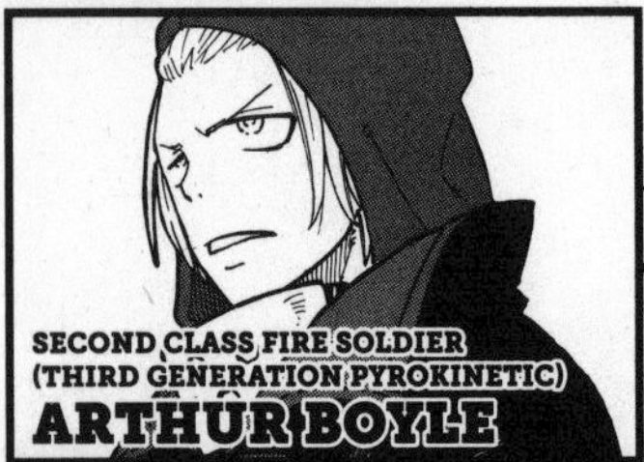

SECOND CLASS FIRE SOLDIER (THIRD GENERATION PYROKINETIC)

ARTHUR BOYLE

Trained at the academy with Shinra. He follows his own personal code of chivalry as the self-proclaimed Knight King. He's a blockhead who is bad at mental exercise. But girls love him. He creates a fire sword with a blade that can cut through most anything. He's a weirdo who grows stronger the more delusional he gets.

CAPTAIN (NON-POWERED)

AKITARU ŌBI

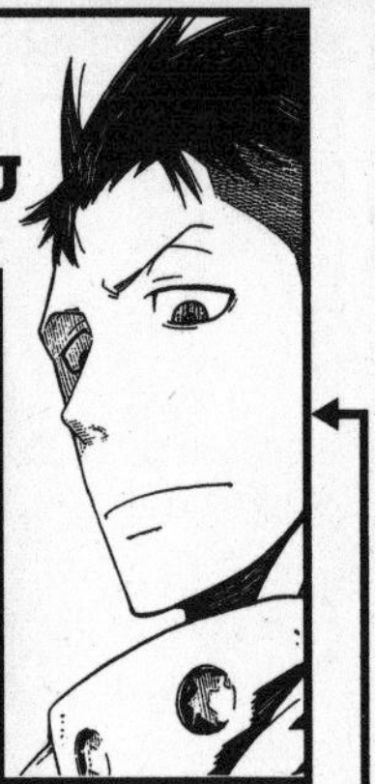

The caring leader of the newly established Company 8. His goal is to investigate the other companies and uncover the truth about spontaneous human combustion. He has no powers, but uses his finely honed muscles as a weapon in a battle style that makes him worthy of the Captain title. A man of character respected even in other companies.

WATCHES OUT FOR

TRUSTS

IDIOT!!

WATCHES OUT FOR

TRUSTS

STRONG BOND

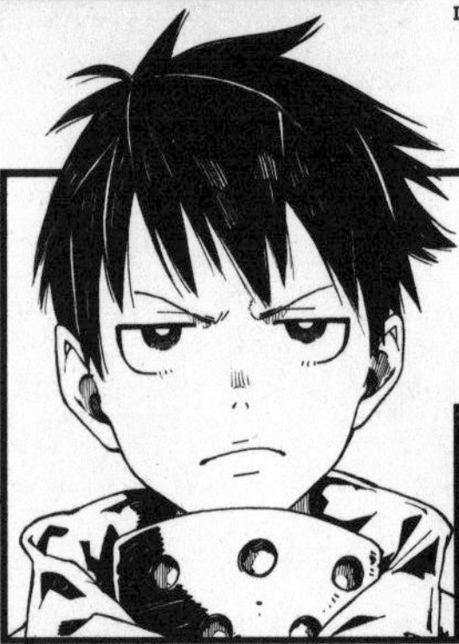

SECOND CLASS FIRE SOLDIER (THIRD GENERATION PYROKINETIC)

SHINRA KUSAKABE

The bizarre smile that shows on his face when he gets nervous has earned him the derisive nickname of "devil," but he dreams of becoming a hero who saves people from spontaneous combustion! His weapon is a fiery kick. He wields a special flame called the Adolla Burst. Before entering the training academy, he was kept in the custody of Haijima Industries' Power Development Facility.

A NICE GIRL

LOOKS AWESOME ON THE JOB

A TOUGH BUT WEIRD LADY

HANG IN THERE, ROOKIE!

TERRIFIED

STRICT DISCIPLINARIAN

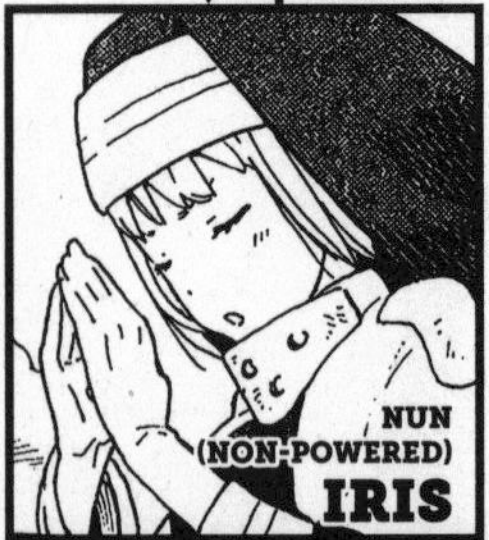

NUN (NON-POWERED)

IRIS

A sister of the Holy Sol Temple, her prayers are an indispensable part of extinguishing Infernals. Personality-wise, she is no less than an angel. Her boobs are big. Very big. She demonstrated incredible resilience in facing the Infernal hordes.

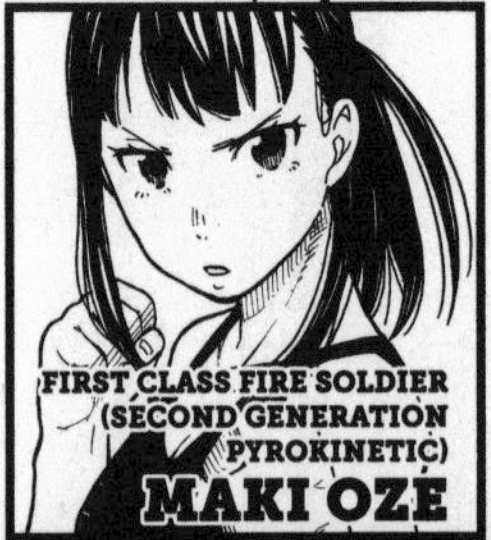

FIRST CLASS FIRE SOLDIER (SECOND GENERATION PYROKINETIC)

MAKI OZE

A former member of the military, she is an excellent fighter who controls fire. She's a cool lady, but is mad about love stories, and her beauty is overshadowed by her "head full of flowers and wedding bells." She's friendly, but goes berserk when anyone comments on her muscles. Powerful enough to control a firestorm.

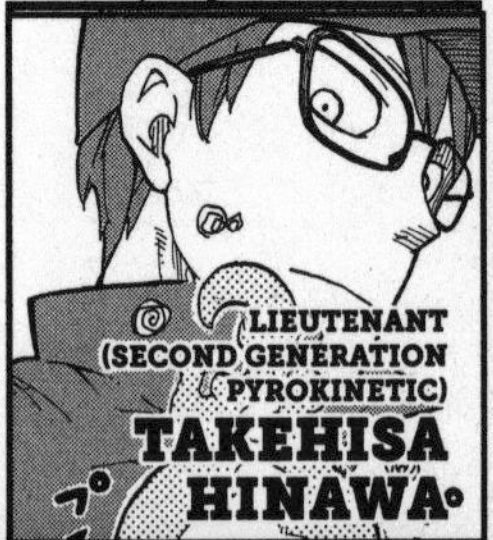

LIEUTENANT (SECOND GENERATION PYROKINETIC)

TAKEHISA HINAWA

A dry, unemotional ex-military man, whose stern discipline is feared among the new recruits. He helped Obi to found Company 8. He never allows the soldiers to play with fire. The gun he uses is a cherished memento from his friend who became an Infernal.

THE GIRLS' CLUB

RESPECTS

FOLLOWERS OF THE EVANGELIST

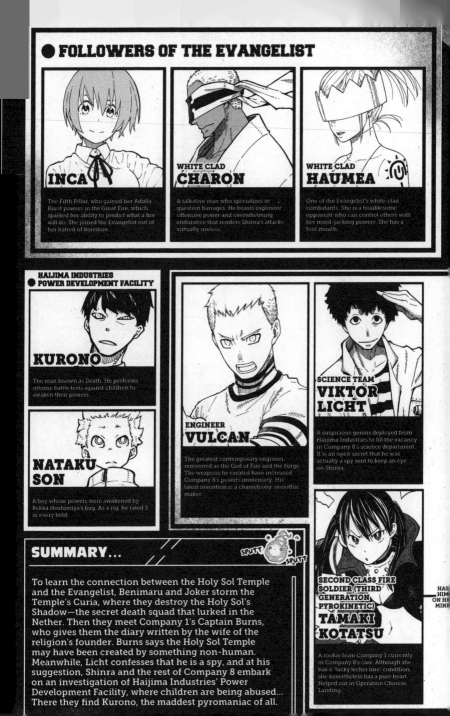

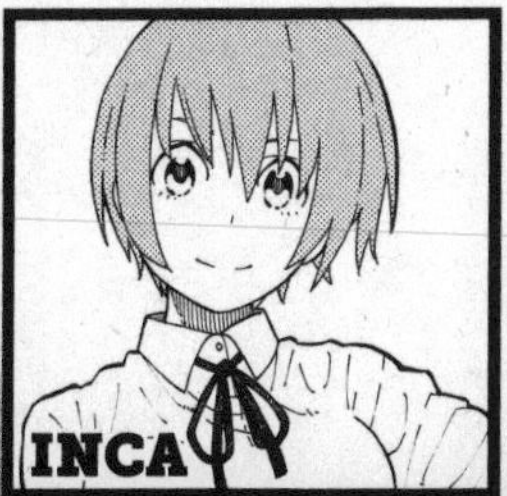
INCA

The Fifth Pillar, who gained her Adolla Burst powers in the Great Fire, which sparked her ability to predict what a fire will do. She joined the Evangelist out of her hatred of boredom.

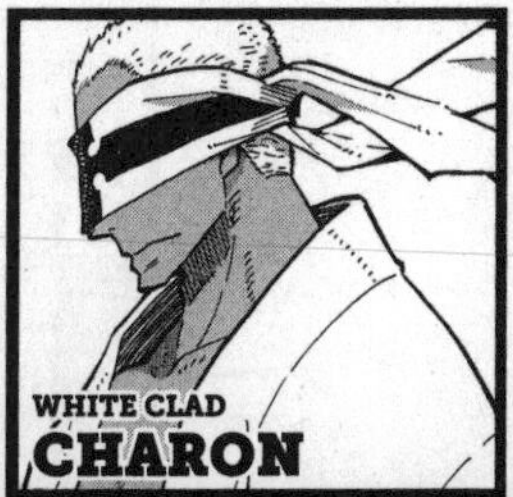
WHITE CLAD
CHARON

A talkative man who specializes in question barrages. He boasts explosive offensive power and overwhelming endurance that renders Shinra's attacks virtually useless.

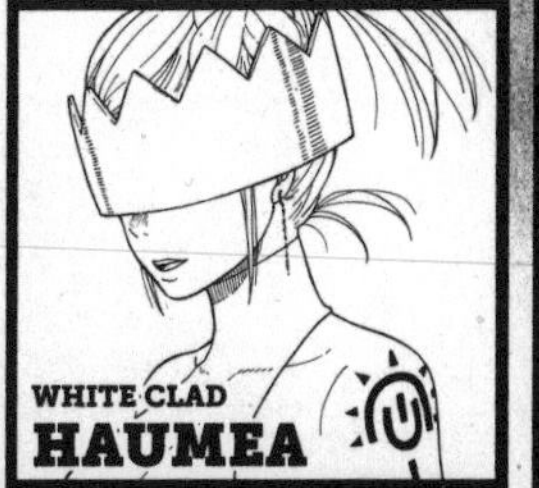
WHITE CLAD
HAUMEA

One of the Evangelist's white-clad combatants. She is a troublesome opponent who can control others with her mind-jacking powers. She has a foul mouth.

HAIJIMA INDUSTRIES POWER DEVELOPMENT FACILITY

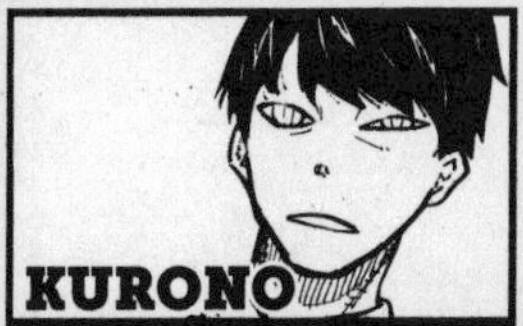
KURONO

The man known as Death. He performs intense battle tests against children to awaken their powers.

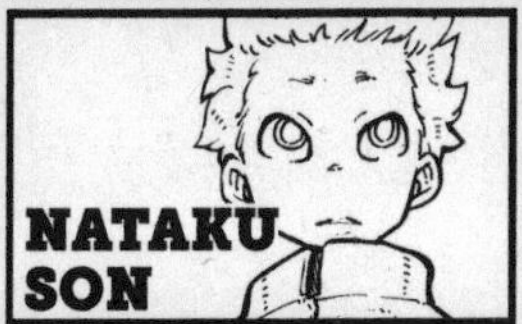
NATAKU
SON

A boy whose powers were awakened by Rekka Hoshimiya's bug. As a rig, he rated S in every field.

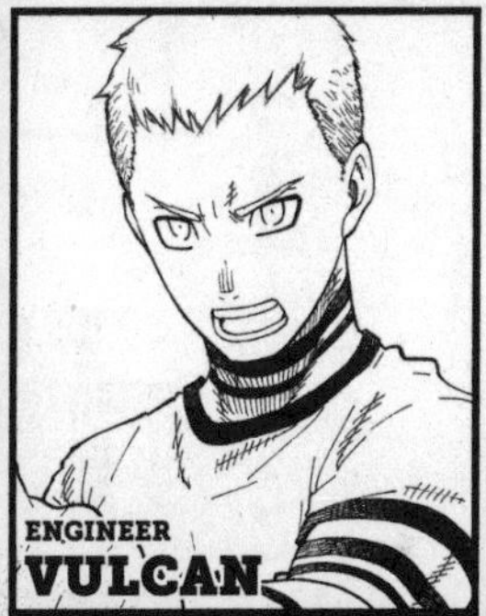
ENGINEER
VULCAN

The greatest contemporary engineer, renowned as the God of Fire and the Forge. The weapons he created have increased Company 8's powers immensely. His latest invention is a chameleony smoothie maker.

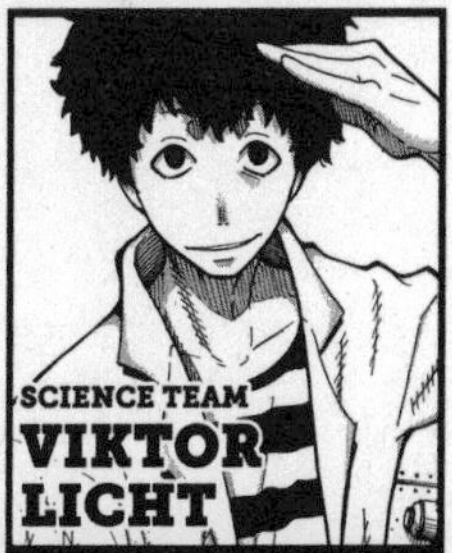
SCIENCE TEAM
VIKTOR
LICHT

A suspicious genius deployed from Haijima Industries to fill the vacancy in Company 8's science department. It is an open secret that he was actually a spy sent to keep an eye on Shinra.

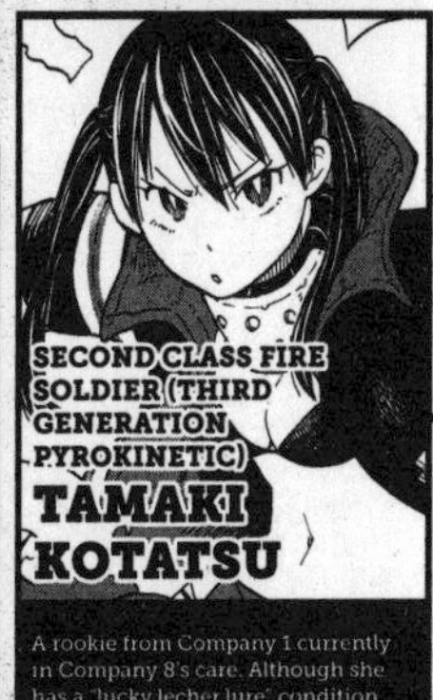
SECOND CLASS FIRE
SOLDIER (THIRD
GENERATION
PYROKINETIC)
TAMAKI
KOTATSU

A rookie from Company 1 currently in Company 8's care. Although she has a "lucky lecher lure" condition, she nevertheless has a pure heart. Helped out in Operation Chinese Landing.

SUMMARY...

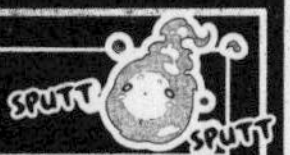
SPUTT
SPUTT

To learn the connection between the Holy Sol Temple and the Evangelist, Benimaru and Joker storm the Temple's Curia, where they destroy the Holy Sol's Shadow—the secret death squad that lurked in the Nether. Then they meet Company 1's Captain Burns, who gives them the diary written by the wife of the religion's founder. Burns says the Holy Sol Temple may have been created by something non-human. Meanwhile, Licht confesses that he is a spy, and at his suggestion, Shinra and the rest of Company 8 embark on an investigation of Haijima Industries' Power Development Facility, where children are being abused... There they find Kurono, the maddest pyromaniac of all.

FIRE FORCE 16
CONTENTS

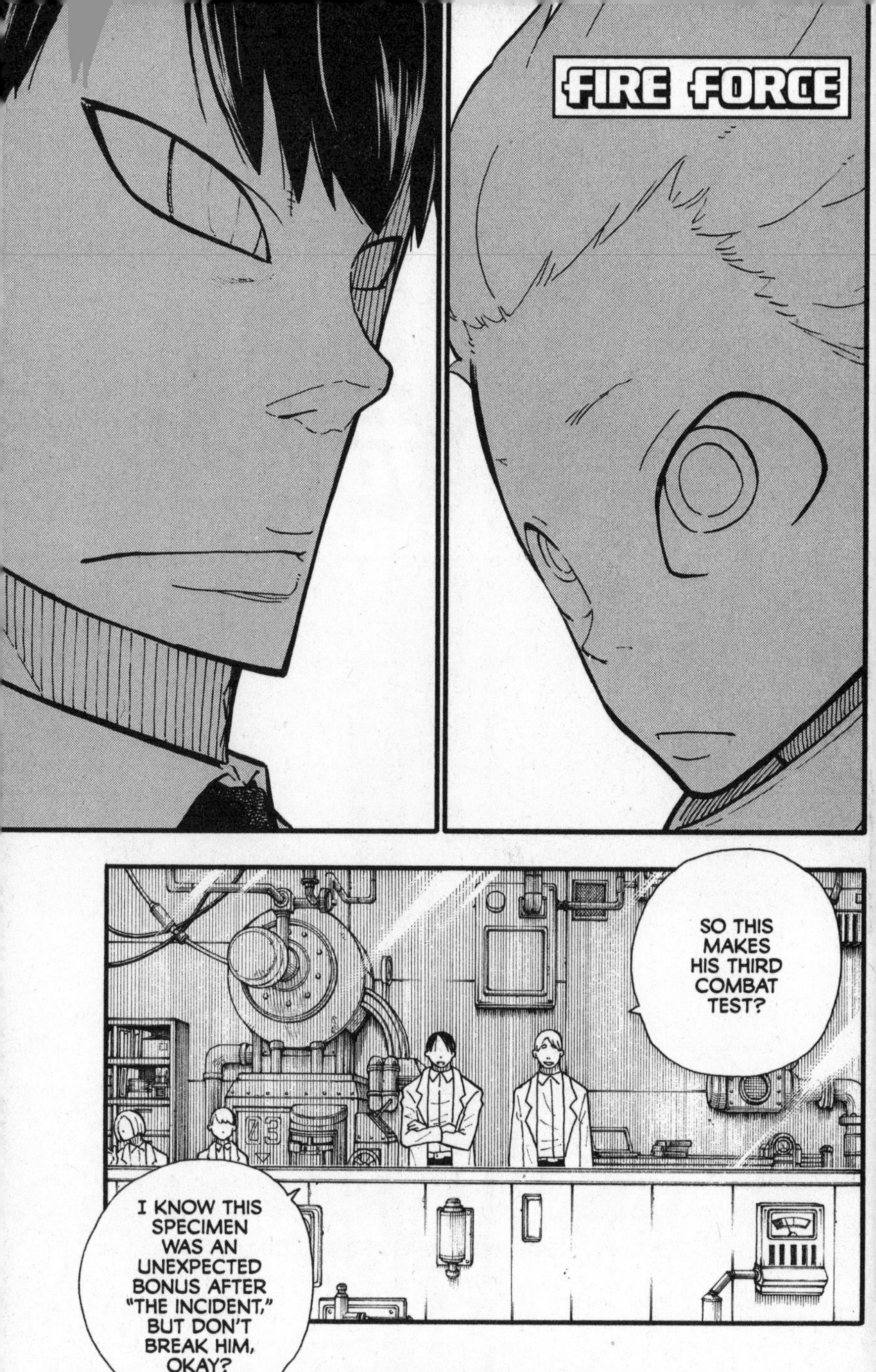
FIRE FORCE
SO THIS MAKES HIS THIRD COMBAT TEST?
I KNOW THIS SPECIMEN WAS AN UNEXPECTED BONUS AFTER "THE INCIDENT," BUT DON'T BREAK HIM, OKAY?

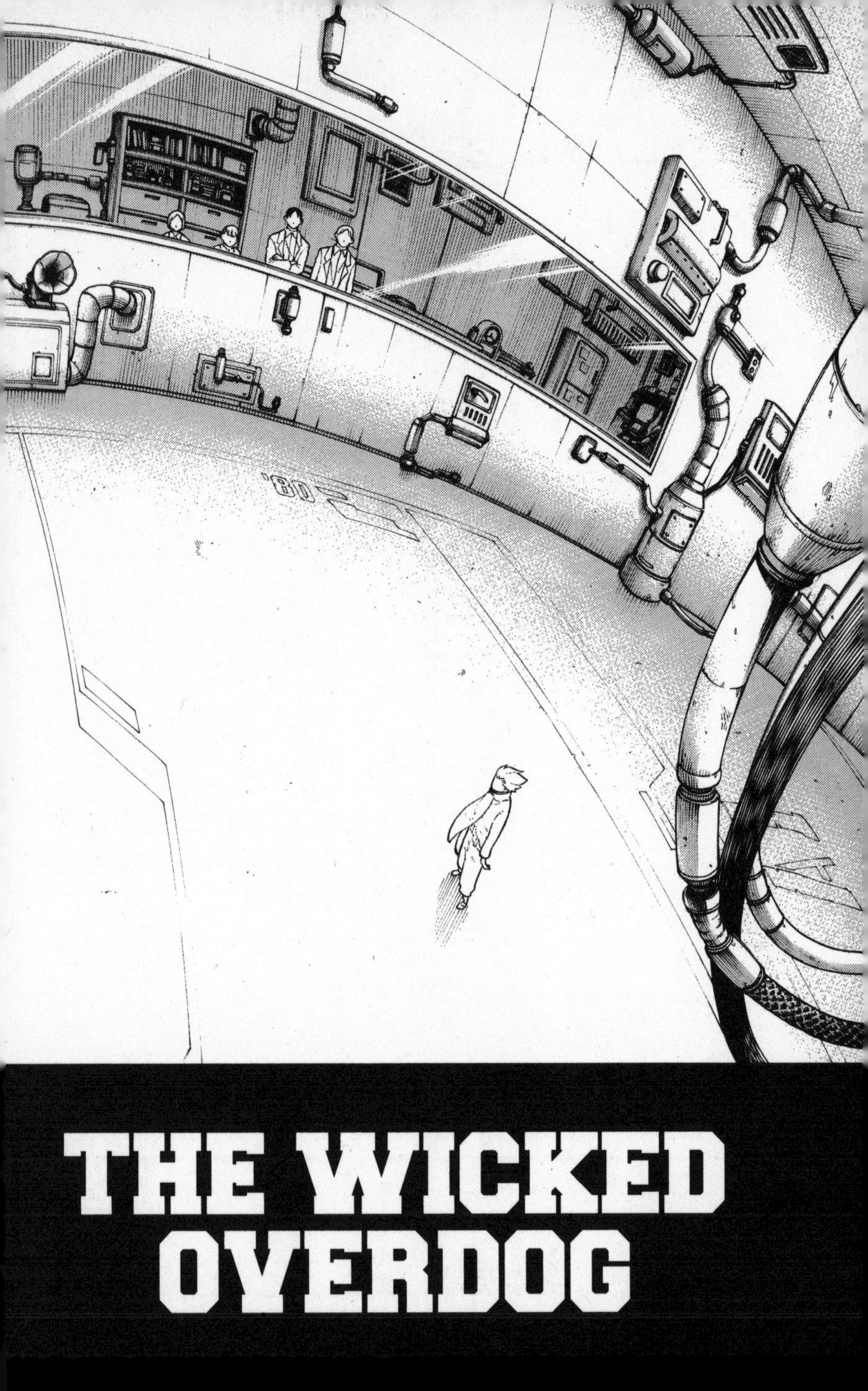

THE WICKED OVERDOG

CHAPTER CXXXIII:

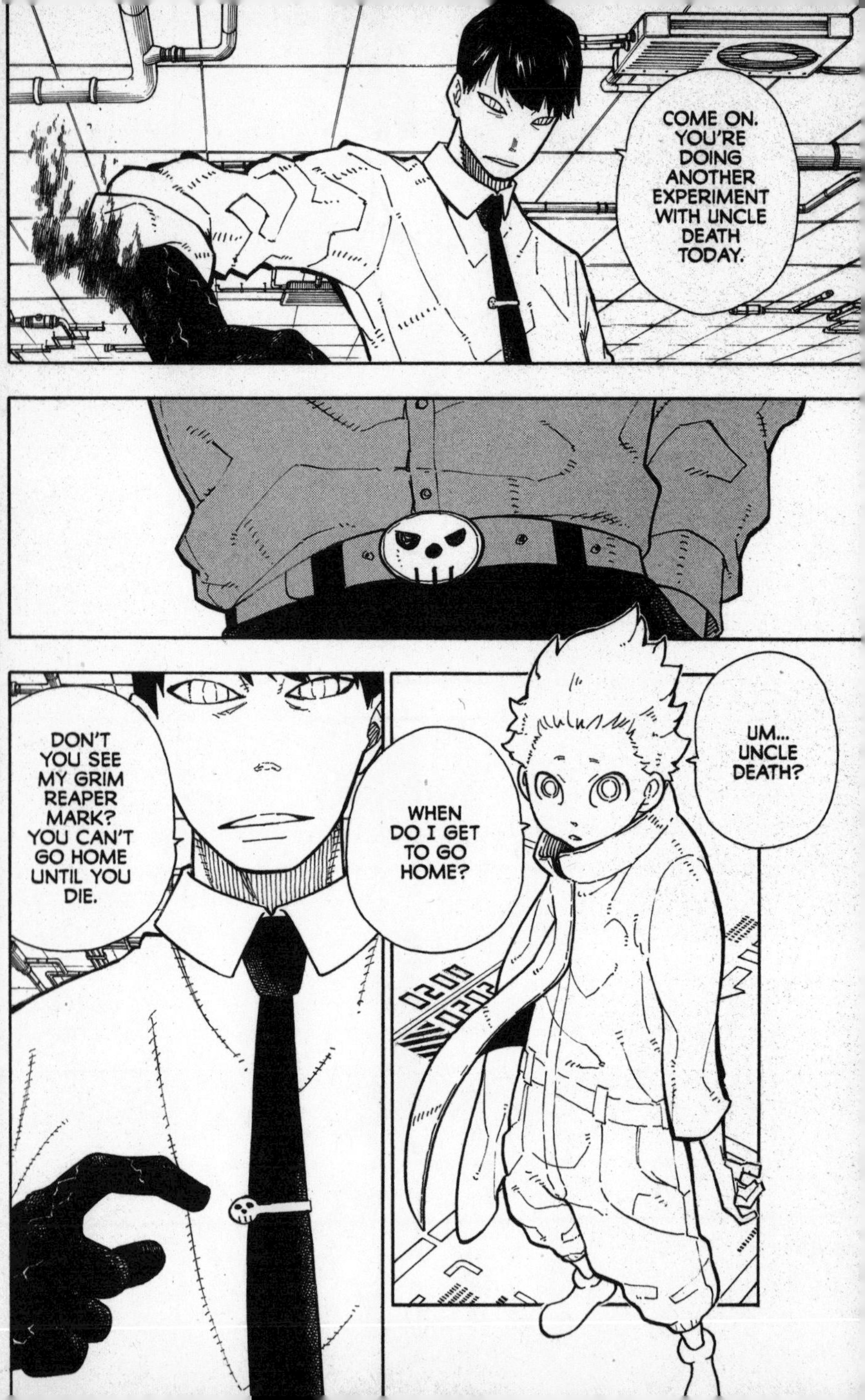
COME ON. YOU'RE DOING ANOTHER EXPERIMENT WITH UNCLE DEATH TODAY.
UM... UNCLE DEATH?
WHEN DO I GET TO GO HOME?
DON'T YOU SEE MY GRIM REAPER MARK? YOU CAN'T GO HOME UNTIL YOU DIE.

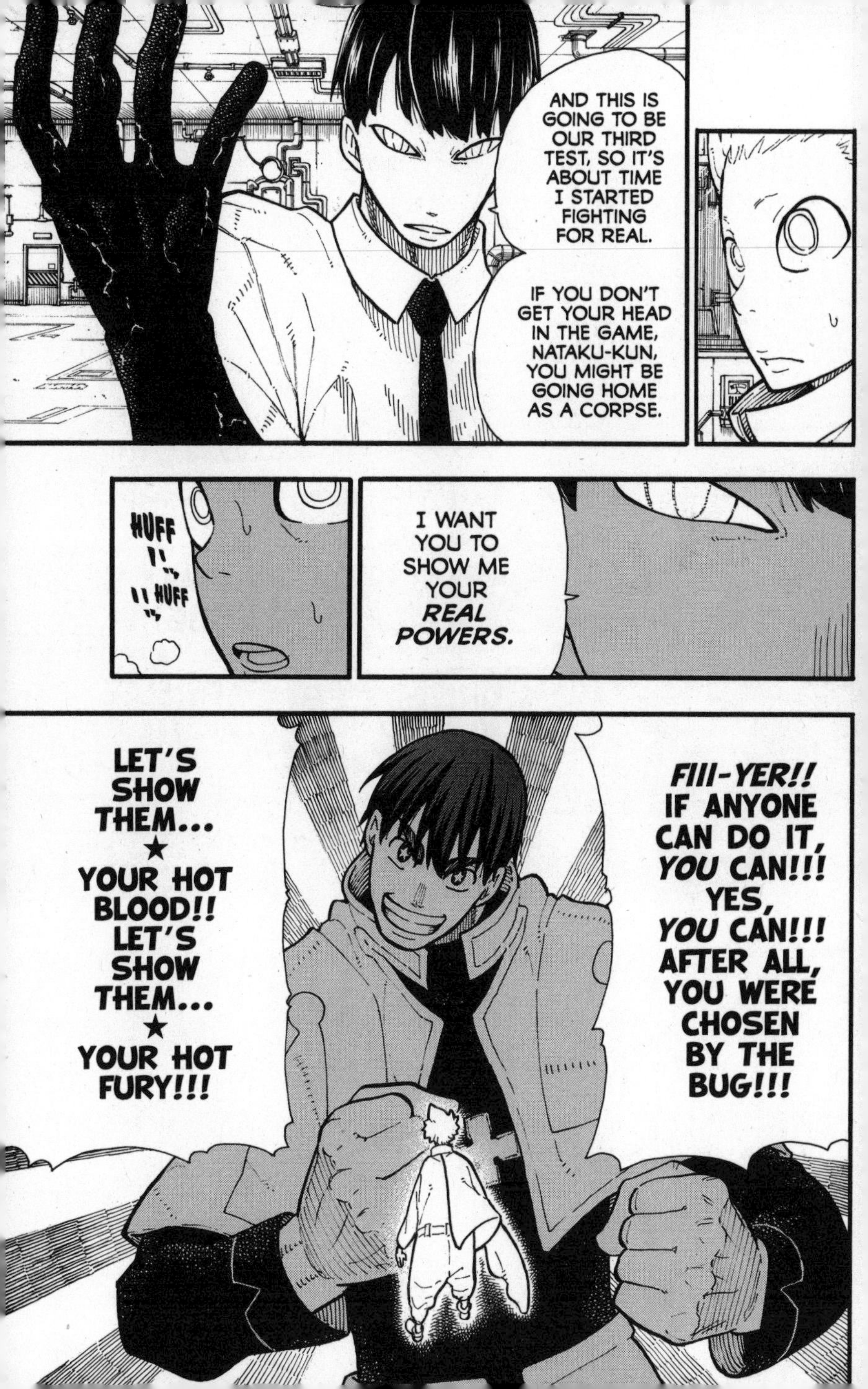
AND THIS IS GOING TO BE OUR THIRD TEST, SO IT'S ABOUT TIME I STARTED FIGHTING FOR REAL.
IF YOU DON'T GET YOUR HEAD IN THE GAME, NATAKU-KUN, YOU MIGHT BE GOING HOME AS A CORPSE.
I WANT YOU TO SHOW ME YOUR *REAL POWERS.*
HUFF
HUFF
FIII-YER!! IF ANYONE CAN DO IT, *YOU* CAN!!! YES, *YOU* CAN!!! AFTER ALL, YOU WERE CHOSEN BY THE BUG!!!
LET'S SHOW THEM... ★ YOUR HOT BLOOD!! LET'S SHOW THEM... ★ YOUR HOT FURY!!!

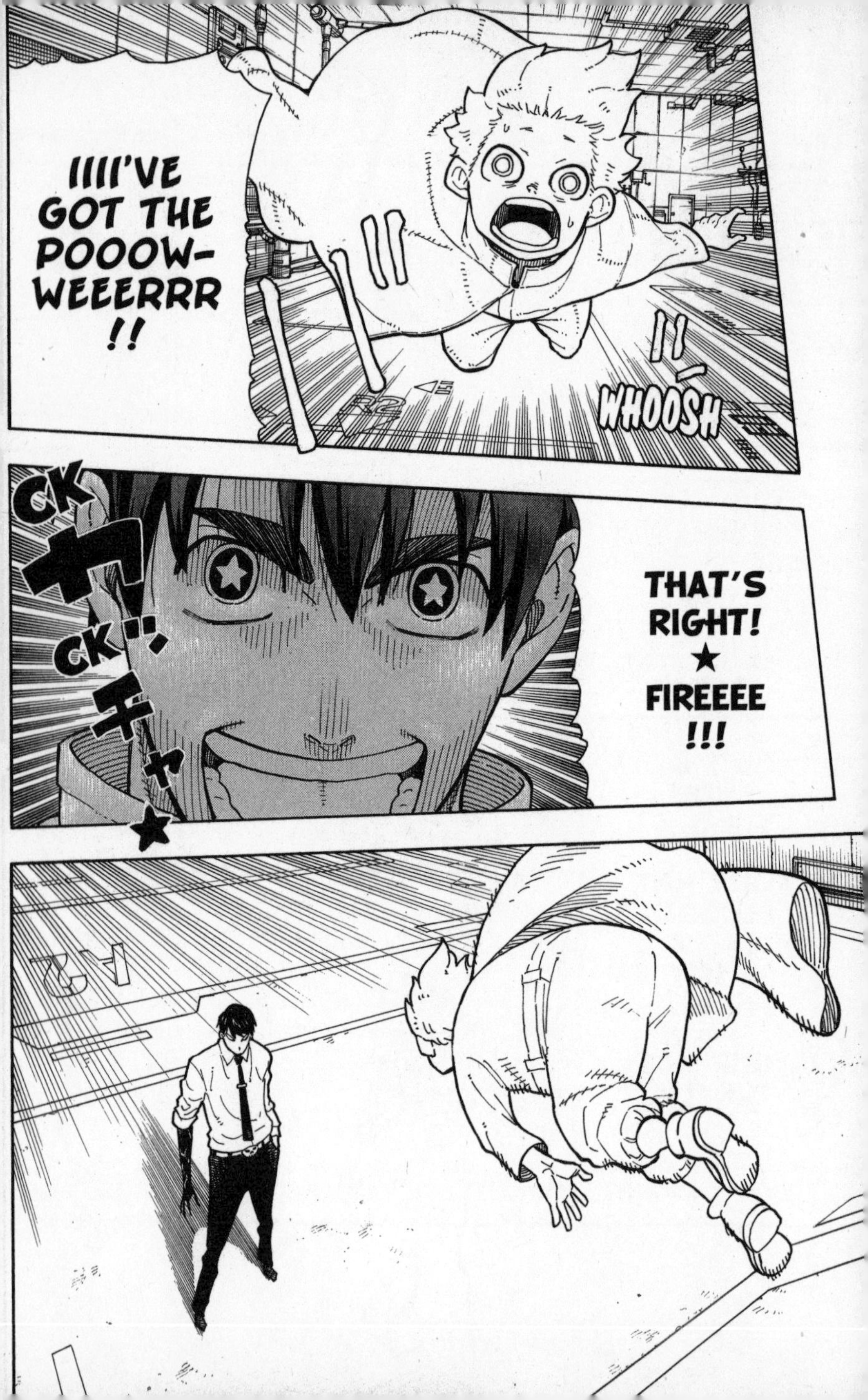
IIIII'VE GOT THE POOOW-WEEERRR !!
WHOOSH
THAT'S RIGHT! ★ FIREEEE !!!
CK
CK

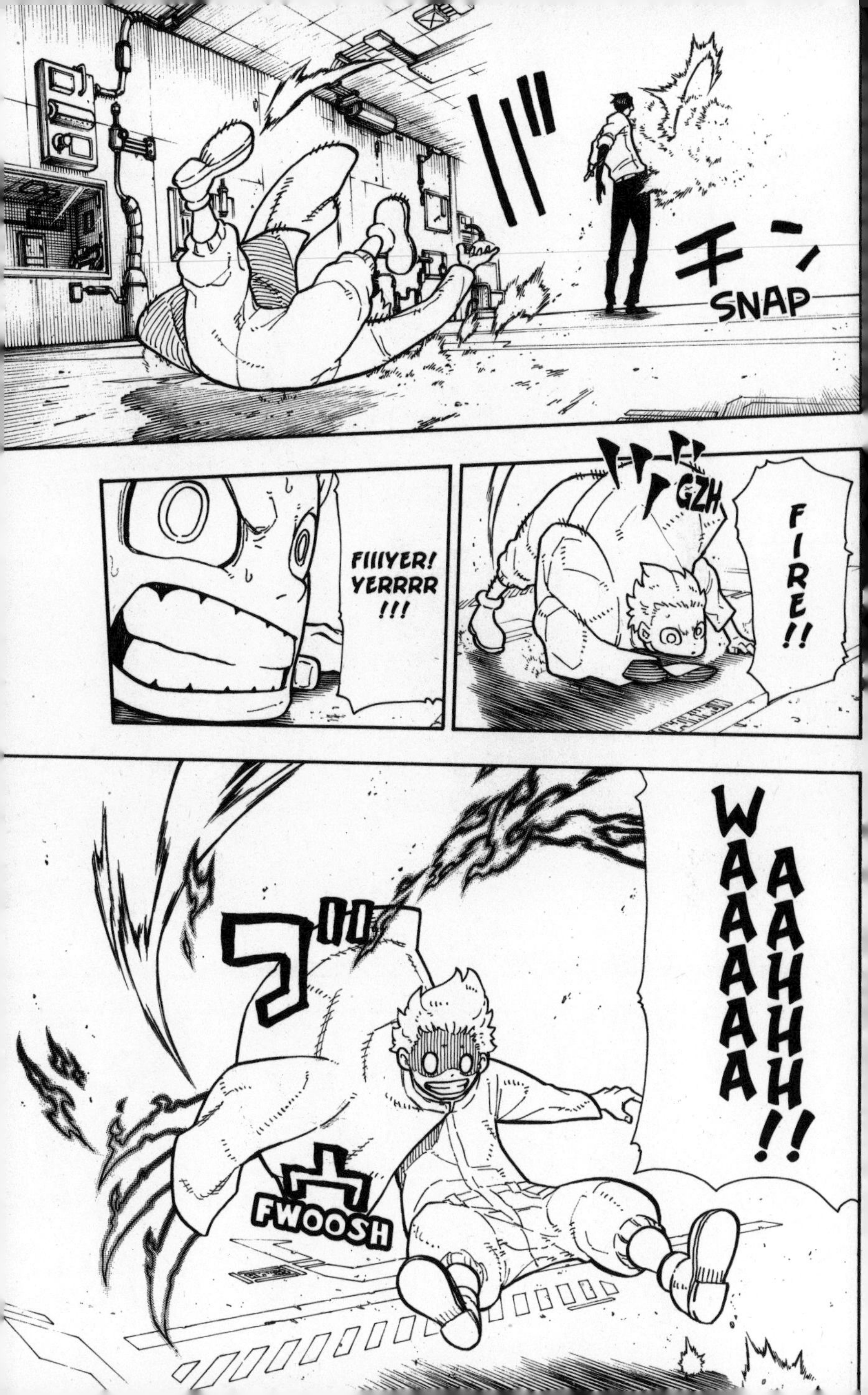
ド
チン
SNAP
GZH
FIRE!!
FIIIYER! YERRRR!!!
WAAAAAAAHHH!!
ゴッ
ボ
FWOOSH

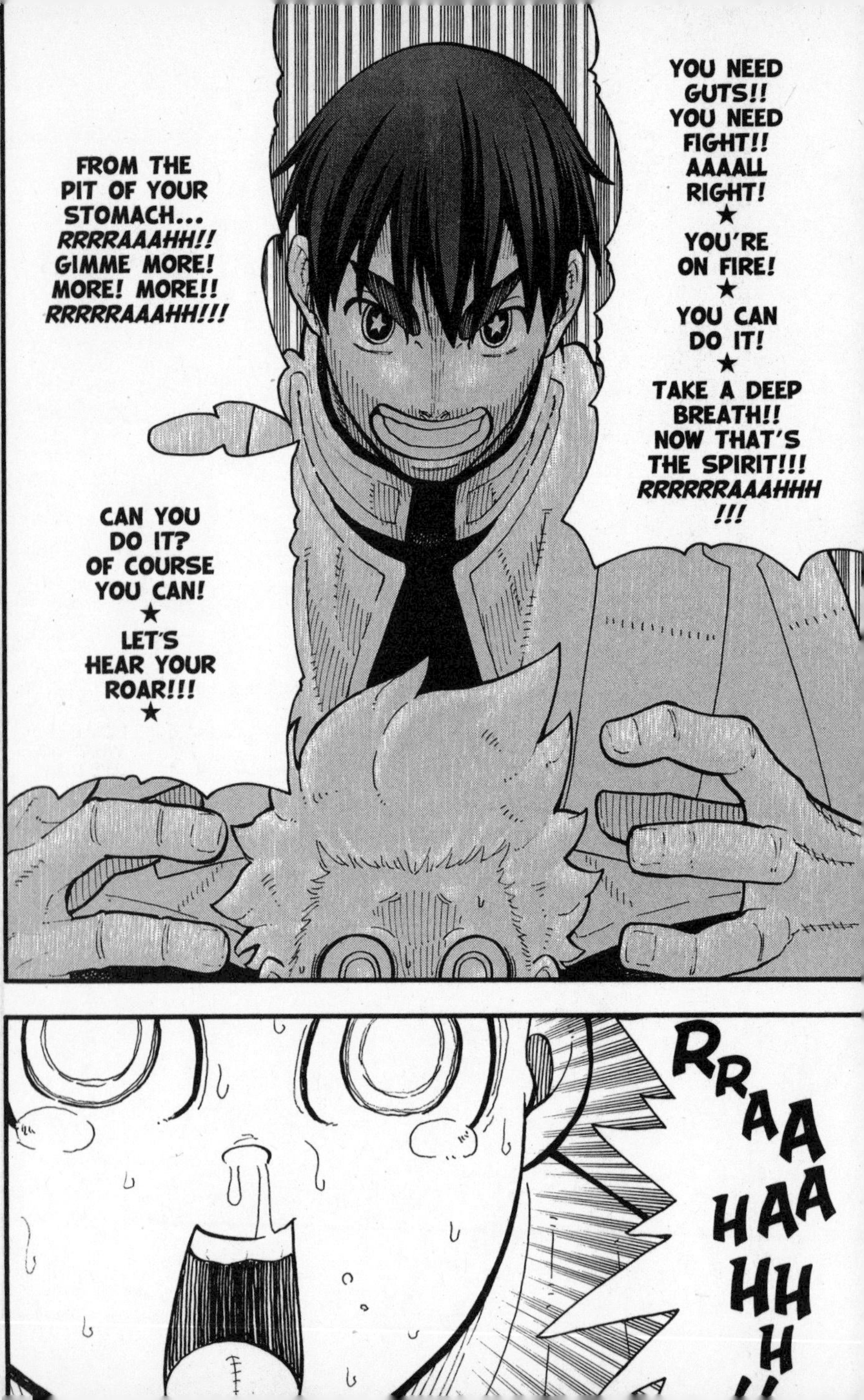
YOU NEED GUTS!! YOU NEED FIGHT!! AAAALL RIGHT! ★ YOU'RE ON FIRE! ★ YOU CAN DO IT! ★ TAKE A DEEP BREATH!! NOW THAT'S THE SPIRIT!!! *RRRRRRAAAHHH!!!*
FROM THE PIT OF YOUR STOMACH... *RRRRAAAHH!!* GIMME MORE! MORE! MORE!! *RRRRRAAAHH!!!*
CAN YOU DO IT? OF COURSE YOU CAN! ★ LET'S HEAR YOUR ROAR!!! ★
RRAAHAAHHH!!

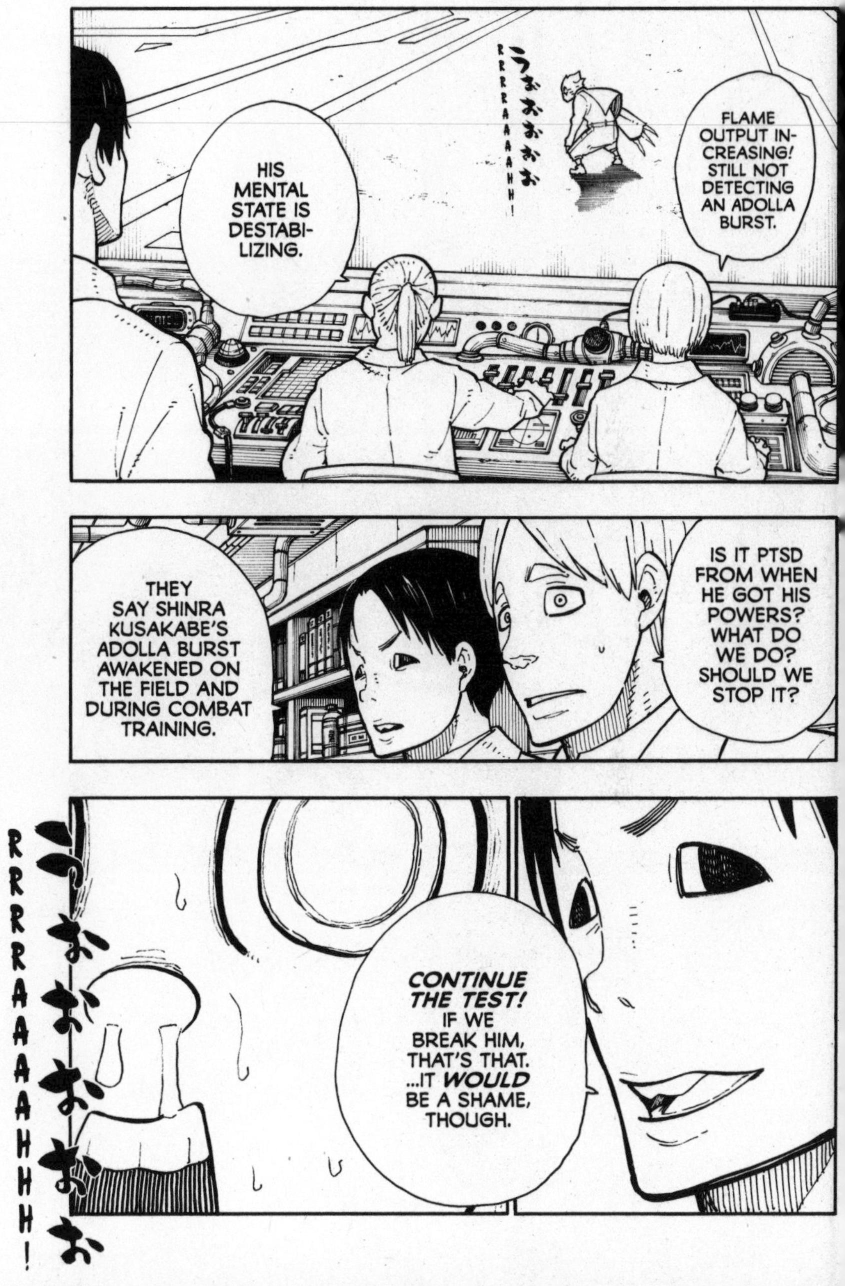
FLAME OUTPUT IN-CREASING! STILL NOT DETECTING AN ADOLLA BURST.
うおおおお
RRRRAAAAHH!
HIS MENTAL STATE IS DESTABI-LIZING.
IS IT PTSD FROM WHEN HE GOT HIS POWERS? WHAT DO WE DO? SHOULD WE STOP IT?
THEY SAY SHINRA KUSAKABE'S ADOLLA BURST AWAKENED ON THE FIELD AND DURING COMBAT TRAINING.
CONTINUE THE TEST! IF WE BREAK HIM, THAT'S THAT. ...IT WOULD BE A SHAME, THOUGH.
うおおおお
RRRRAAAAHHH!

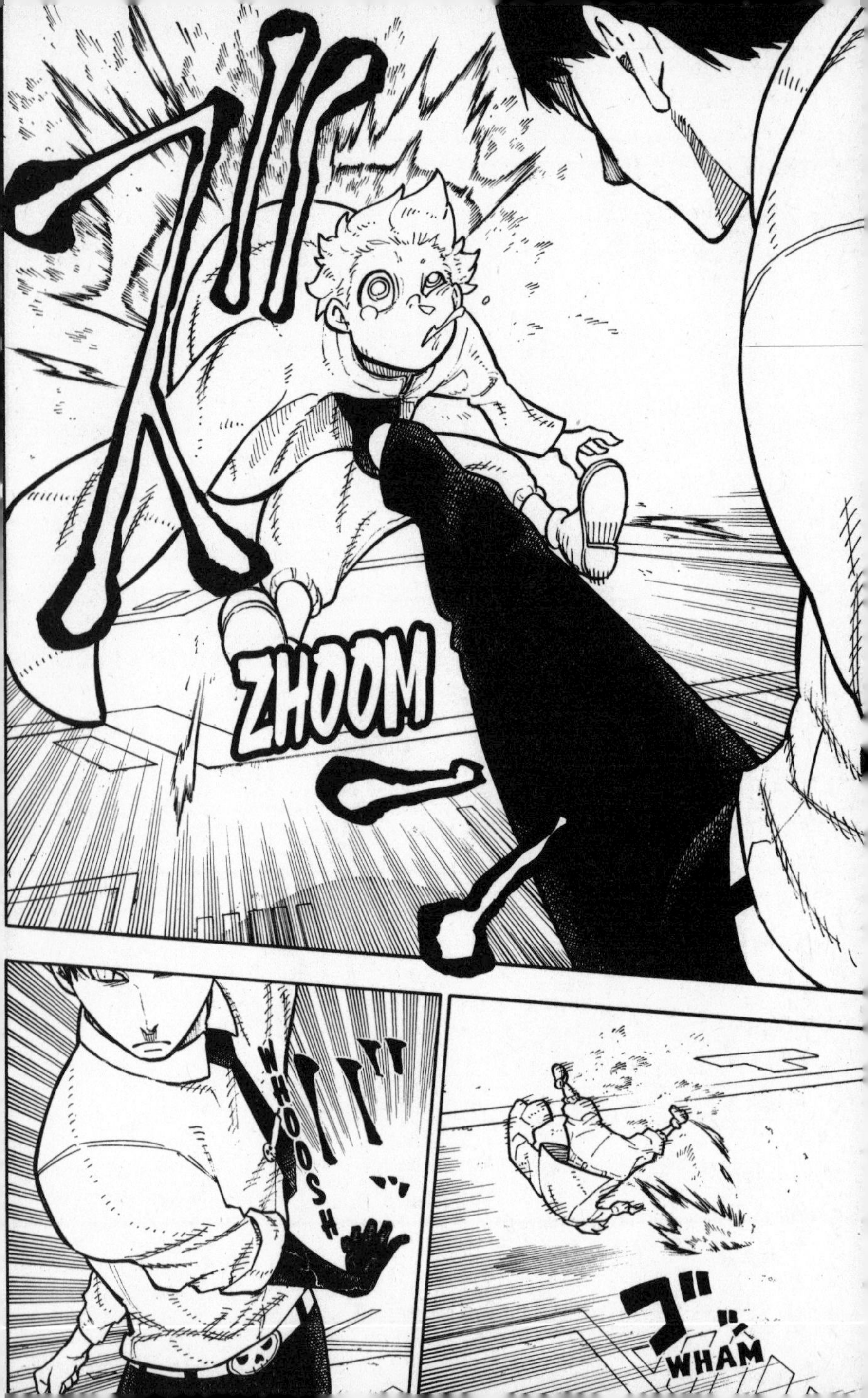
ZHOOM
ゴッ
WHAM
WHOOOSH

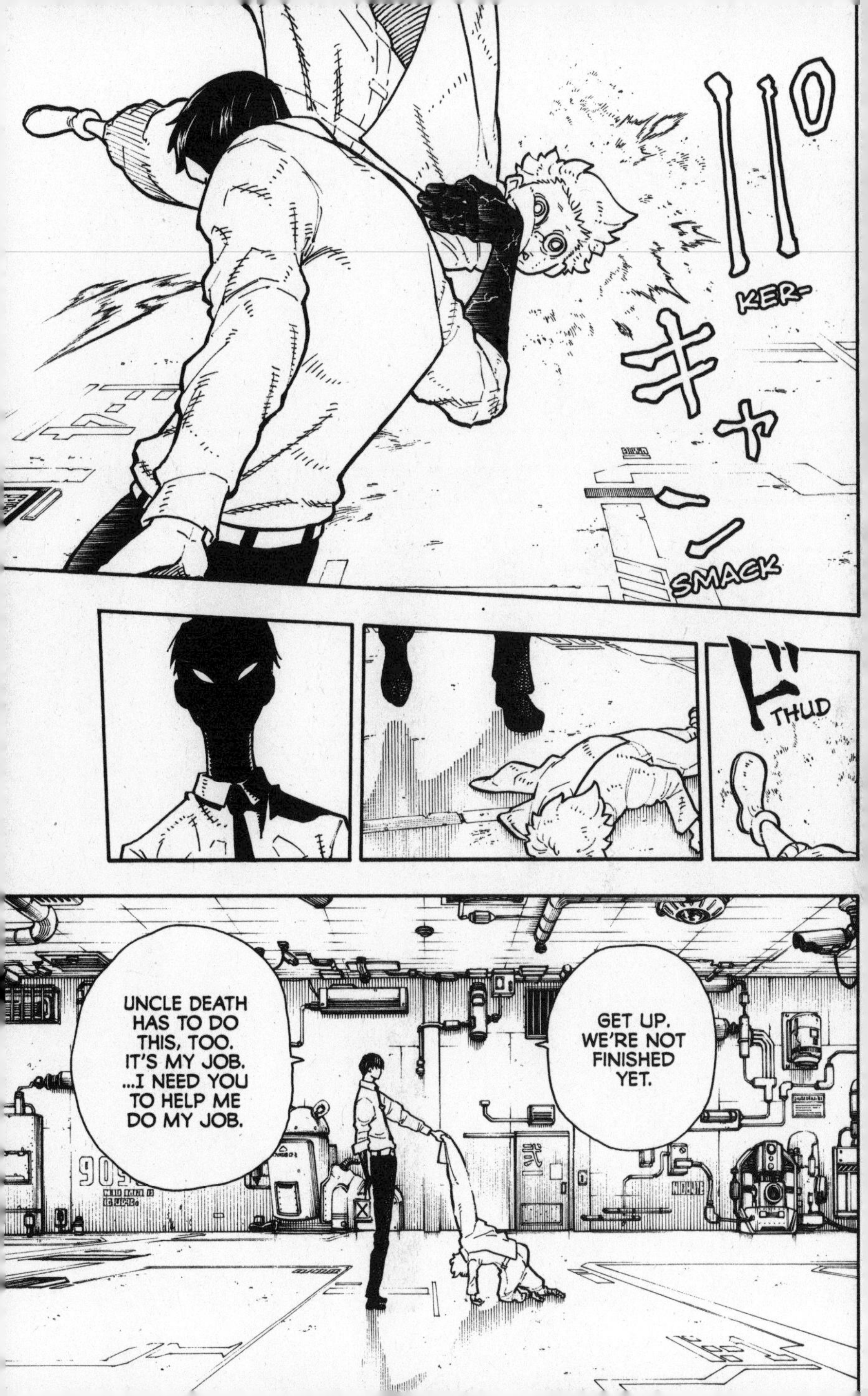

KER-
SMACK
THUD
GET UP. WE'RE NOT FINISHED YET.
UNCLE DEATH HAS TO DO THIS, TOO. IT'S MY JOB. ...I NEED YOU TO HELP ME DO MY JOB.

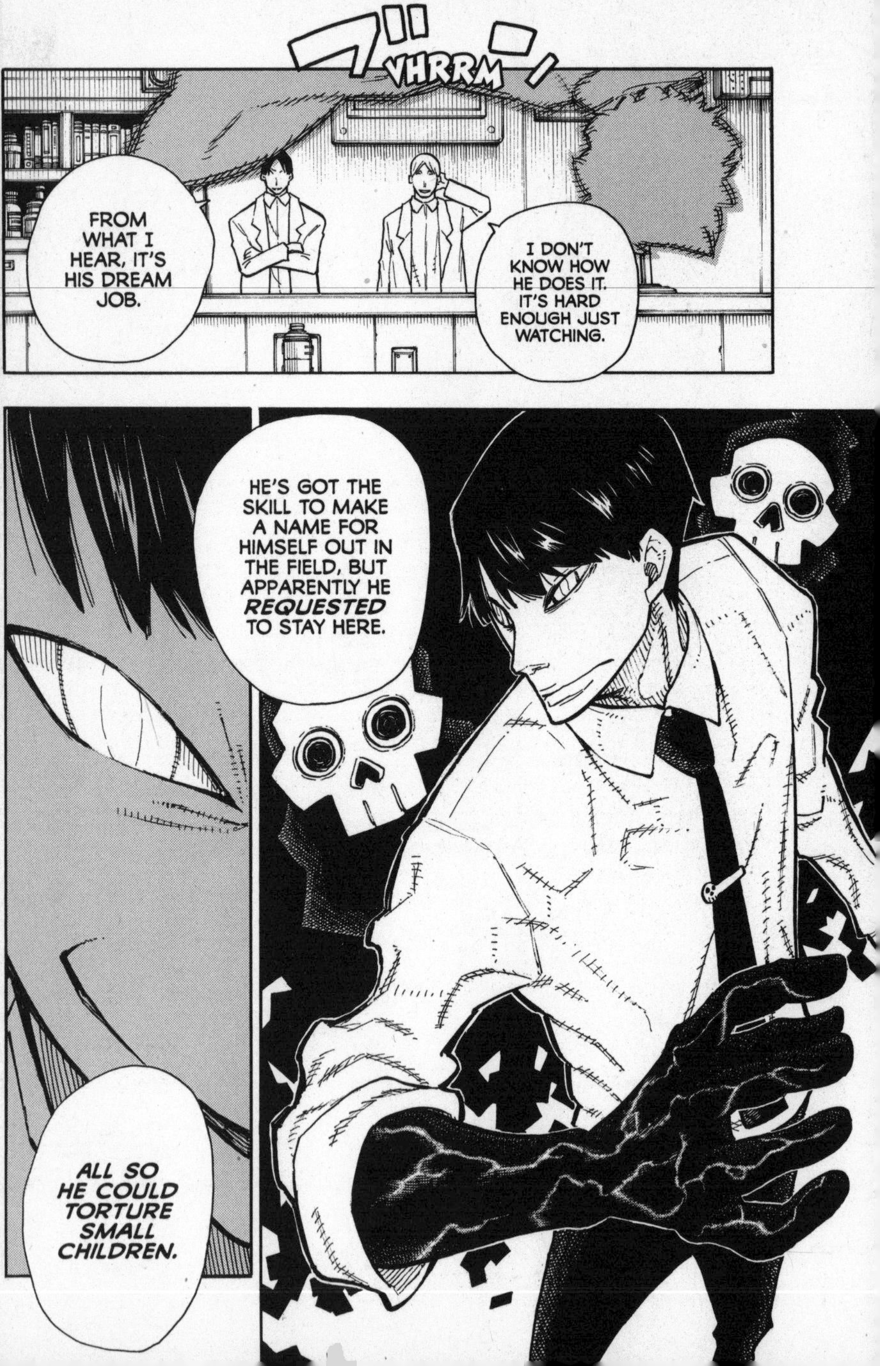
VHRRM
I DON'T KNOW HOW HE DOES IT. IT'S HARD ENOUGH JUST WATCHING.
FROM WHAT I HEAR, IT'S HIS DREAM JOB.
HE'S GOT THE SKILL TO MAKE A NAME FOR HIMSELF OUT IN THE FIELD, BUT APPARENTLY HE ***REQUESTED*** TO STAY HERE.
ALL SO HE COULD TORTURE SMALL CHILDREN.

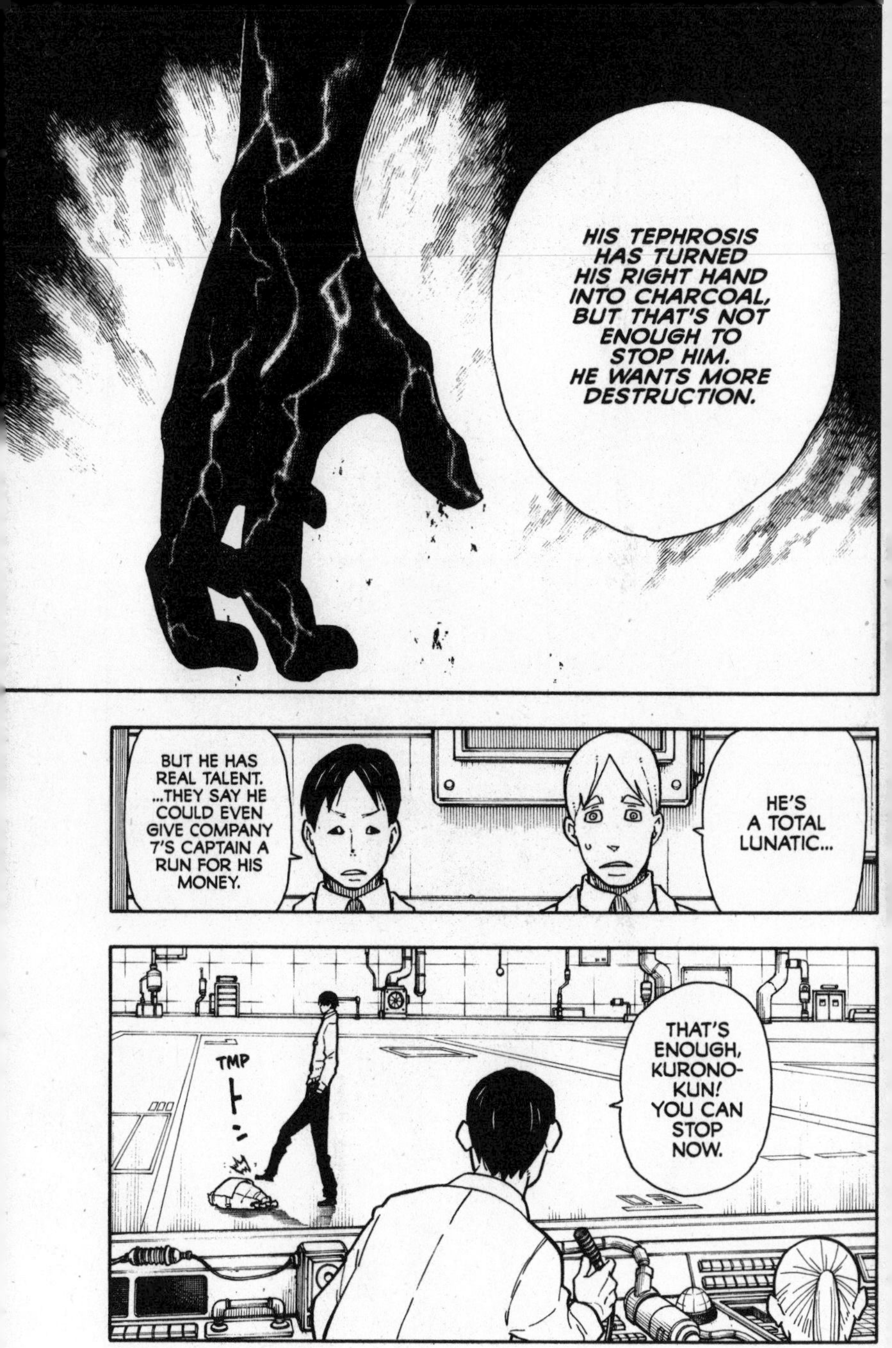
HIS TEPHROSIS HAS TURNED HIS RIGHT HAND INTO CHARCOAL, BUT THAT'S NOT ENOUGH TO STOP HIM. HE WANTS MORE DESTRUCTION.
HE'S A TOTAL LUNATIC...
BUT HE HAS REAL TALENT. ...THEY SAY HE COULD EVEN GIVE COMPANY 7'S CAPTAIN A RUN FOR HIS MONEY.
THAT'S ENOUGH, KURONO-KUN! YOU CAN STOP NOW.
TMP

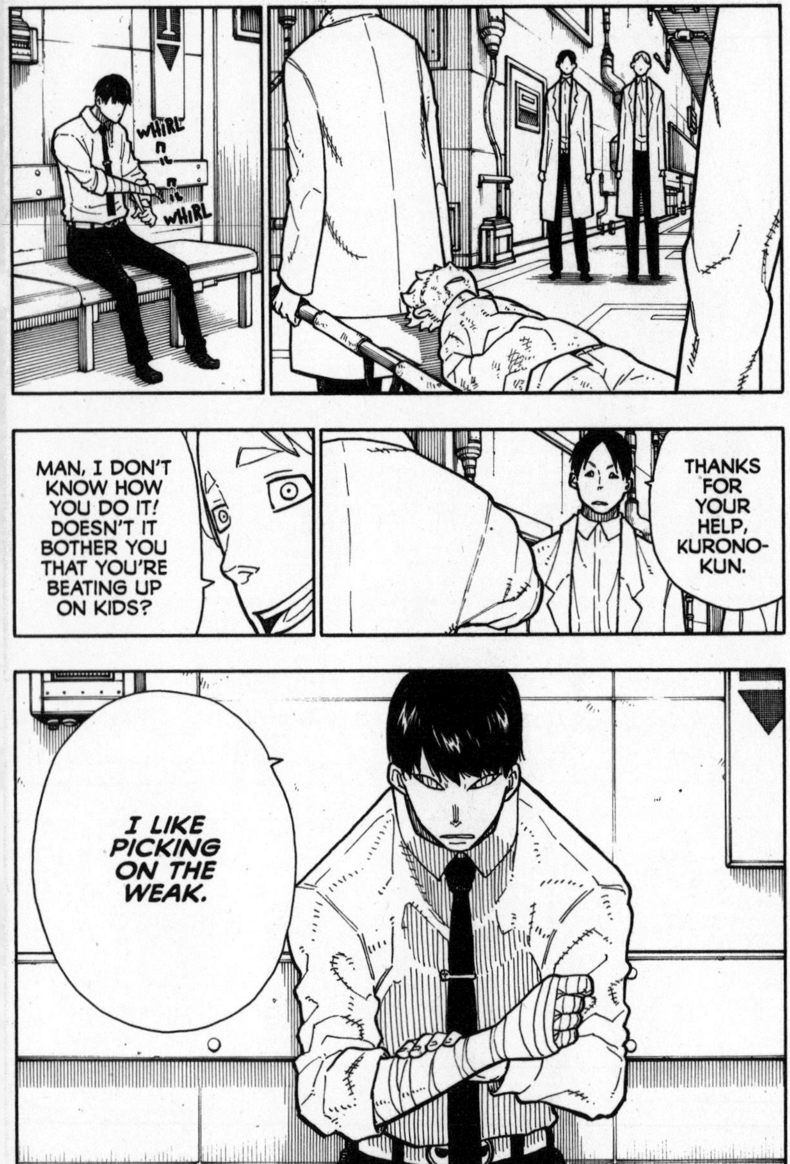
WHIRL
WHIRL
THANKS FOR YOUR HELP, KURONO-KUN.
MAN, I DON'T KNOW HOW YOU DO IT! DOESN'T IT BOTHER YOU THAT YOU'RE BEATING UP ON KIDS?
I LIKE PICKING ON THE WEAK.

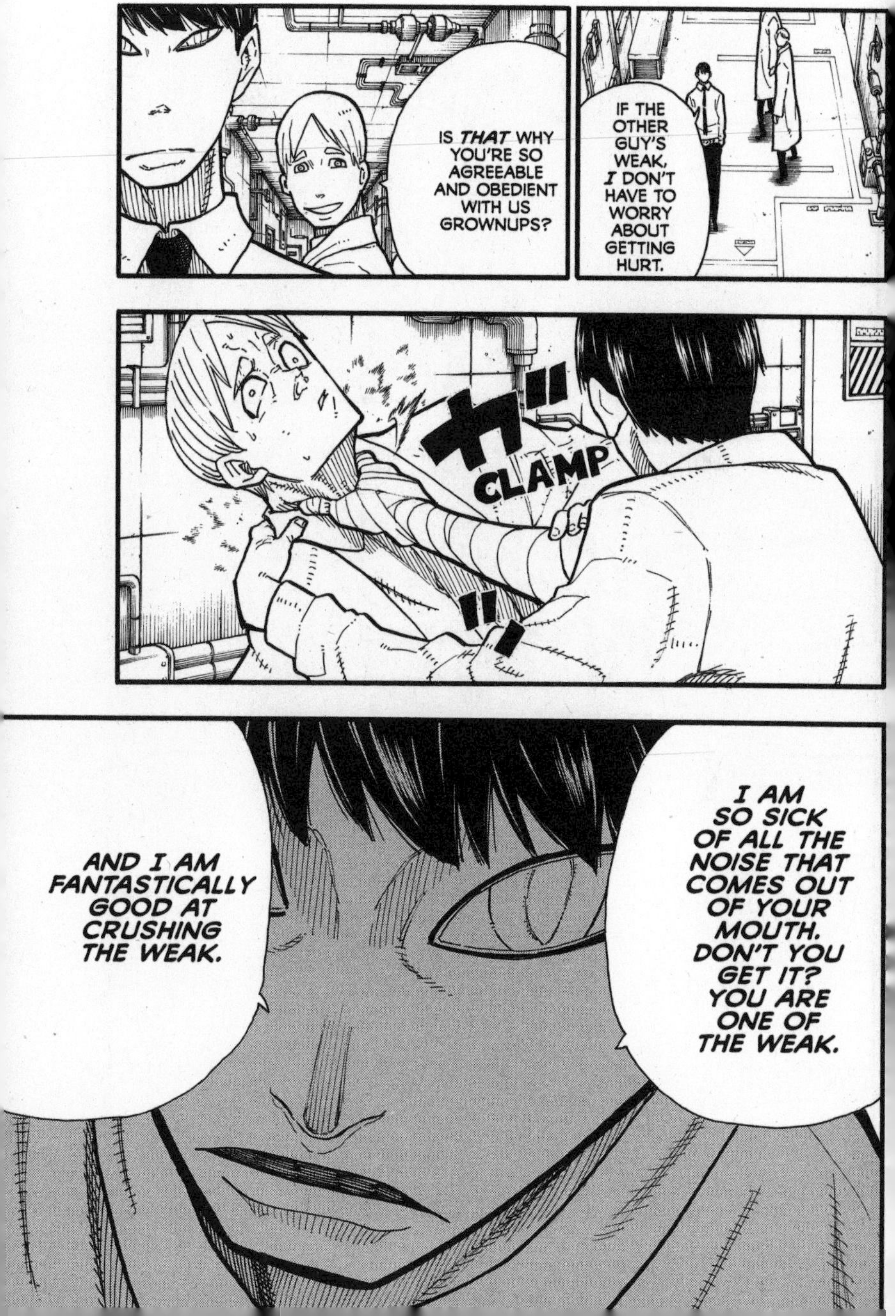
IF THE OTHER GUY'S WEAK, *I* DON'T HAVE TO WORRY ABOUT GETTING HURT.
IS *THAT* WHY YOU'RE SO AGREEABLE AND OBEDIENT WITH US GROWNUPS?
ガ CLAMP
I AM SO SICK OF ALL THE NOISE THAT COMES OUT OF YOUR MOUTH. DON'T YOU GET IT? YOU ARE ONE OF THE WEAK.
AND I AM FANTASTICALLY GOOD AT CRUSHING THE WEAK.

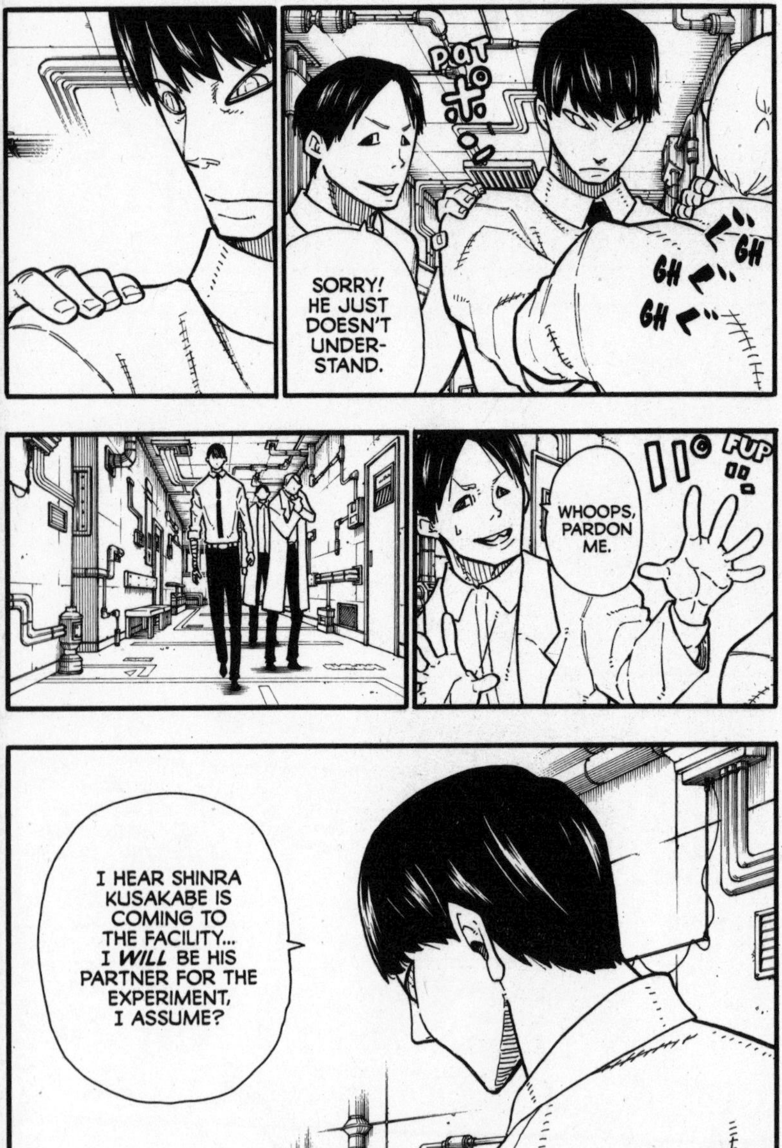

PAT
SORRY! HE JUST DOESN'T UNDER-STAND.
GH
GH
GH
FUP
WHOOPS, PARDON ME.
I HEAR SHINRA KUSAKABE IS COMING TO THE FACILITY... I WILL BE HIS PARTNER FOR THE EXPERIMENT, I ASSUME?

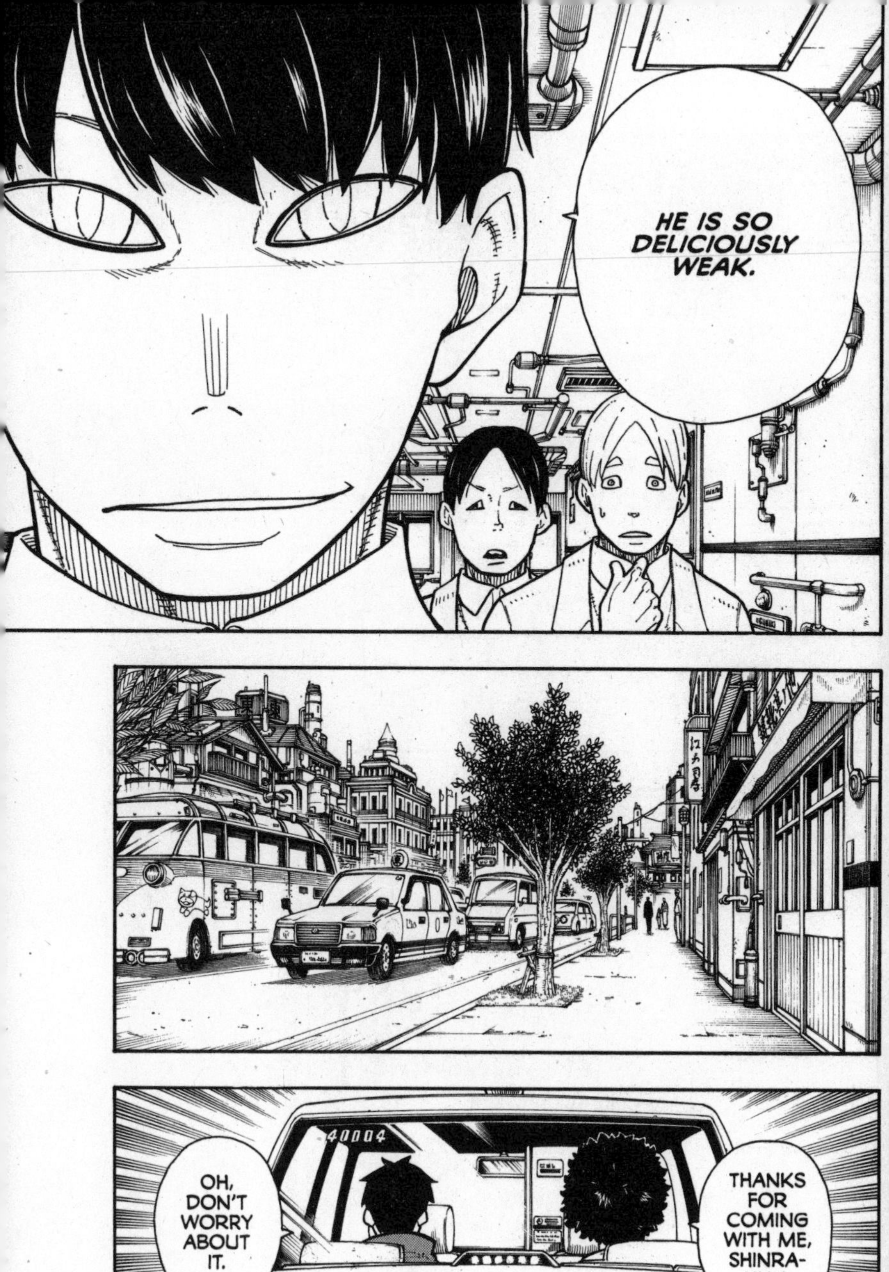
HE IS SO DELICIOUSLY WEAK.
THANKS FOR COMING WITH ME, SHINRA-KUN.
OH, DON'T WORRY ABOUT IT.

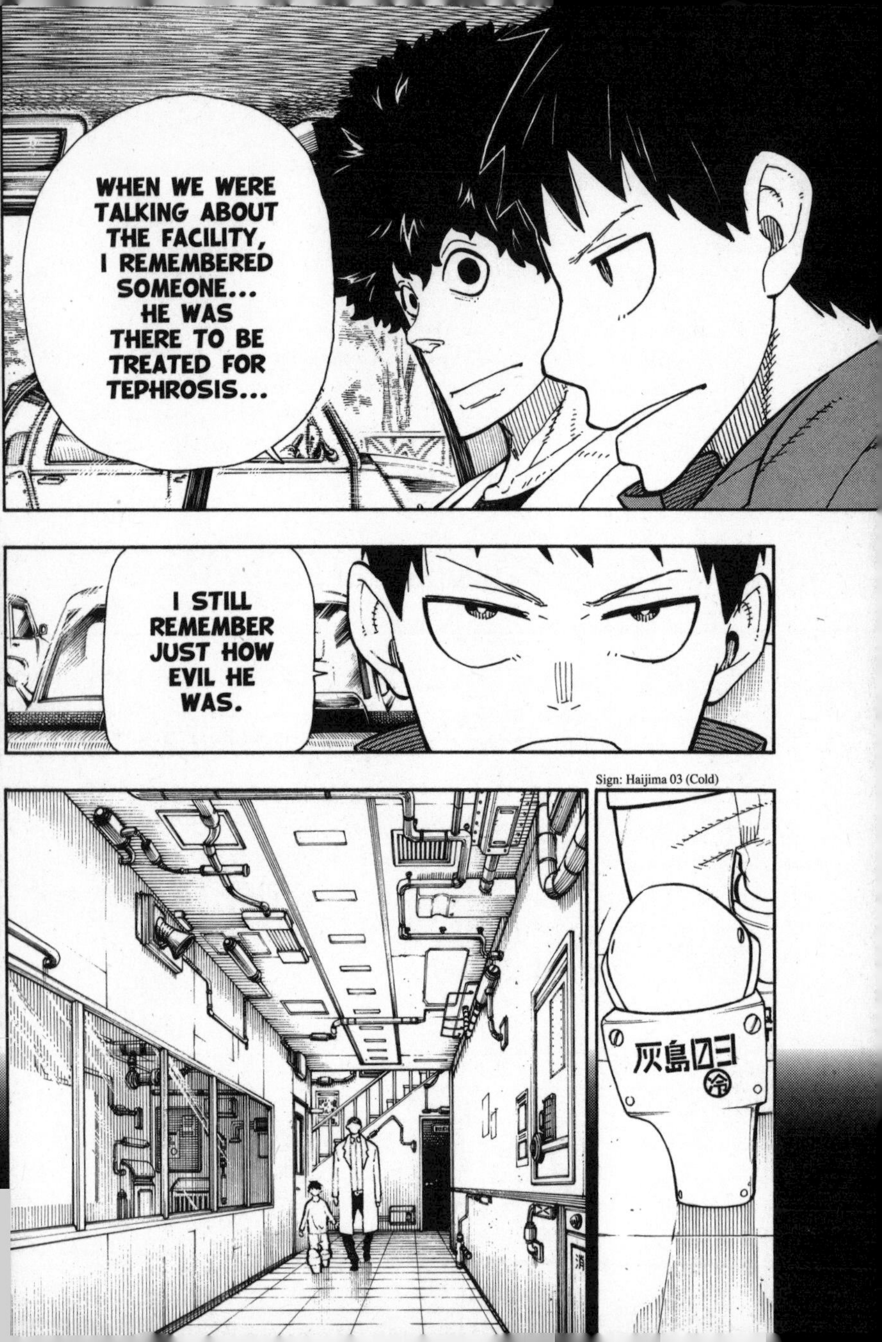
WHEN WE WERE TALKING ABOUT THE FACILITY, I REMEMBERED SOMEONE... HE WAS THERE TO BE TREATED FOR TEPHROSIS...
I STILL REMEMBER JUST HOW EVIL HE WAS.
Sign: Haijima 03 (Cold)
灰島03
冷

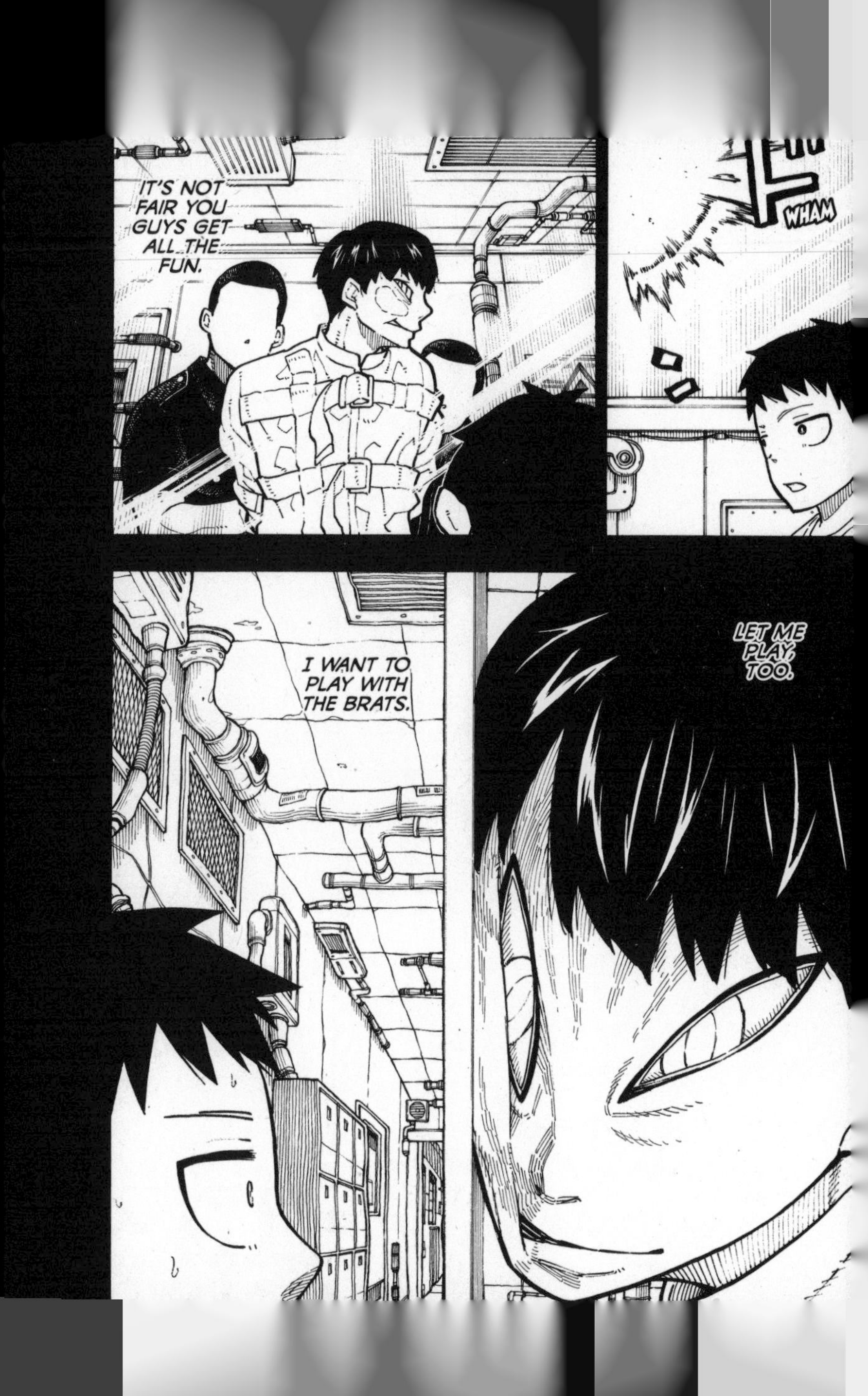
WHAM
IT'S NOT FAIR YOU GUYS GET ALL THE FUN.
LET ME PLAY, TOO.
I WANT TO PLAY WITH THE BRATS.

FIRE FORCE

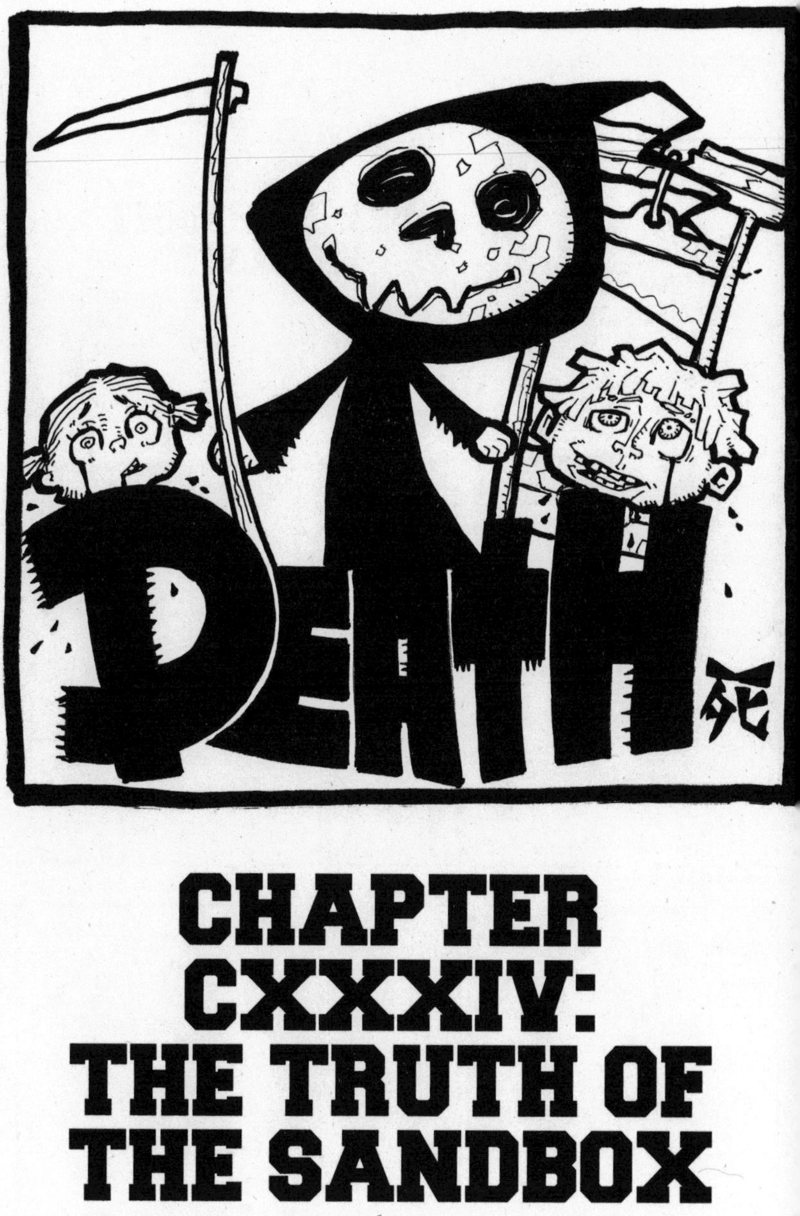
DEATH
死

CHAPTER CXXXIV: THE TRUTH OF THE SANDBOX

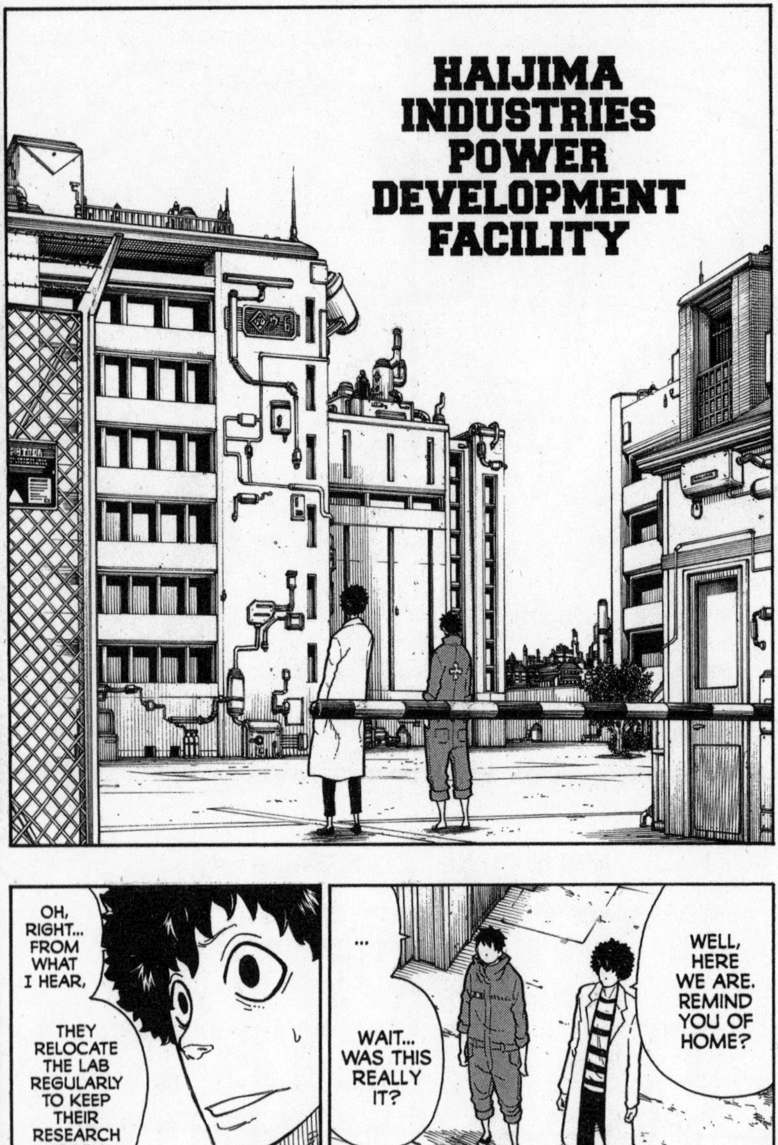
HAIJIMA INDUSTRIES POWER DEVELOPMENT FACILITY
WELL, HERE WE ARE. REMIND YOU OF HOME?
...
WAIT... WAS THIS REALLY IT?
OH, RIGHT... FROM WHAT I HEAR,
THEY RELOCATE THE LAB REGULARLY TO KEEP THEIR RESEARCH HIDDEN.

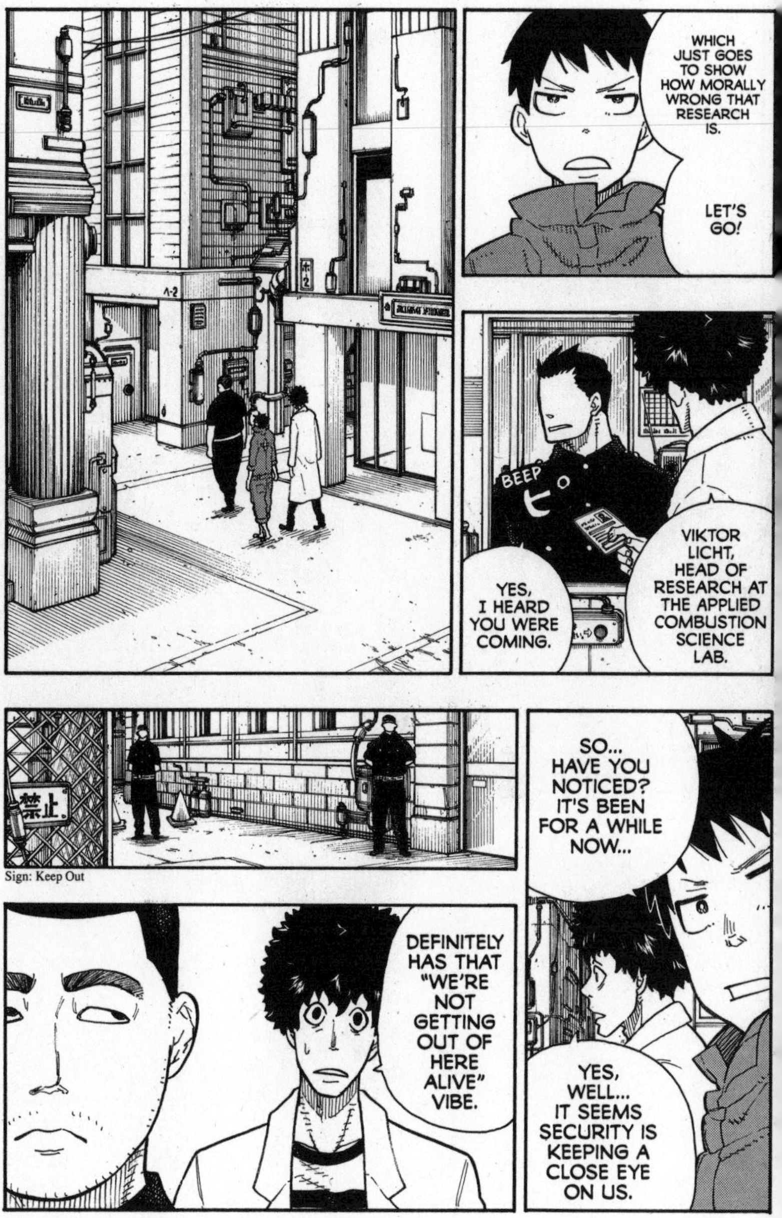
WHICH JUST GOES TO SHOW HOW MORALLY WRONG THAT RESEARCH IS.
LET'S GO!
VIKTOR LICHT, HEAD OF RESEARCH AT THE APPLIED COMBUSTION SCIENCE LAB.
BEEP
YES, I HEARD YOU WERE COMING.
SO... HAVE YOU NOTICED? IT'S BEEN FOR A WHILE NOW...
YES, WELL... IT SEEMS SECURITY IS KEEPING A CLOSE EYE ON US.
禁止
DEFINITELY HAS THAT "WE'RE NOT GETTING OUT OF HERE ALIVE" VIBE.
Sign: Keep Out

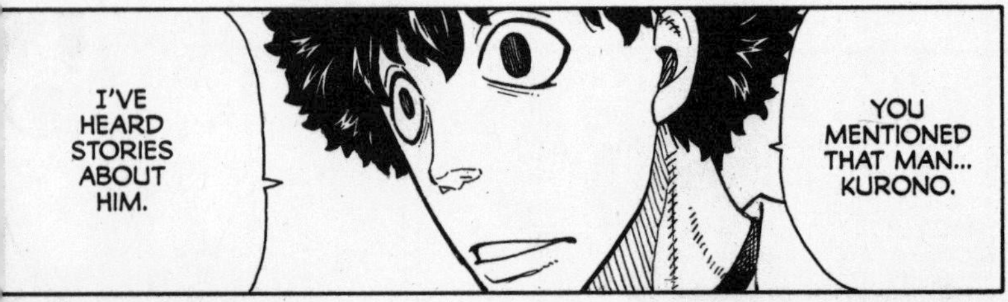
YOU MENTIONED THAT MAN... KURONO.
I'VE HEARD STORIES ABOUT HIM.

Signs: Tephrosis, Carbonization, Black

Signs: Bully, Glories in Abuse, Craves the Weak, Grim Reaper

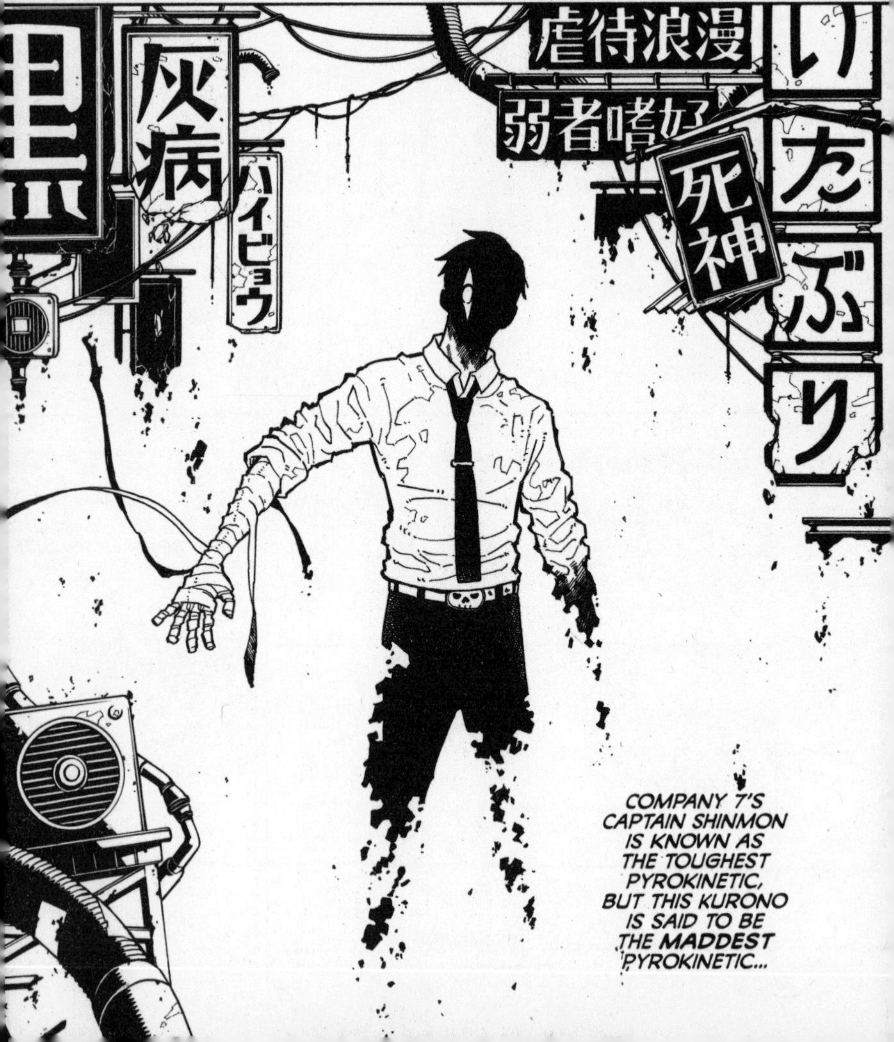
いたぶり
虐待浪漫
弱者嗜好
死神
ハイビョウ
灰病
黒
COMPANY 7'S CAPTAIN SHINMON IS KNOWN AS THE TOUGHEST PYROKINETIC, BUT THIS KURONO IS SAID TO BE THE *MADDEST* PYROKINETIC...

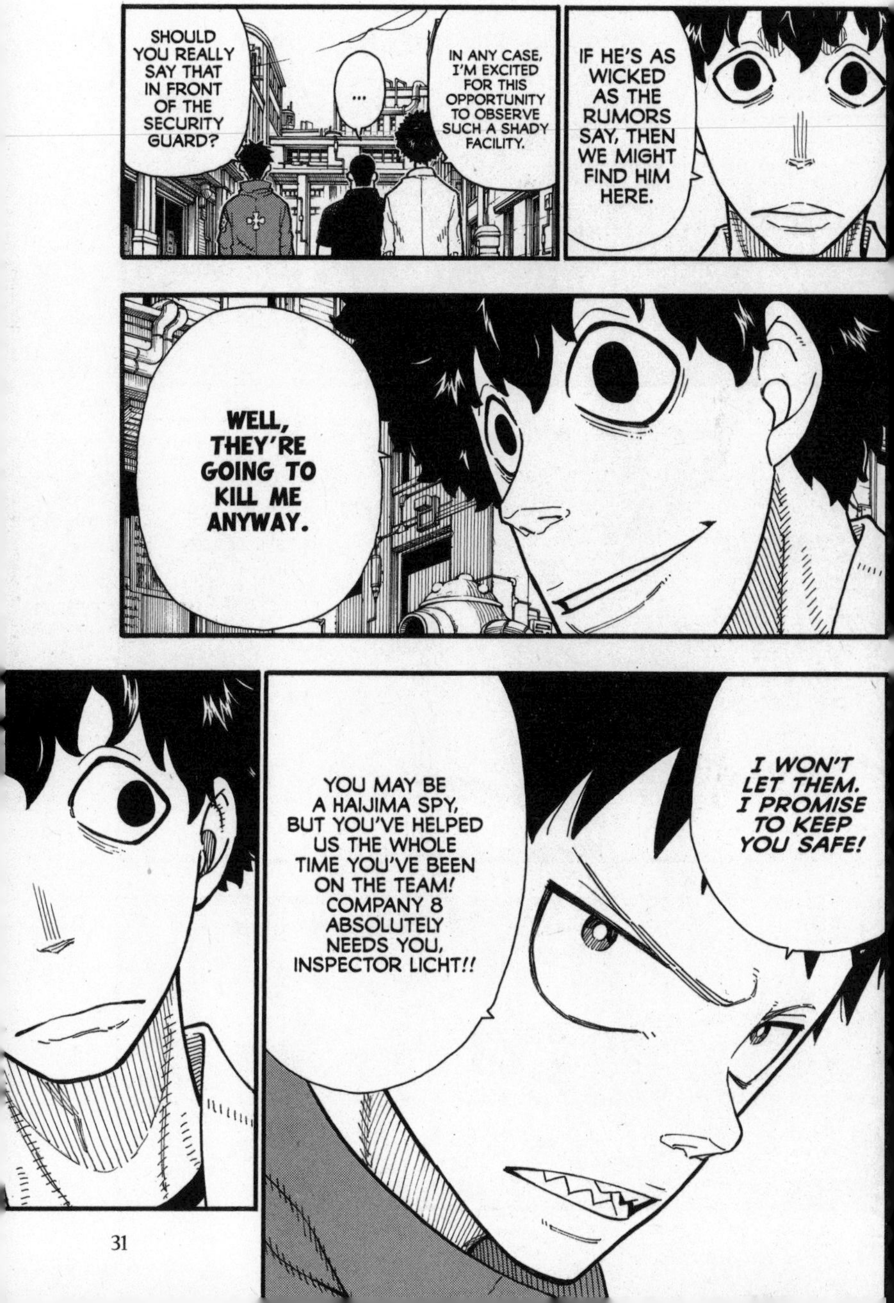
IF HE'S AS WICKED AS THE RUMORS SAY, THEN WE MIGHT FIND HIM HERE.
IN ANY CASE, I'M EXCITED FOR THIS OPPORTUNITY TO OBSERVE SUCH A SHADY FACILITY.
...
SHOULD YOU REALLY SAY THAT IN FRONT OF THE SECURITY GUARD?
WELL, THEY'RE GOING TO KILL ME ANYWAY.
I WON'T LET THEM. I PROMISE TO KEEP YOU SAFE!
YOU MAY BE A HAIJIMA SPY, BUT YOU'VE HELPED US THE WHOLE TIME YOU'VE BEEN ON THE TEAM! COMPANY 8 ABSOLUTELY NEEDS YOU, INSPECTOR LICHT!!

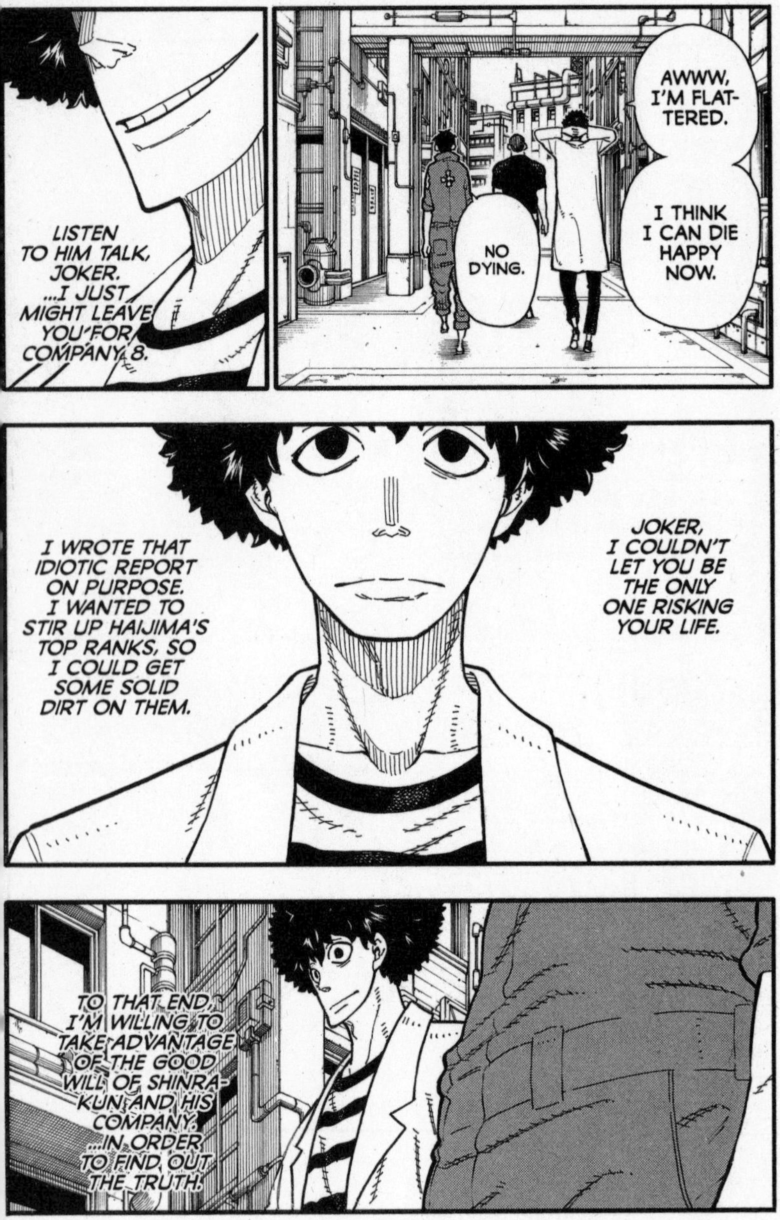
AWWW, I'M FLAT-TERED.
I THINK I CAN DIE HAPPY NOW.
NO DYING.
LISTEN TO HIM TALK, JOKER. ...I JUST MIGHT LEAVE YOU FOR COMPANY 8.
JOKER, I COULDN'T LET YOU BE THE ONLY ONE RISKING YOUR LIFE.
I WROTE THAT IDIOTIC REPORT ON PURPOSE. I WANTED TO STIR UP HAIJIMA'S TOP RANKS, SO I COULD GET SOME SOLID DIRT ON THEM.
TO THAT END, I'M WILLING TO TAKE ADVANTAGE OF THE GOOD WILL OF SHINRA-KUN AND HIS COMPANY ...IN ORDER TO FIND OUT THE TRUTH.

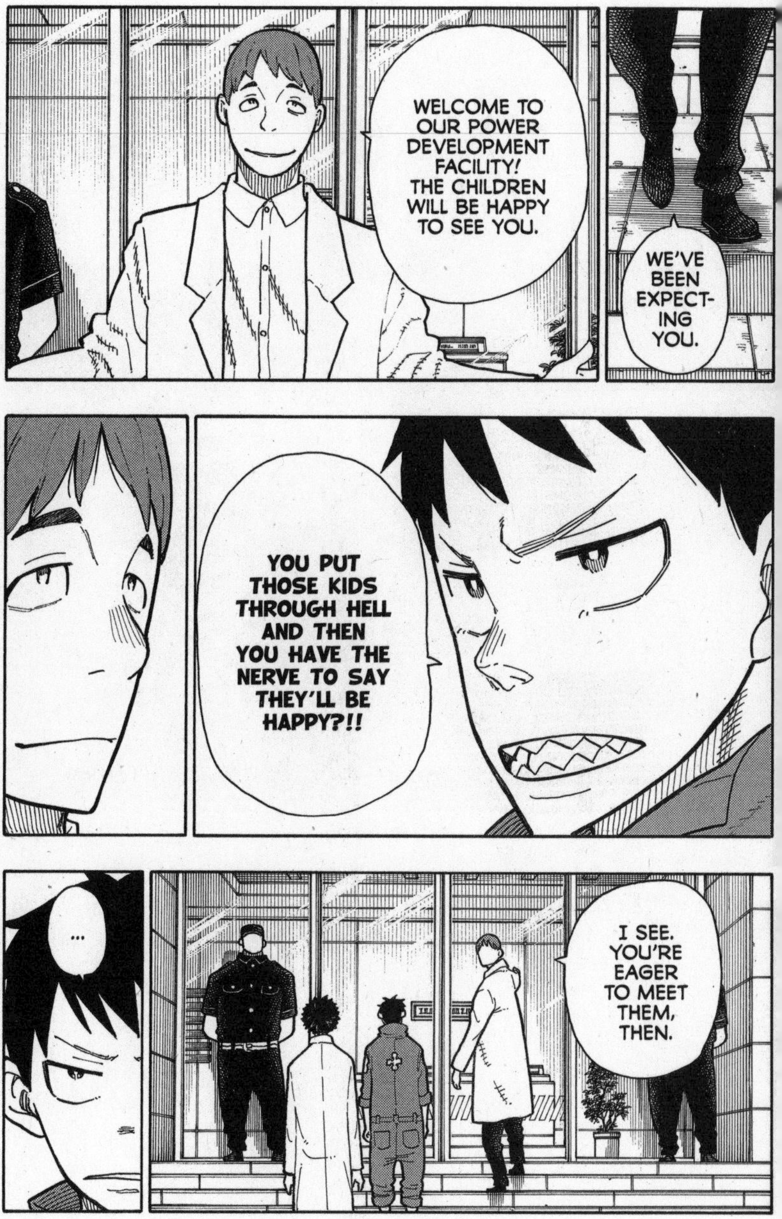
WE'VE BEEN EXPECT-ING YOU.
WELCOME TO OUR POWER DEVELOPMENT FACILITY! THE CHILDREN WILL BE HAPPY TO SEE YOU.
YOU PUT THOSE KIDS THROUGH HELL AND THEN YOU HAVE THE NERVE TO SAY THEY'LL BE HAPPY?!!
I SEE. YOU'RE EAGER TO MEET THEM, THEN.
...

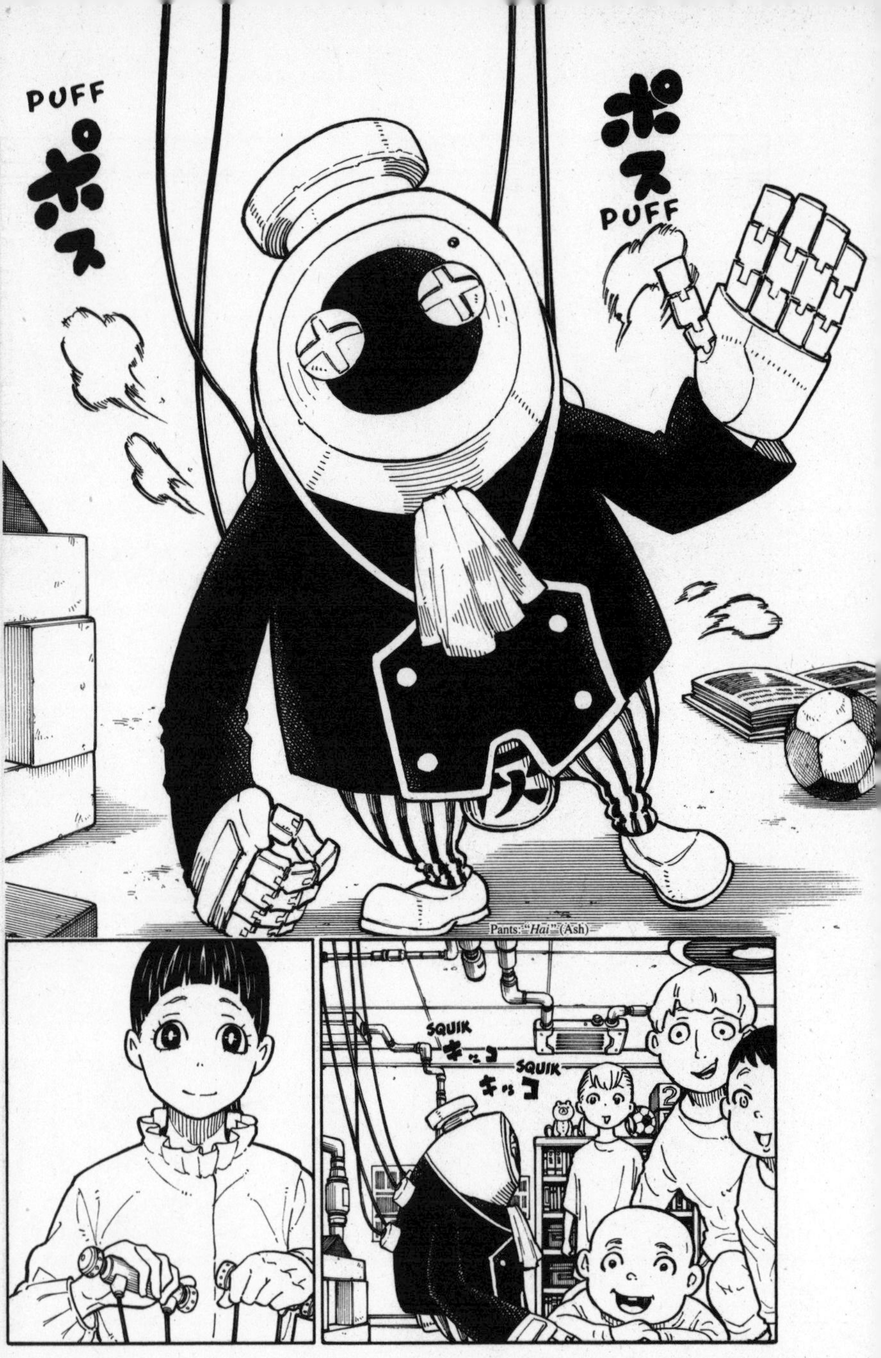
ポス
PUFF
PUFF
ポス
Pants: "Hai" (Ash)
SQUIK
キッコ
SQUIK
キッコ

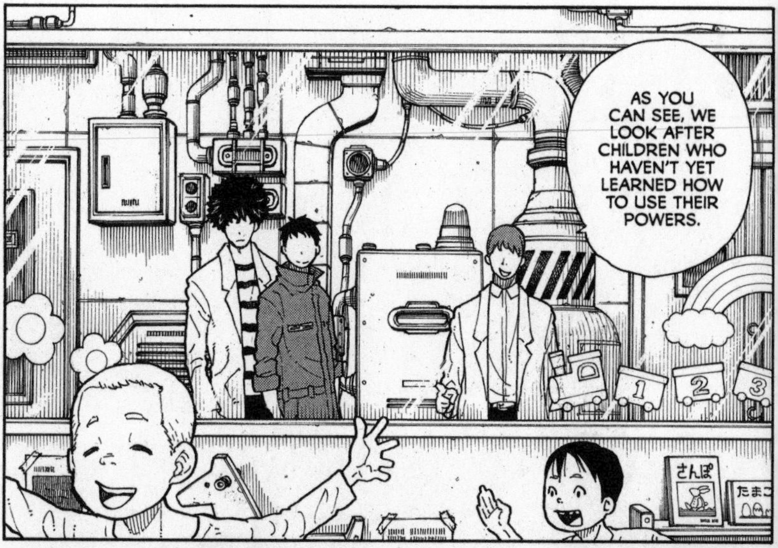
AS YOU CAN SEE, WE LOOK AFTER CHILDREN WHO HAVEN'T YET LEARNED HOW TO USE THEIR POWERS.
さんぽ

Books: Walk (L), Egg (R)

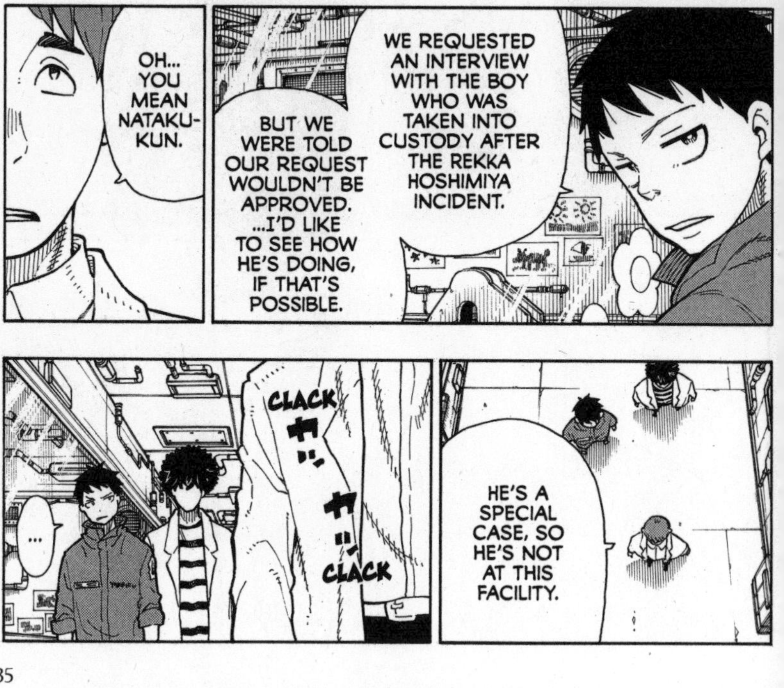
WE REQUESTED AN INTERVIEW WITH THE BOY WHO WAS TAKEN INTO CUSTODY AFTER THE REKKA HOSHIMIYA INCIDENT.
BUT WE WERE TOLD OUR REQUEST WOULDN'T BE APPROVED. ...I'D LIKE TO SEE HOW HE'S DOING, IF THAT'S POSSIBLE.
OH... YOU MEAN NATAKU-KUN.
HE'S A SPECIAL CASE, SO HE'S NOT AT THIS FACILITY.
CLACK
CLACK
...

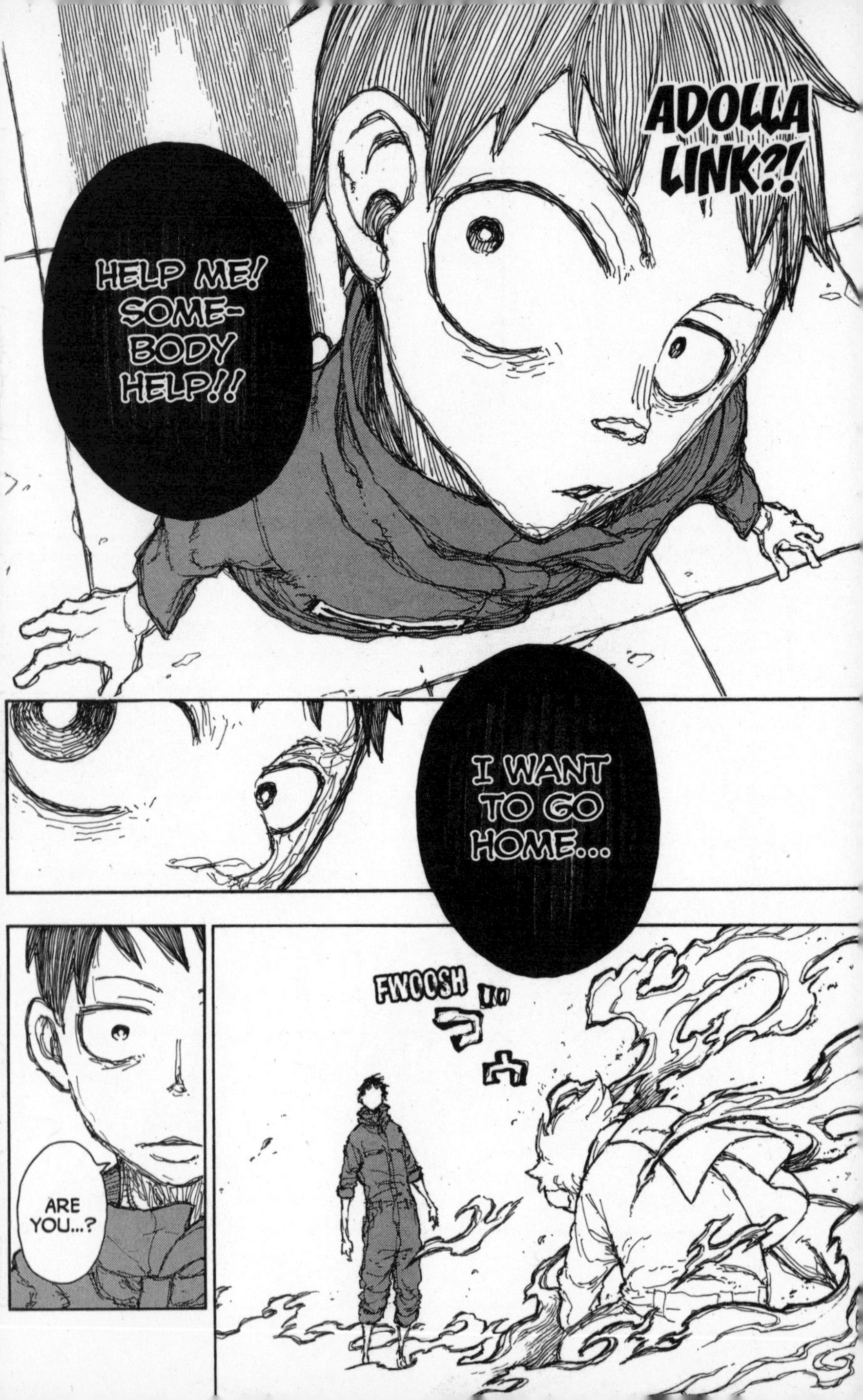
ADOLLA LINK?!
HELP ME! SOME-BODY HELP!!
I WANT TO GO HOME...
FWOOSH
ゴウ
ARE YOU...?

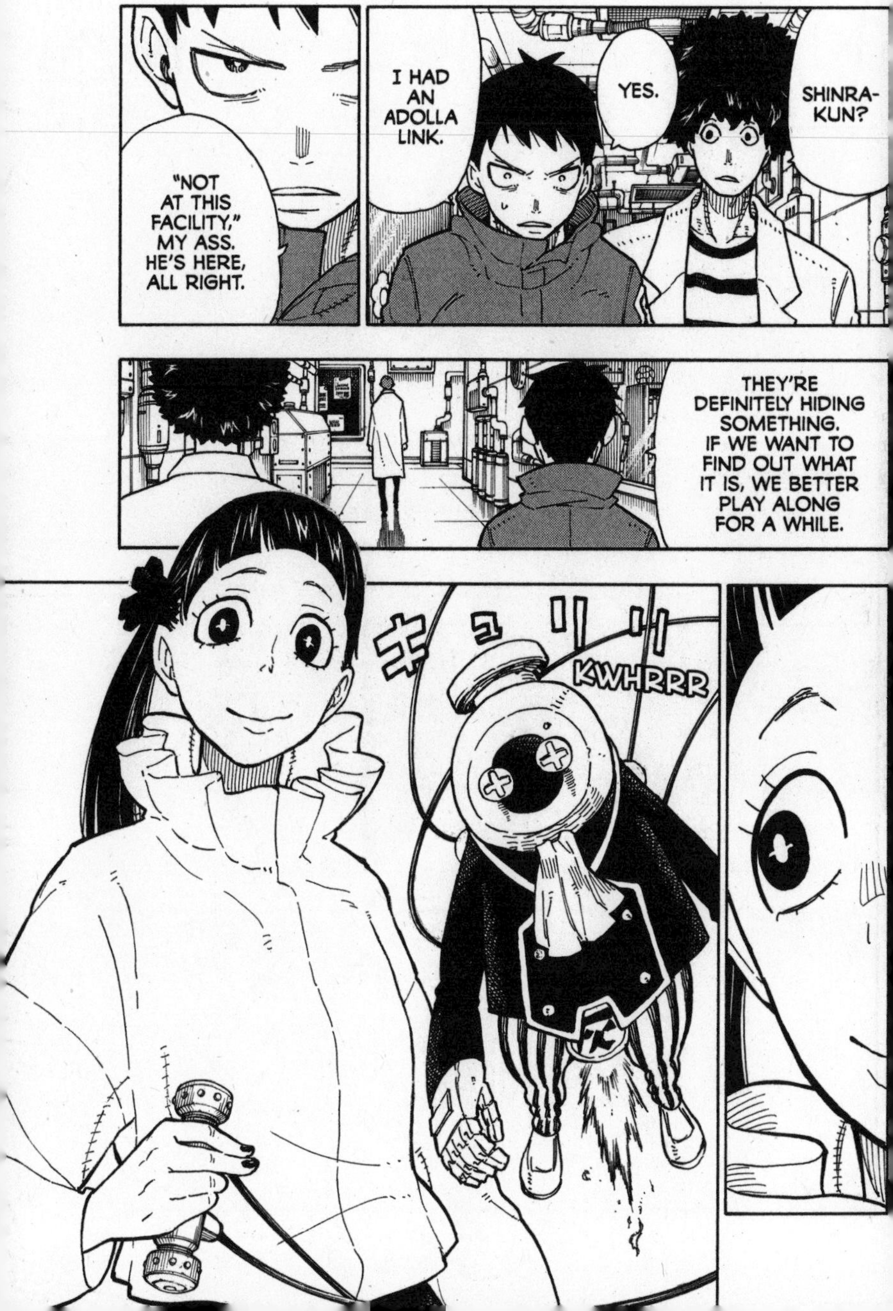
SHINRA-KUN?
YES.
I HAD AN ADOLLA LINK.
"NOT AT THIS FACILITY," MY ASS. HE'S HERE, ALL RIGHT.
THEY'RE DEFINITELY HIDING SOMETHING. IF WE WANT TO FIND OUT WHAT IT IS, WE BETTER PLAY ALONG FOR A WHILE.
KWHRRR

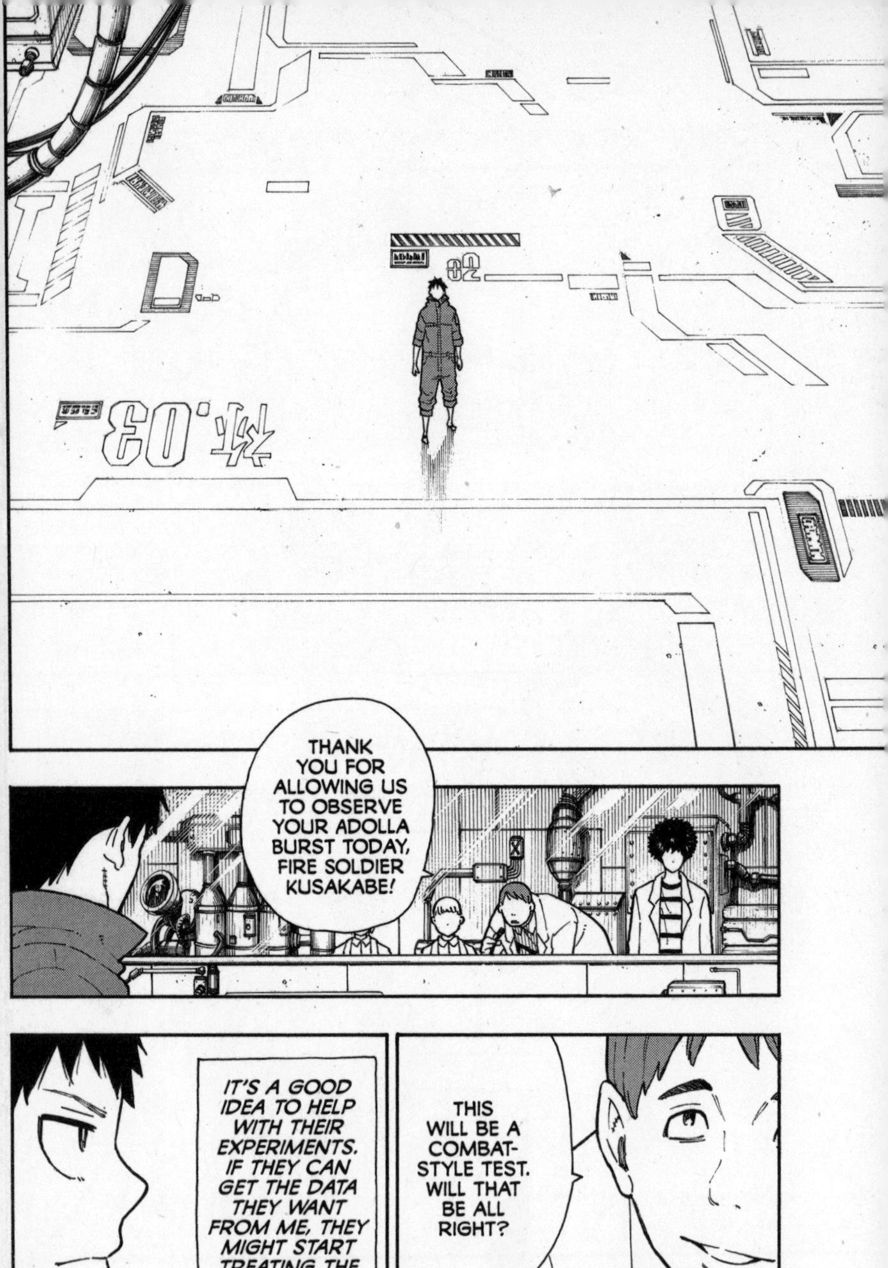
THANK YOU FOR ALLOWING US TO OBSERVE YOUR ADOLLA BURST TODAY, FIRE SOLDIER KUSAKABE!
THIS WILL BE A COMBAT-STYLE TEST. WILL THAT BE ALL RIGHT?
IT'S A GOOD IDEA TO HELP WITH THEIR EXPERIMENTS. IF THEY CAN GET THE DATA THEY WANT FROM ME, THEY MIGHT START TREATING THE KIDS BETTER.

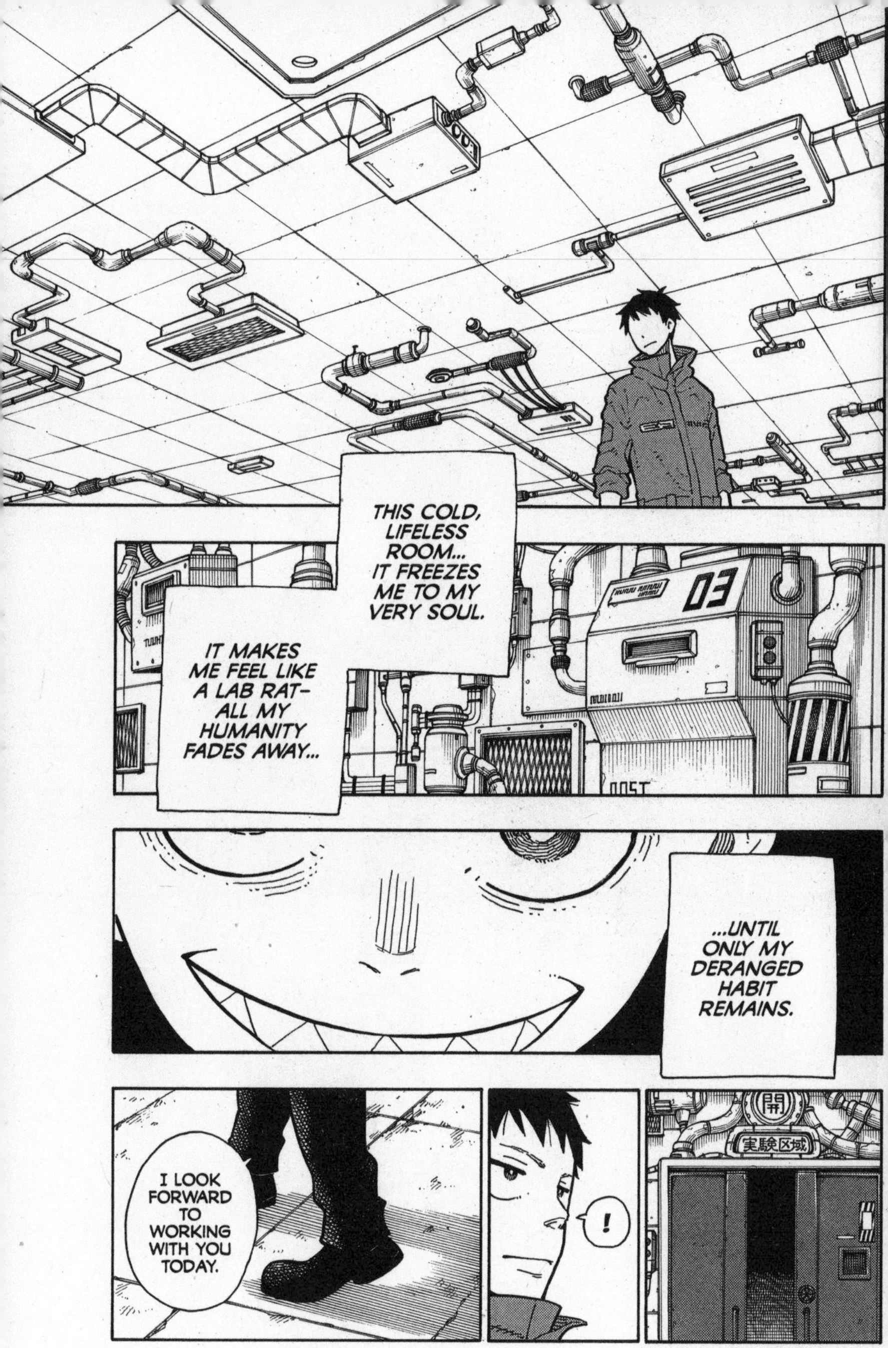
THIS COLD, LIFELESS ROOM... IT FREEZES ME TO MY VERY SOUL.
IT MAKES ME FEEL LIKE A LAB RAT— ALL MY HUMANITY FADES AWAY...
...UNTIL ONLY MY DERANGED HABIT REMAINS.
開
実験区域
!
I LOOK FORWARD TO WORKING WITH YOU TODAY.
Sign: (ENTER) Testing Zone

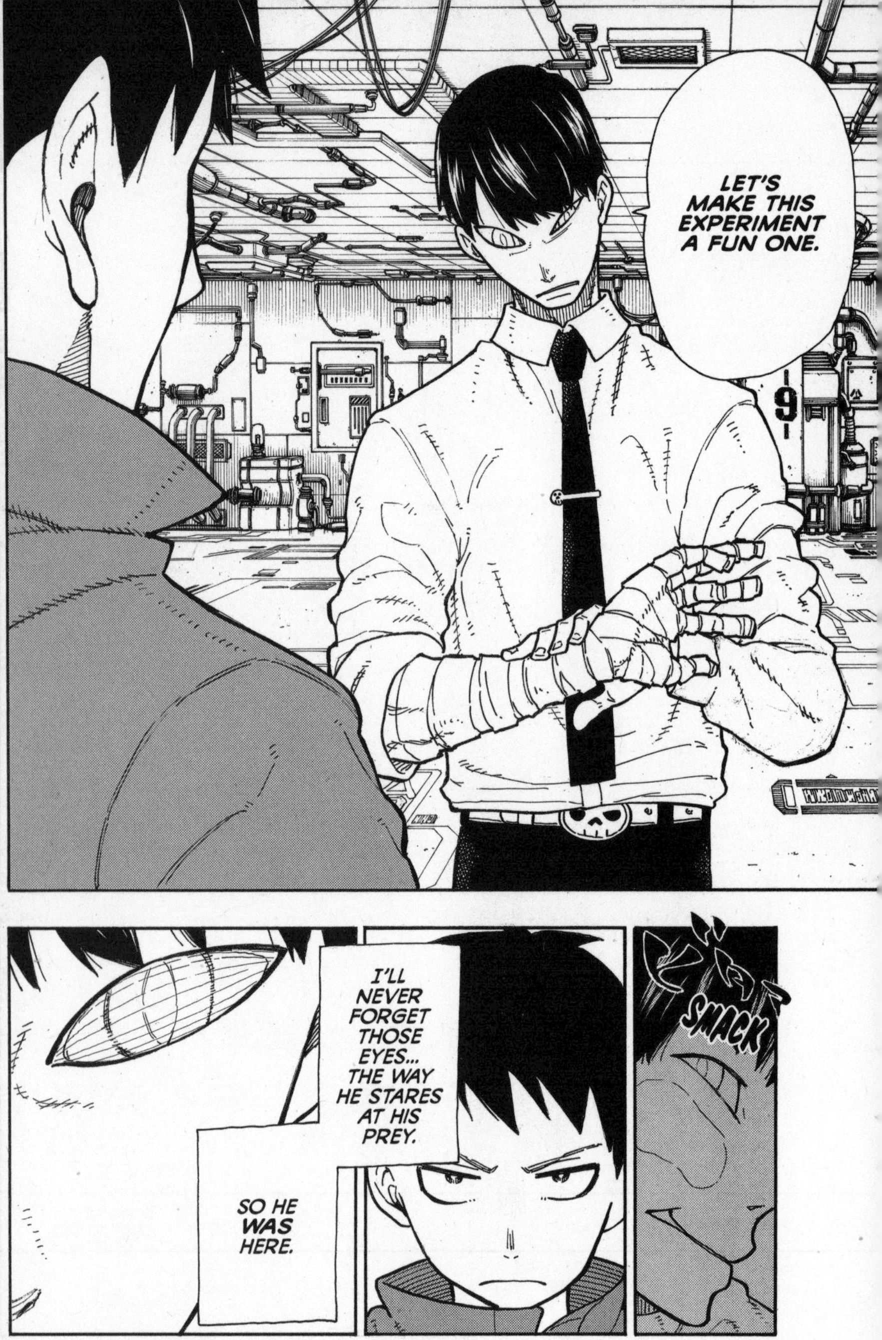
LET'S MAKE THIS EXPERIMENT A FUN ONE.
SMACK
I'LL NEVER FORGET THOSE EYES... THE WAY HE STARES AT HIS PREY.
SO HE WAS HERE.

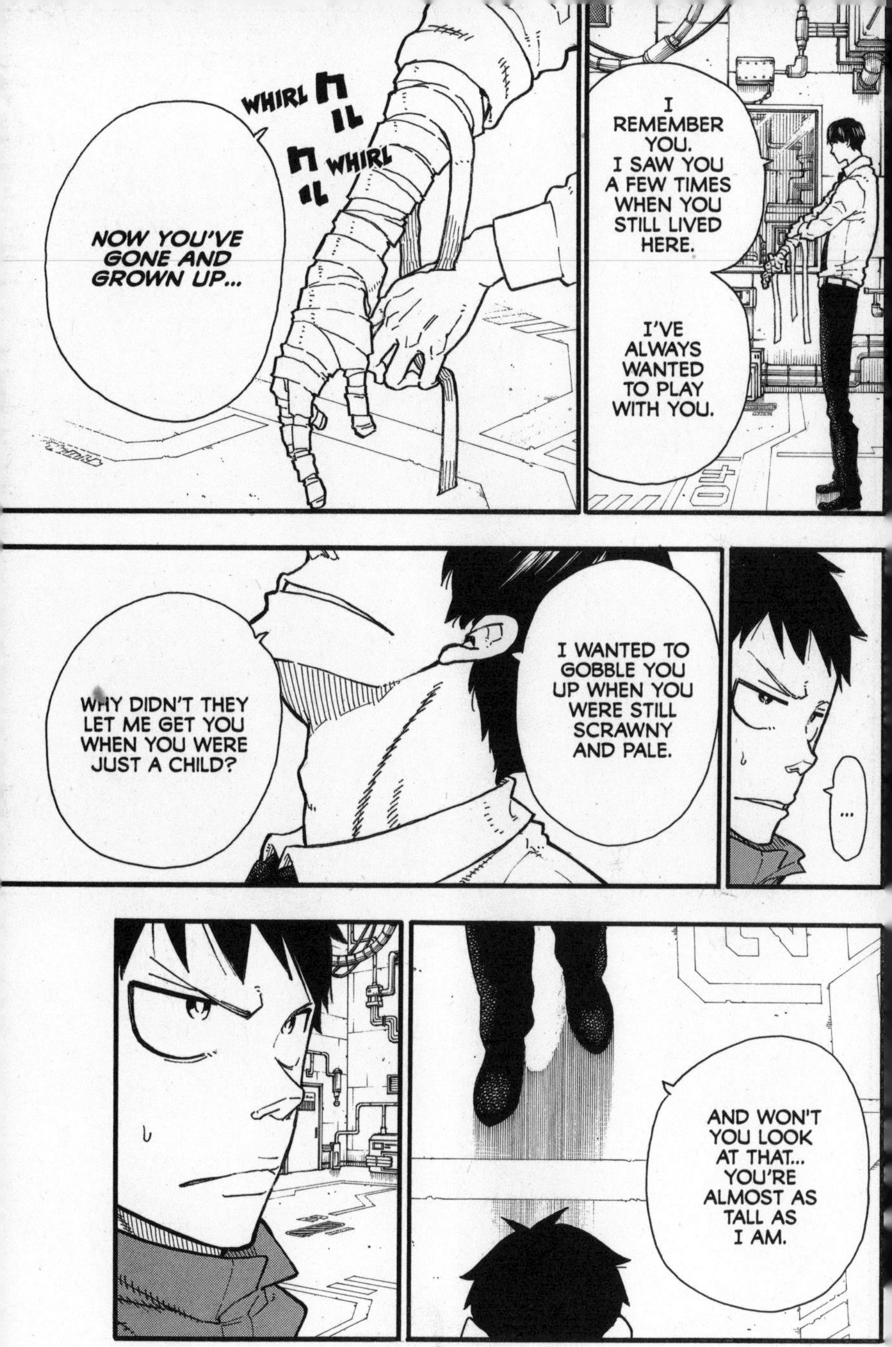
I REMEMBER YOU. I SAW YOU A FEW TIMES WHEN YOU STILL LIVED HERE.
I'VE ALWAYS WANTED TO PLAY WITH YOU.
WHIRL
WHIRL
NOW YOU'VE GONE AND GROWN UP...
...
I WANTED TO GOBBLE YOU UP WHEN YOU WERE STILL SCRAWNY AND PALE.
WHY DIDN'T THEY LET ME GET YOU WHEN YOU WERE JUST A CHILD?
AND WON'T YOU LOOK AT THAT... YOU'RE ALMOST AS TALL AS I AM.

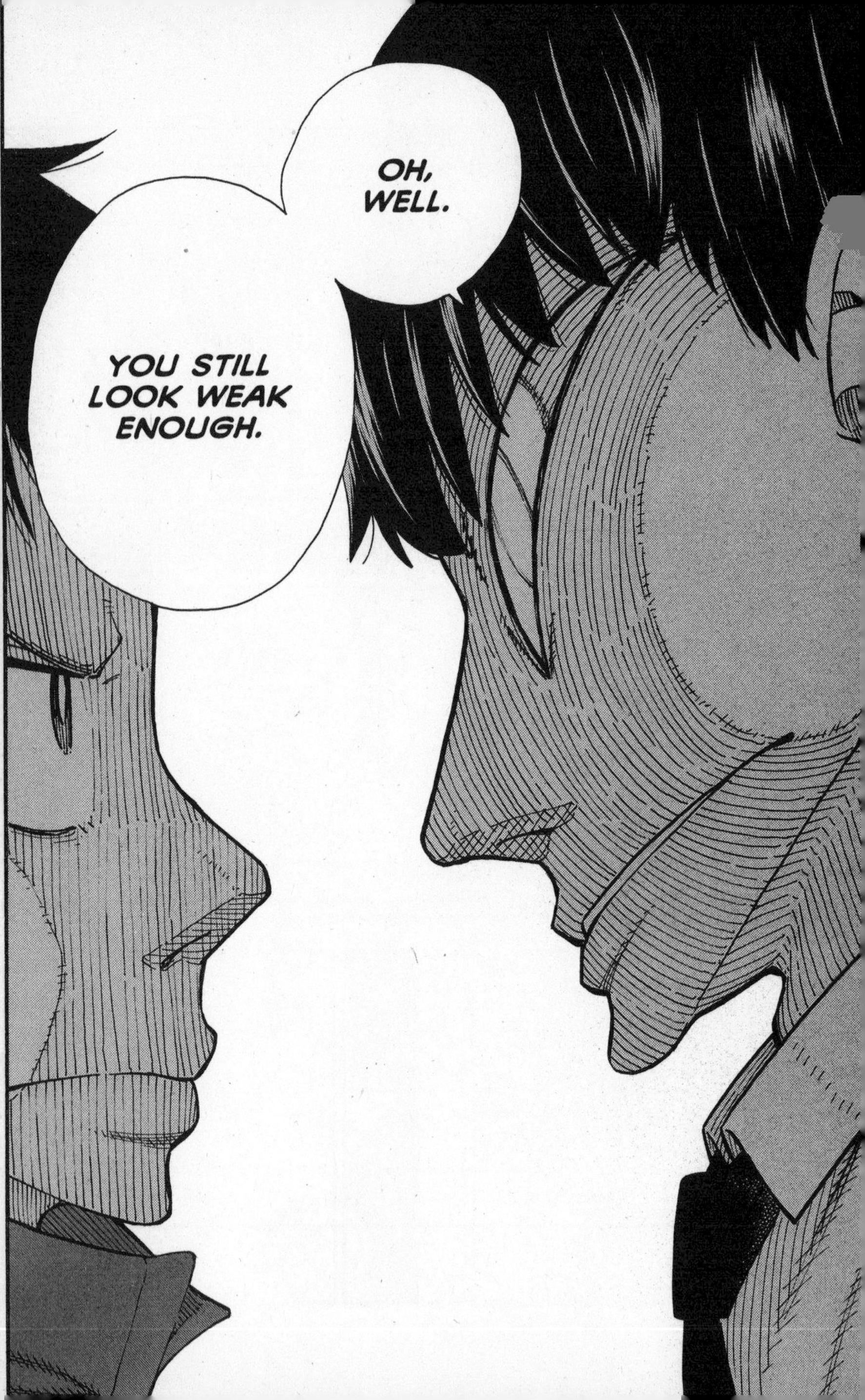
OH, WELL.
YOU STILL LOOK WEAK ENOUGH.

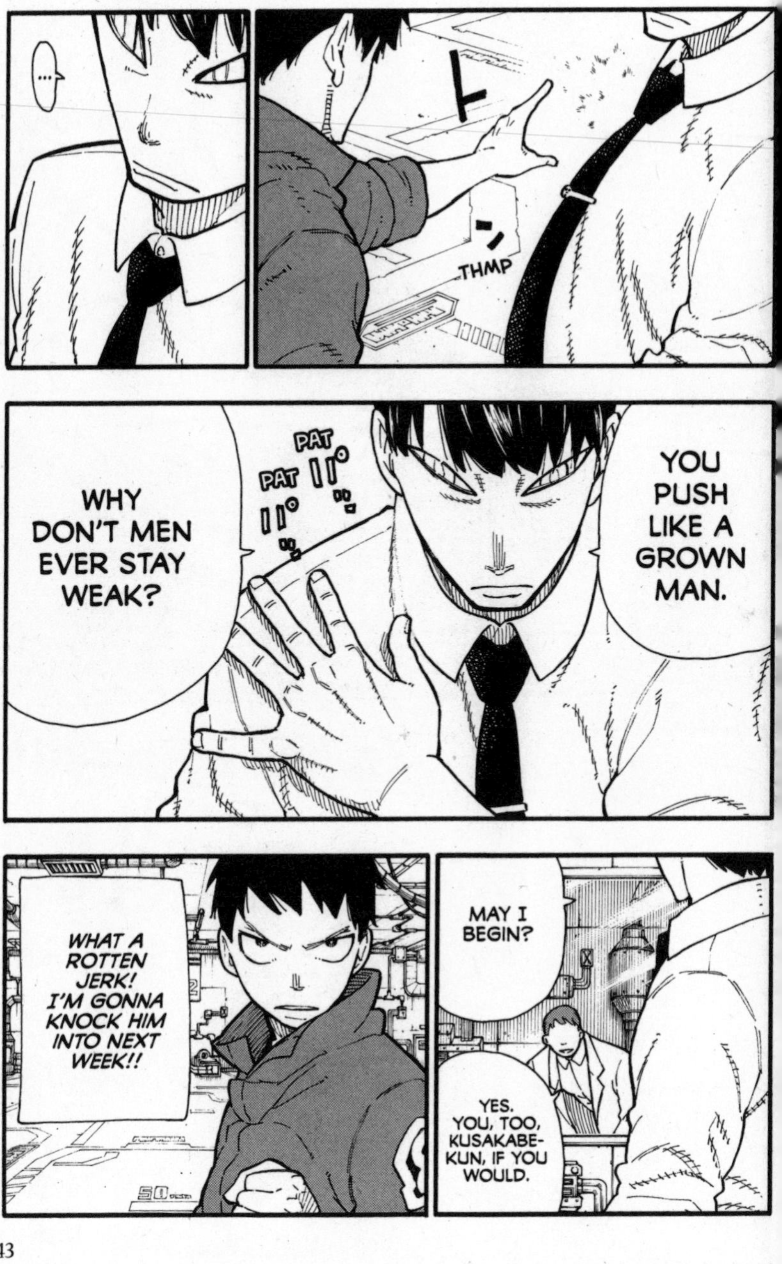
THMP
...
YOU PUSH LIKE A GROWN MAN.
PAT PAT
WHY DON'T MEN EVER STAY WEAK?
MAY I BEGIN?
YES. YOU, TOO, KUSAKABE-KUN, IF YOU WOULD.
WHAT A ROTTEN JERK! I'M GONNA KNOCK HIM INTO NEXT WEEK!!

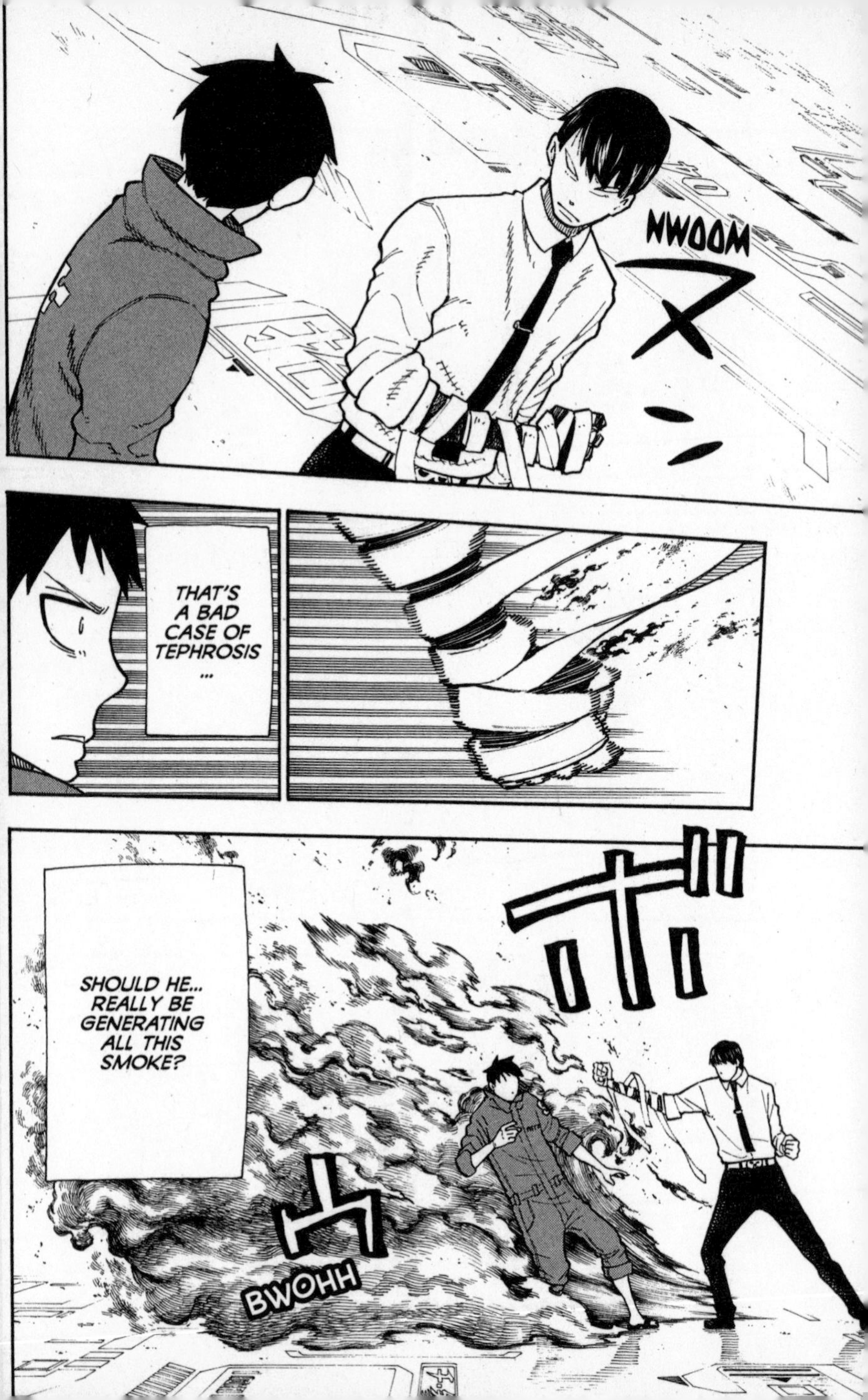
NWOOM
THAT'S A BAD CASE OF TEPHROSIS ...
SHOULD HE... REALLY BE GENERATING ALL THIS SMOKE?
BWOHH

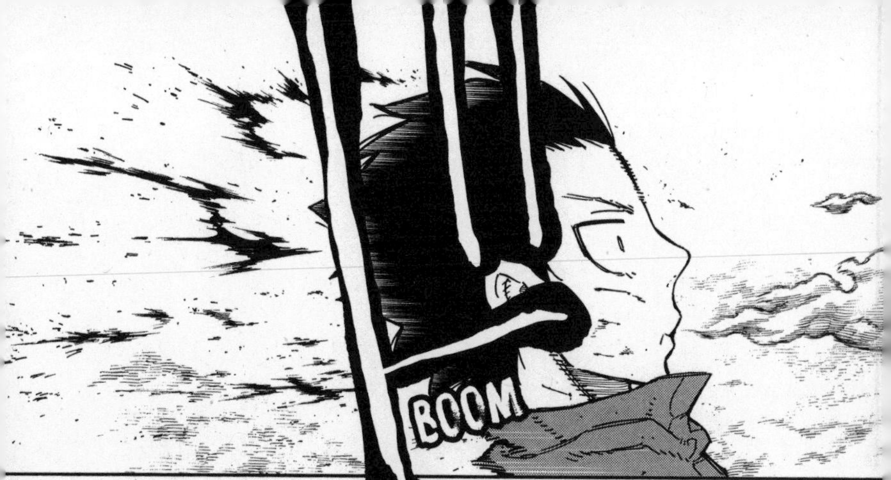
BOOM
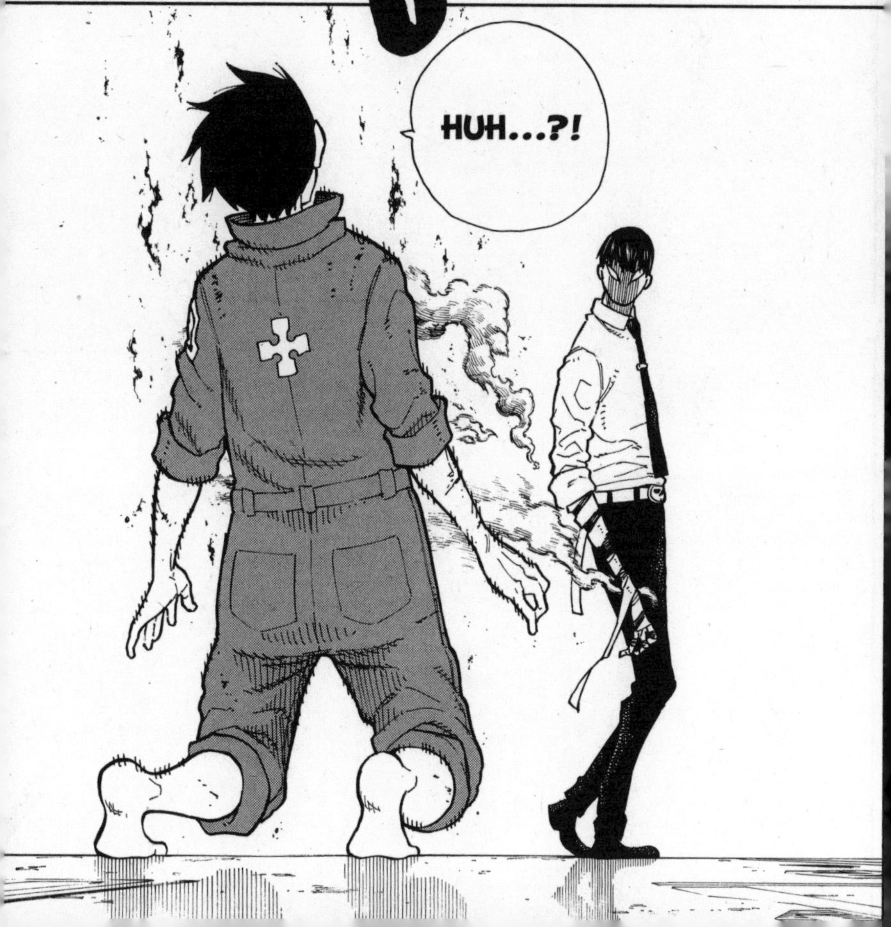
HUH...?!

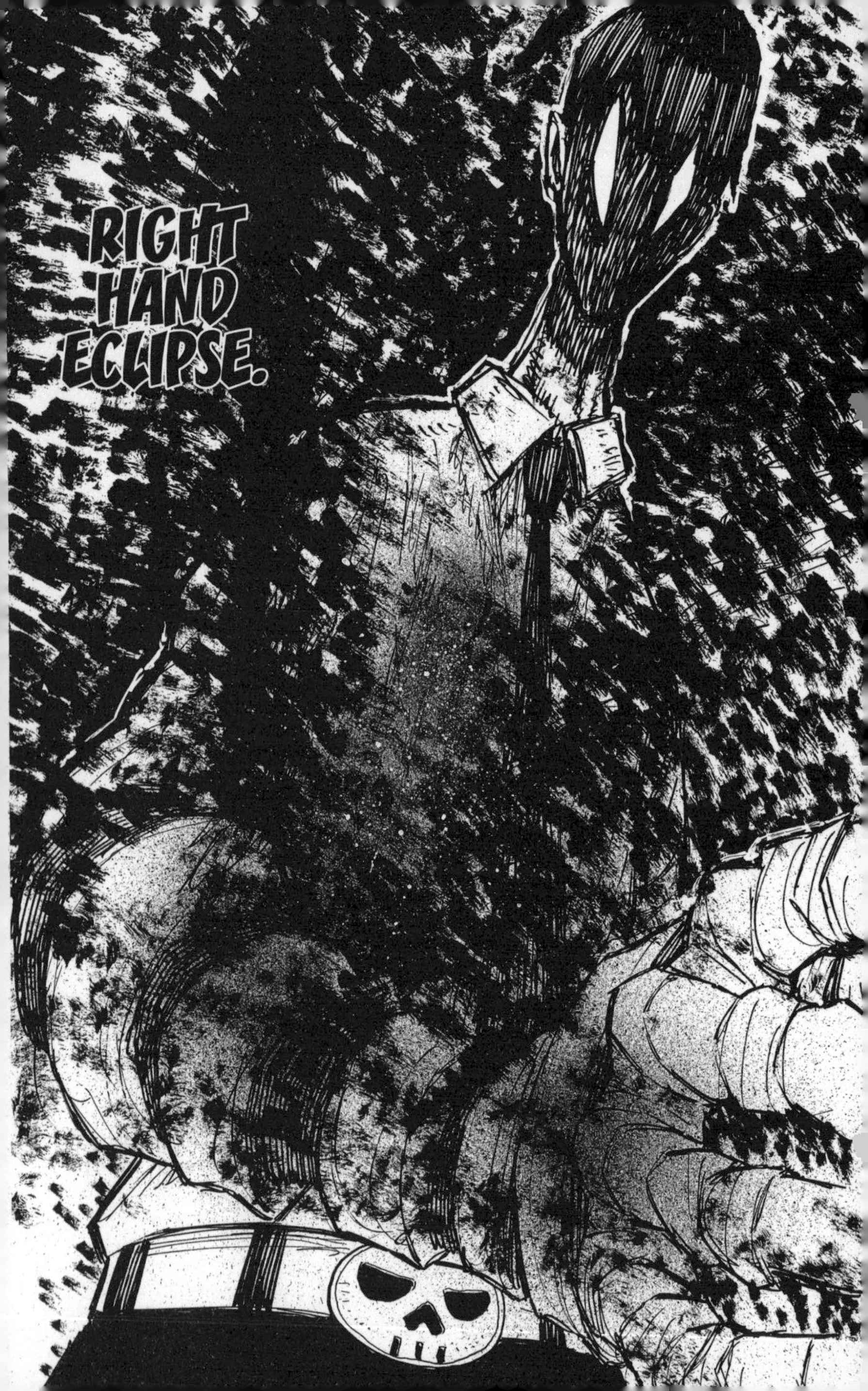
RIGHT HAND ECLIPSE.

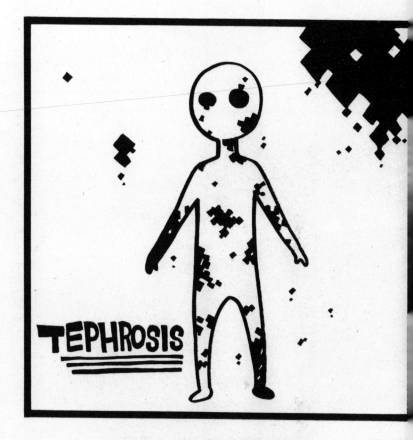

CHAPTER CXXXV: ASHEN DEATH

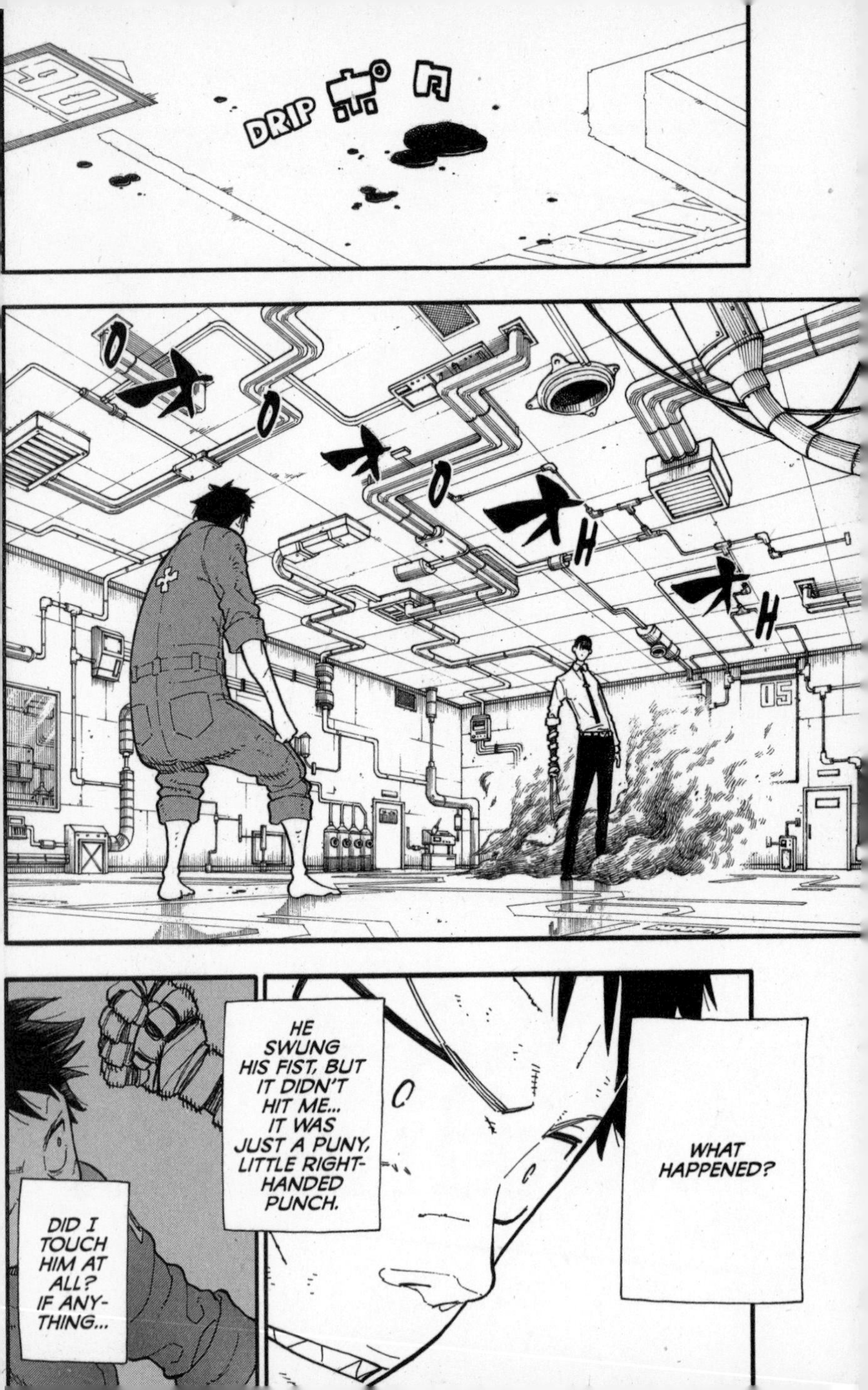
DRIP
WHAT HAPPENED?
HE SWUNG HIS FIST, BUT IT DIDN'T HIT ME... IT WAS JUST A PUNY, LITTLE RIGHT-HANDED PUNCH.
DID I TOUCH HIM AT ALL? IF ANYTHING...

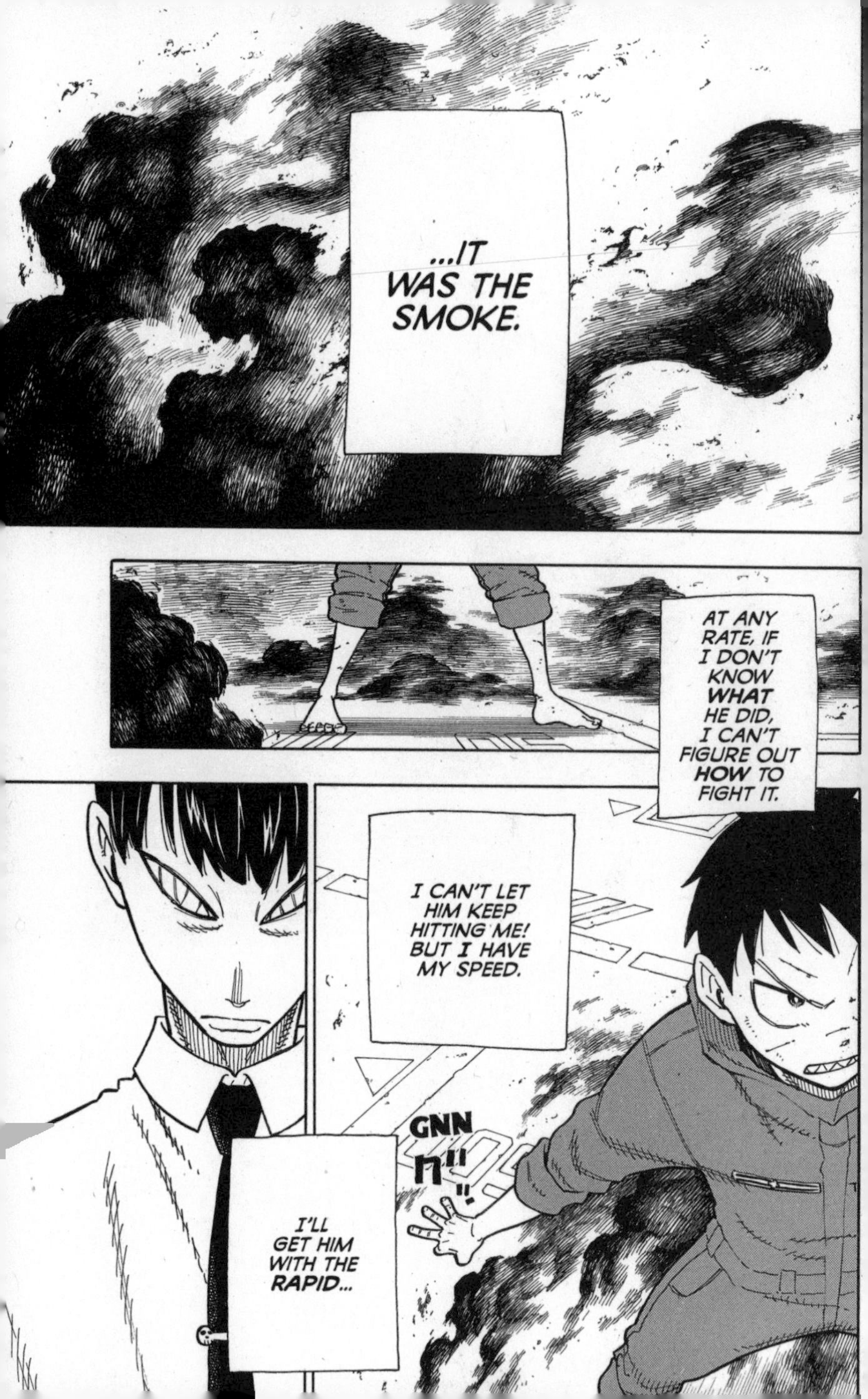
...IT WAS THE SMOKE.
AT ANY RATE, IF I DON'T KNOW WHAT HE DID, I CAN'T FIGURE OUT HOW TO FIGHT IT.
I CAN'T LET HIM KEEP HITTING ME! BUT I HAVE MY SPEED.
GNN
I'LL GET HIM WITH THE RAPID...

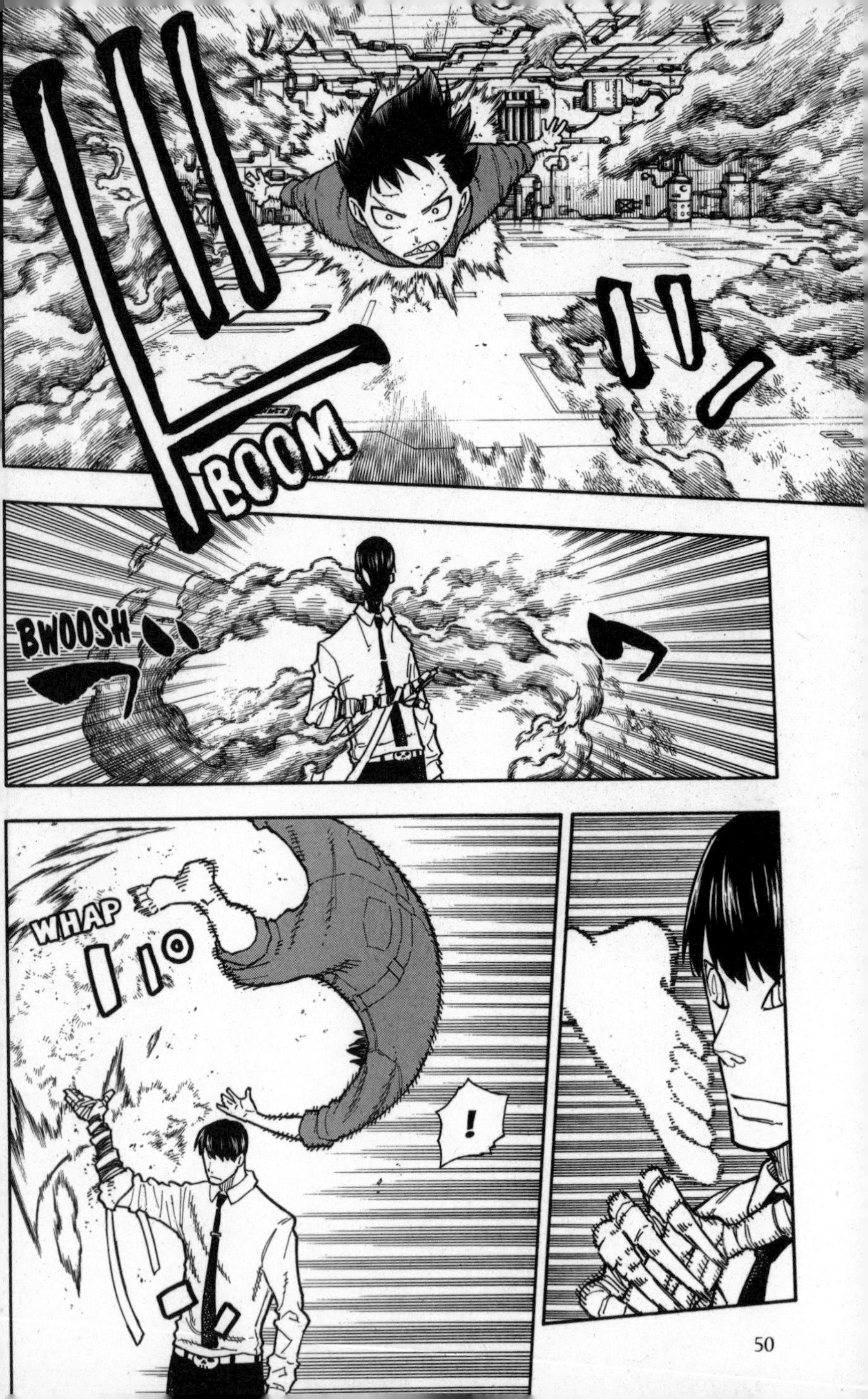
BOOM
BWOOSH
!
WHAP

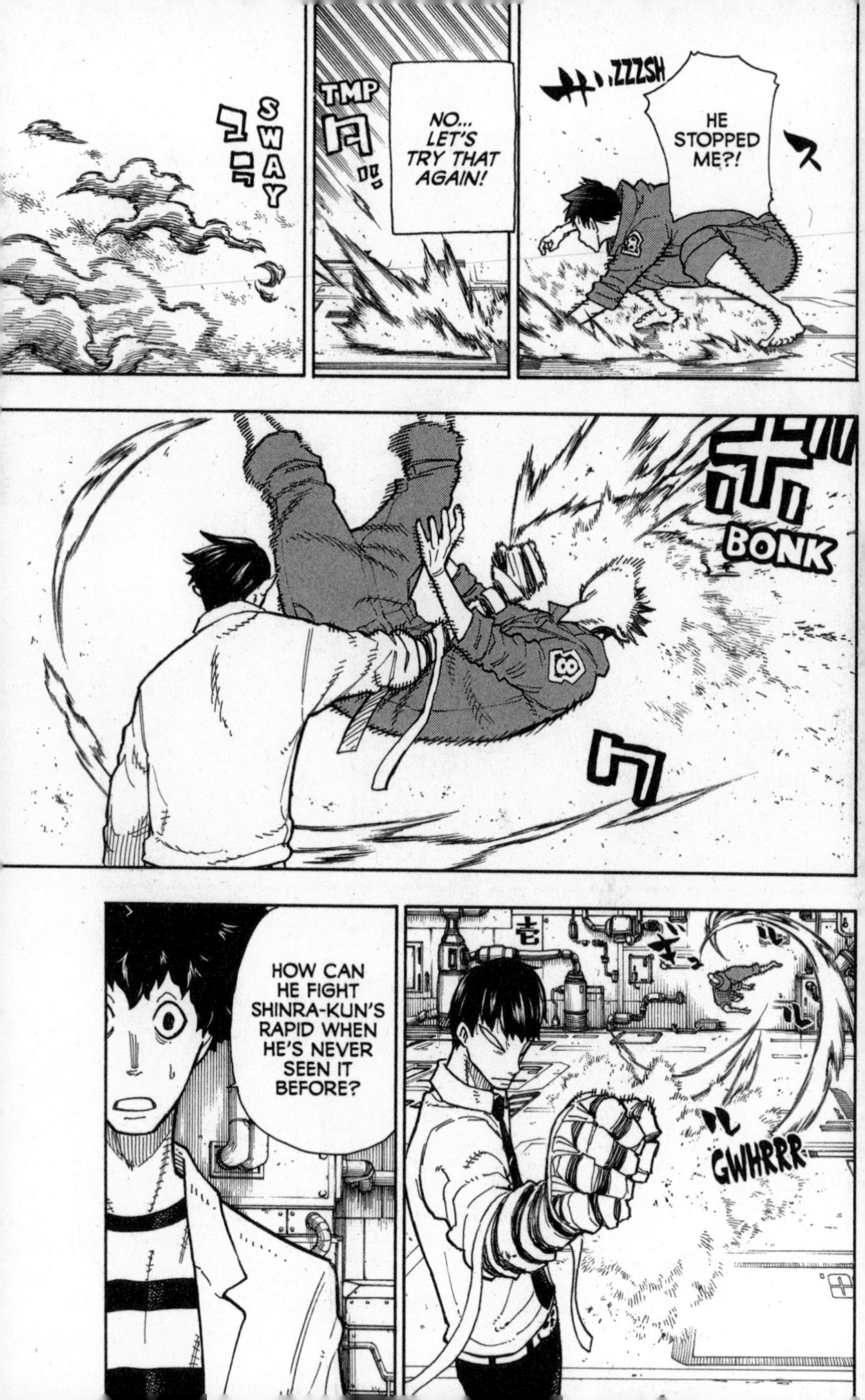
ZZZSH
HE STOPPED ME?!
TMP
NO... LET'S TRY THAT AGAIN!
SWAY
BONK
GWHRRR
HOW CAN HE FIGHT SHINRA-KUN'S RAPID WHEN HE'S NEVER SEEN IT BEFORE?

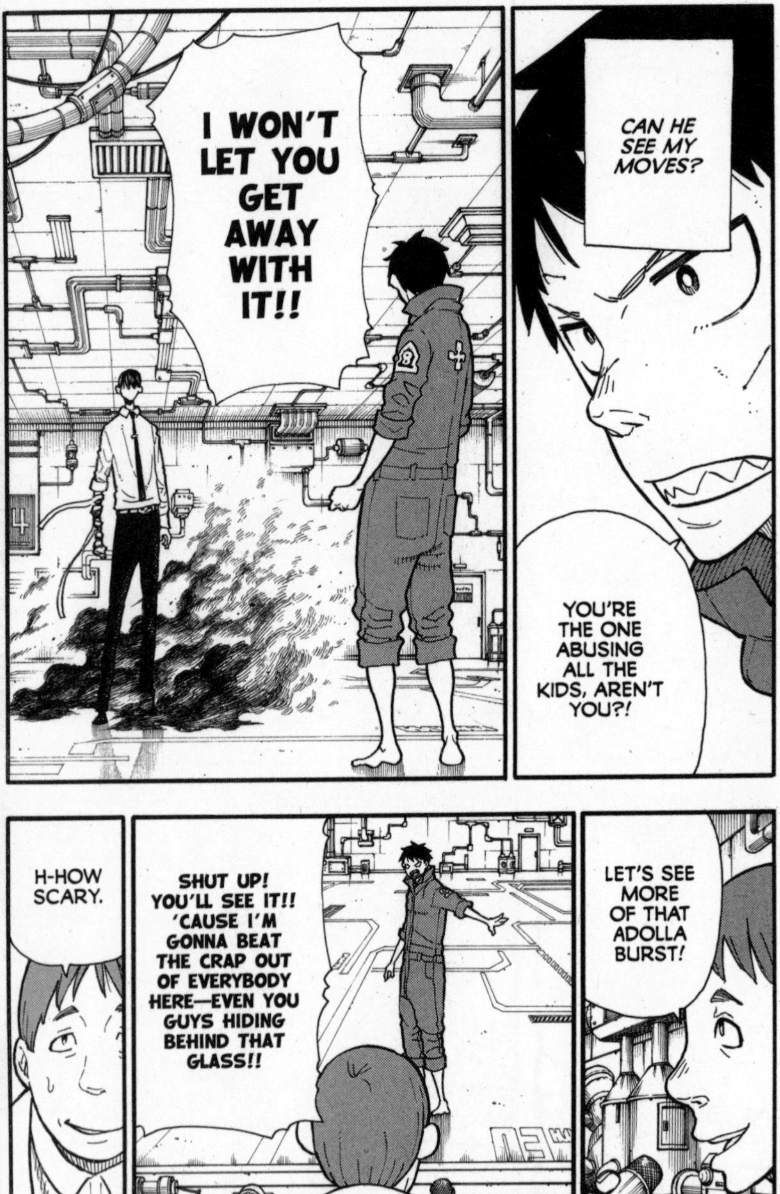
CAN HE SEE MY MOVES?
YOU'RE THE ONE ABUSING ALL THE KIDS, AREN'T YOU?!
I WON'T LET YOU GET AWAY WITH IT!!
LET'S SEE MORE OF THAT ADOLLA BURST!
SHUT UP! YOU'LL SEE IT!! 'CAUSE I'M GONNA BEAT THE CRAP OUT OF EVERYBODY HERE—EVEN YOU GUYS HIDING BEHIND THAT GLASS!!
H-HOW SCARY.

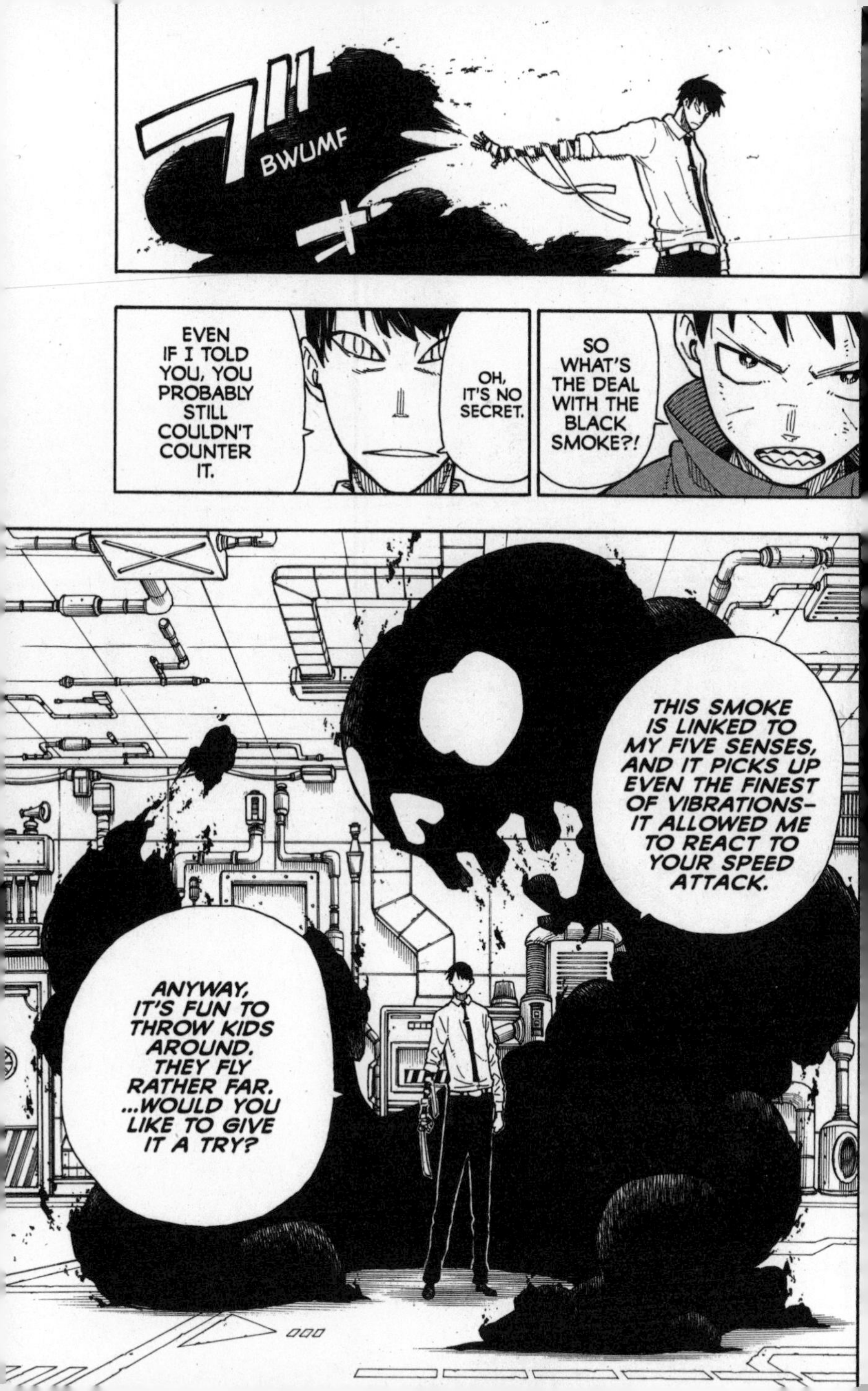
BWUMF
SO WHAT'S THE DEAL WITH THE BLACK SMOKE?!
OH, IT'S NO SECRET.
EVEN IF I TOLD YOU, YOU PROBABLY STILL COULDN'T COUNTER IT.
THIS SMOKE IS LINKED TO MY FIVE SENSES, AND IT PICKS UP EVEN THE FINEST OF VIBRATIONS— IT ALLOWED ME TO REACT TO YOUR SPEED ATTACK.
ANYWAY, IT'S FUN TO THROW KIDS AROUND. THEY FLY RATHER FAR. ...WOULD YOU LIKE TO GIVE IT A TRY?

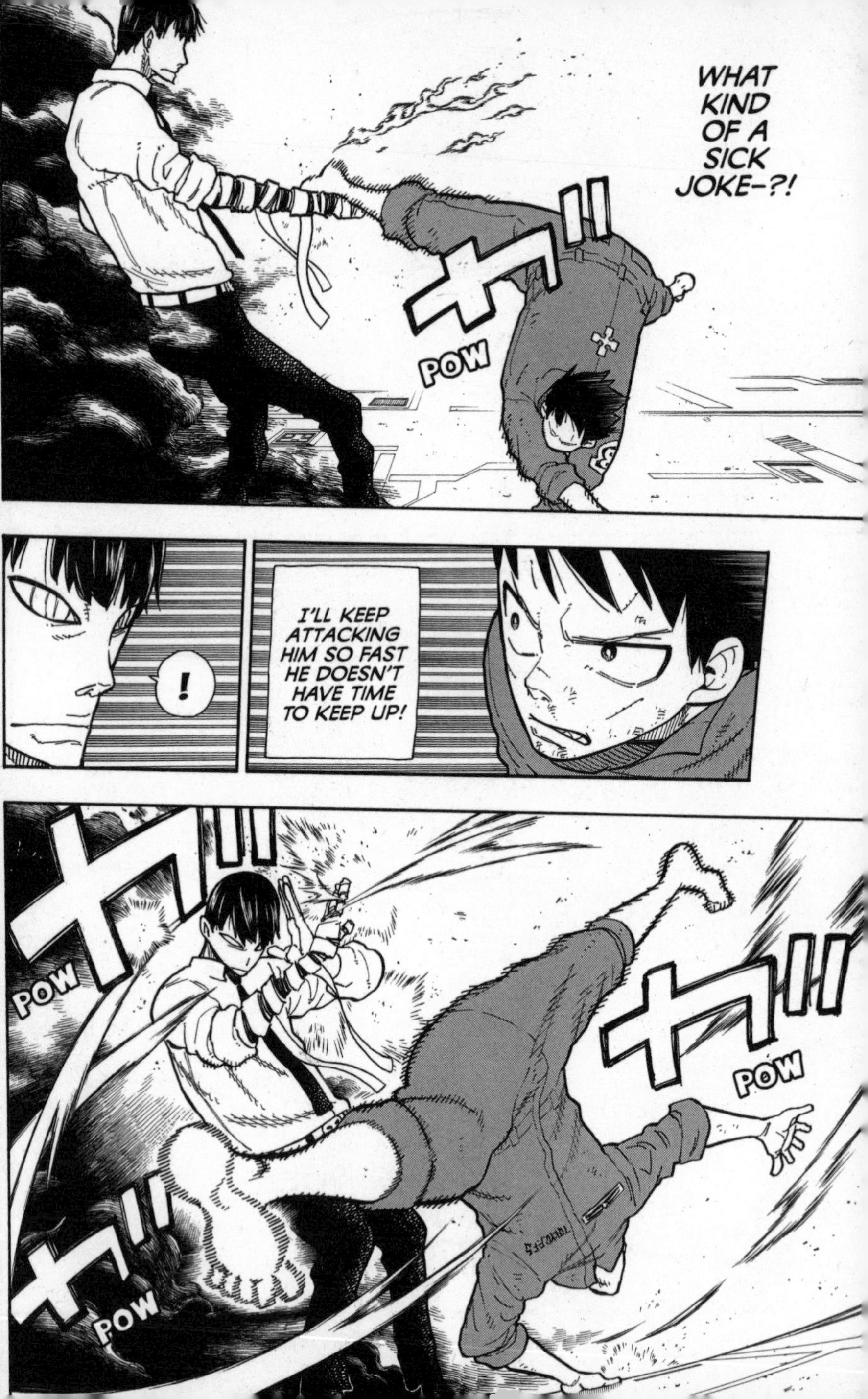
WHAT KIND OF A SICK JOKE-?!
POW
I'LL KEEP ATTACKING HIM SO FAST HE DOESN'T HAVE TIME TO KEEP UP!
!
POW
POW
POW

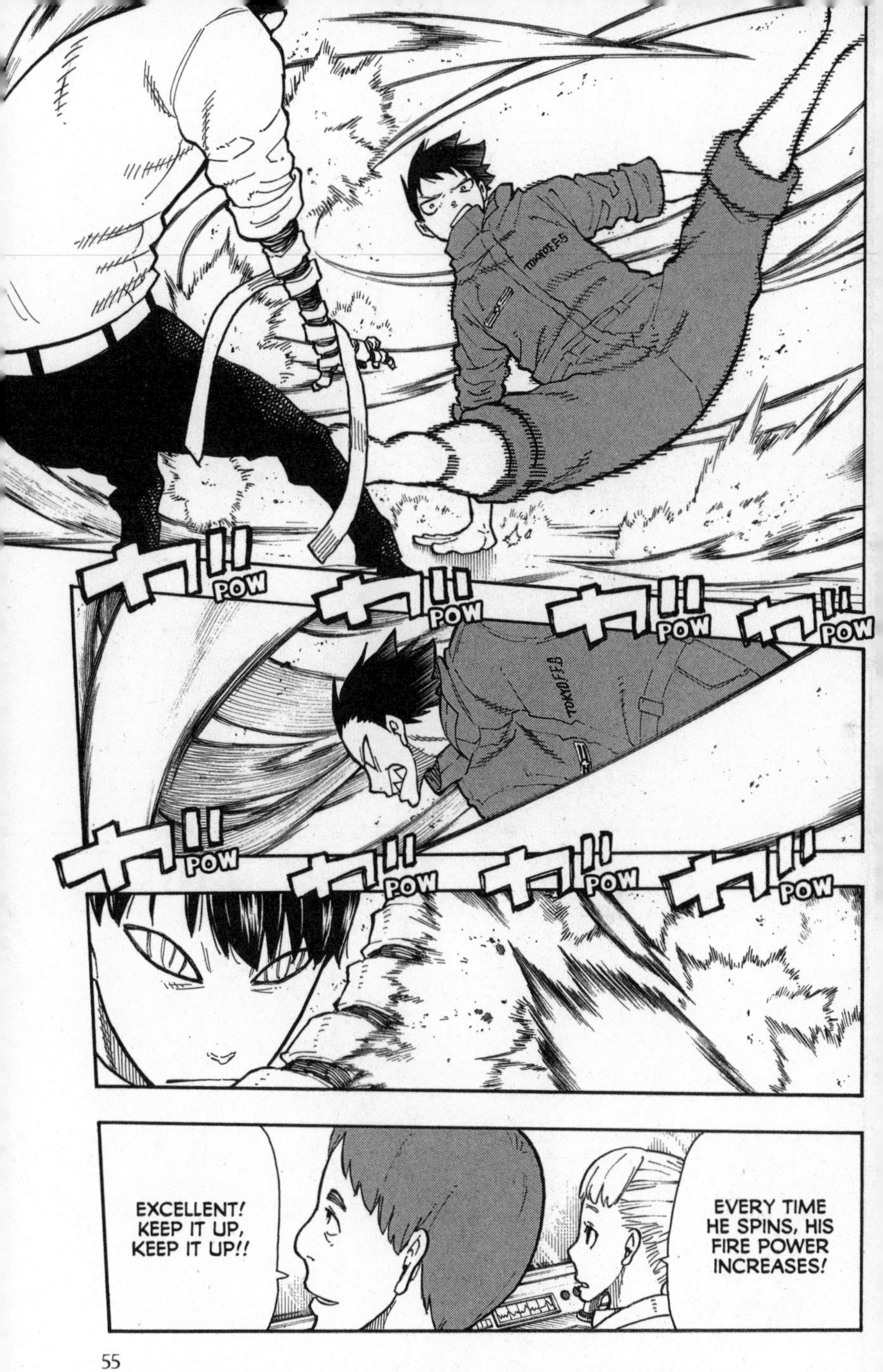
ガ POW
ガ POW
ガ POW
ガ POW
ガ POW
ガ POW
ガ POW
ガ POW
EVERY TIME HE SPINS, HIS FIRE POWER INCREASES!
EXCELLENT! KEEP IT UP, KEEP IT UP!!

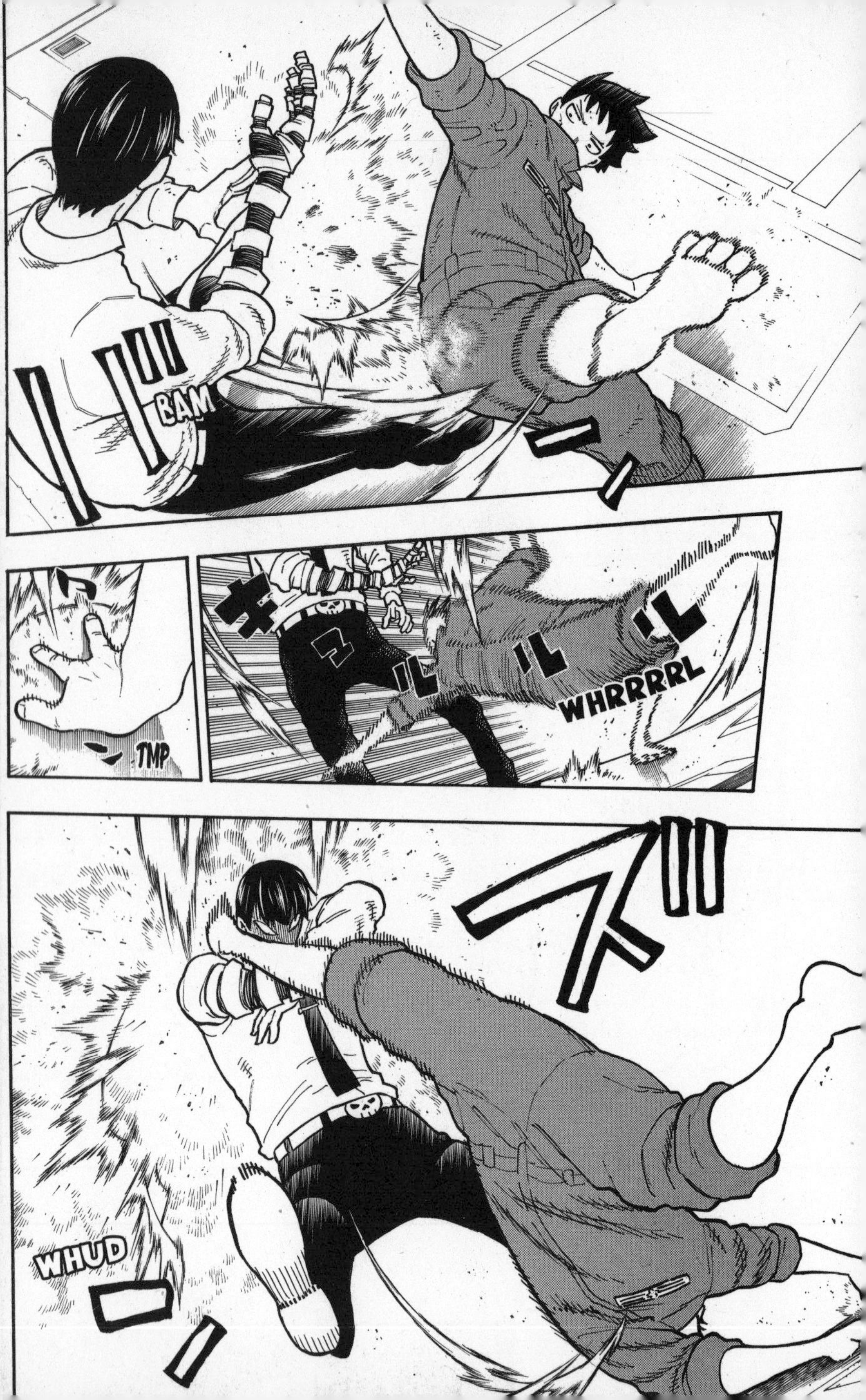
BAM
WHRRRRL
TMP
WHUD

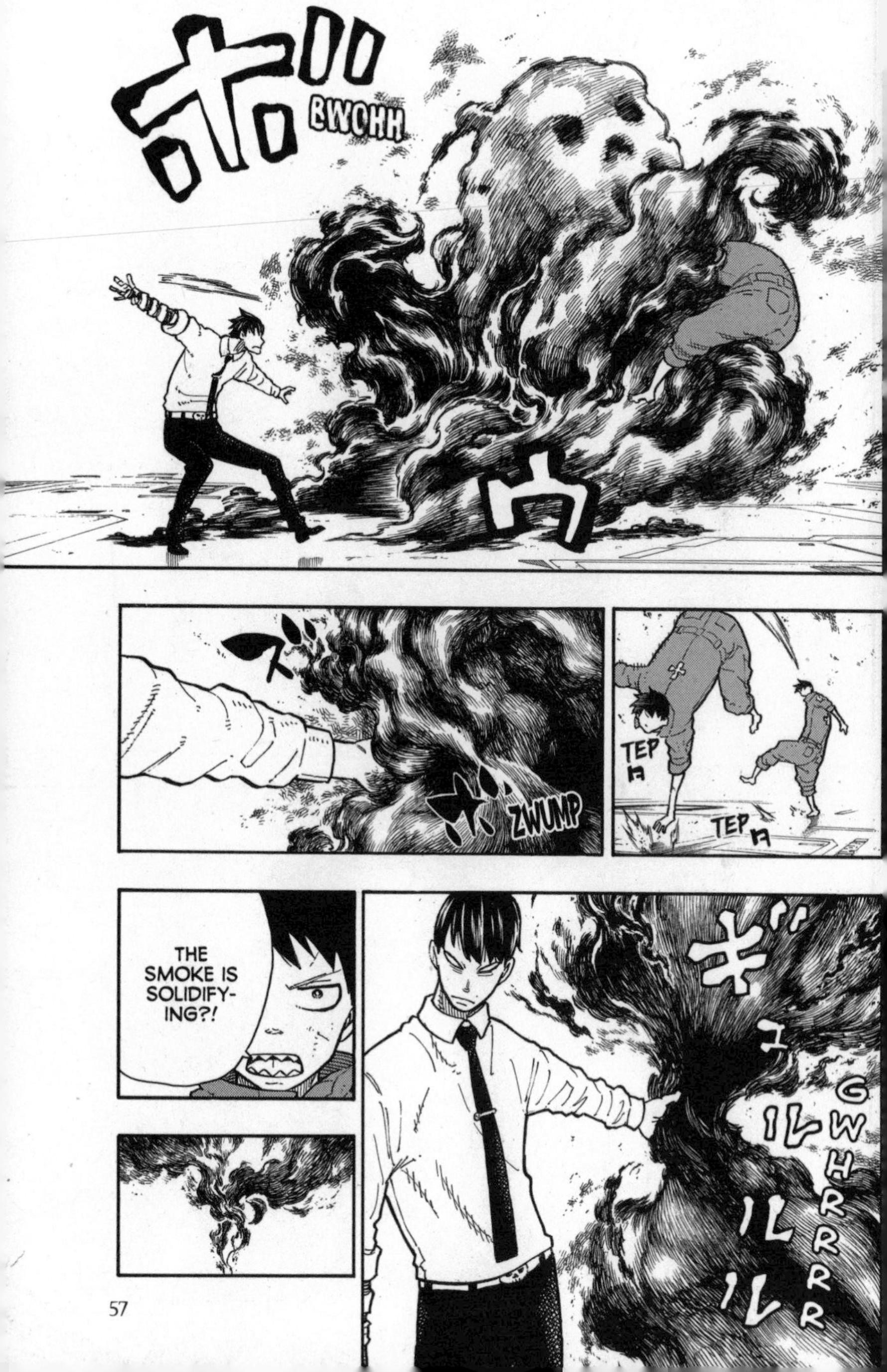
BWOHH
TEP
TEP
ZWUMP
GWHRRRR
THE SMOKE IS SOLIDIFY-ING?!

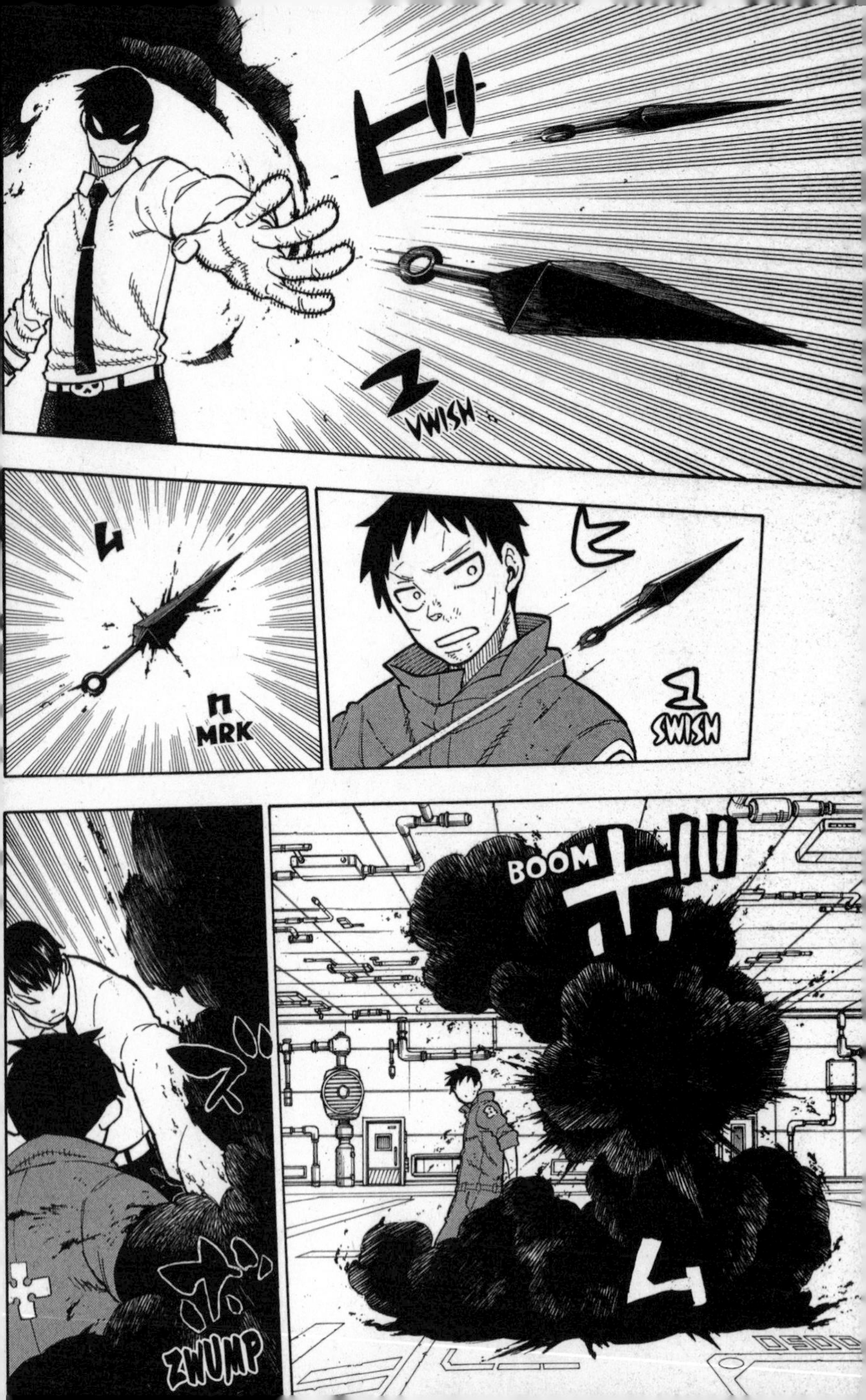
VWISH
SWISH
MRK
BOOM
ZWUMP

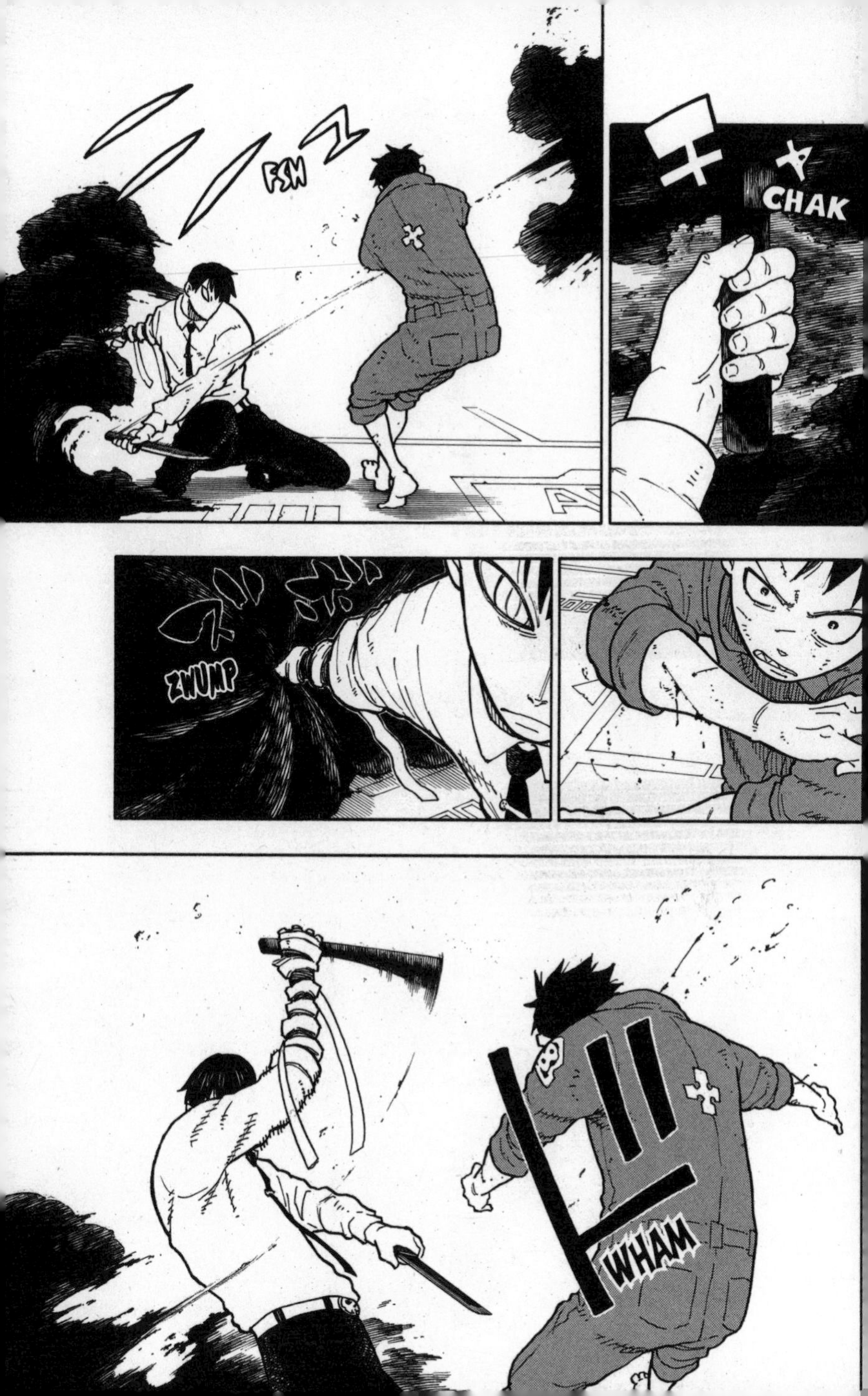
CHAK
FSH
ZWUMP
WHAM

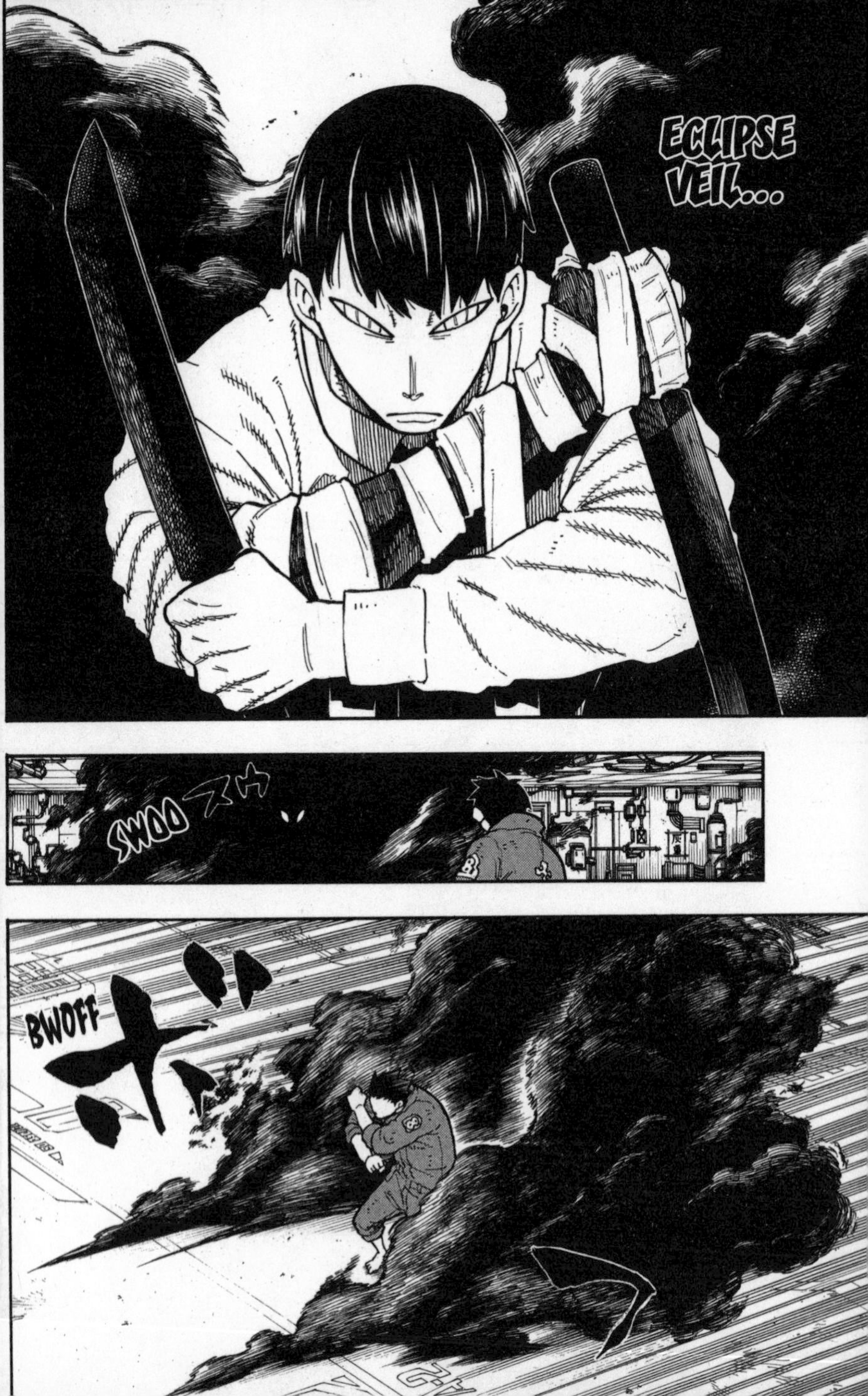
ECLIPSE VEIL...
SWOO スゥ
BWOFF

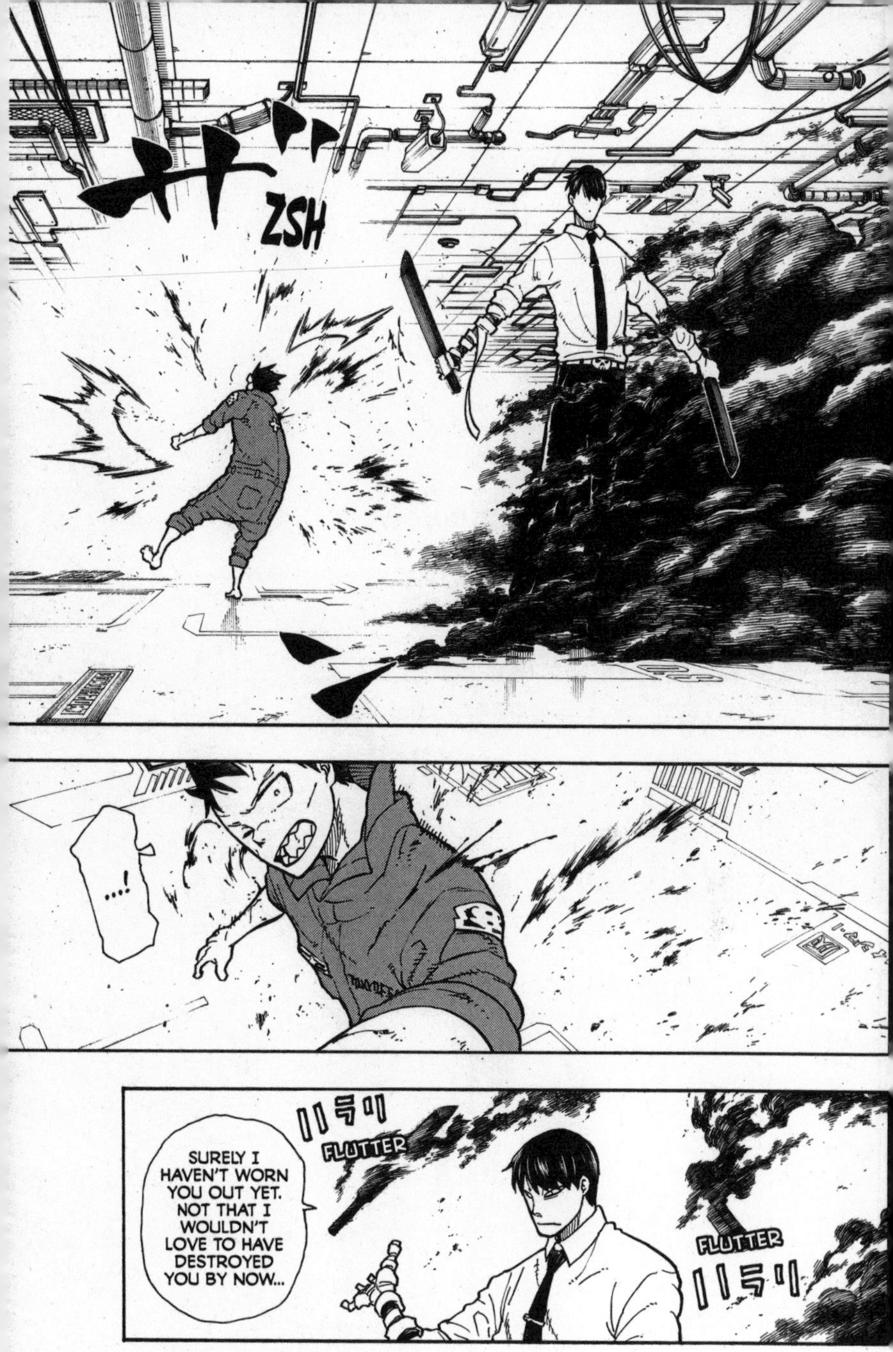
ZSH
...!
FLUTTER
SURELY I HAVEN'T WORN YOU OUT YET. NOT THAT I WOULDN'T LOVE TO HAVE DESTROYED YOU BY NOW...
FLUTTER

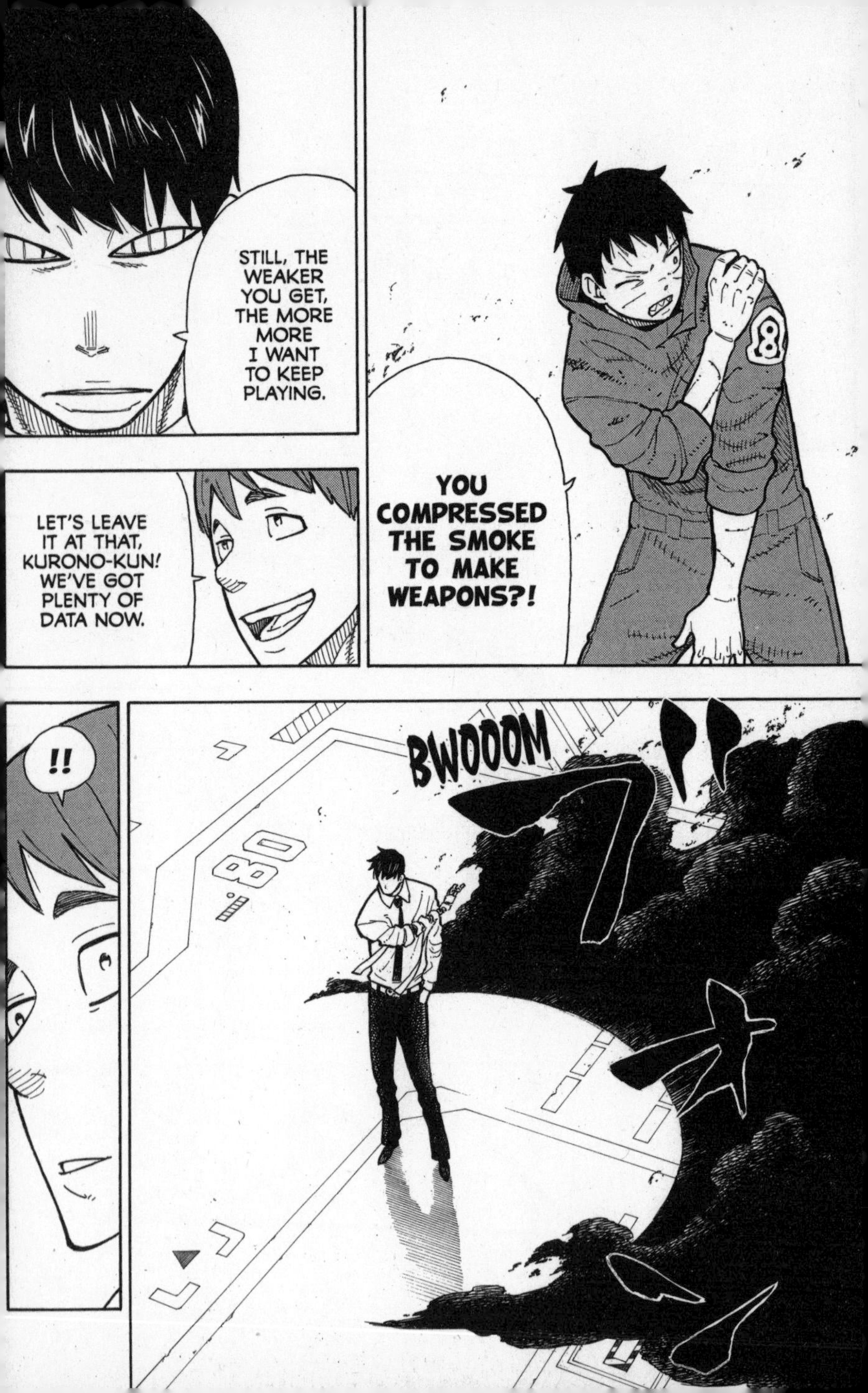
YOU COMPRESSED THE SMOKE TO MAKE WEAPONS?!
STILL, THE WEAKER YOU GET, THE MORE MORE I WANT TO KEEP PLAYING.
LET'S LEAVE IT AT THAT, KURONO-KUN! WE'VE GOT PLENTY OF DATA NOW.
BWOOOM
!!

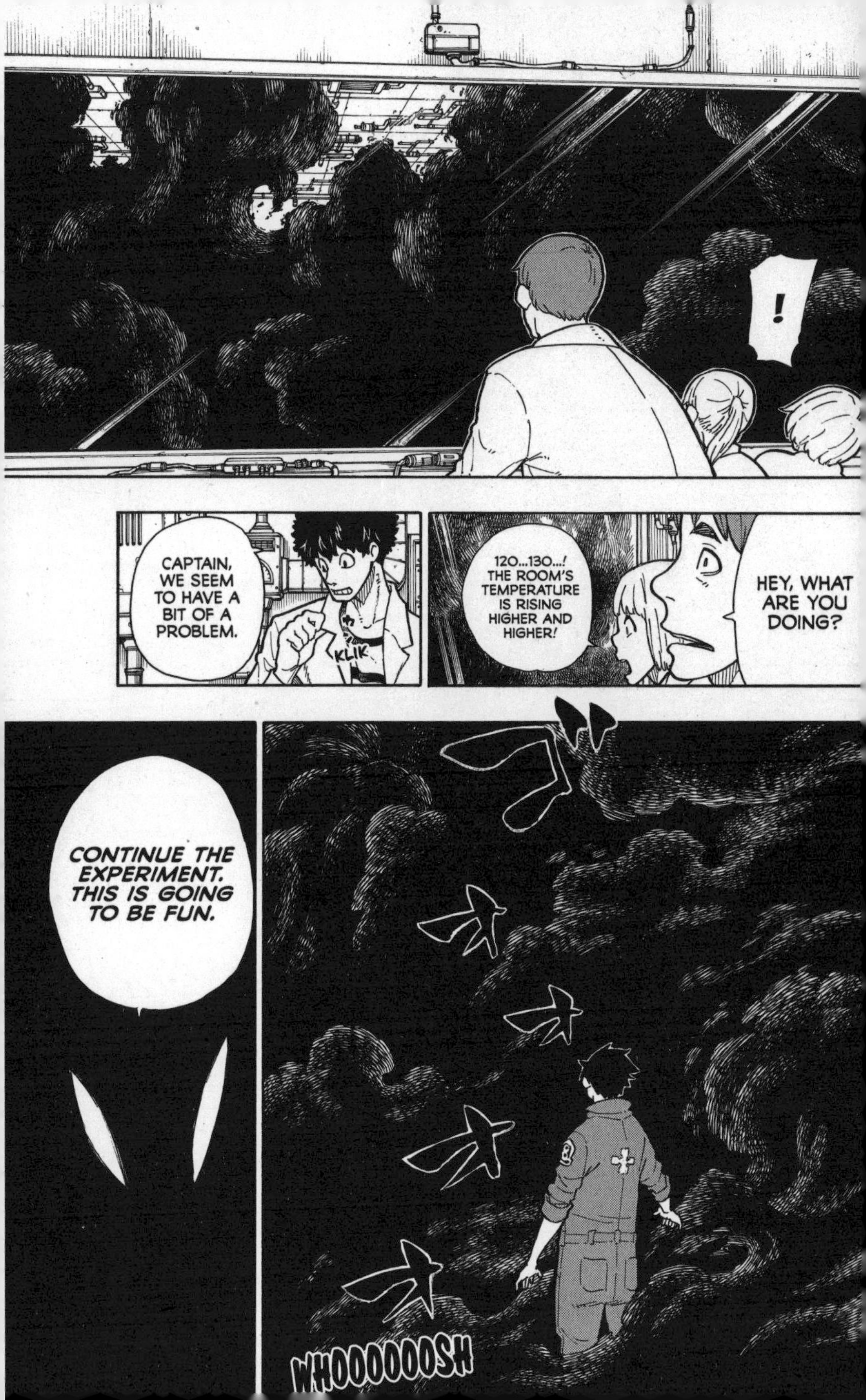
!
HEY, WHAT ARE YOU DOING?
120...130...! THE ROOM'S TEMPERATURE IS RISING HIGHER AND HIGHER!
CAPTAIN, WE SEEM TO HAVE A BIT OF A PROBLEM.
KLIK
WHOOOOOOSH
CONTINUE THE EXPERIMENT. THIS IS GOING TO BE FUN.

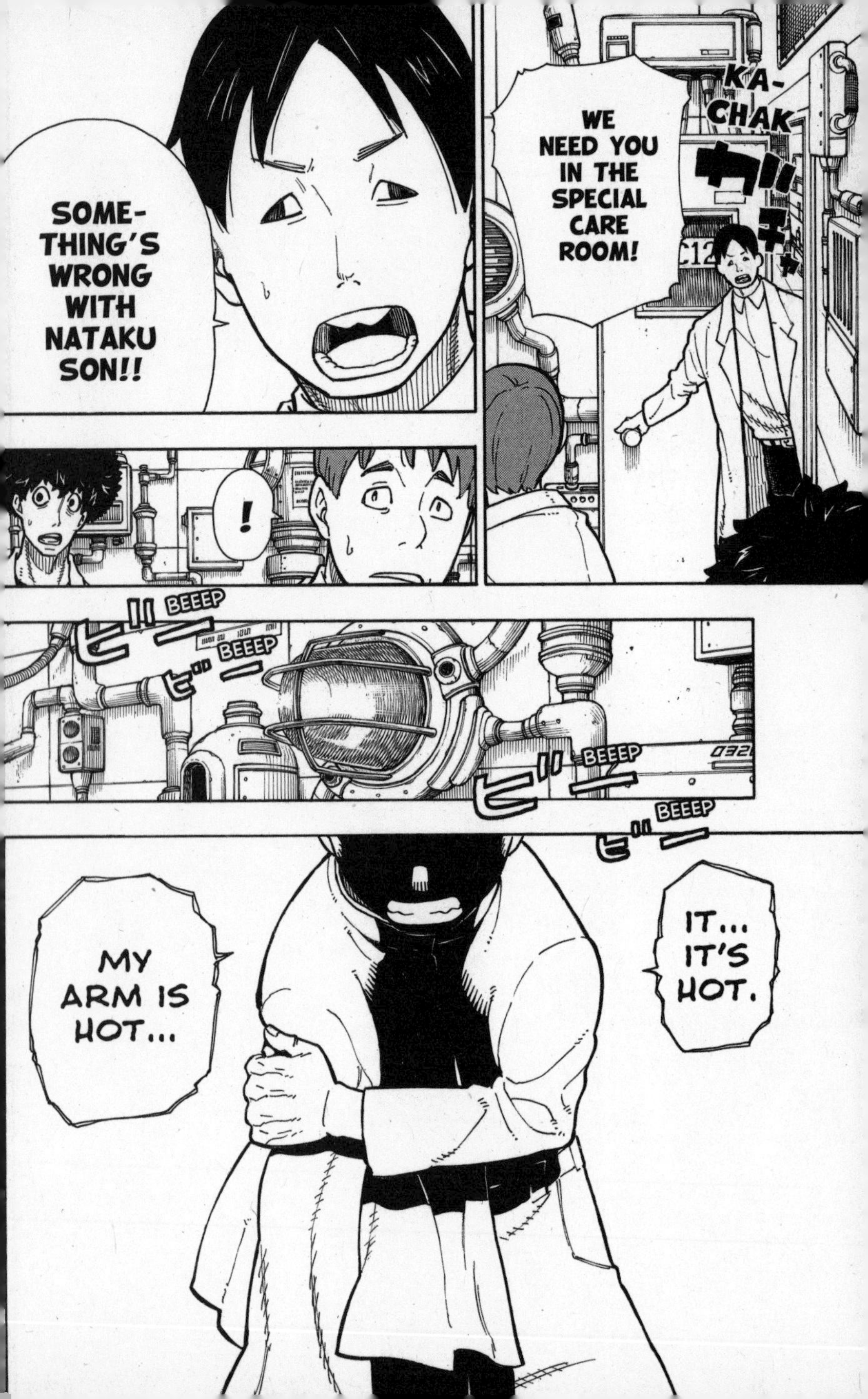
KA-CHAK
WE NEED YOU IN THE SPECIAL CARE ROOM!
SOME-THING'S WRONG WITH NATAKU SON!!
!
BEEEP
BEEEP
BEEEP
BEEEP
IT... IT'S HOT.
MY ARM IS HOT...

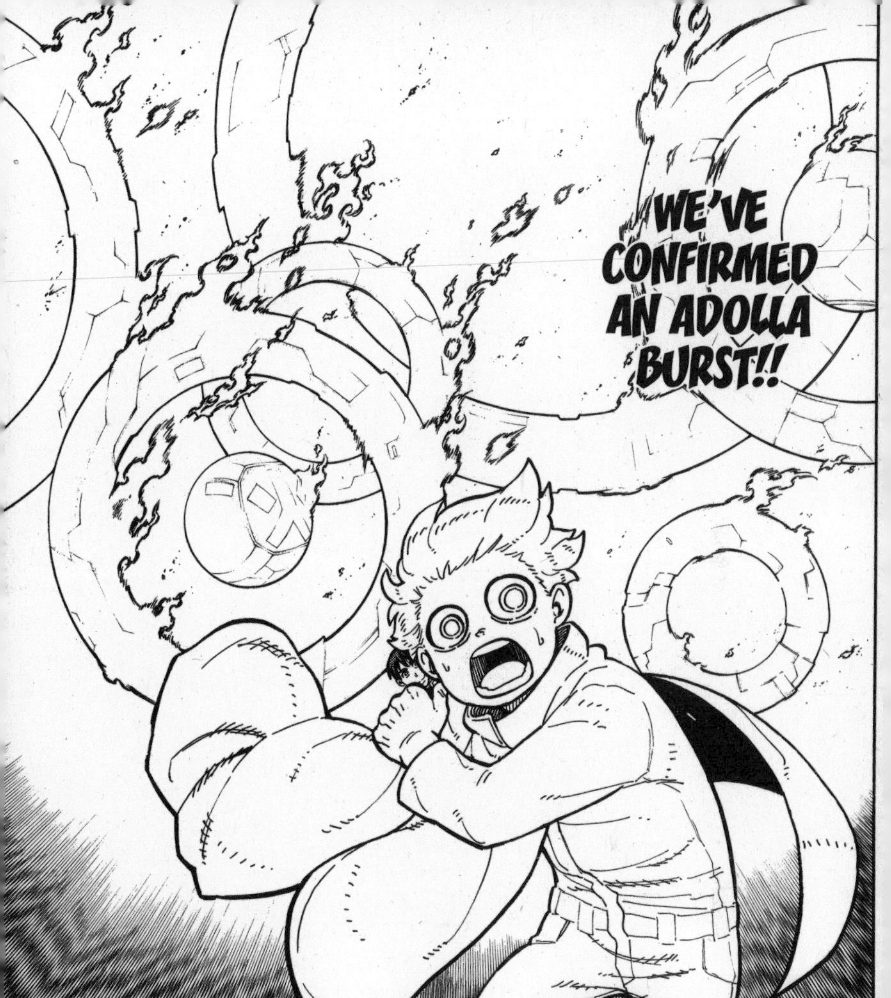
WE'VE CONFIRMED AN ADOLLA BURST!!
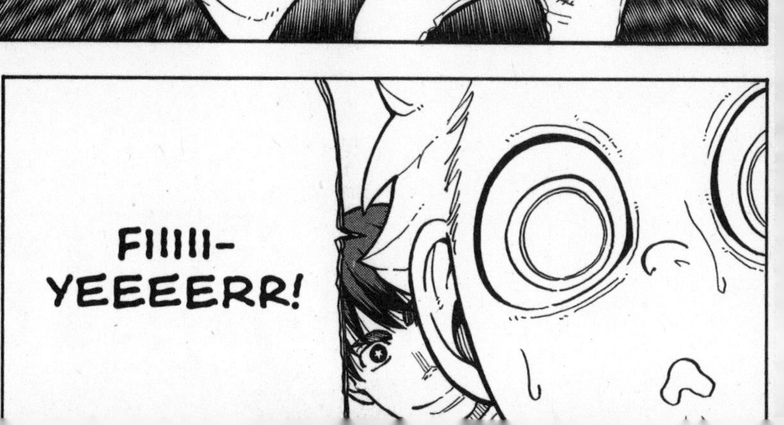
FIIIII-
YEEEEERR!

FIRE FORCE

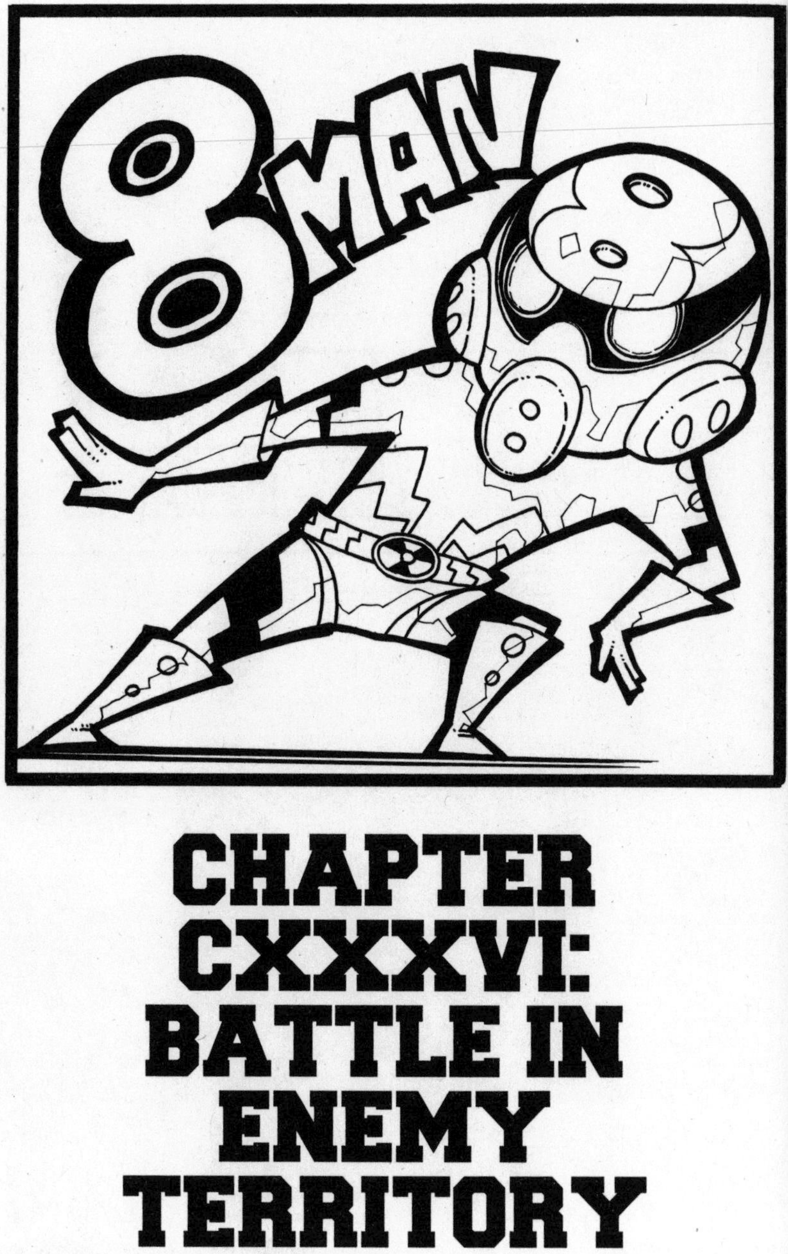
8MAN

CHAPTER CXXXVI: BATTLE IN ENEMY TERRITORY

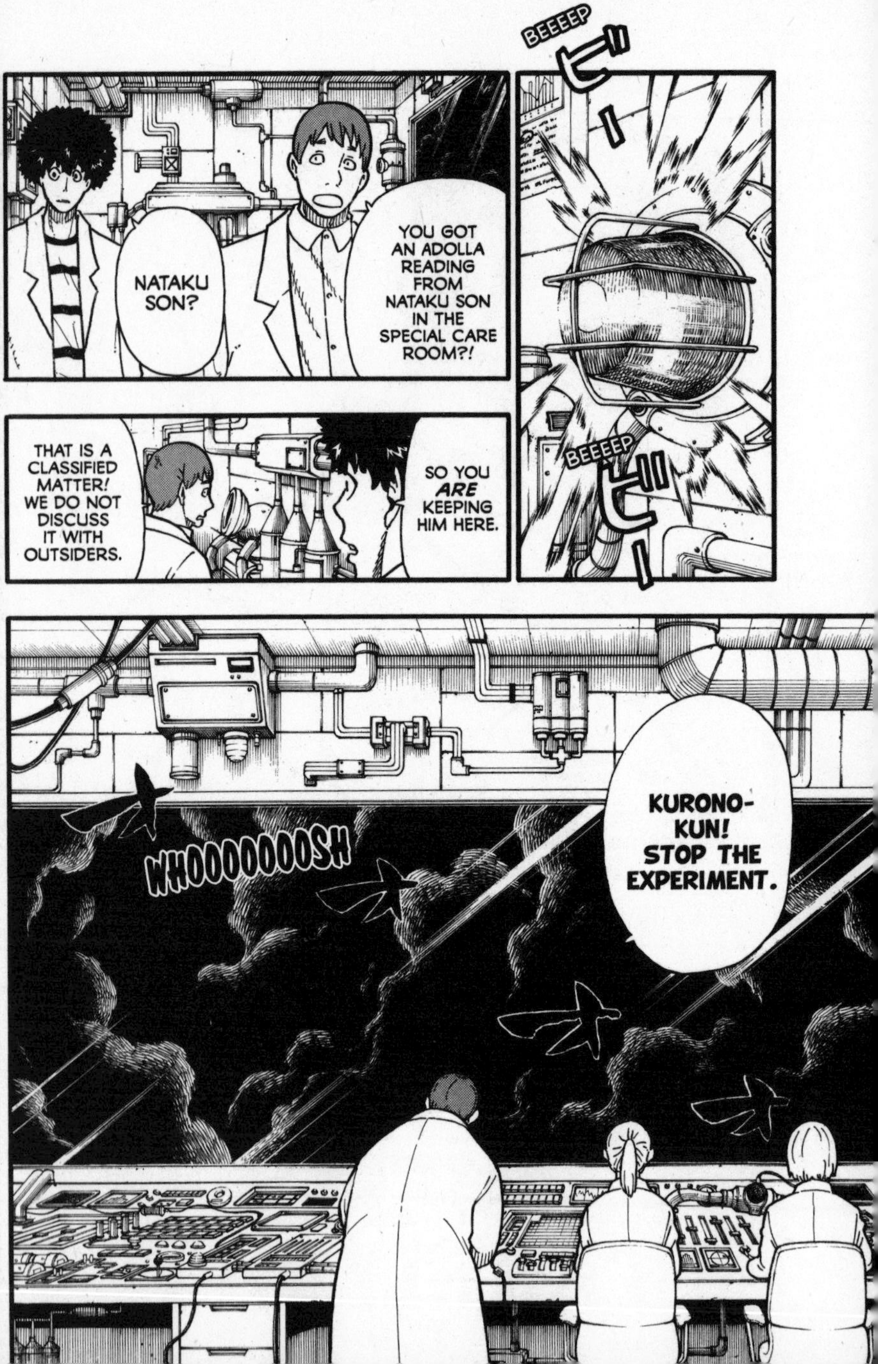
BEEEEP
BEEEEP
YOU GOT AN ADOLLA READING FROM NATAKU SON IN THE SPECIAL CARE ROOM?!
NATAKU SON?
SO YOU *ARE* KEEPING HIM HERE.
THAT IS A CLASSIFIED MATTER! WE DO NOT DISCUSS IT WITH OUTSIDERS.
KURONO-KUN! STOP THE EXPERIMENT.
WHOOOOOOOSH

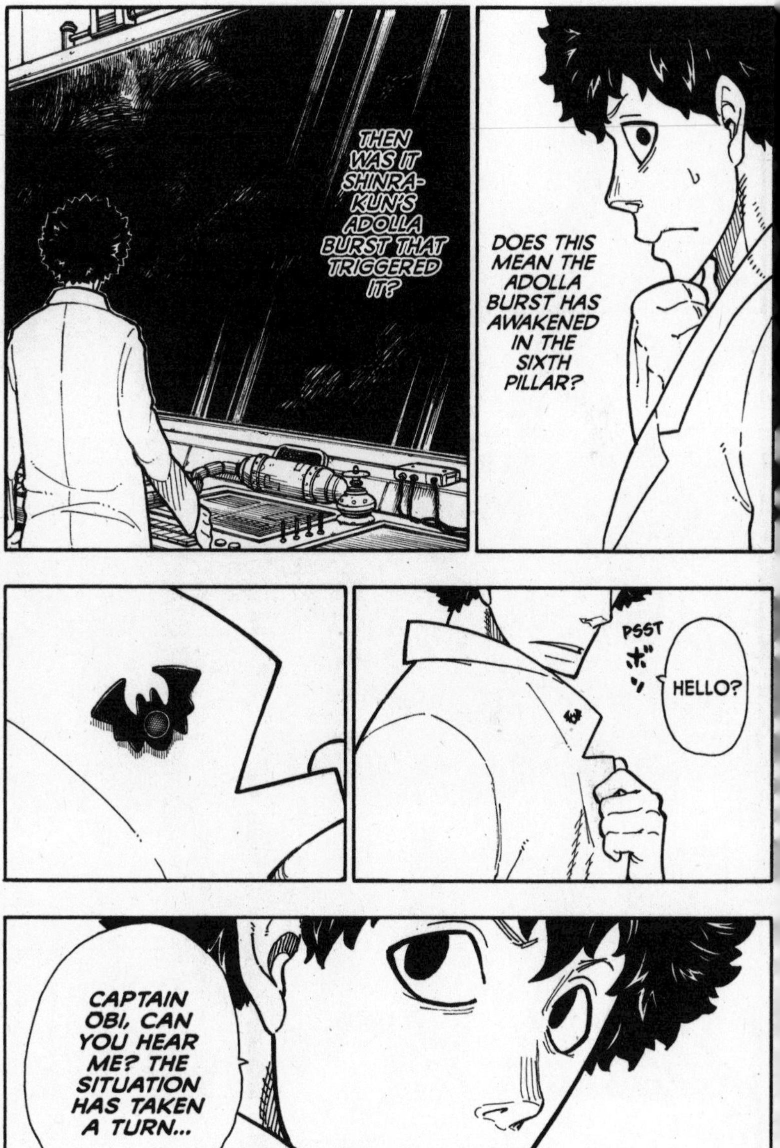
DOES THIS MEAN THE ADOLLA BURST HAS AWAKENED IN THE SIXTH PILLAR?
THEN WAS IT SHINRA-KUN'S ADOLLA BURST THAT TRIGGERED IT?
PSST
ボッ
HELLO?
CAPTAIN OBI, CAN YOU HEAR ME? THE SITUATION HAS TAKEN A TURN...

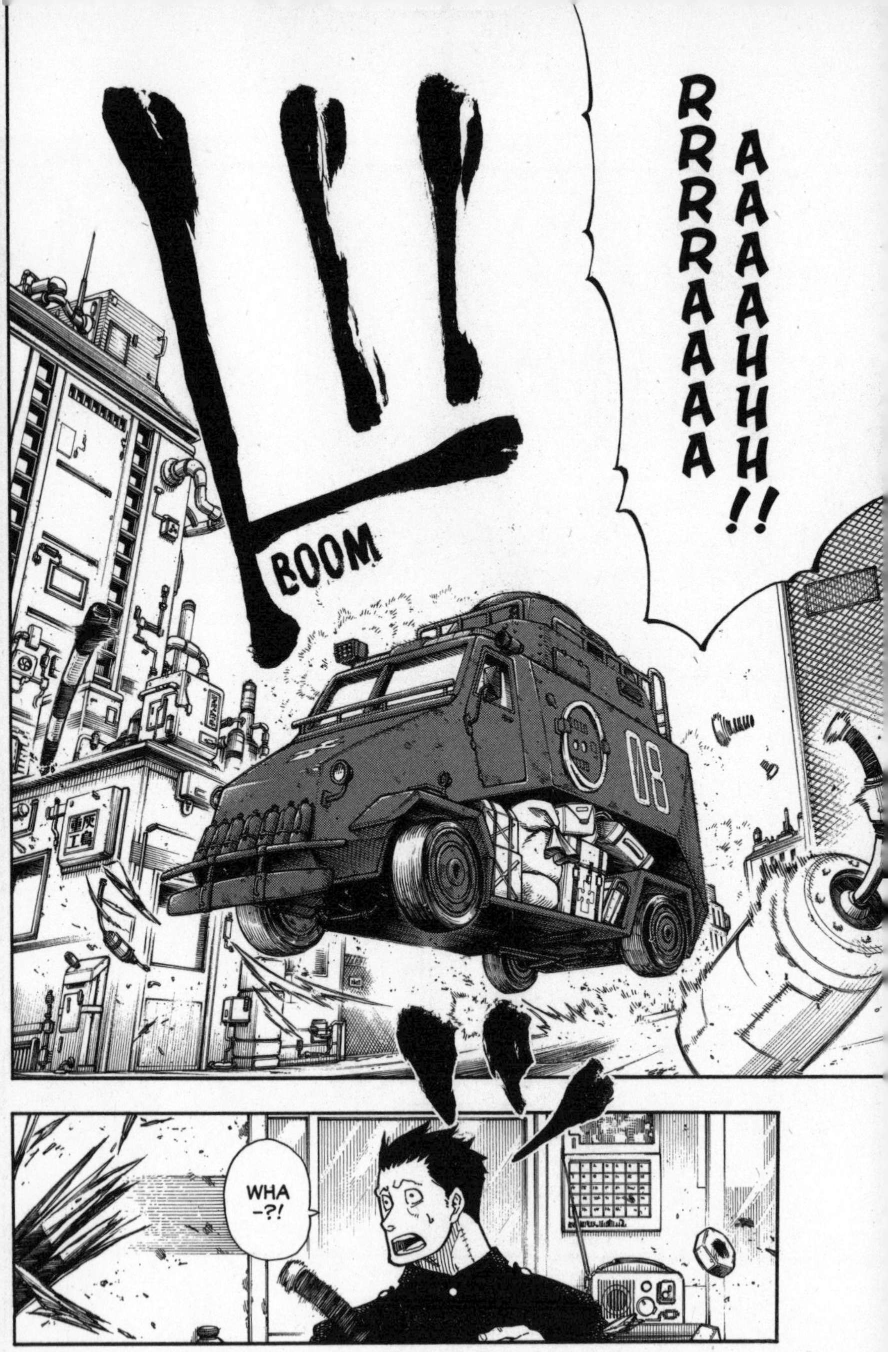
RRRRAAAA AAAAAHHH!!
BOOM
WHA-?!

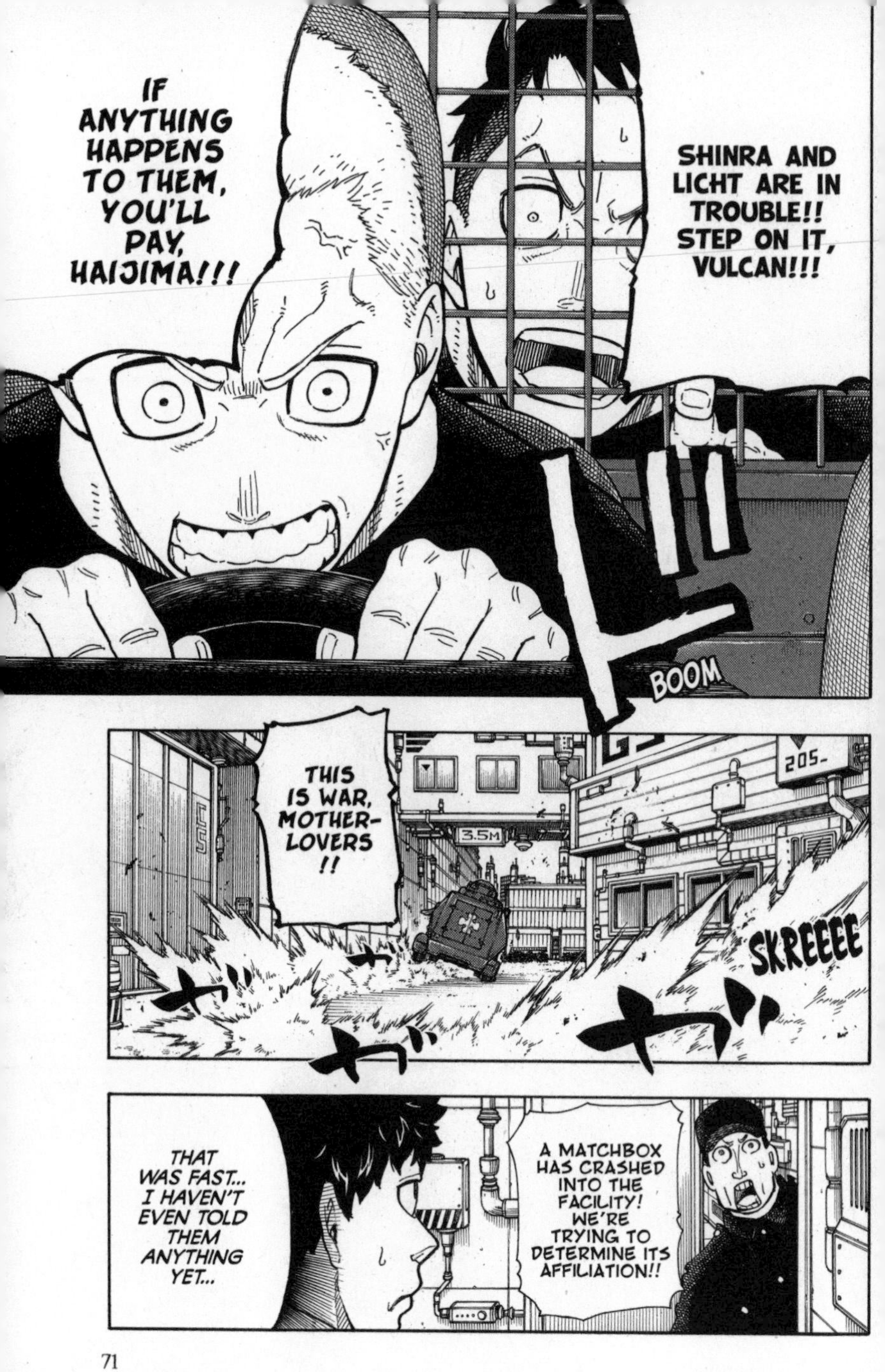
SHINRA AND LICHT ARE IN TROUBLE!! STEP ON IT, VULCAN!!!
IF ANYTHING HAPPENS TO THEM, YOU'LL PAY, HAIJIMA!!!
BOOM
THIS IS WAR, MOTHER-LOVERS!!
SKREEEE
A MATCHBOX HAS CRASHED INTO THE FACILITY! WE'RE TRYING TO DETERMINE ITS AFFILIATION!!
THAT WAS FAST... I HAVEN'T EVEN TOLD THEM ANYTHING YET...

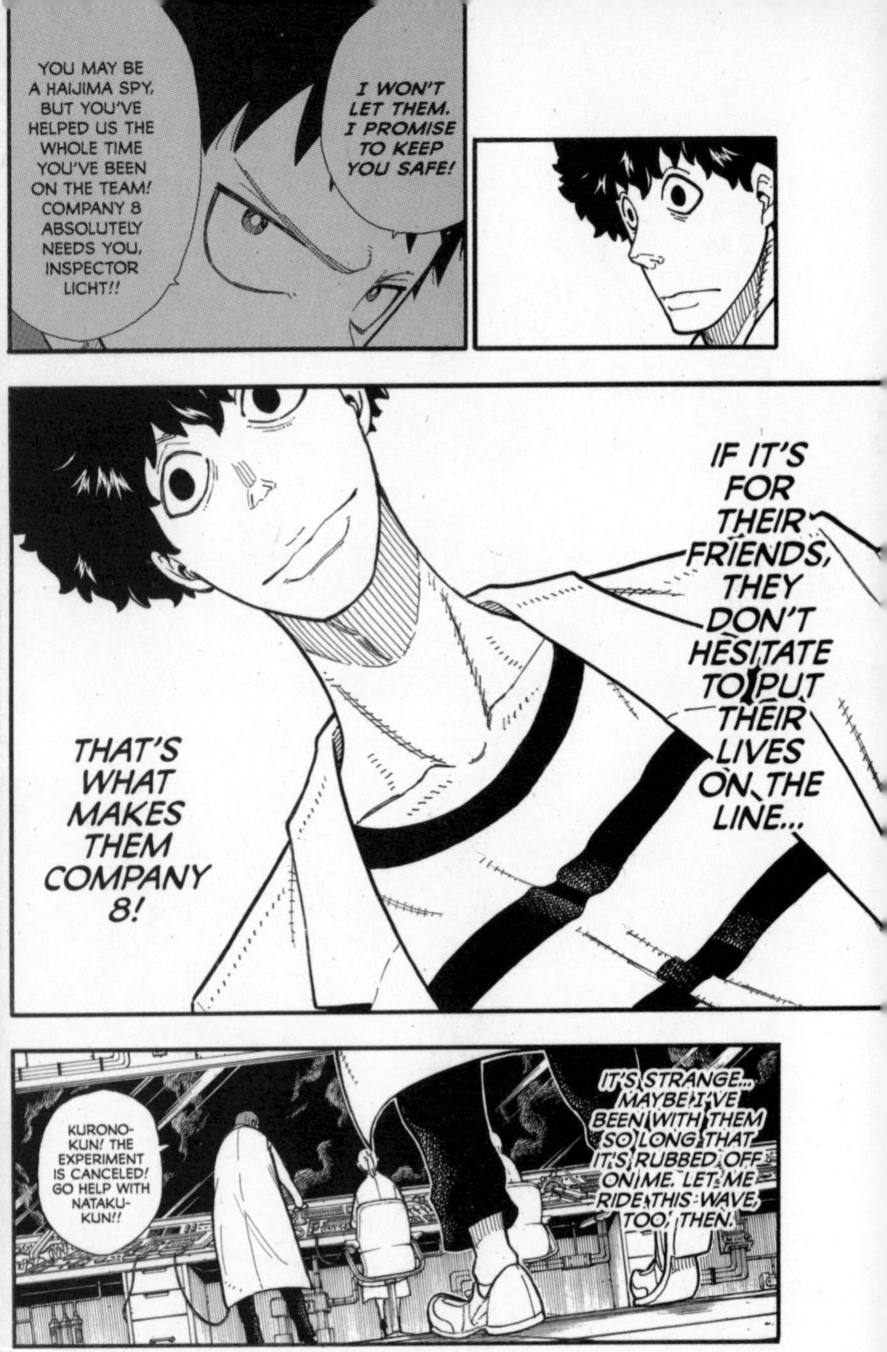
I WON'T LET THEM. I PROMISE TO KEEP YOU SAFE!
YOU MAY BE A HAIJIMA SPY, BUT YOU'VE HELPED US THE WHOLE TIME YOU'VE BEEN ON THE TEAM! COMPANY 8 ABSOLUTELY NEEDS YOU, INSPECTOR LICHT!!
IF IT'S FOR THEIR FRIENDS, THEY DON'T HESITATE TO PUT THEIR LIVES ON THE LINE...
THAT'S WHAT MAKES THEM COMPANY 8!
IT'S STRANGE... MAYBE I'VE BEEN WITH THEM SO LONG THAT IT'S RUBBED OFF ON ME. LET ME RIDE THIS WAVE, TOO, THEN.
KURONO-KUN! THE EXPERIMENT IS CANCELED! GO HELP WITH NATAKU-KUN!!

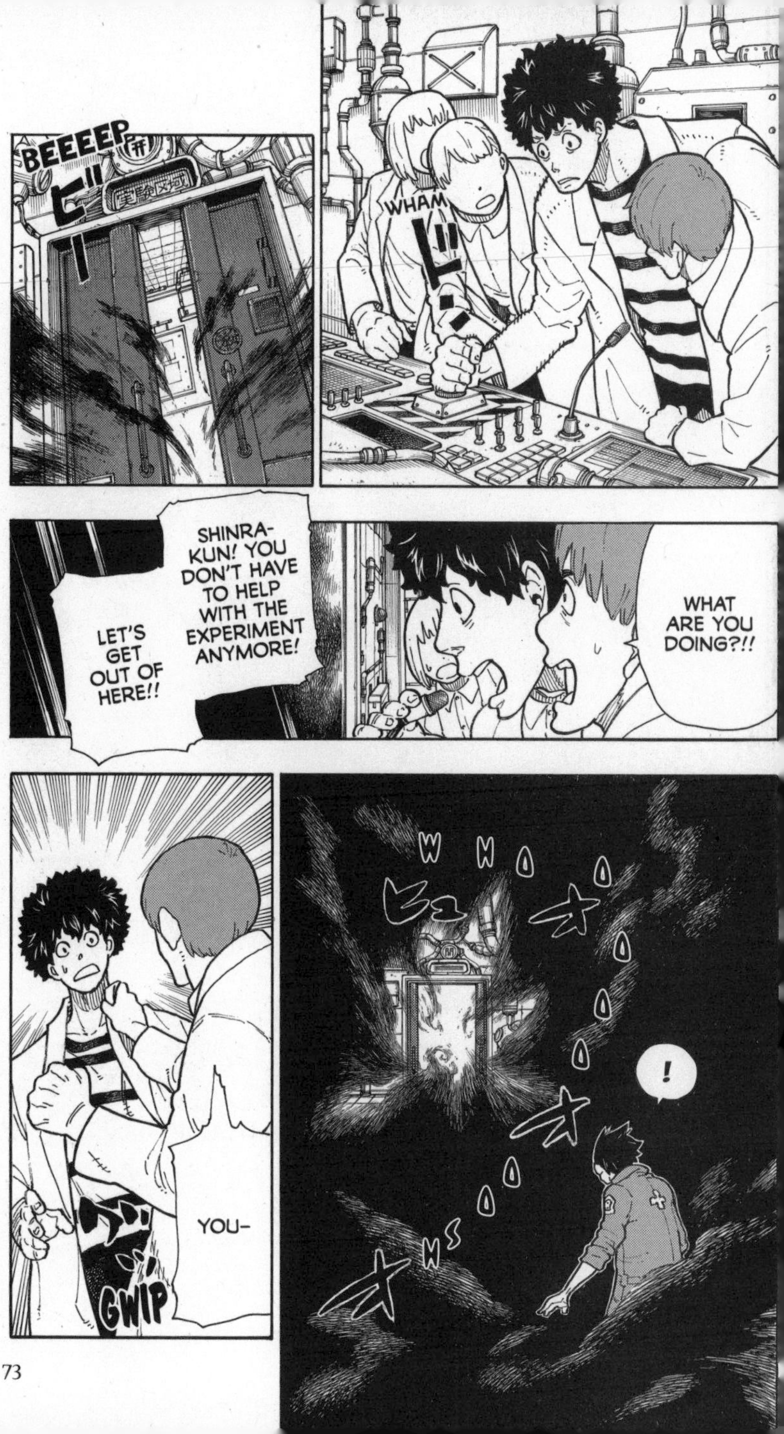
WHAM
BEEEEP
WHAT ARE YOU DOING?!!
SHINRA-KUN! YOU DON'T HAVE TO HELP WITH THE EXPERIMENT ANYMORE!
LET'S GET OUT OF HERE!!
WHOOOOSH
!
YOU-
GWIP

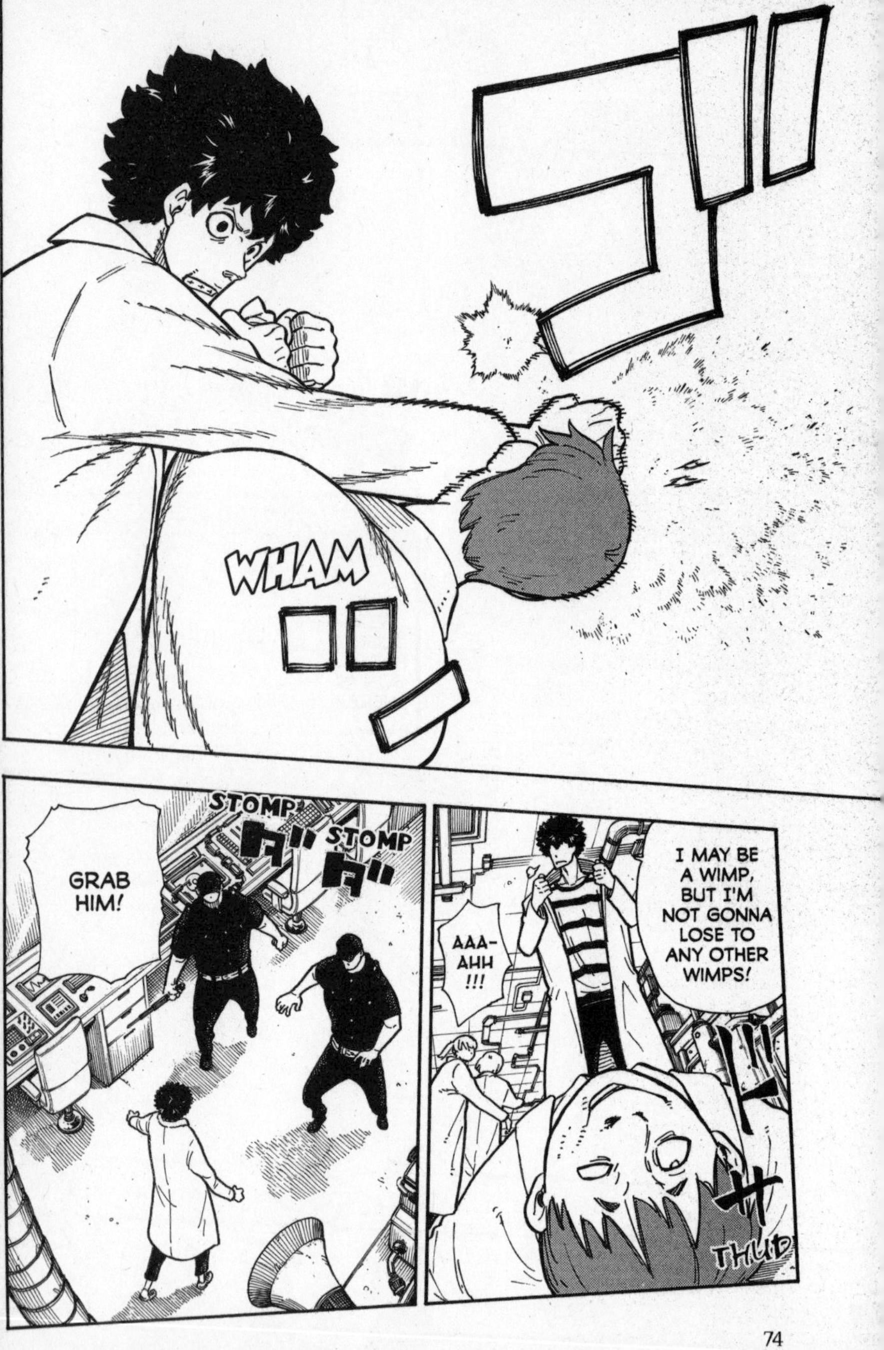
WHAM
I MAY BE A WIMP, BUT I'M NOT GONNA LOSE TO ANY OTHER WIMPS!
AAA-AHH !!!
THUD
STOMP
STOMP
GRAB HIM!

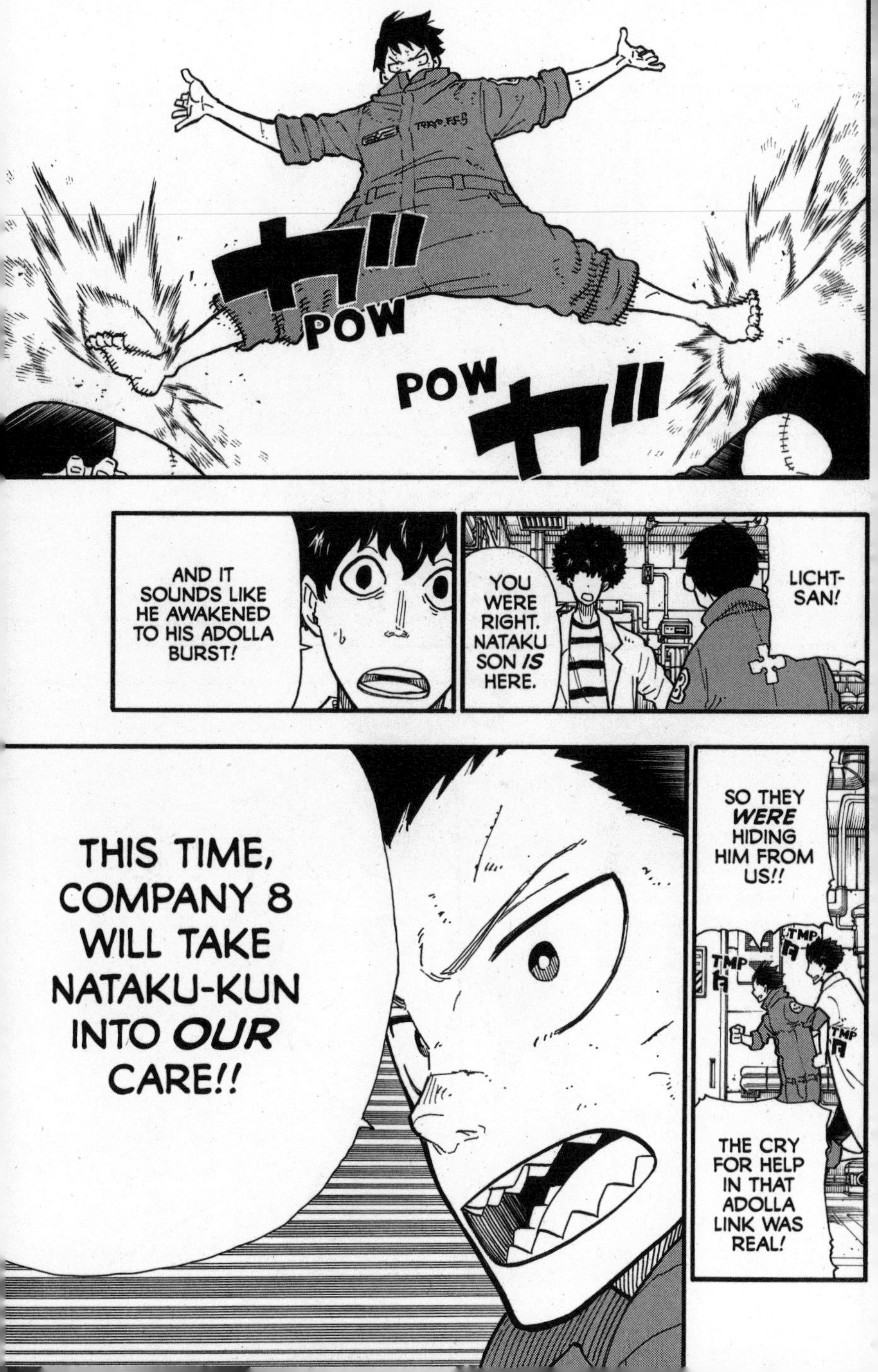
ヤ゛
POW
POW
ヤ゛
LICHT-SAN!
YOU WERE RIGHT. NATAKU SON *IS* HERE.
AND IT SOUNDS LIKE HE AWAKENED TO HIS ADOLLA BURST!
SO THEY *WERE* HIDING HIM FROM US!!
TMP
TMP
TMP
THE CRY FOR HELP IN THAT ADOLLA LINK WAS REAL!
THIS TIME, COMPANY 8 WILL TAKE NATAKU-KUN INTO *OUR* CARE!!

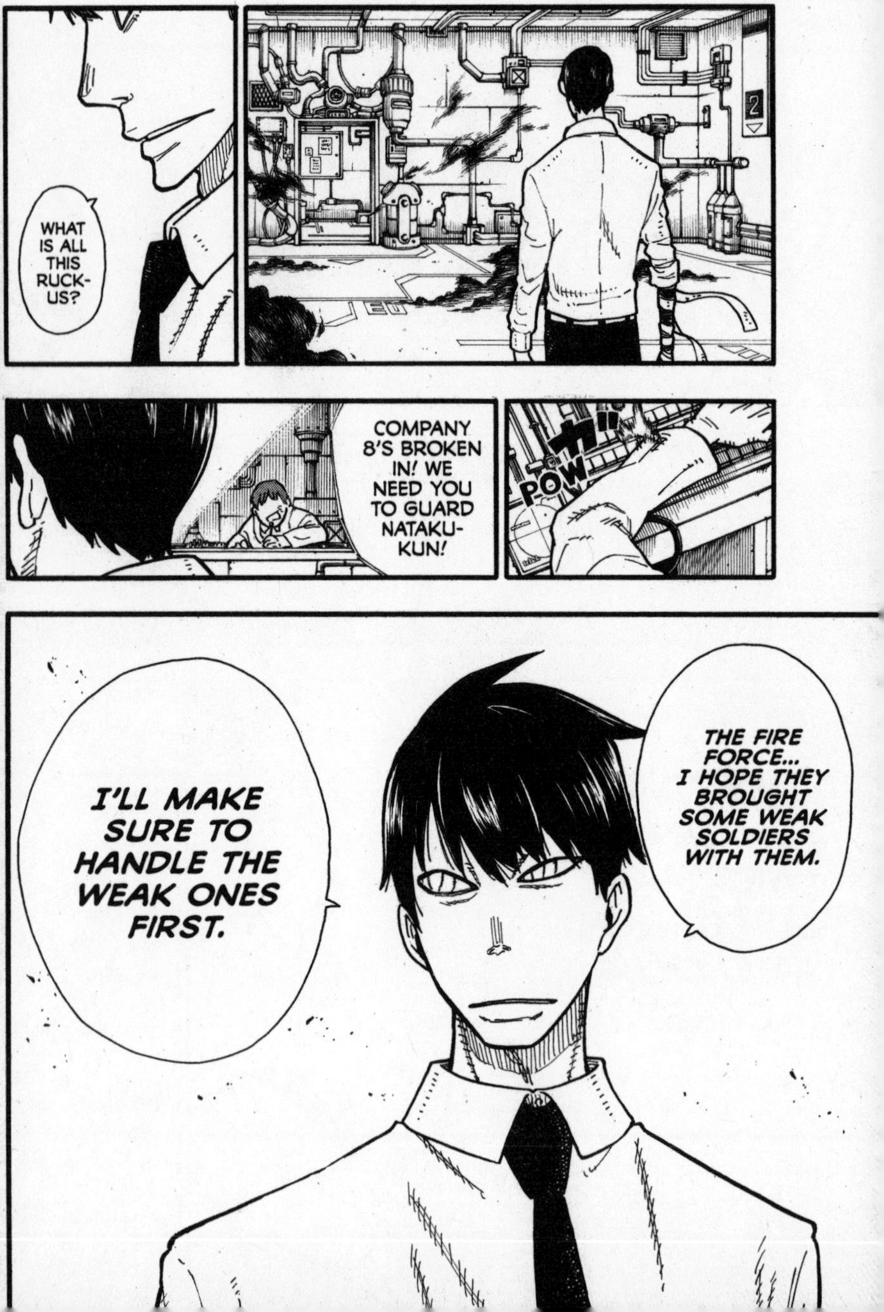
WHAT IS ALL THIS RUCK-US?
POW
COMPANY 8'S BROKEN IN! WE NEED YOU TO GUARD NATAKU-KUN!
THE FIRE FORCE... I HOPE THEY BROUGHT SOME WEAK SOLDIERS WITH THEM.
I'LL MAKE SURE TO HANDLE THE WEAK ONES FIRST.

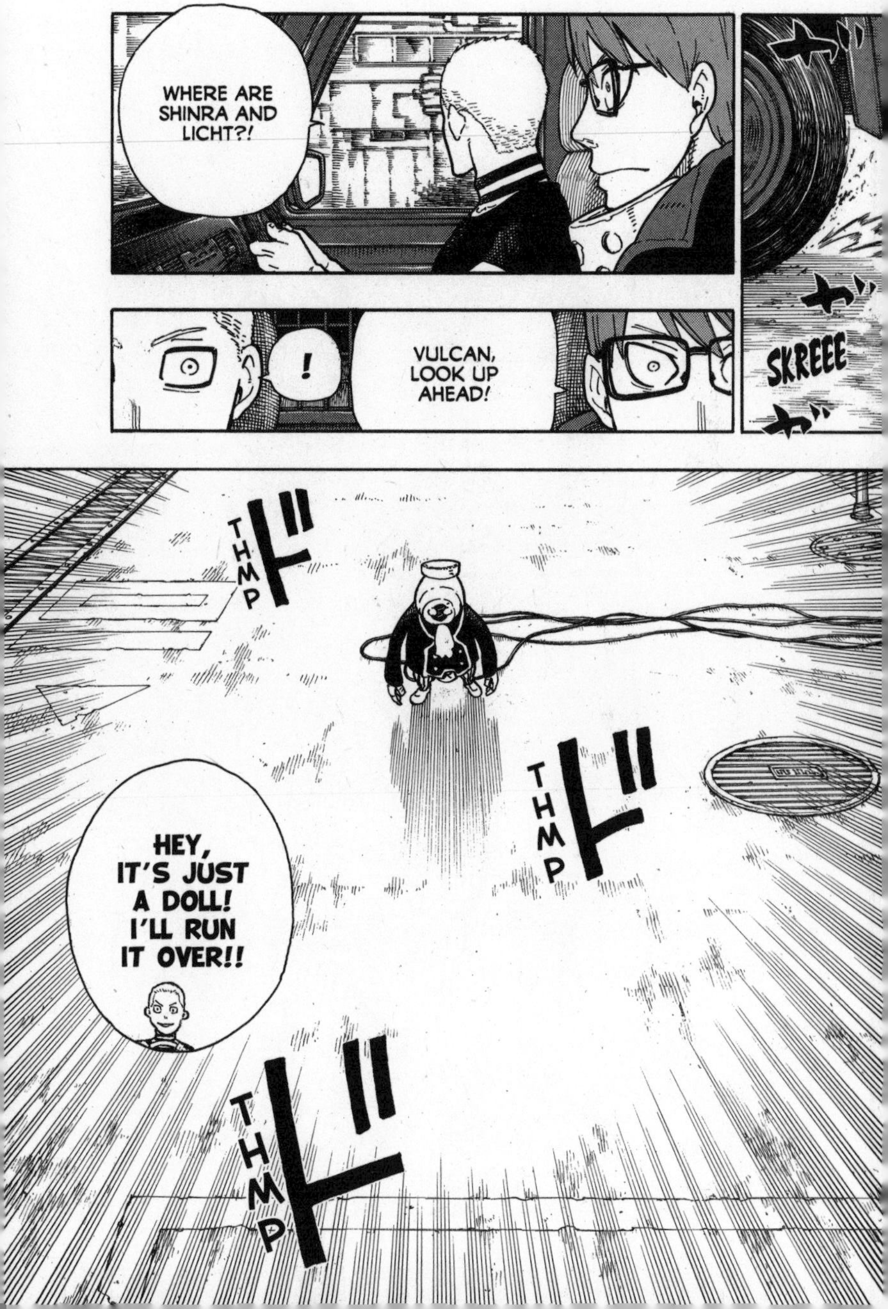
SKREEE
WHERE ARE SHINRA AND LICHT?!
VULCAN, LOOK UP AHEAD!
!
THMP
THMP
HEY, IT'S JUST A DOLL! I'LL RUN IT OVER!!
THMP

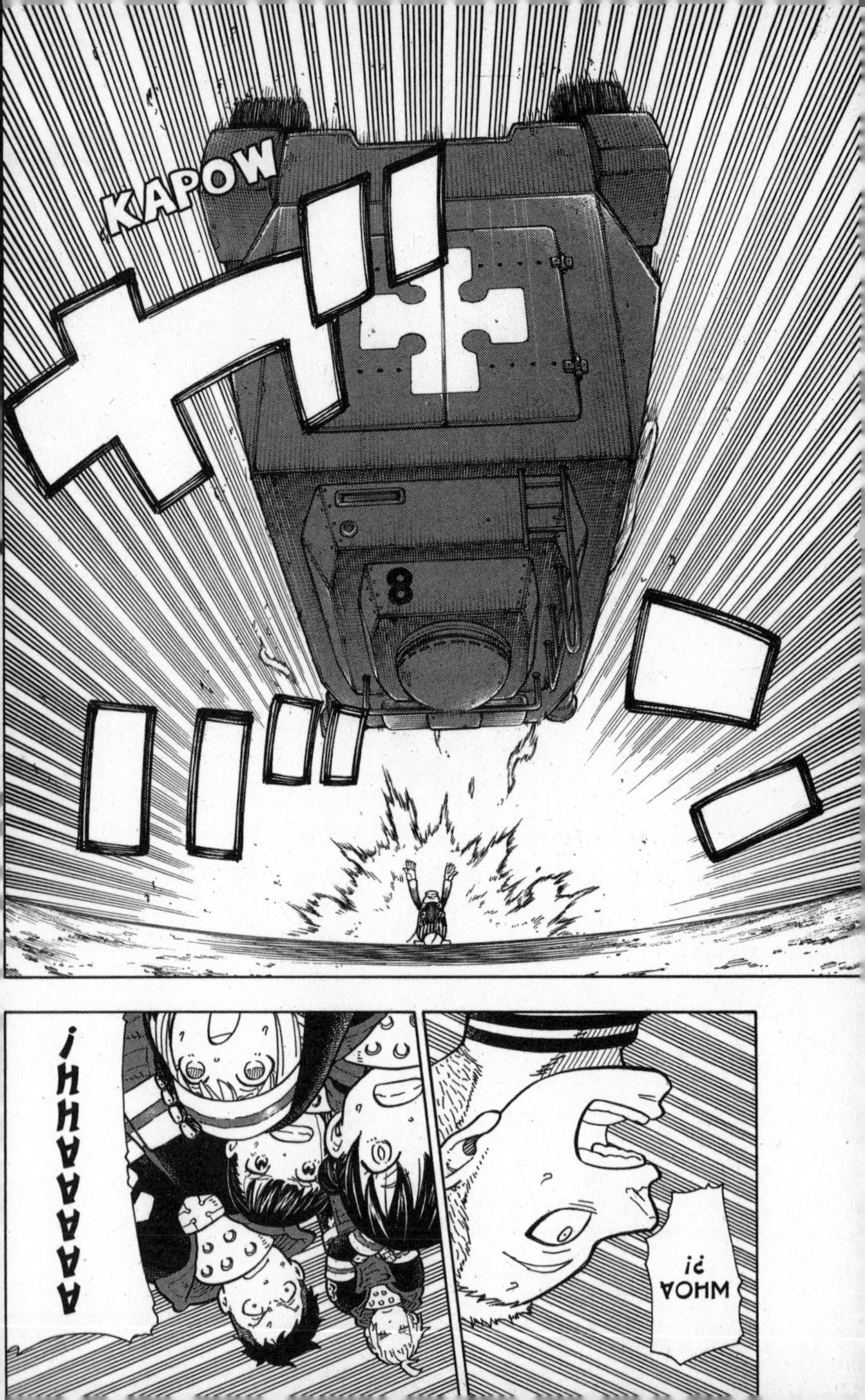
KAPOW
WHOA?!
AAAAAHH!

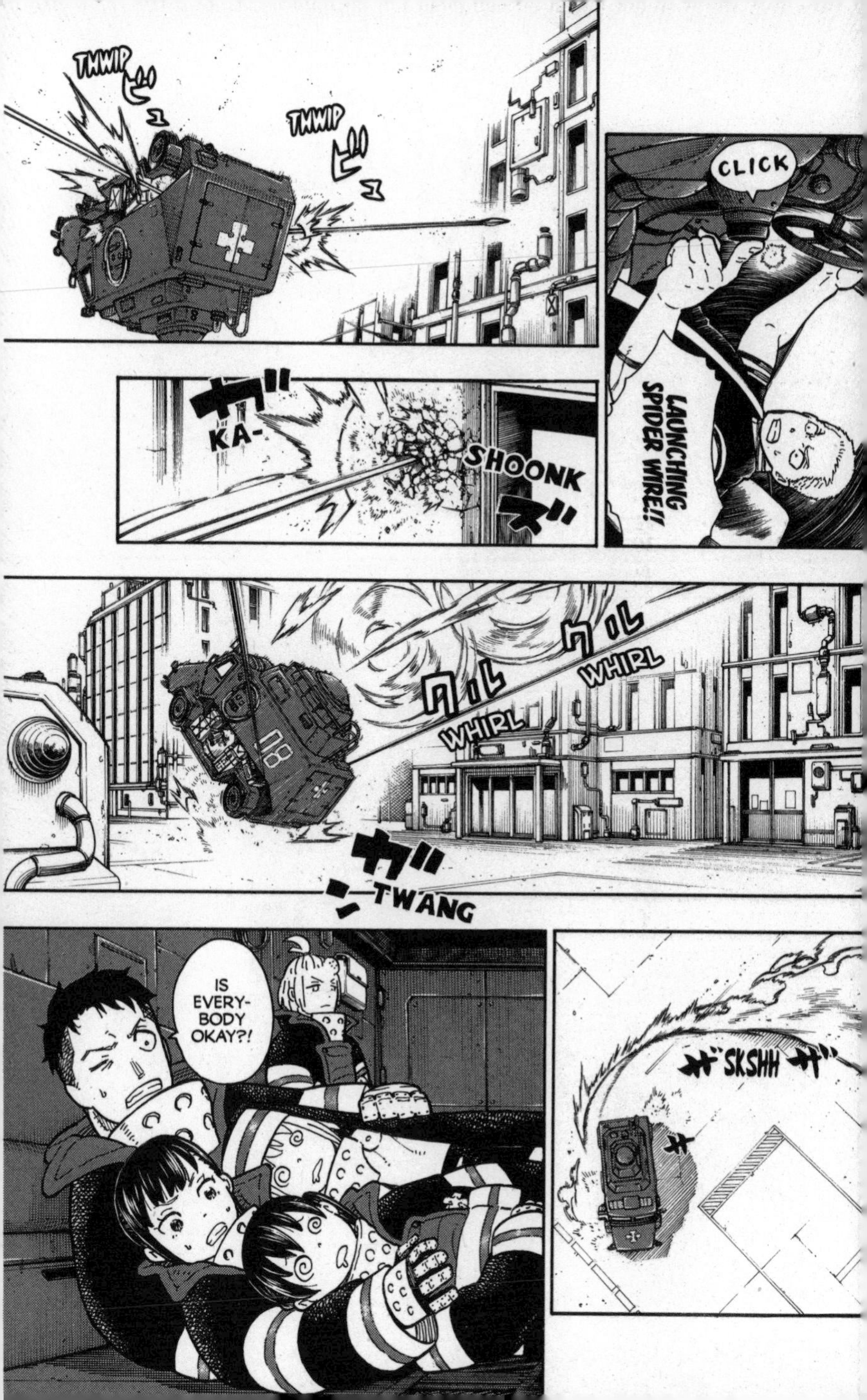

CLICK
LAUNCHING SPIDER WIRE!!
THWIP
THWIP
KA-
SHOONK
WHIRL
WHIRL
TWANG
SKSHH
IS EVERY-BODY OKAY?!

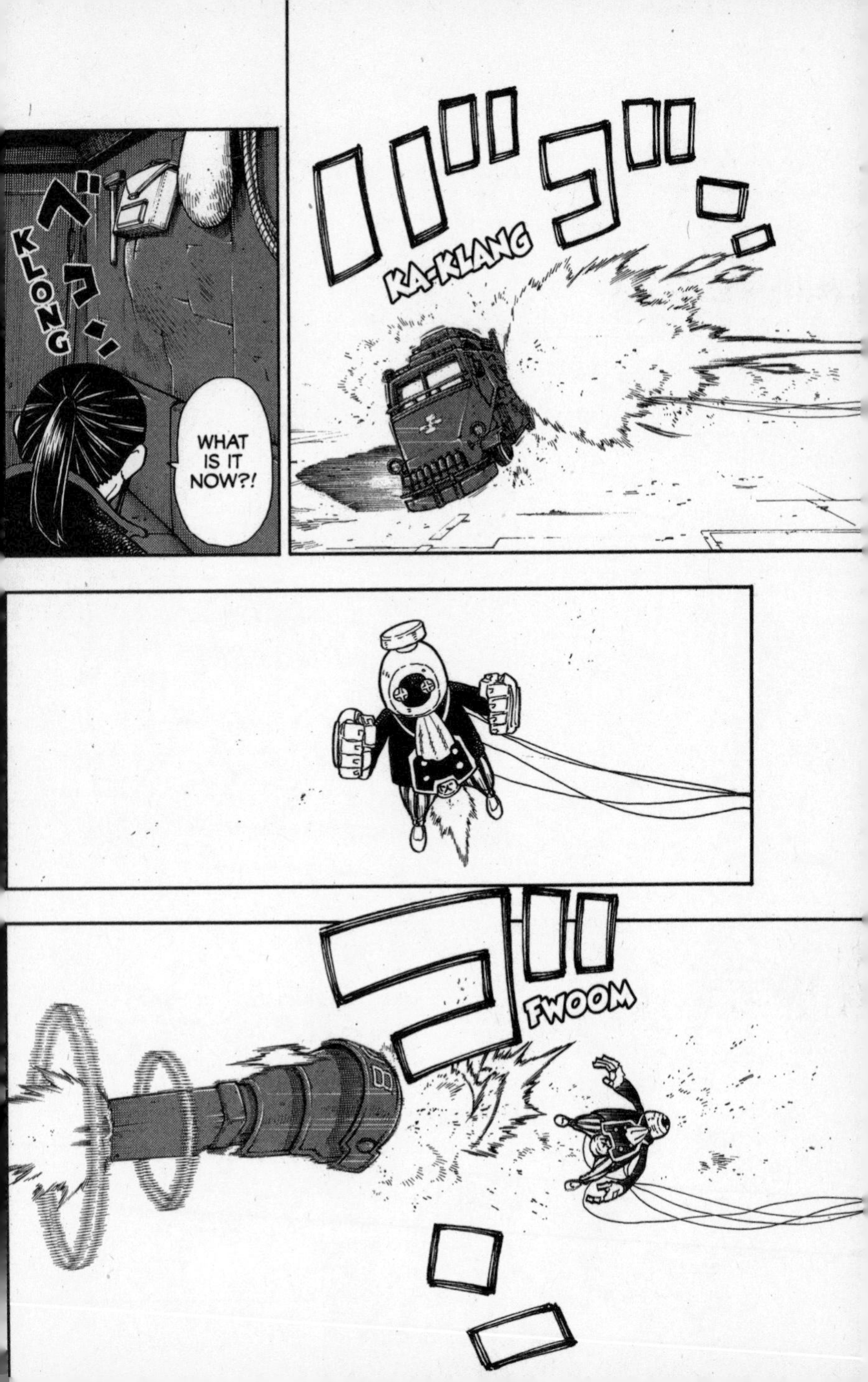

KA-KLANG
KLONG
WHAT IS IT NOW?!
FWOOM

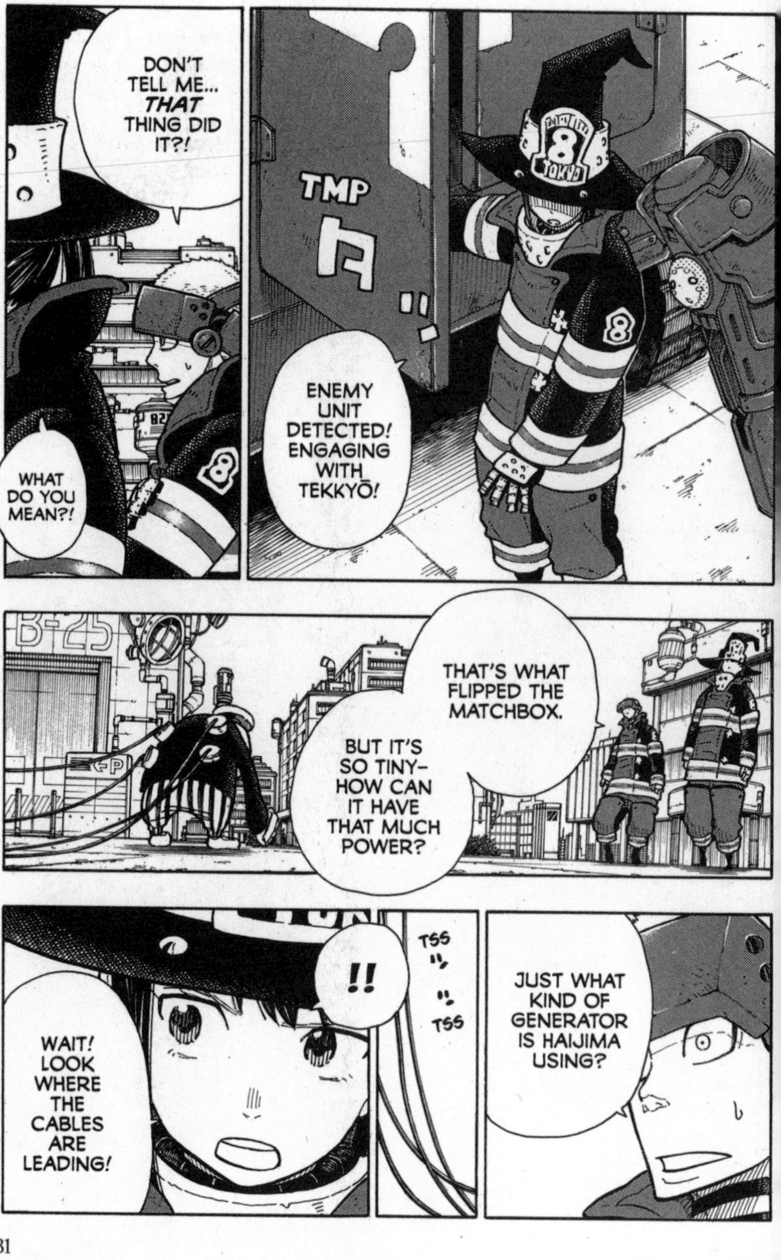
TMP
ENEMY UNIT DETECTED! ENGAGING WITH TEKKYŌ!
DON'T TELL ME... *THAT* THING DID IT?!
WHAT DO YOU MEAN?!
THAT'S WHAT FLIPPED THE MATCHBOX.
BUT IT'S SO TINY– HOW CAN IT HAVE THAT MUCH POWER?
JUST WHAT KIND OF GENERATOR IS HAIJIMA USING?
TSS
TSS
!!
WAIT! LOOK WHERE THE CABLES ARE LEADING!

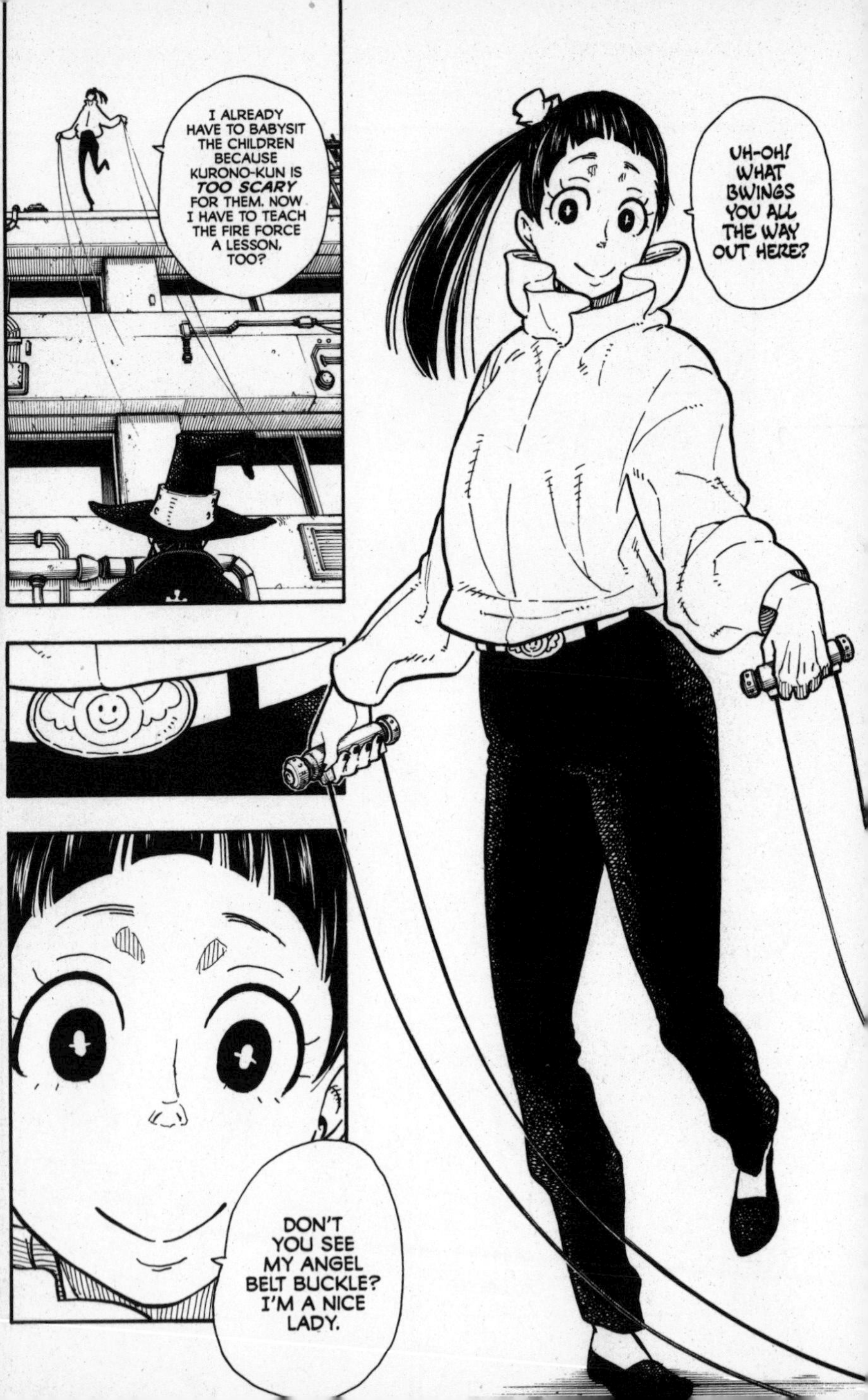
UH-OH! WHAT BWINGS YOU ALL THE WAY OUT HERE?
I ALREADY HAVE TO BABYSIT THE CHILDREN BECAUSE KURONO-KUN IS ***TOO SCARY*** FOR THEM. NOW I HAVE TO TEACH THE FIRE FORCE A LESSON, TOO?
DON'T YOU SEE MY ANGEL BELT BUCKLE? I'M A NICE LADY.

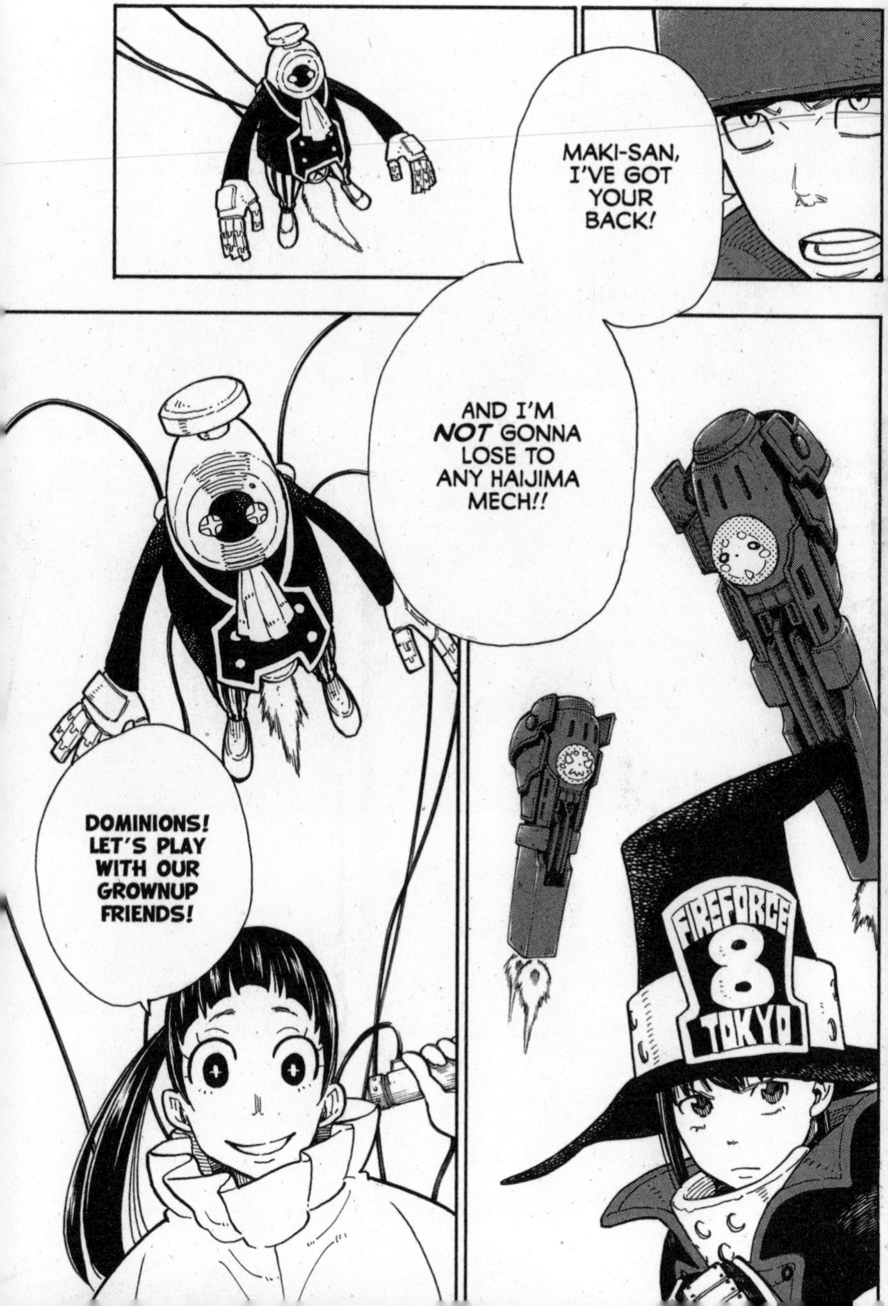
MAKI-SAN, I'VE GOT YOUR BACK!
AND I'M *NOT* GONNA LOSE TO ANY HAIJIMA MECH!!
FIREFORCE 8 TOKYO
DOMINIONS! LET'S PLAY WITH OUR GROWNUP FRIENDS!

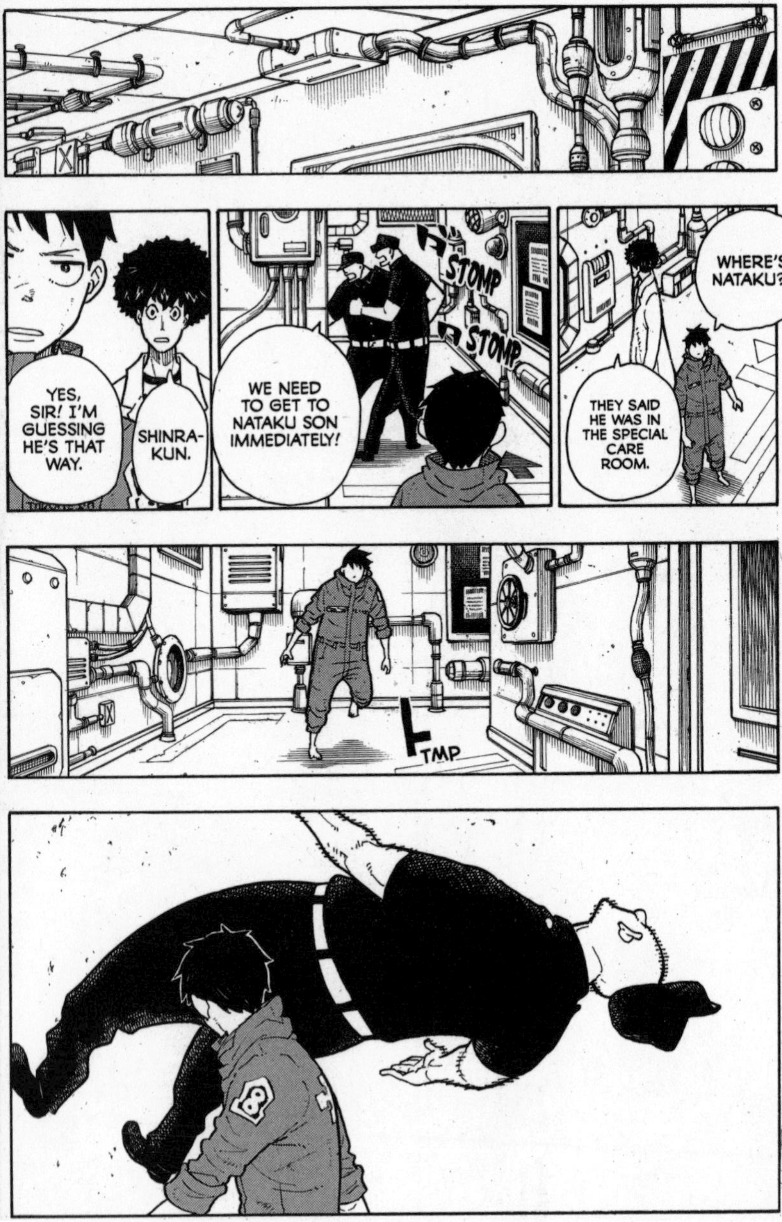
WHERE'S NATAKU?!
THEY SAID HE WAS IN THE SPECIAL CARE ROOM.
STOMP
STOMP
WE NEED TO GET TO NATAKU SON IMMEDIATELY!
SHINRA-KUN.
YES, SIR! I'M GUESSING HE'S THAT WAY.
TMP

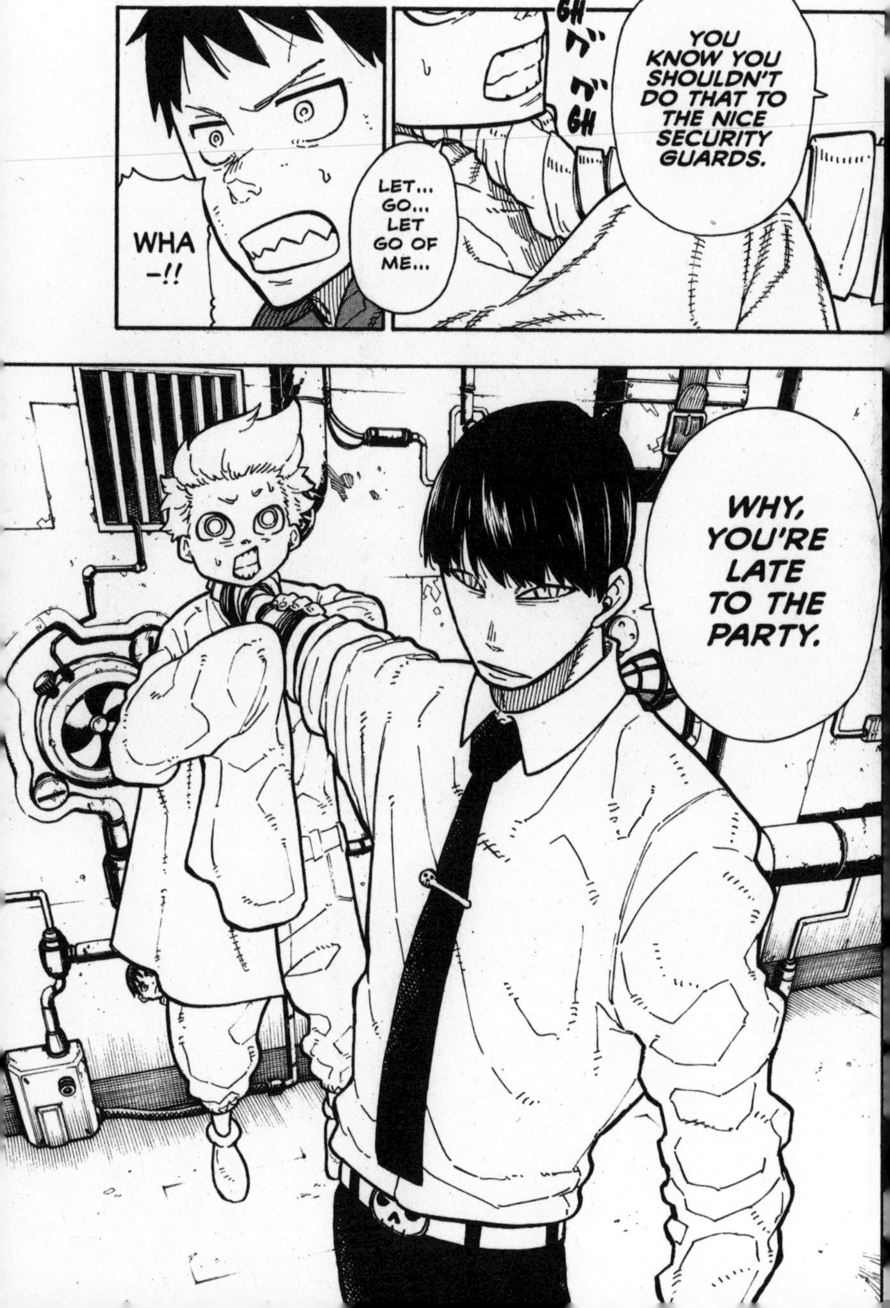
GH
GH
YOU KNOW YOU SHOULDN'T DO THAT TO THE NICE SECURITY GUARDS.
LET... GO... LET GO OF ME...
WHA-!!
WHY, YOU'RE LATE TO THE PARTY.

FIRE FORCE

CATER-
PILLAR

08

CHAPTER CXXXVII: THE ANGEL VS. THE WITCH

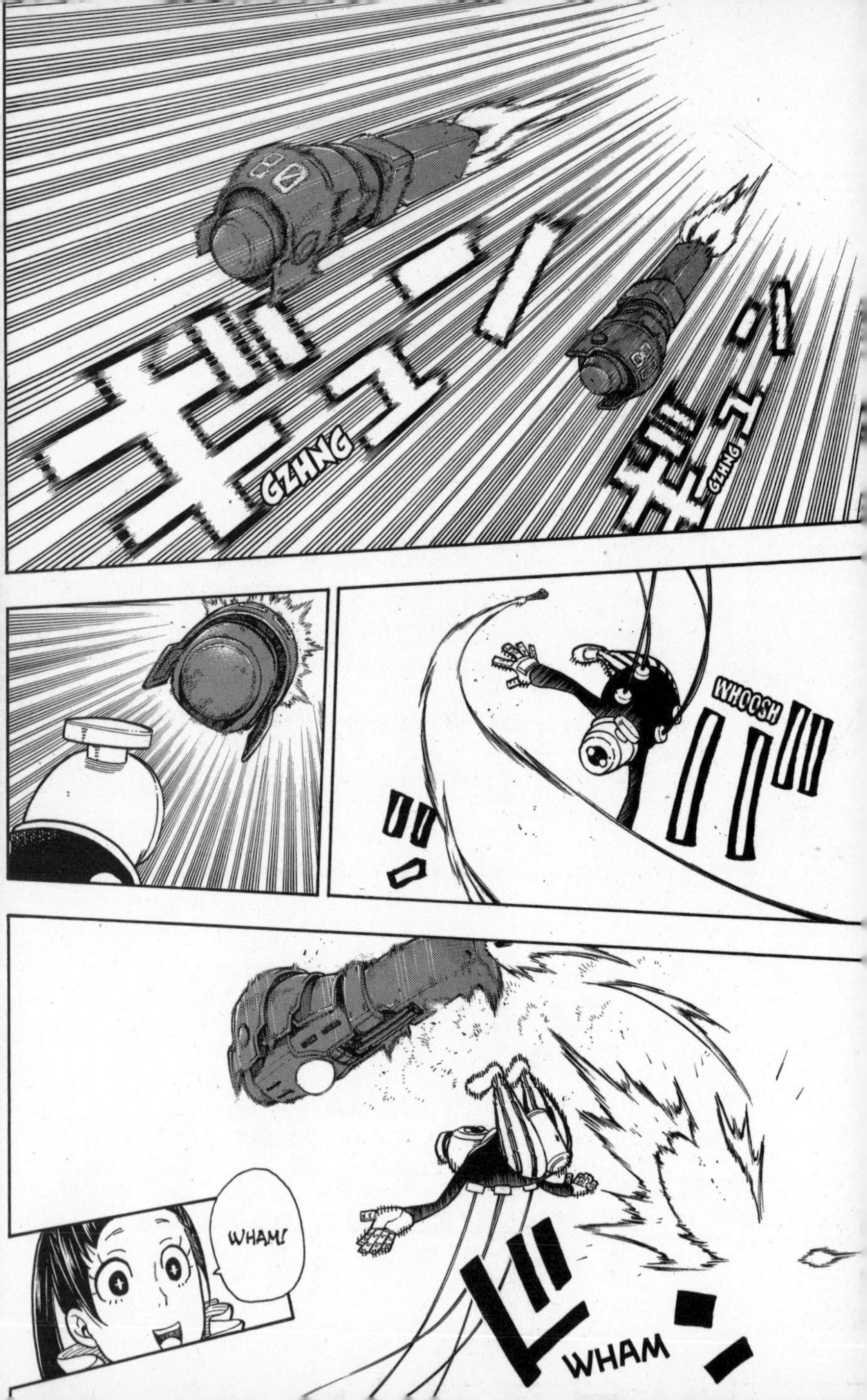
GZHNG
GZHNG
WHOOSH
WHAM!
WHAM

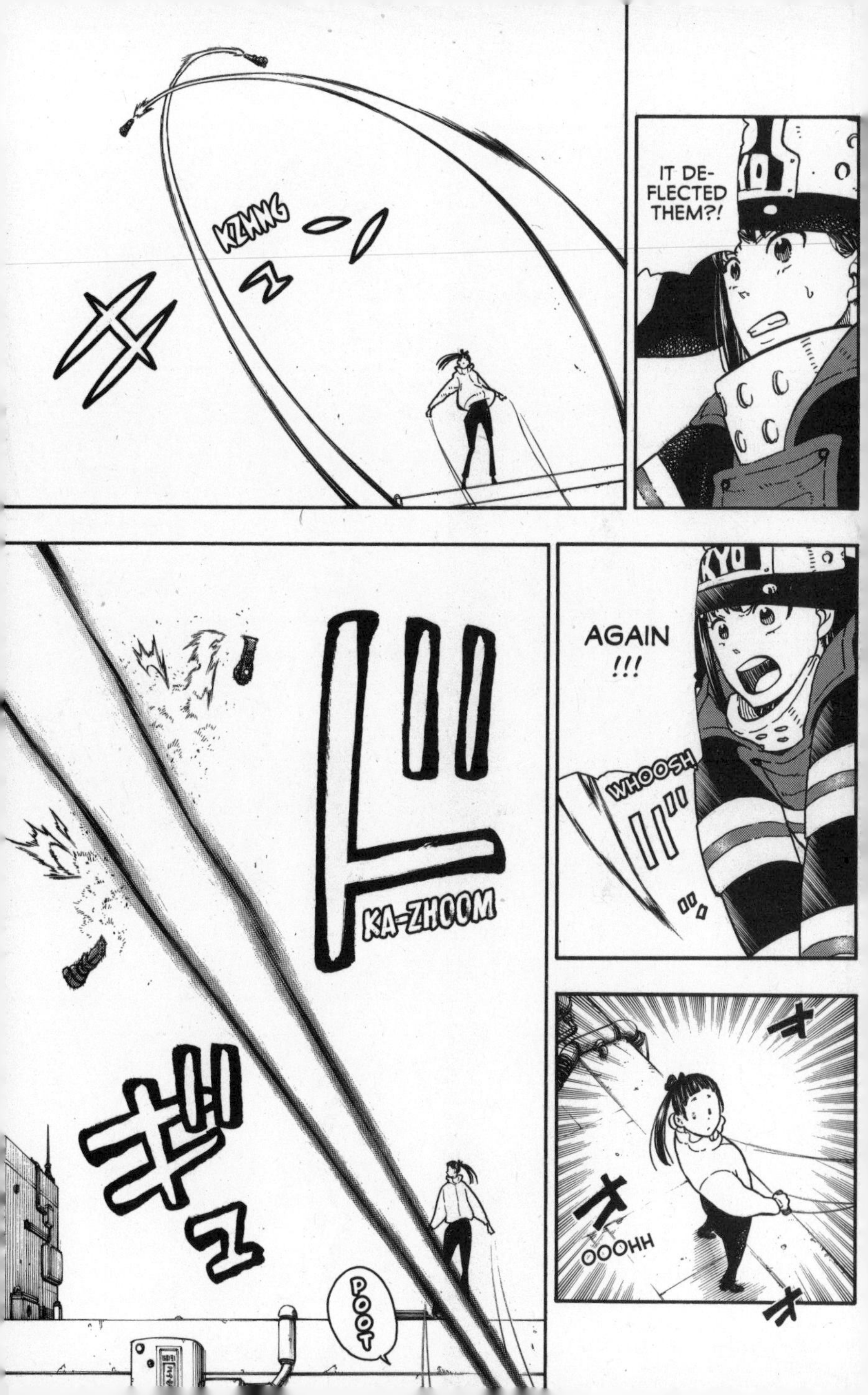
IT DE-FLECTED THEM?!
KZHNG
AGAIN!!!
WHOOSH
OOOHH
KA-ZHOOM
POOT

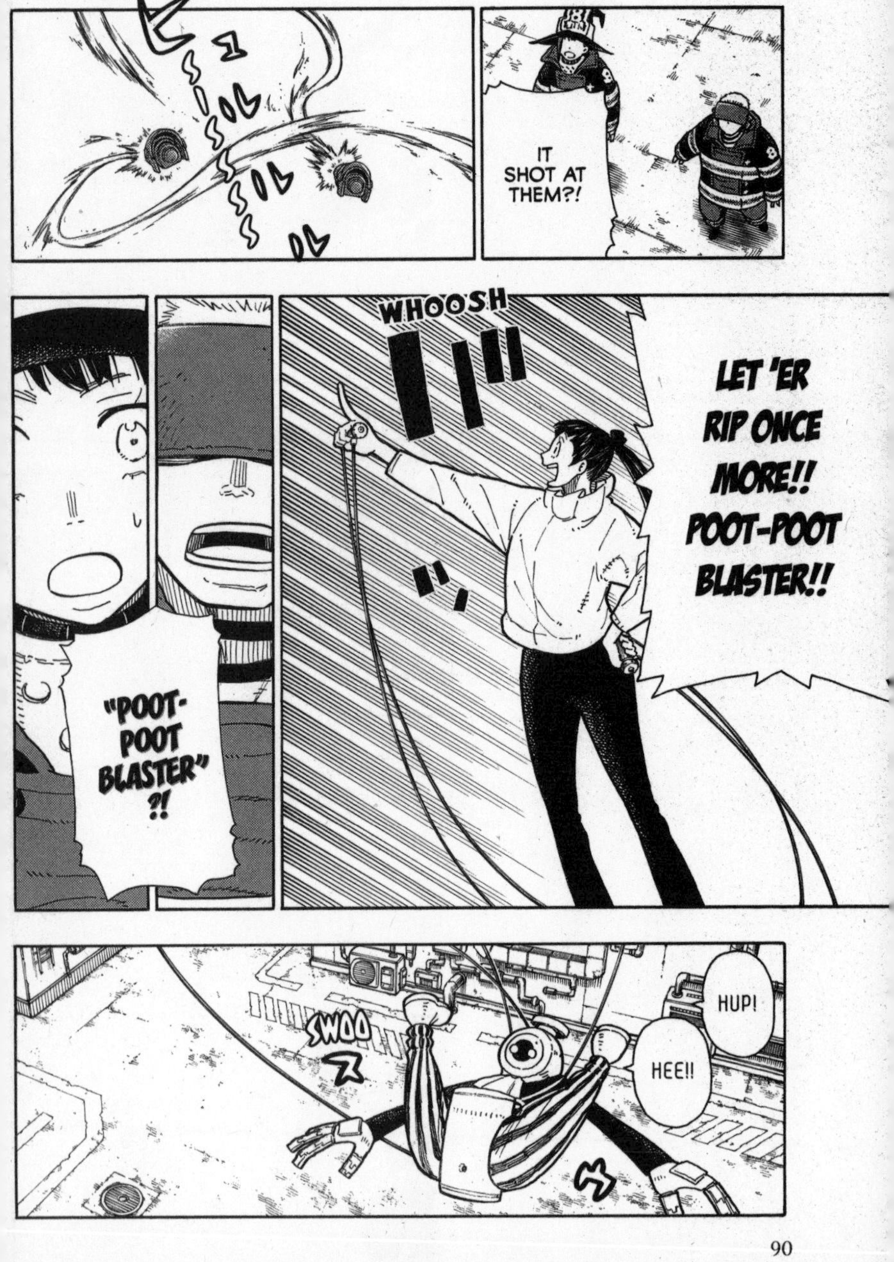
IT SHOT AT THEM?!
WHOOSH
LET 'ER RIP ONCE MORE!! POOT-POOT BLASTER!!
"POOT-POOT BLASTER"?!
HUP!
HEE!!
SWOO

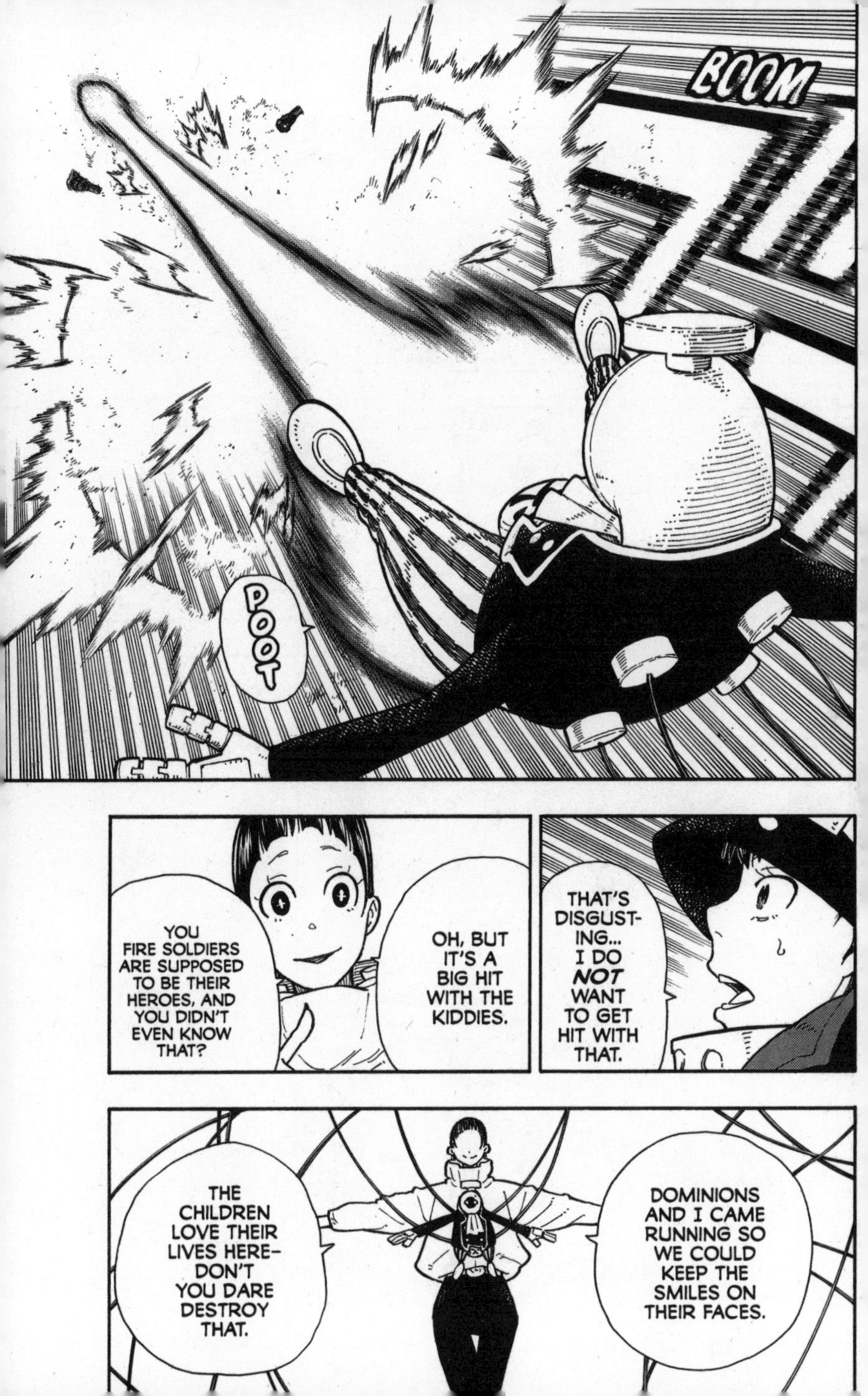
BOOM
POOT
THAT'S DISGUSTING... I DO *NOT* WANT TO GET HIT WITH THAT.
OH, BUT IT'S A BIG HIT WITH THE KIDDIES.
YOU FIRE SOLDIERS ARE SUPPOSED TO BE THEIR HEROES, AND YOU DIDN'T EVEN KNOW THAT?
DOMINIONS AND I CAME RUNNING SO WE COULD KEEP THE SMILES ON THEIR FACES.
THE CHILDREN LOVE THEIR LIVES HERE–DON'T YOU DARE DESTROY THAT.

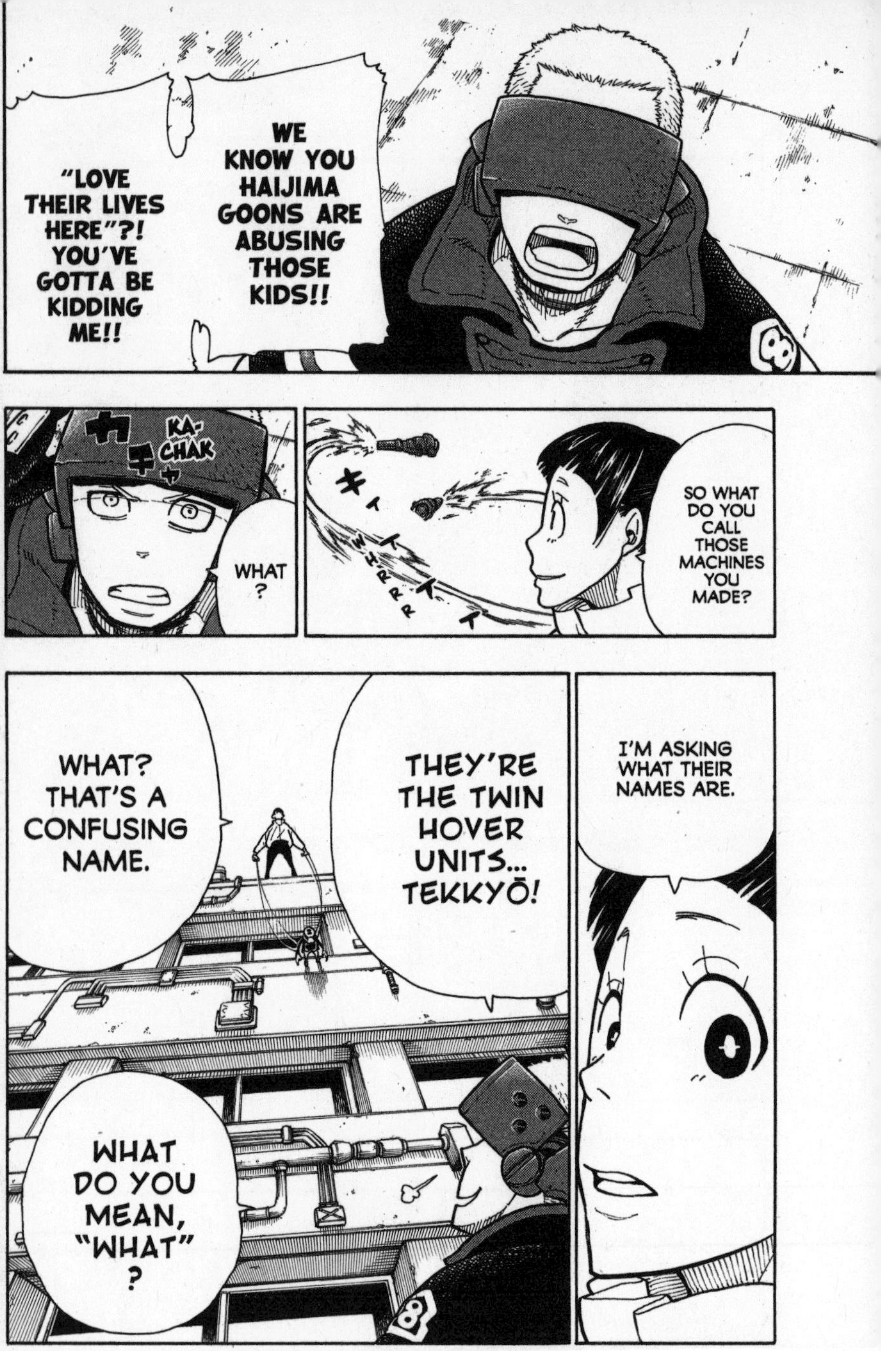
WE KNOW YOU HAIJIMA GOONS ARE ABUSING THOSE KIDS!!
"LOVE THEIR LIVES HERE"?! YOU'VE GOTTA BE KIDDING ME!!
SO WHAT DO YOU CALL THOSE MACHINES YOU MADE?
WHRRR
KA-CHAK
WHAT?
I'M ASKING WHAT THEIR NAMES ARE.
THEY'RE THE TWIN HOVER UNITS... TEKKYŌ!
WHAT? THAT'S A CONFUSING NAME.
WHAT DO YOU MEAN, "WHAT"?

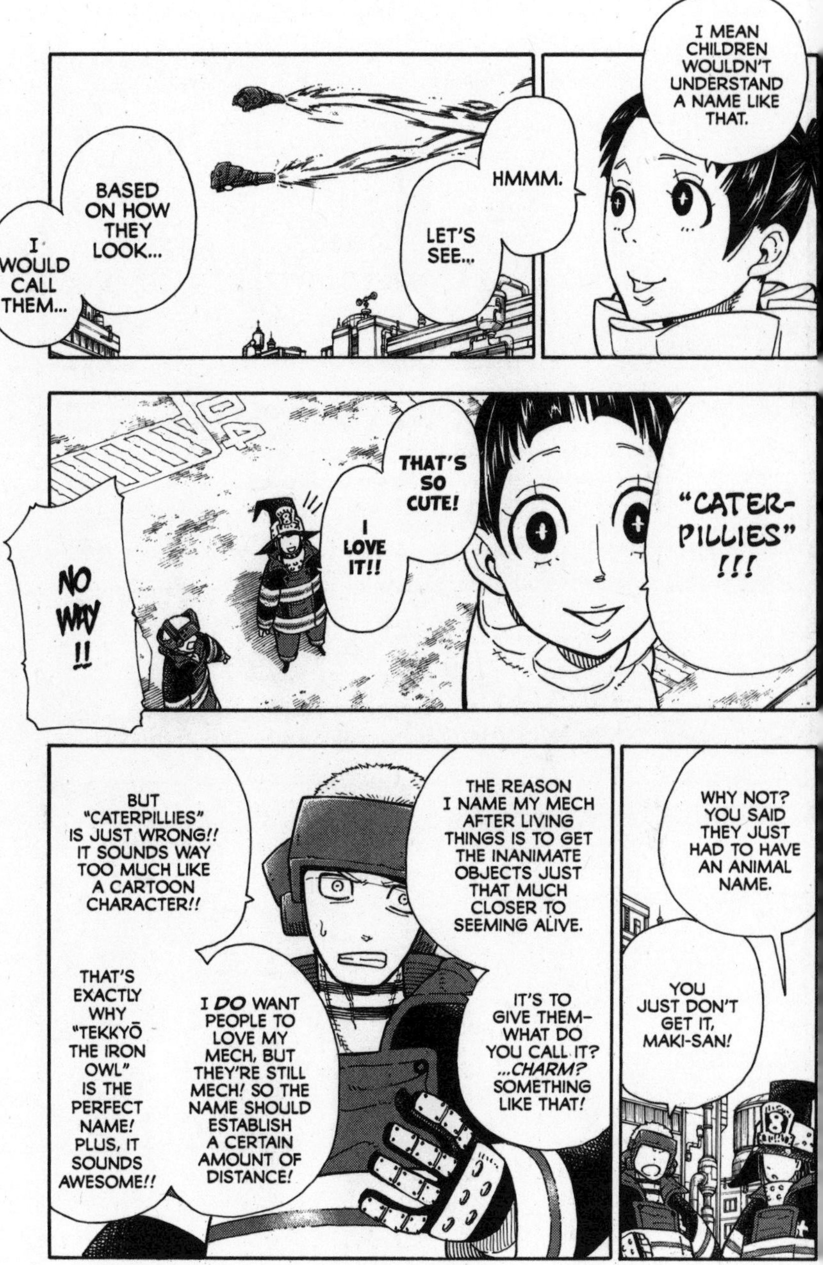
I MEAN CHILDREN WOULDN'T UNDERSTAND A NAME LIKE THAT.
HMMM.
LET'S SEE...
BASED ON HOW THEY LOOK...
I WOULD CALL THEM...
"CATER-PILLIES" !!!
THAT'S SO CUTE!
I LOVE IT!!
NO WAY!!
WHY NOT? YOU SAID THEY JUST HAD TO HAVE AN ANIMAL NAME.
YOU JUST DON'T GET IT, MAKI-SAN!
THE REASON I NAME MY MECH AFTER LIVING THINGS IS TO GET THE INANIMATE OBJECTS JUST THAT MUCH CLOSER TO SEEMING ALIVE.
IT'S TO GIVE THEM– WHAT DO YOU CALL IT? ...CHARM? SOMETHING LIKE THAT!
BUT "CATERPILLIES" IS JUST WRONG!! IT SOUNDS WAY TOO MUCH LIKE A CARTOON CHARACTER!!
I DO WANT PEOPLE TO LOVE MY MECH, BUT THEY'RE STILL MECH! SO THE NAME SHOULD ESTABLISH A CERTAIN AMOUNT OF DISTANCE!
THAT'S EXACTLY WHY "TEKKYŌ THE IRON OWL" IS THE PERFECT NAME! PLUS, IT SOUNDS AWESOME!!

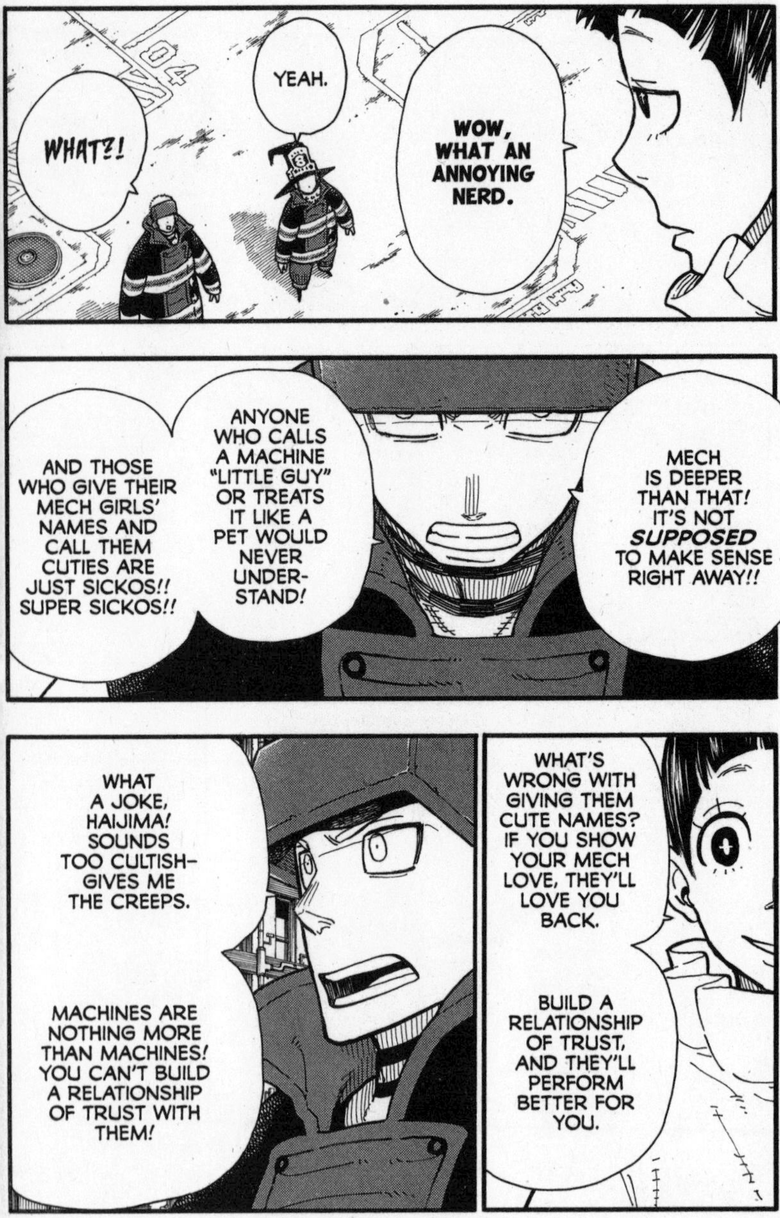
WOW, WHAT AN ANNOYING NERD.
YEAH.
WHAT?!
MECH IS DEEPER THAN THAT! IT'S NOT *SUPPOSED* TO MAKE SENSE RIGHT AWAY!!
ANYONE WHO CALLS A MACHINE "LITTLE GUY" OR TREATS IT LIKE A PET WOULD NEVER UNDER-STAND!
AND THOSE WHO GIVE THEIR MECH GIRLS' NAMES AND CALL THEM CUTIES ARE JUST SICKOS!! SUPER SICKOS!!
WHAT'S WRONG WITH GIVING THEM CUTE NAMES? IF YOU SHOW YOUR MECH LOVE, THEY'LL LOVE YOU BACK.
BUILD A RELATIONSHIP OF TRUST, AND THEY'LL PERFORM BETTER FOR YOU.
WHAT A JOKE, HAIJIMA! SOUNDS TOO CULTISH–GIVES ME THE CREEPS.
MACHINES ARE NOTHING MORE THAN MACHINES! YOU CAN'T BUILD A RELATIONSHIP OF TRUST WITH THEM!

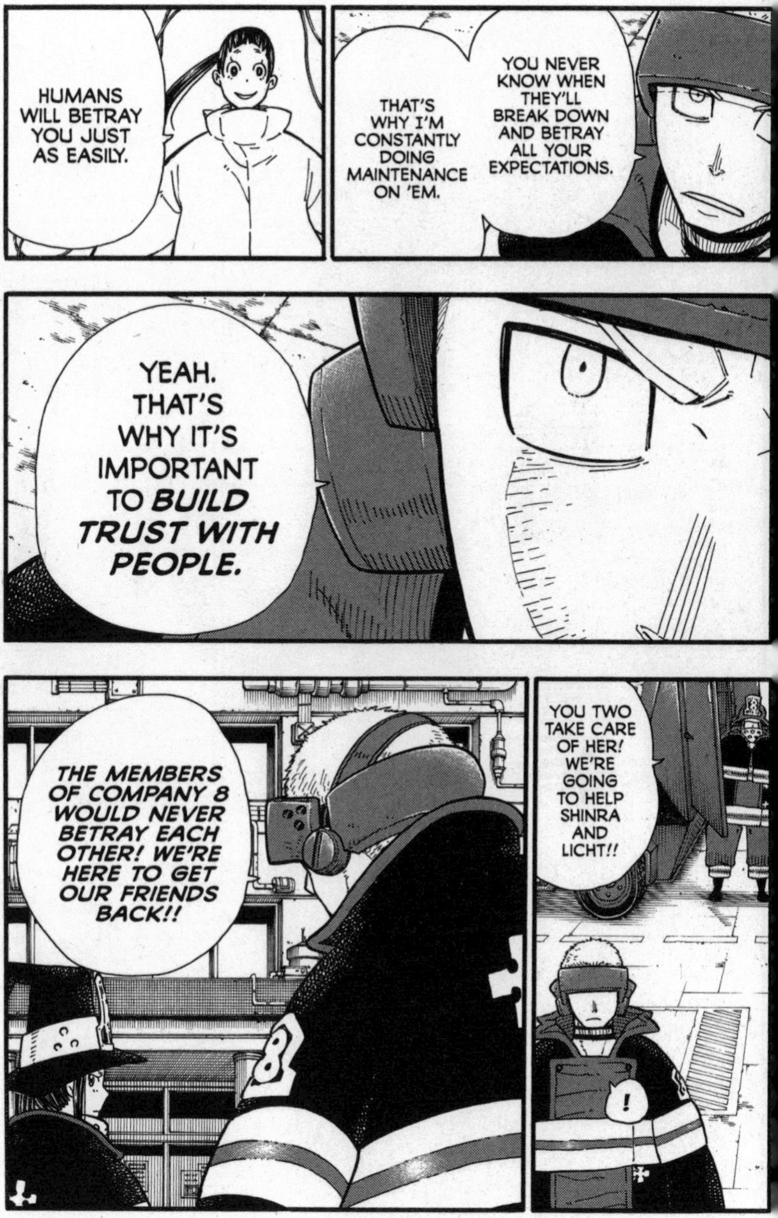
YOU NEVER KNOW WHEN THEY'LL BREAK DOWN AND BETRAY ALL YOUR EXPECTATIONS.
THAT'S WHY I'M CONSTANTLY DOING MAINTENANCE ON 'EM.
HUMANS WILL BETRAY YOU JUST AS EASILY.
YEAH. THAT'S WHY IT'S IMPORTANT TO ***BUILD TRUST WITH PEOPLE.***
YOU TWO TAKE CARE OF HER! WE'RE GOING TO HELP SHINRA AND LICHT!!
!
THE MEMBERS OF COMPANY 8 WOULD NEVER BETRAY EACH OTHER! WE'RE HERE TO GET OUR FRIENDS BACK!!

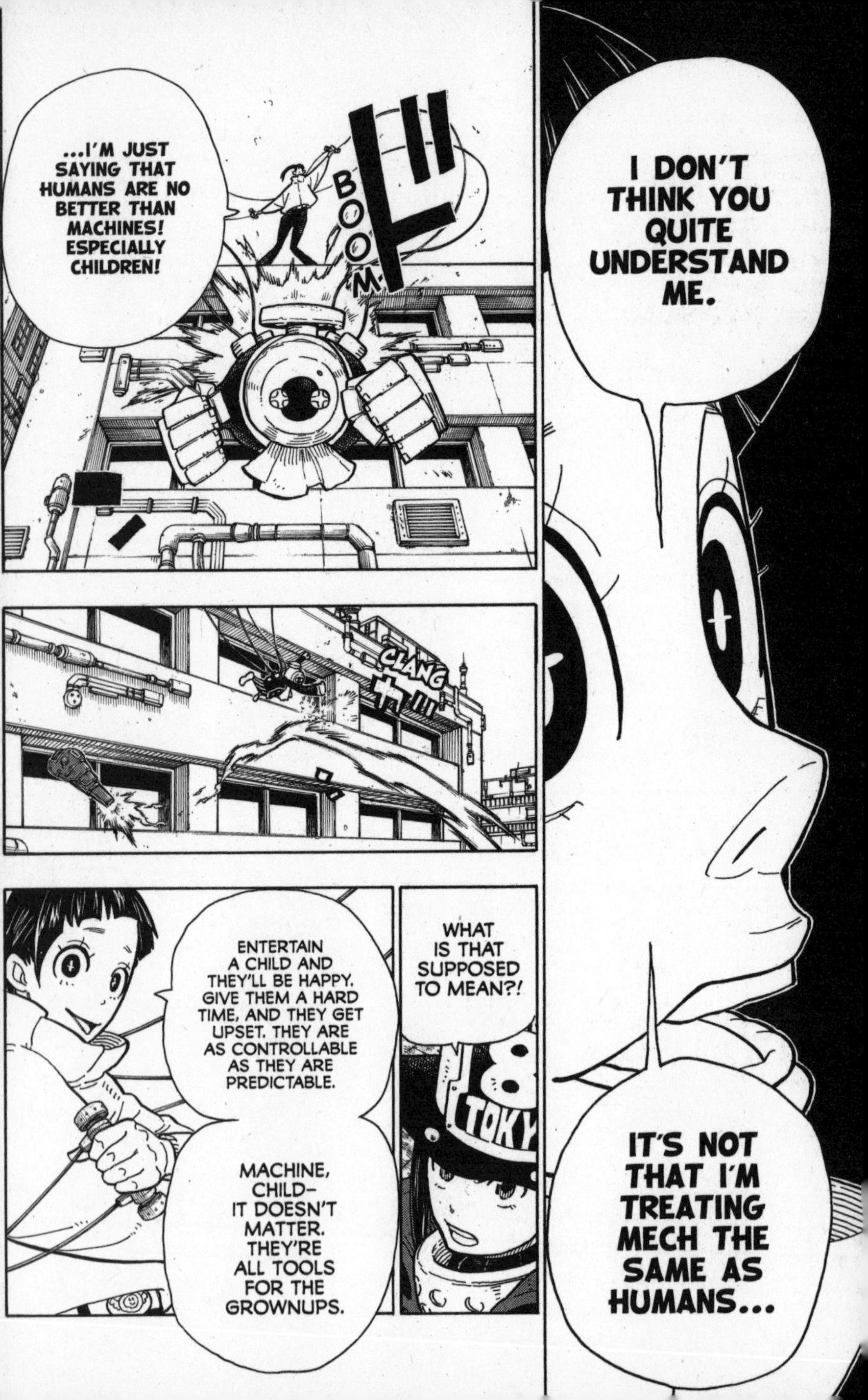
I DON'T THINK YOU QUITE UNDERSTAND ME.
IT'S NOT THAT I'M TREATING MECH THE SAME AS HUMANS...
...I'M JUST SAYING THAT HUMANS ARE NO BETTER THAN MACHINES! ESPECIALLY CHILDREN!
BOOM
CLANG
WHAT IS THAT SUPPOSED TO MEAN?!
TOKY
ENTERTAIN A CHILD AND THEY'LL BE HAPPY. GIVE THEM A HARD TIME, AND THEY GET UPSET. THEY ARE AS CONTROLLABLE AS THEY ARE PREDICTABLE.
MACHINE, CHILD– IT DOESN'T MATTER. THEY'RE ALL TOOLS FOR THE GROWNUPS.

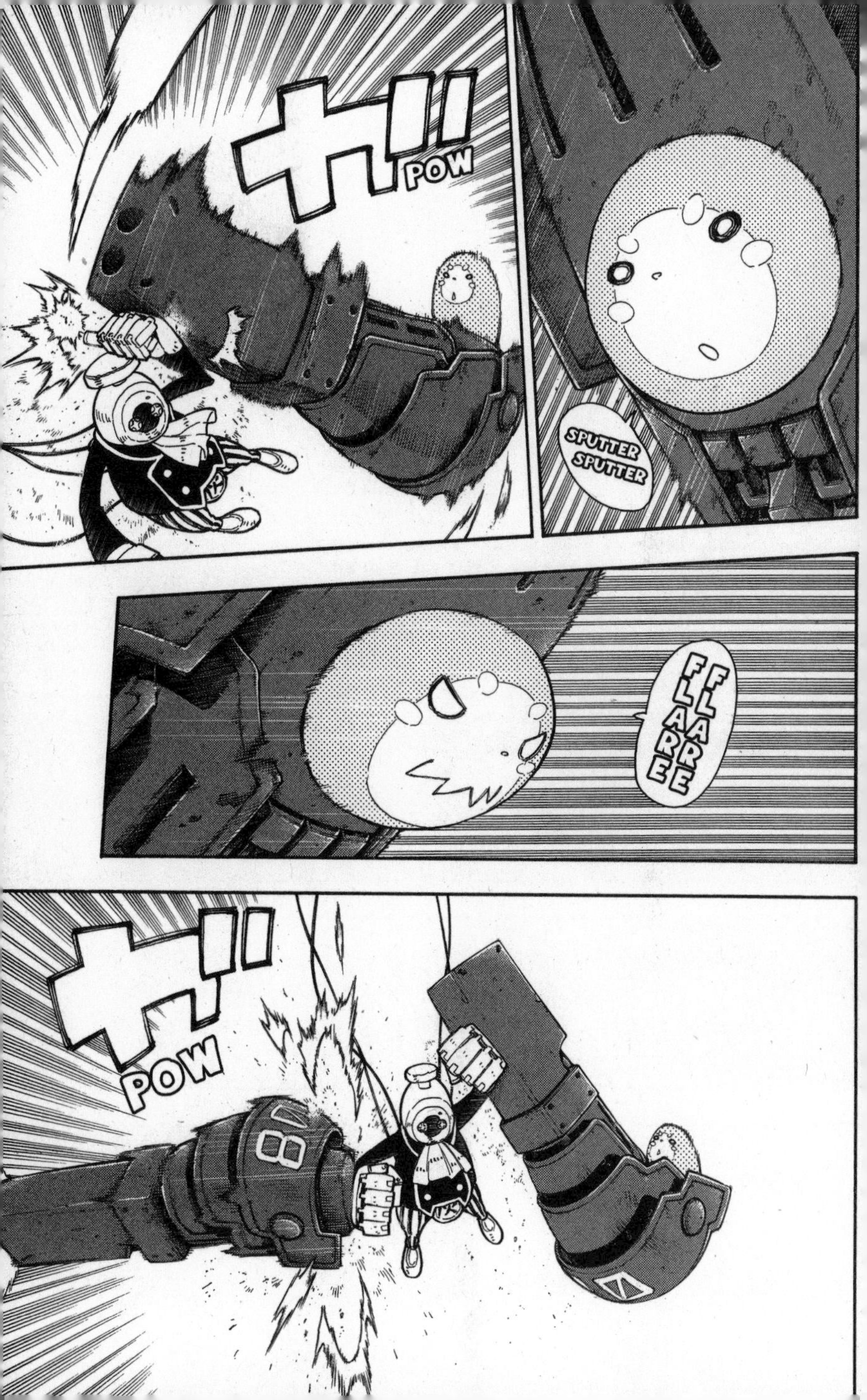
SPUTTER SPUTTER
POW
FLARE FLARE
POW

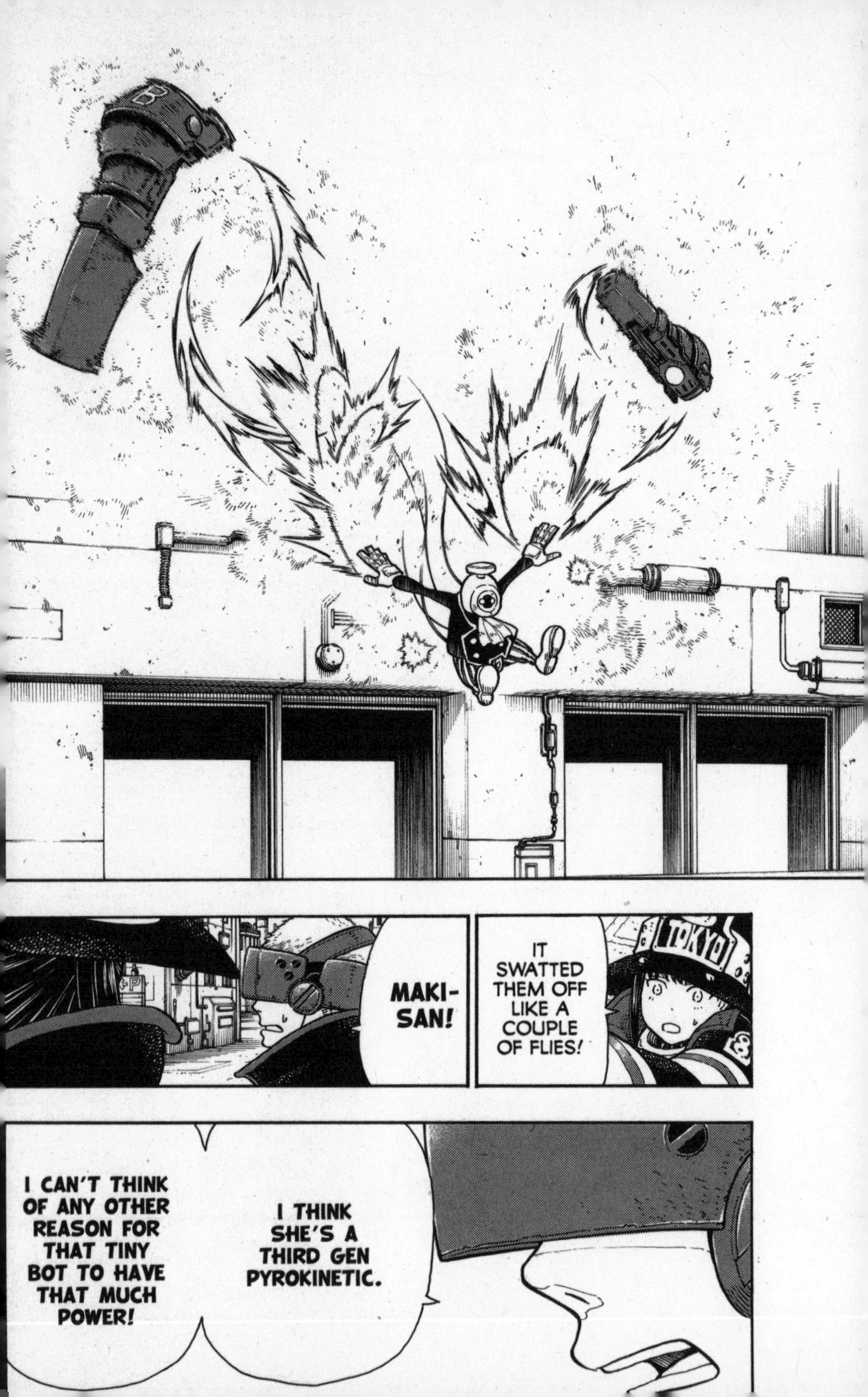
IT SWATTED THEM OFF LIKE A COUPLE OF FLIES!
MAKI-SAN!
I THINK SHE'S A THIRD GEN PYROKINETIC.
I CAN'T THINK OF ANY OTHER REASON FOR THAT TINY BOT TO HAVE THAT MUCH POWER!

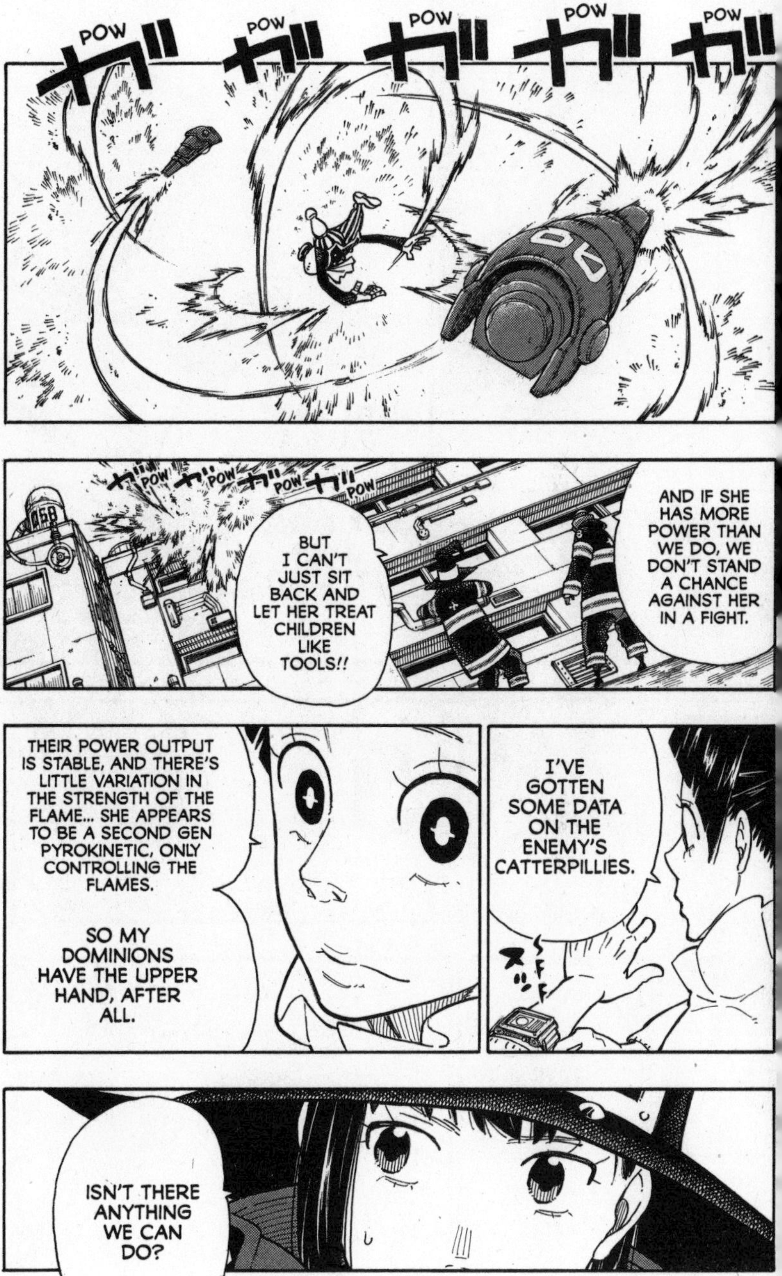
ガ POW ガ POW ガ POW ガ POW ガ POW
AND IF SHE HAS MORE POWER THAN WE DO, WE DON'T STAND A CHANCE AGAINST HER IN A FIGHT.
BUT I CAN'T JUST SIT BACK AND LET HER TREAT CHILDREN LIKE TOOLS!!
ガ POW ガ POW ガ POW ガ POW
I'VE GOTTEN SOME DATA ON THE ENEMY'S CATTERPILLIES.
スッ SFF
THEIR POWER OUTPUT IS STABLE, AND THERE'S LITTLE VARIATION IN THE STRENGTH OF THE FLAME... SHE APPEARS TO BE A SECOND GEN PYROKINETIC, ONLY CONTROLLING THE FLAMES.
SO MY DOMINIONS HAVE THE UPPER HAND, AFTER ALL.
ISN'T THERE ANYTHING WE CAN DO?

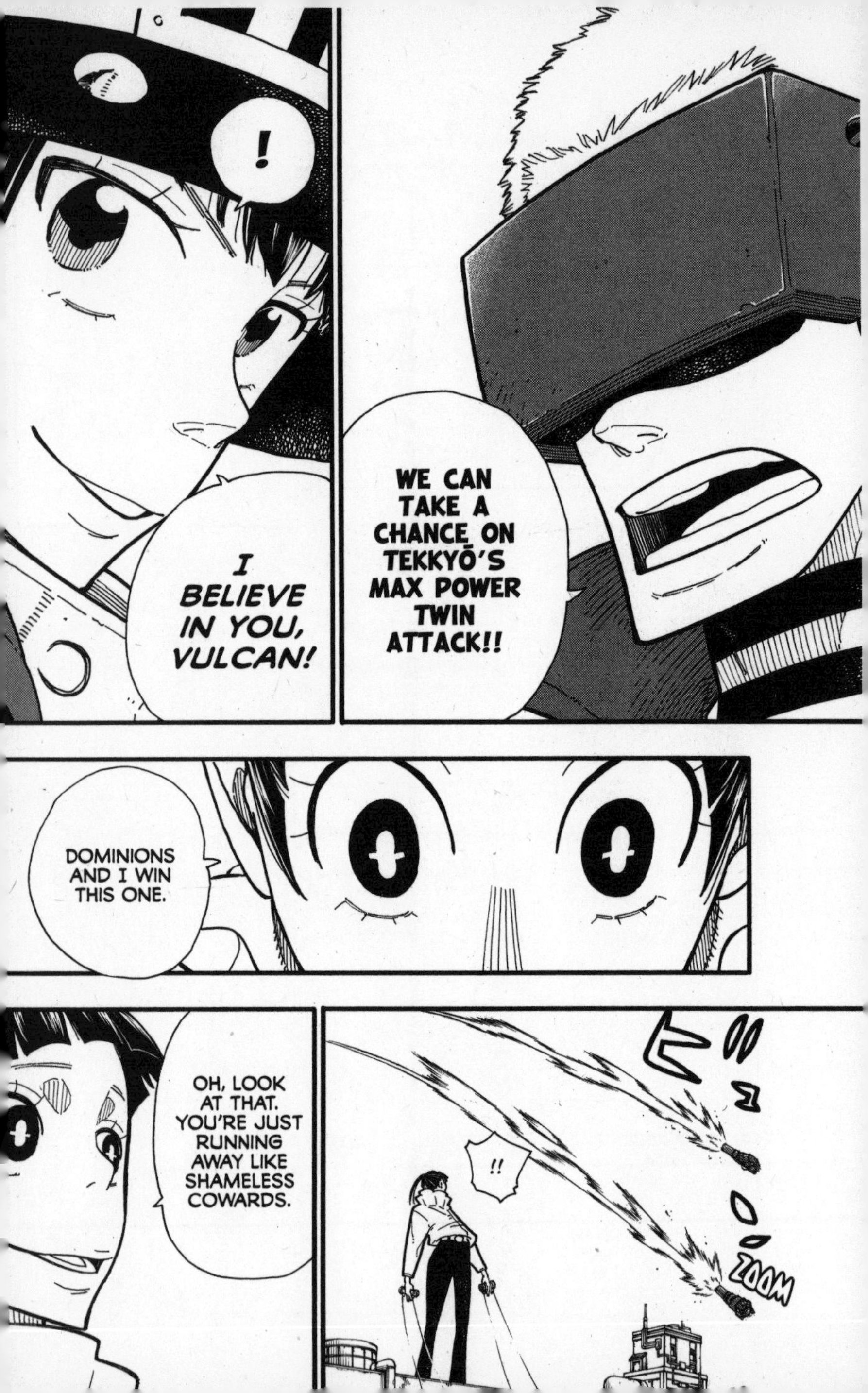
WE CAN TAKE A CHANCE ON TEKKYŌ'S MAX POWER TWIN ATTACK!!
!
I BELIEVE IN YOU, VULCAN!
DOMINIONS AND I WIN THIS ONE.
!!
ZOOM
OH, LOOK AT THAT. YOU'RE JUST RUNNING AWAY LIKE SHAMELESS COWARDS.

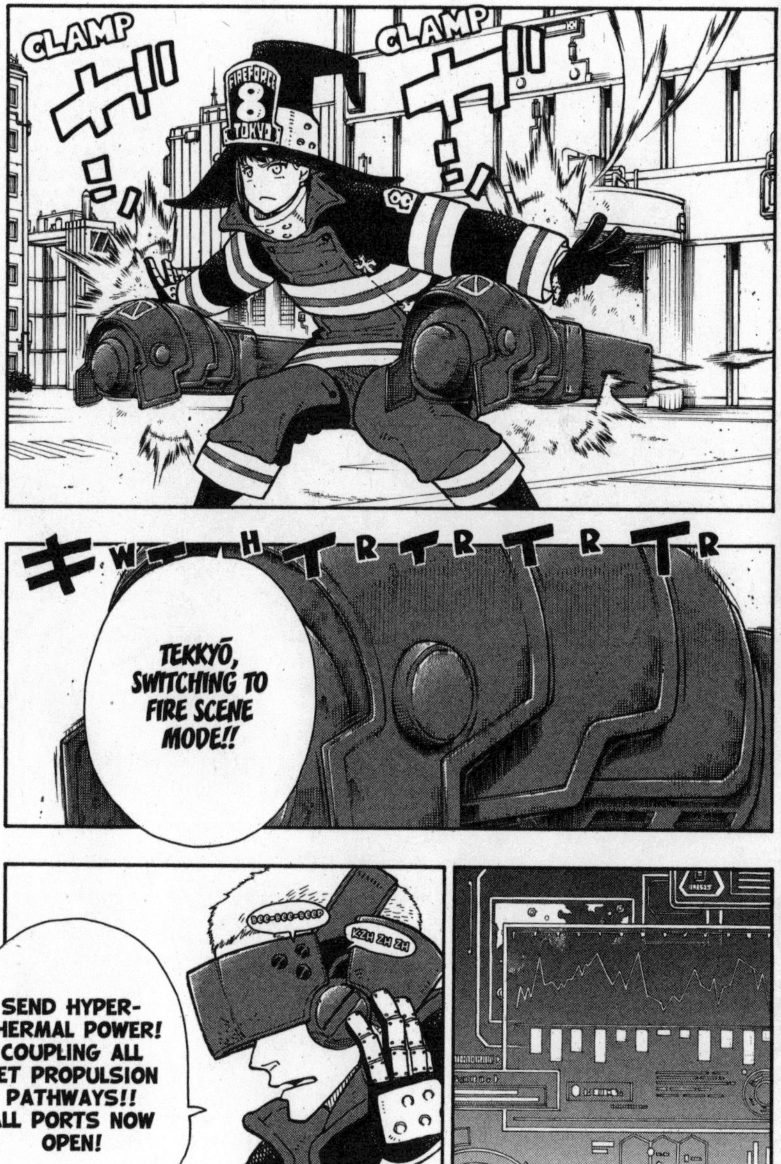
CLAMP
CLAMP
WHRRRR
TEKKYŌ, SWITCHING TO FIRE SCENE MODE!!
BEE-BEE-BEEP
KZH ZH ZH
SEND HYPER-THERMAL POWER! COUPLING ALL JET PROPULSION PATHWAYS!! ALL PORTS NOW OPEN!

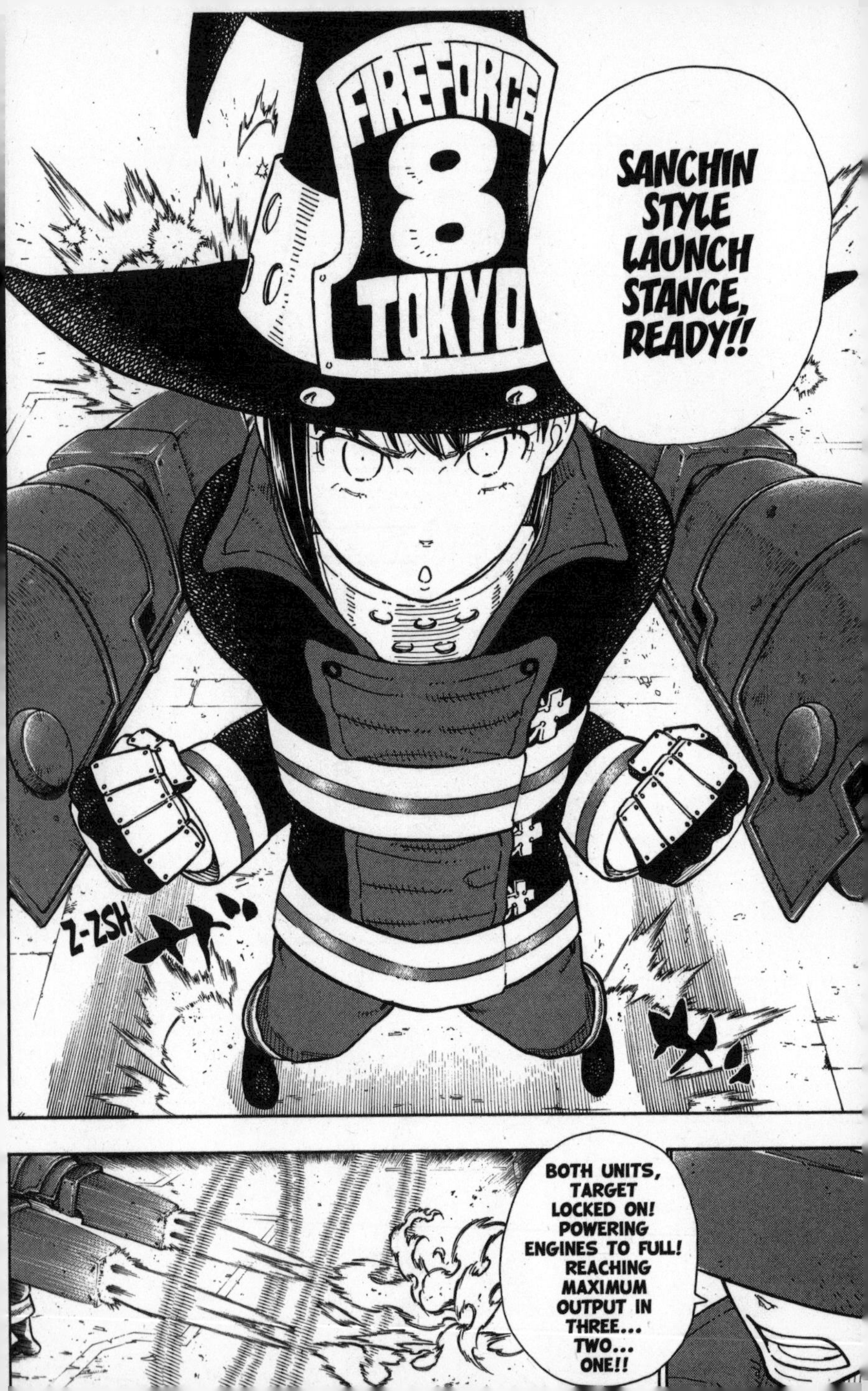
FIREFORCE 8 TOKYO
SANCHIN STYLE LAUNCH STANCE, READY!!
Z-ZSH
BOTH UNITS, TARGET LOCKED ON! POWERING ENGINES TO FULL! REACHING MAXIMUM OUTPUT IN THREE... TWO... ONE!!

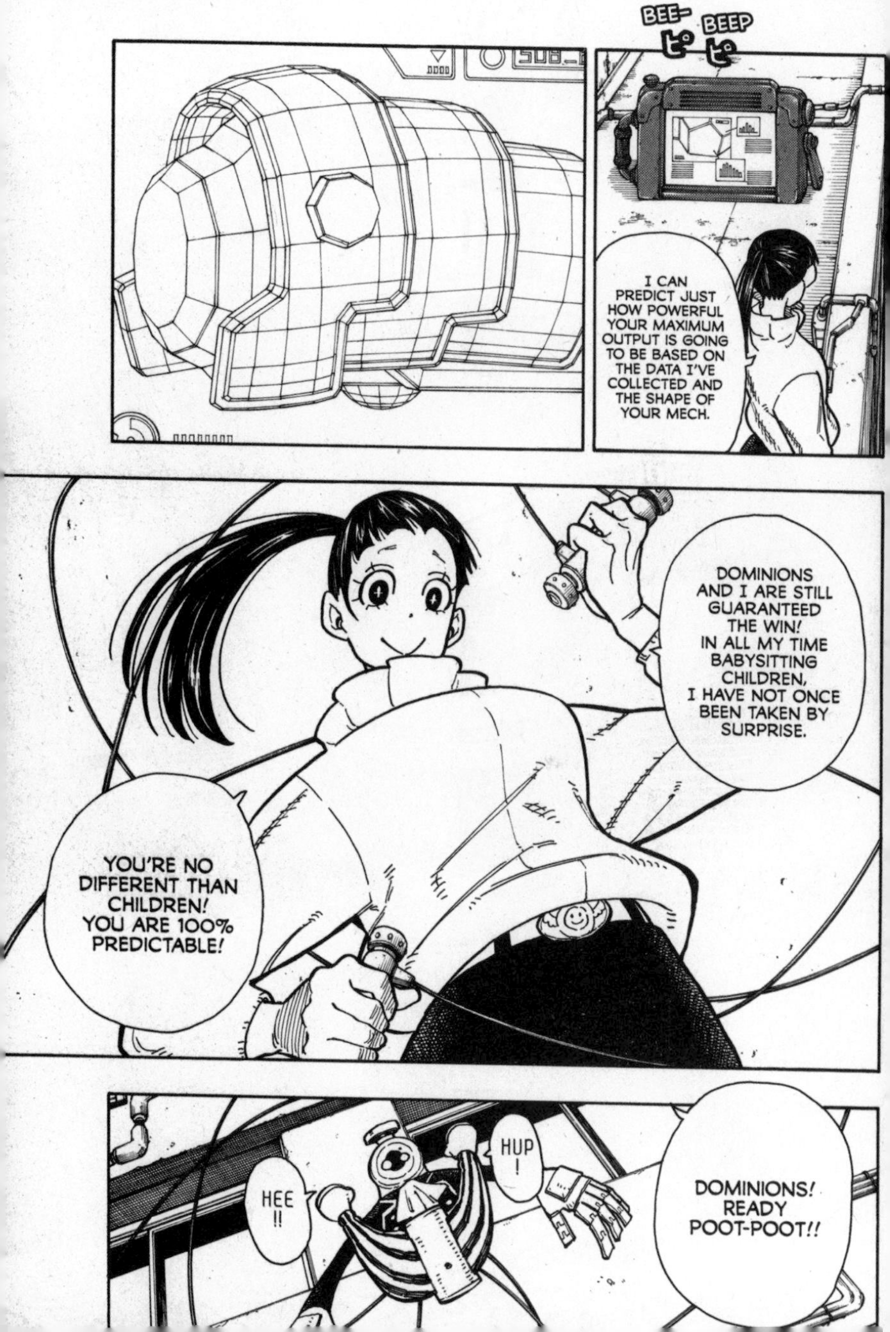
BEE-
BEEP
I CAN PREDICT JUST HOW POWERFUL YOUR MAXIMUM OUTPUT IS GOING TO BE BASED ON THE DATA I'VE COLLECTED AND THE SHAPE OF YOUR MECH.
DOMINIONS AND I ARE STILL GUARANTEED THE WIN! IN ALL MY TIME BABYSITTING CHILDREN, I HAVE NOT ONCE BEEN TAKEN BY SURPRISE.
YOU'RE NO DIFFERENT THAN CHILDREN! YOU ARE 100% PREDICTABLE!
DOMINIONS! READY POOT-POOT!!
HUP!
HEE!!

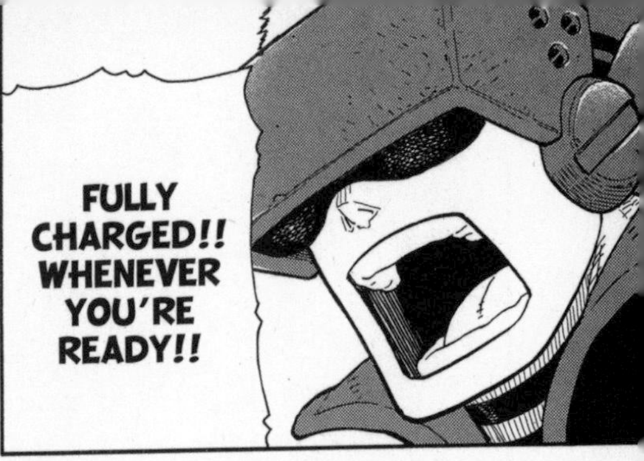
FULLY CHARGED!! WHENEVER YOU'RE READY!!
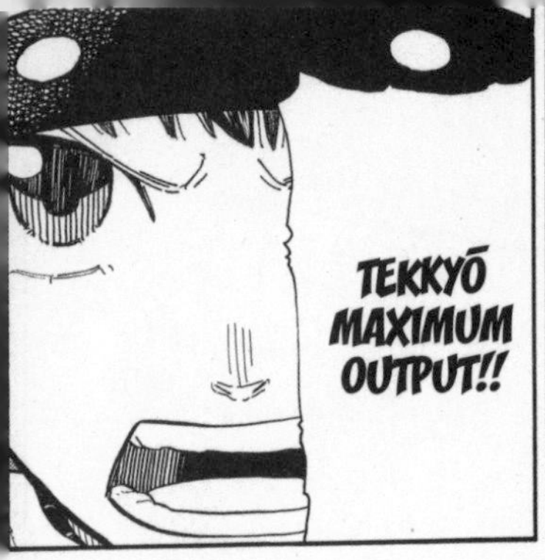
TEKKYŌ MAXIMUM OUTPUT!!
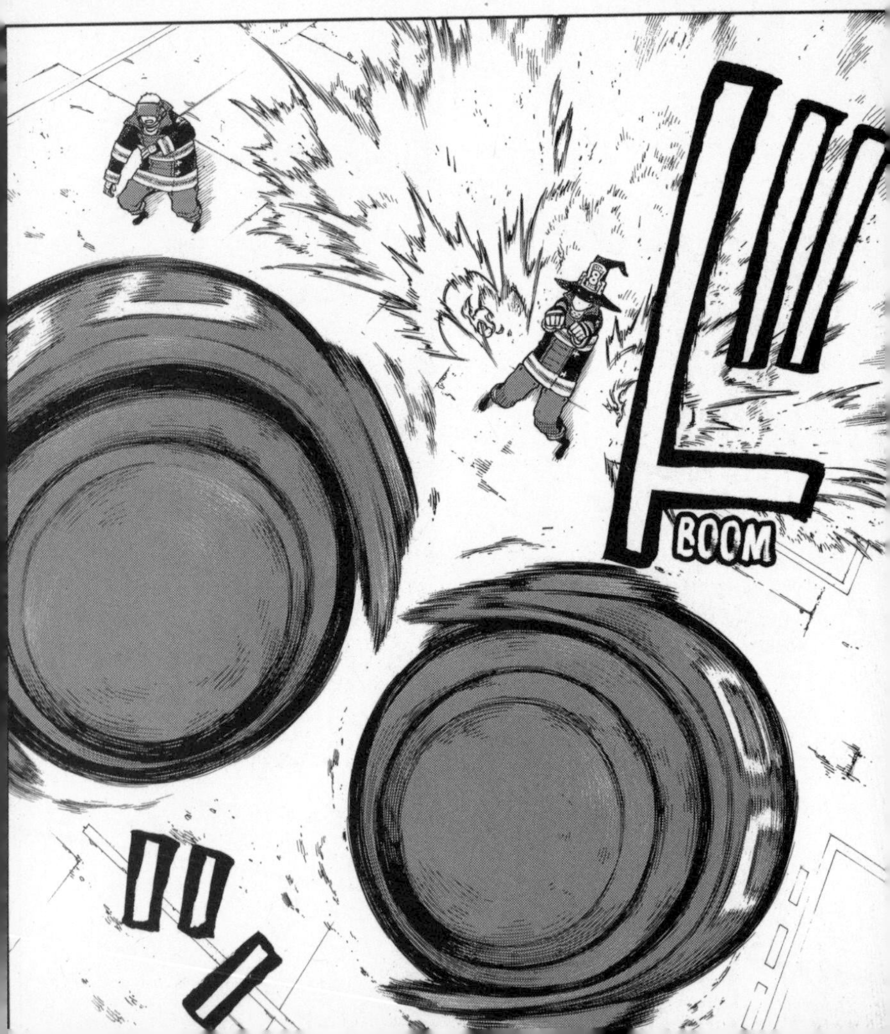
BOOM

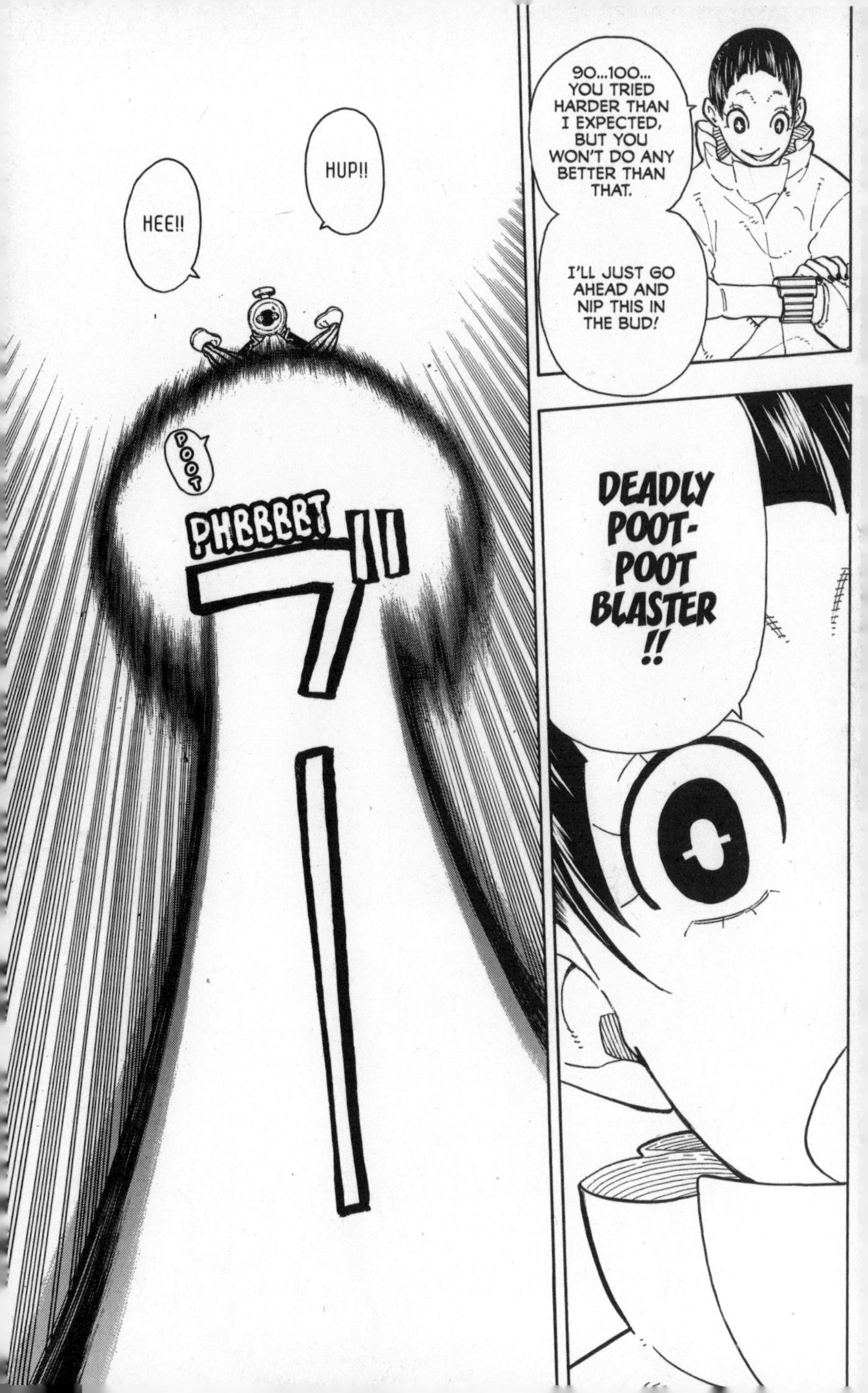
90...100... YOU TRIED HARDER THAN I EXPECTED, BUT YOU WON'T DO ANY BETTER THAN THAT.
I'LL JUST GO AHEAD AND NIP THIS IN THE BUD!
DEADLY POOT-POOT BLASTER!!
HUP!!
HEE!!
POOT
PHBBBBT

FIRE FORCE

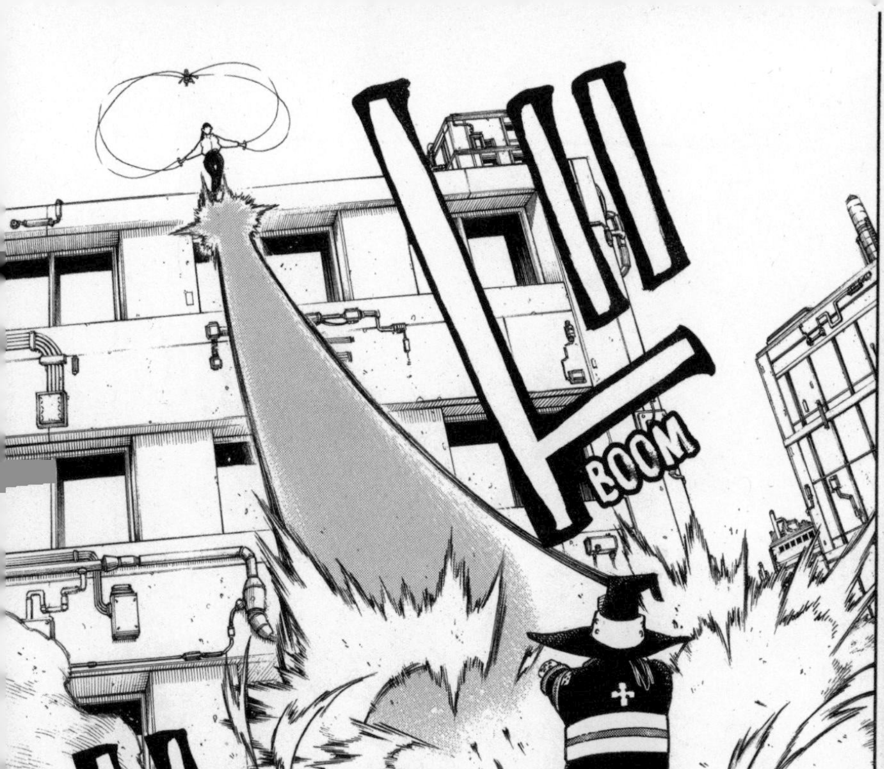
BOOM

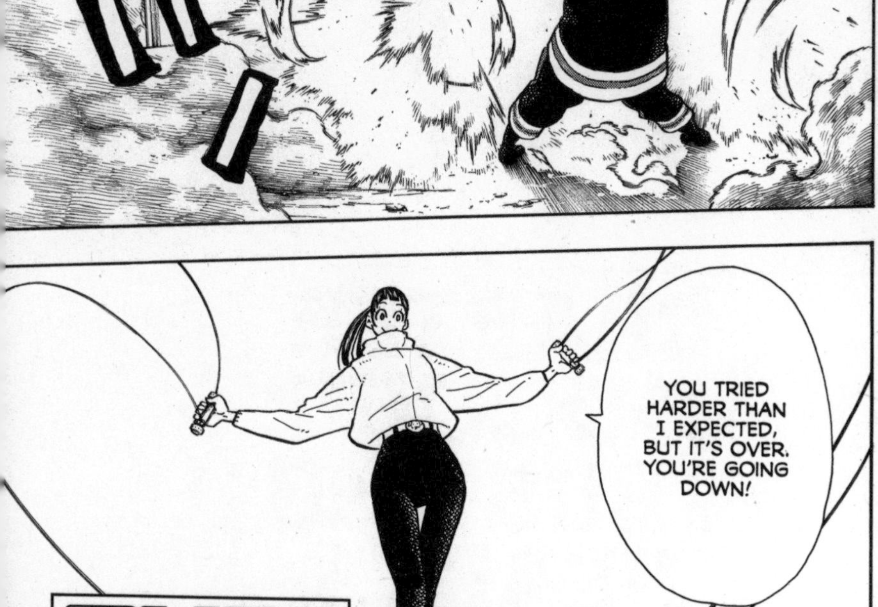
YOU TRIED HARDER THAN I EXPECTED, BUT IT'S OVER. YOU'RE GOING DOWN!

FIRE FORCE

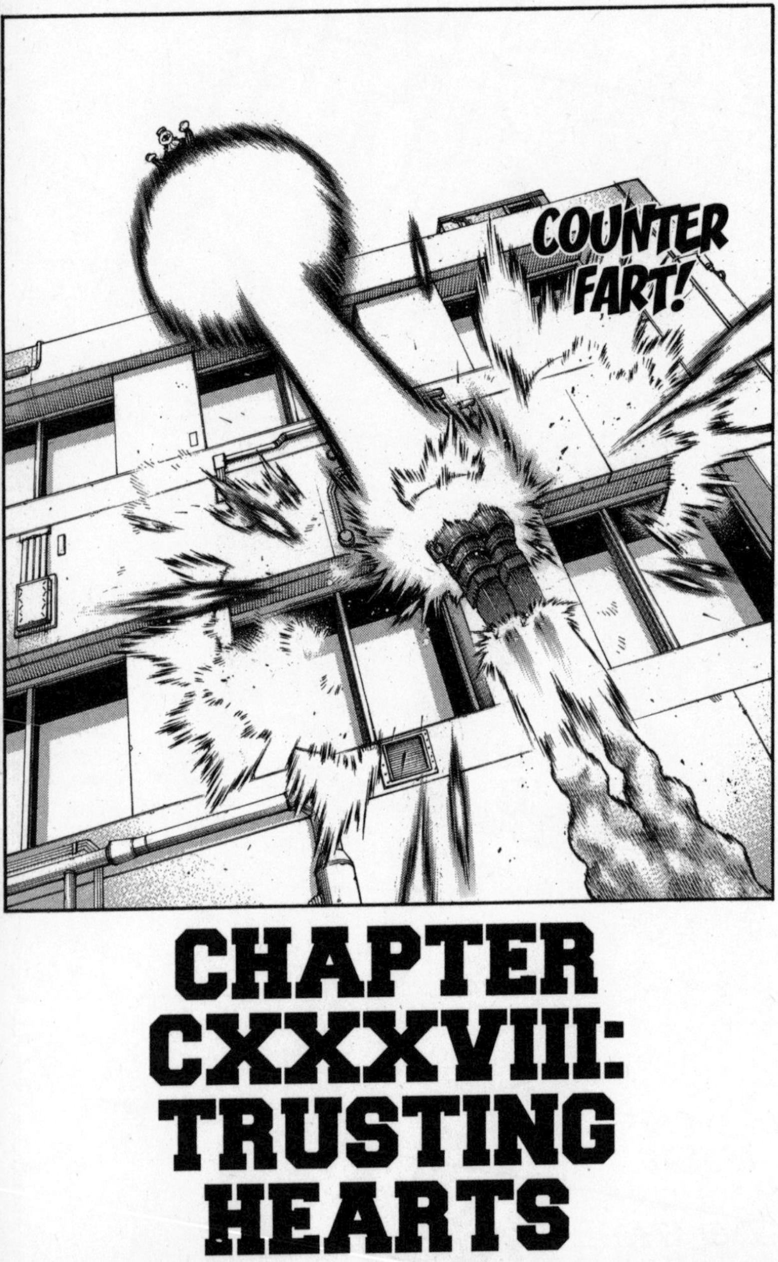
COUNTER FART!

CHAPTER CXXXVIII: TRUSTING HEARTS

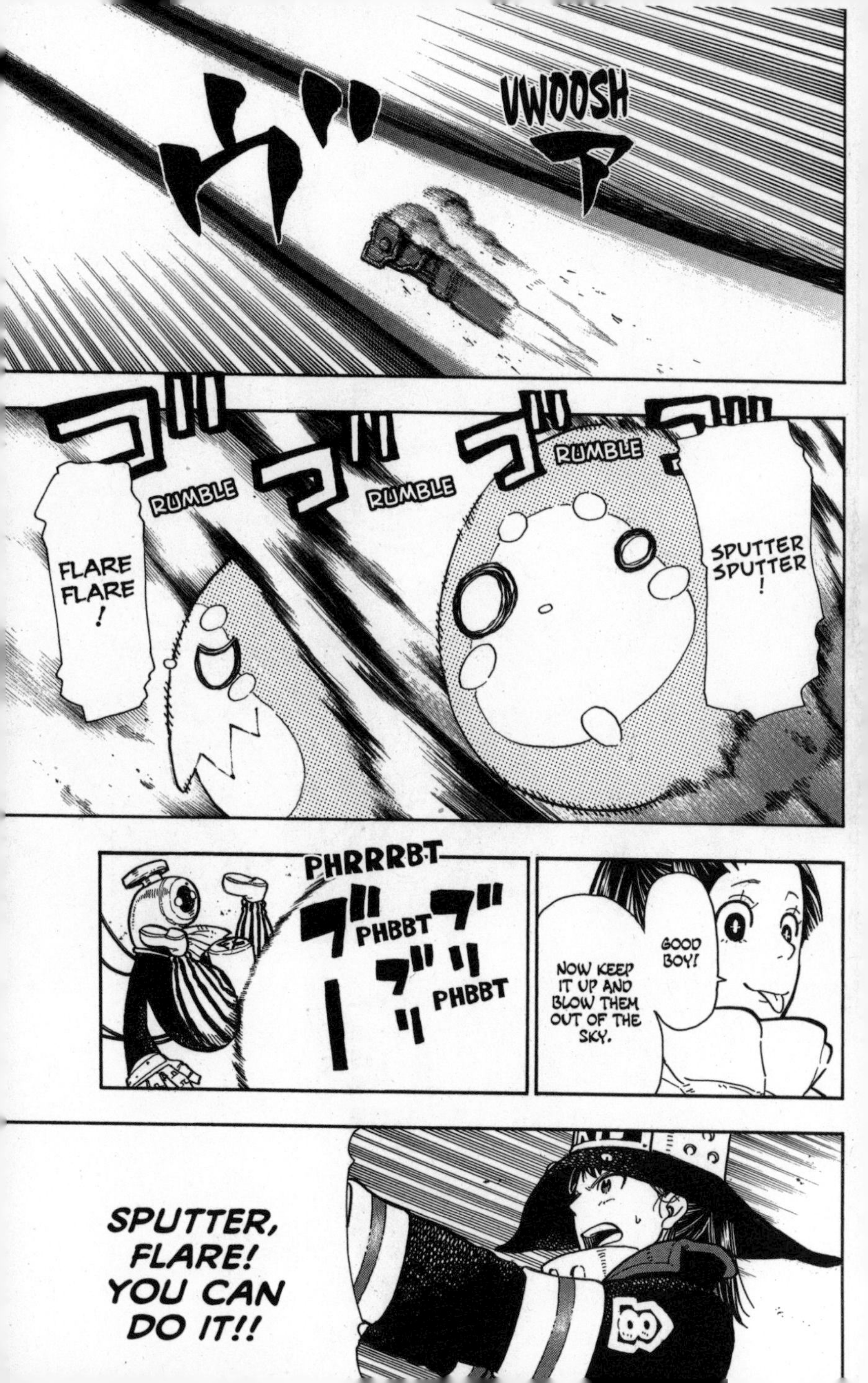
VWOOSH
SPUTTER SPUTTER!
RUMBLE
RUMBLE
RUMBLE
FLARE FLARE!
GOOD BOY!
NOW KEEP IT UP AND BLOW THEM OUT OF THE SKY.
PHRRRBT
PHBBT
PHBBT
SPUTTER, FLARE! YOU CAN DO IT!!

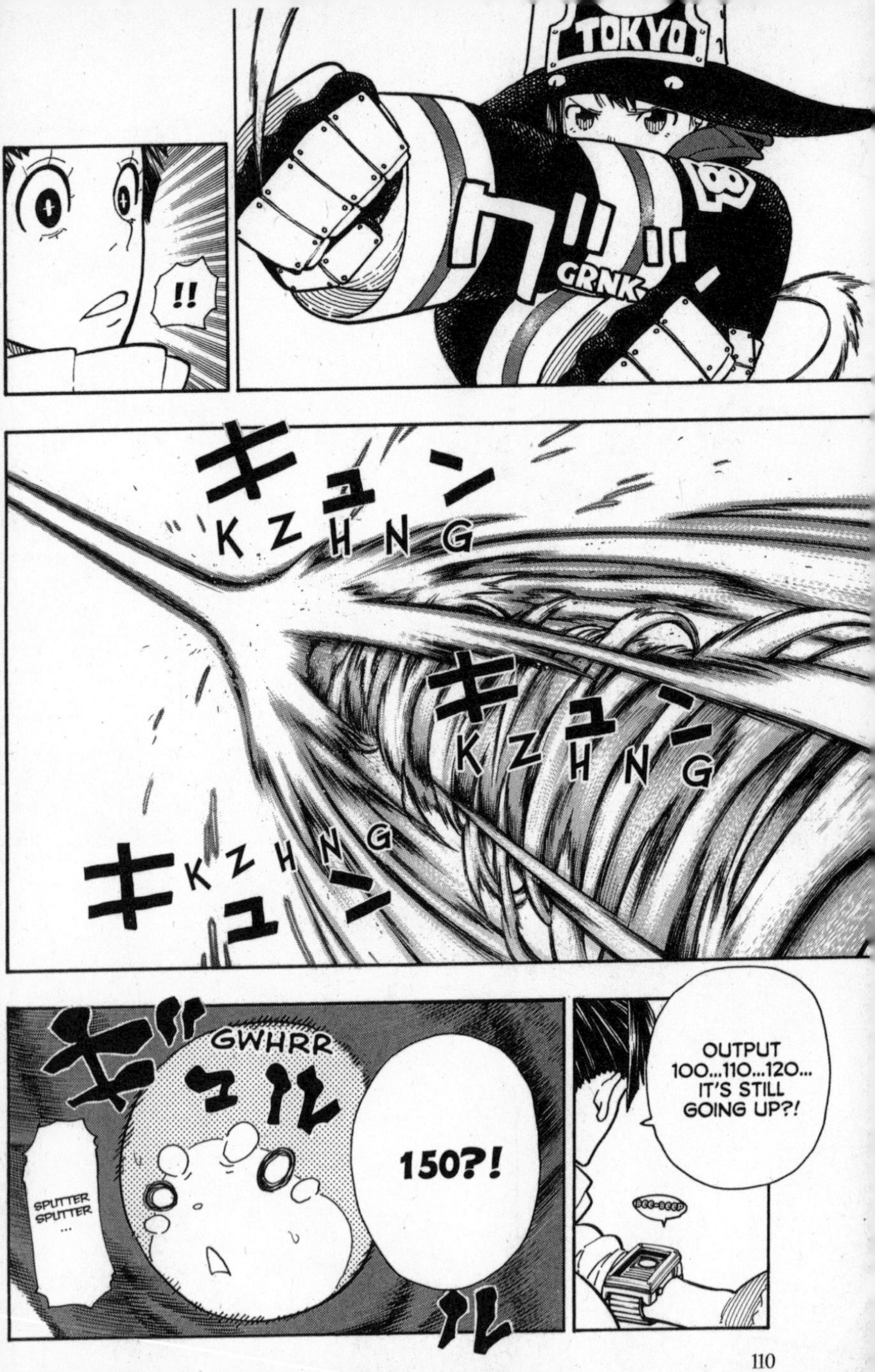
TOKYO
GRNK
!!
KZHNG
KZHNG
KZHNG
OUTPUT 100...110...120... IT'S STILL GOING UP?!
BEE-BEEP
150?!
GWHRR
SPUTTER SPUTTER ...

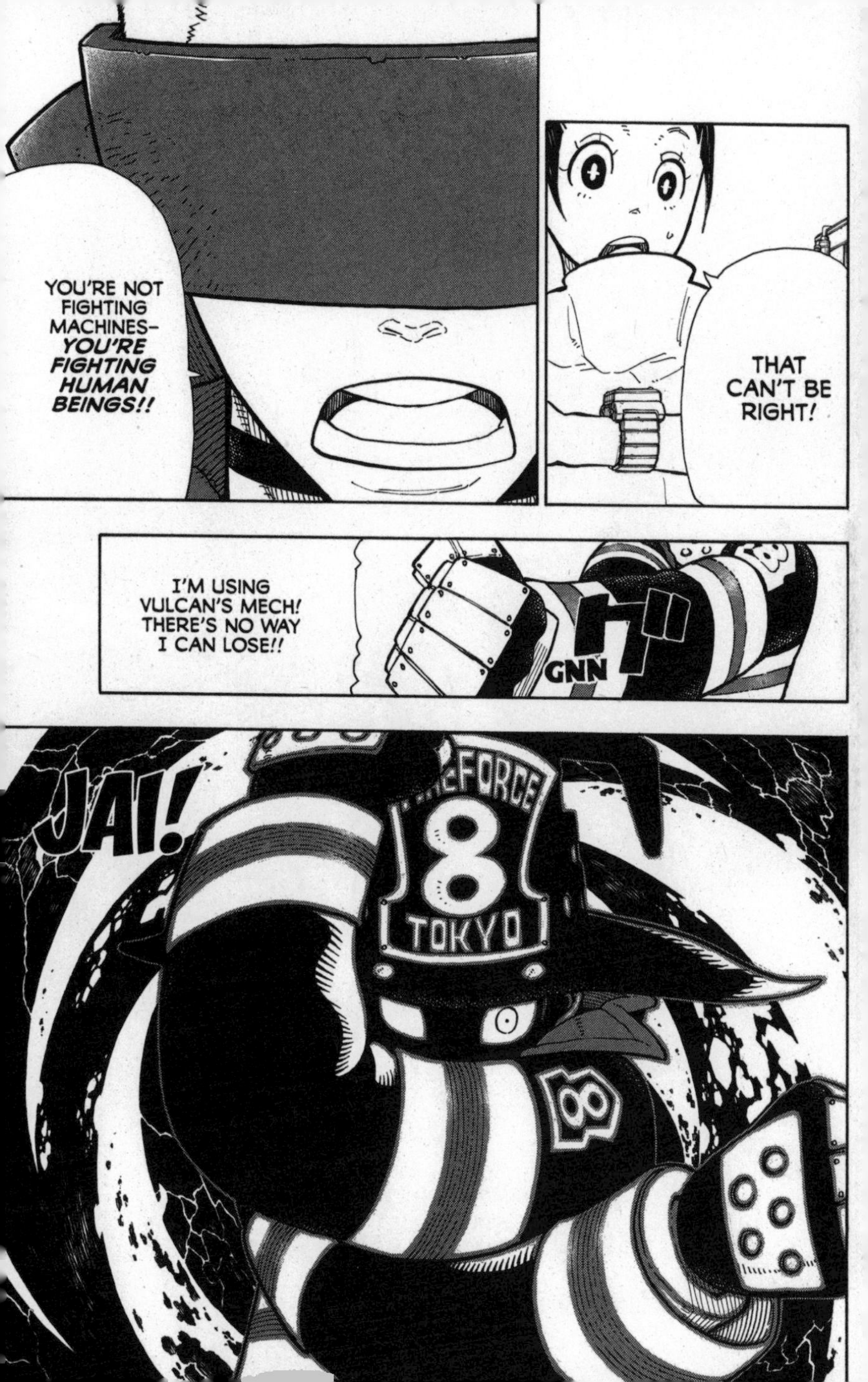
THAT CAN'T BE RIGHT!
YOU'RE NOT FIGHTING MACHINES– *YOU'RE FIGHTING HUMAN BEINGS!!*
I'M USING VULCAN'S MECH! THERE'S NO WAY I CAN LOSE!!
GNN
JAI!
FORCE
8
TOKYO
8

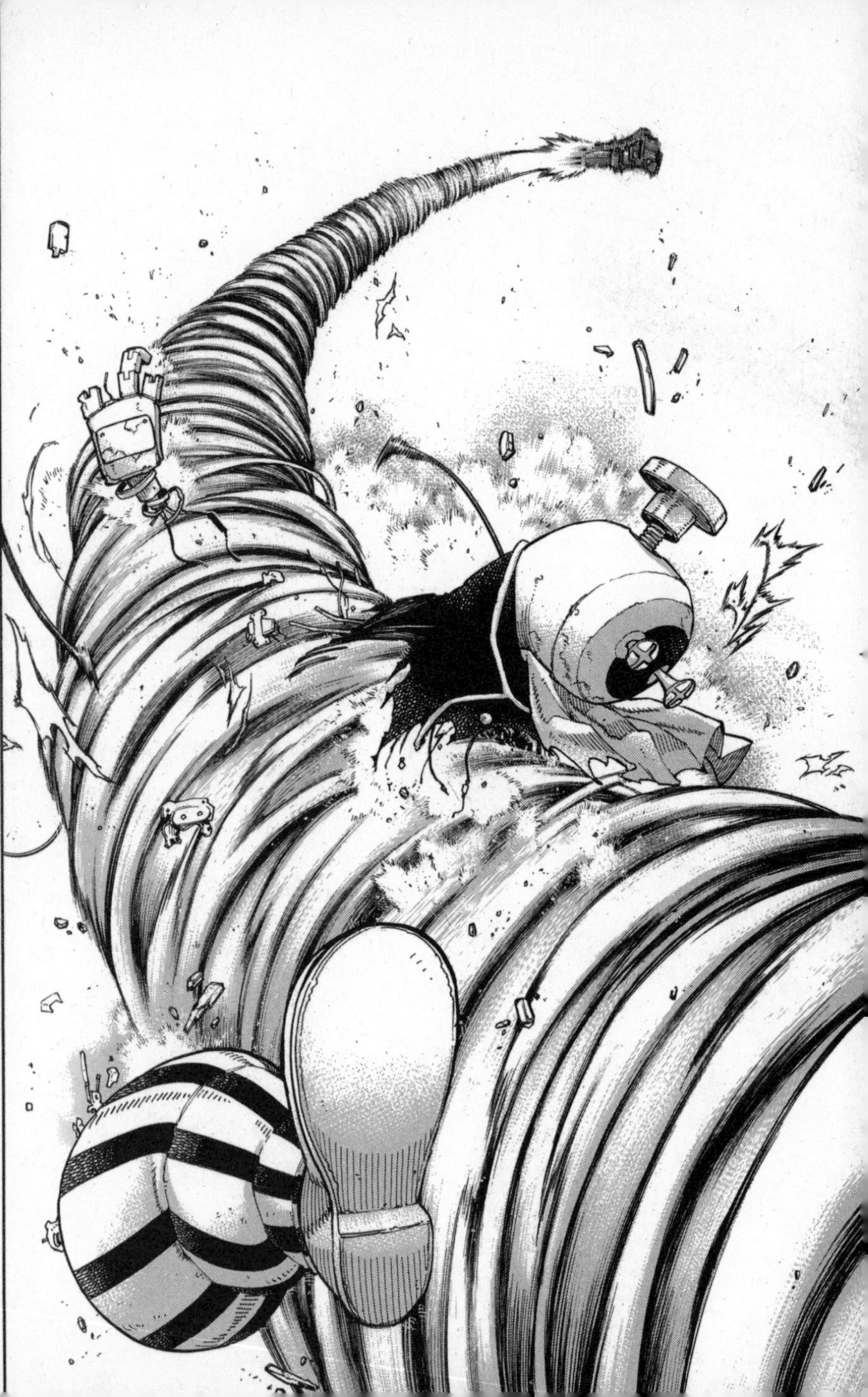

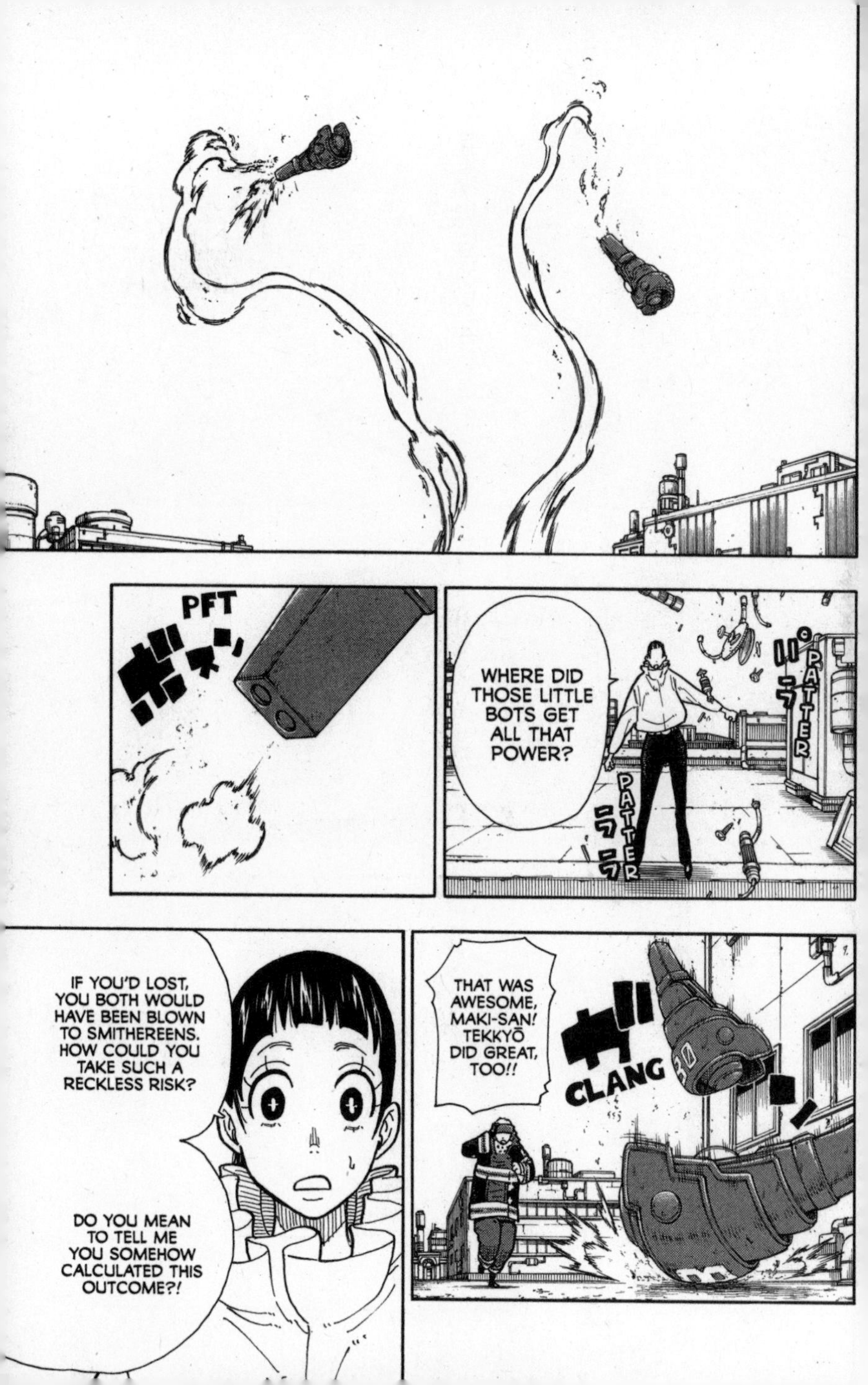
WHERE DID THOSE LITTLE BOTS GET ALL THAT POWER?
PATTER
PATTER
PFT
THAT WAS AWESOME, MAKI-SAN! TEKKYŌ DID GREAT, TOO!!
CLANG
IF YOU'D LOST, YOU BOTH WOULD HAVE BEEN BLOWN TO SMITHEREENS. HOW COULD YOU TAKE SUCH A RECKLESS RISK?
DO YOU MEAN TO TELL ME YOU SOMEHOW CALCULATED THIS OUTCOME?!

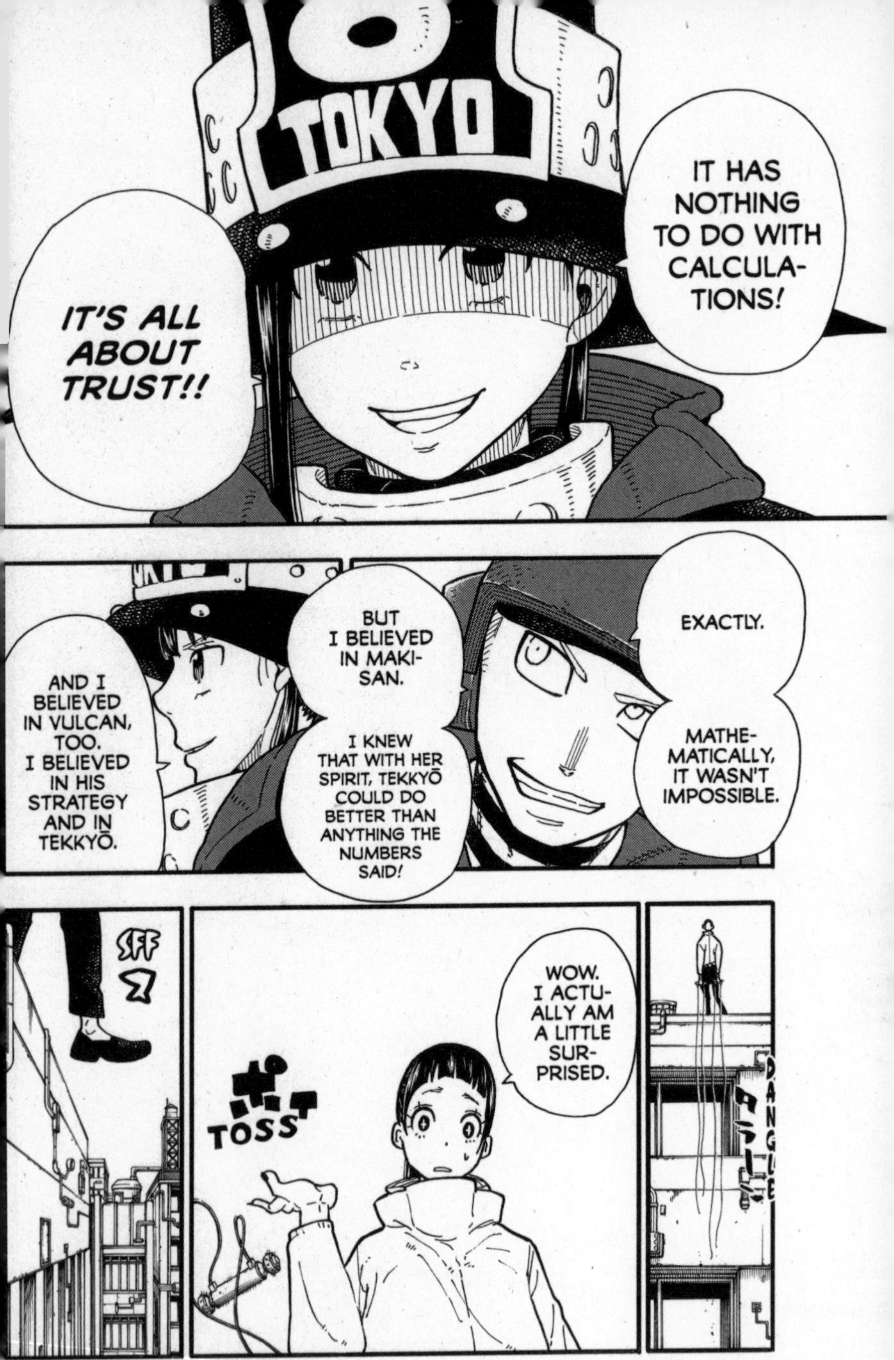
TOKYO
IT HAS NOTHING TO DO WITH CALCULA-TIONS!
IT'S ALL ABOUT TRUST!!
EXACTLY.
MATHE-MATICALLY, IT WASN'T IMPOSSIBLE.
BUT I BELIEVED IN MAKI-SAN.
I KNEW THAT WITH HER SPIRIT, TEKKYŌ COULD DO BETTER THAN ANYTHING THE NUMBERS SAID!
AND I BELIEVED IN VULCAN, TOO. I BELIEVED IN HIS STRATEGY AND IN TEKKYŌ.
DANGLE
WOW. I ACTU-ALLY AM A LITTLE SUR-PRISED.
TOSS
SFF

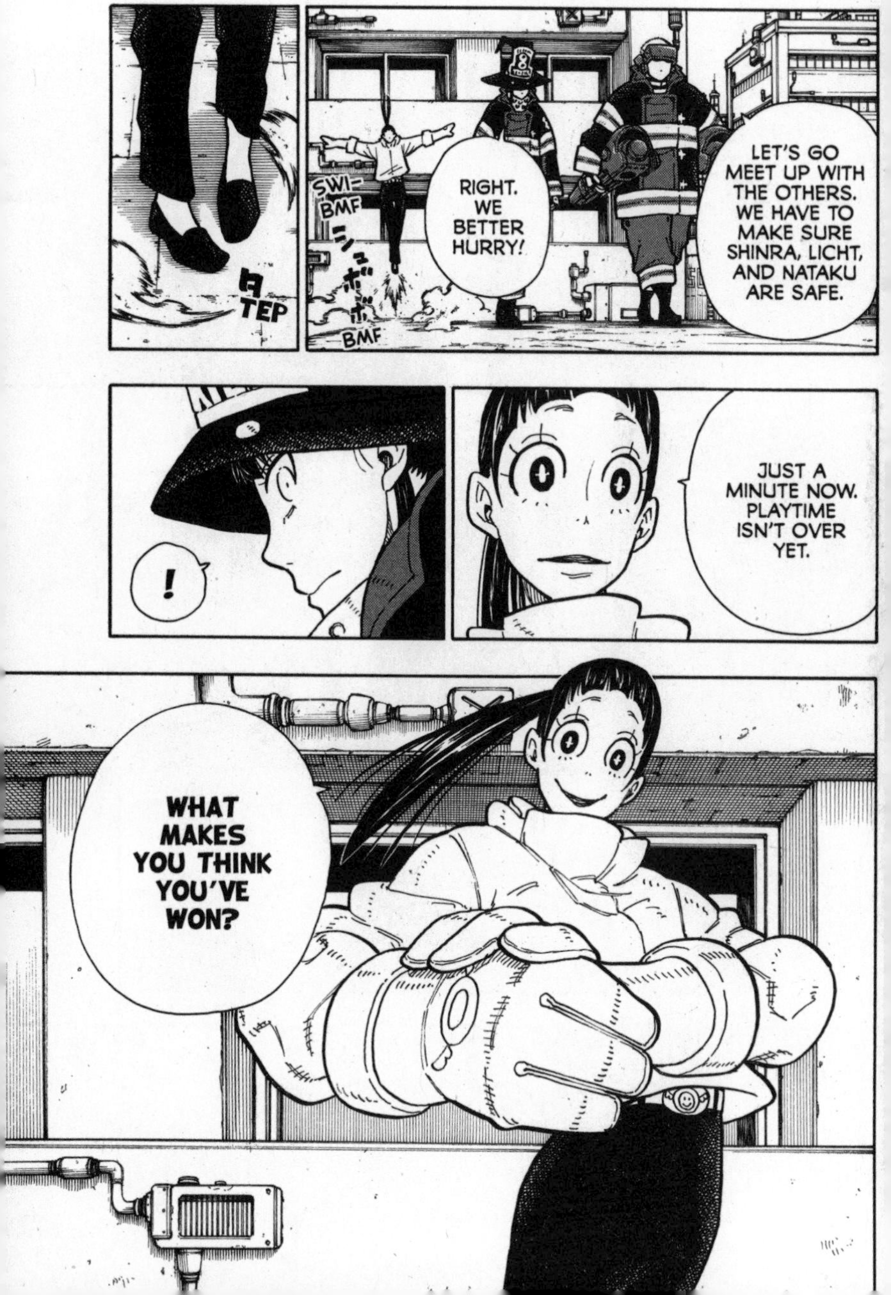
LET'S GO MEET UP WITH THE OTHERS. WE HAVE TO MAKE SURE SHINRA, LICHT, AND NATAKU ARE SAFE.
RIGHT. WE BETTER HURRY!
SWI-BMF
BMF
TEP
JUST A MINUTE NOW. PLAYTIME ISN'T OVER YET.
!
WHAT MAKES YOU THINK YOU'VE WON?

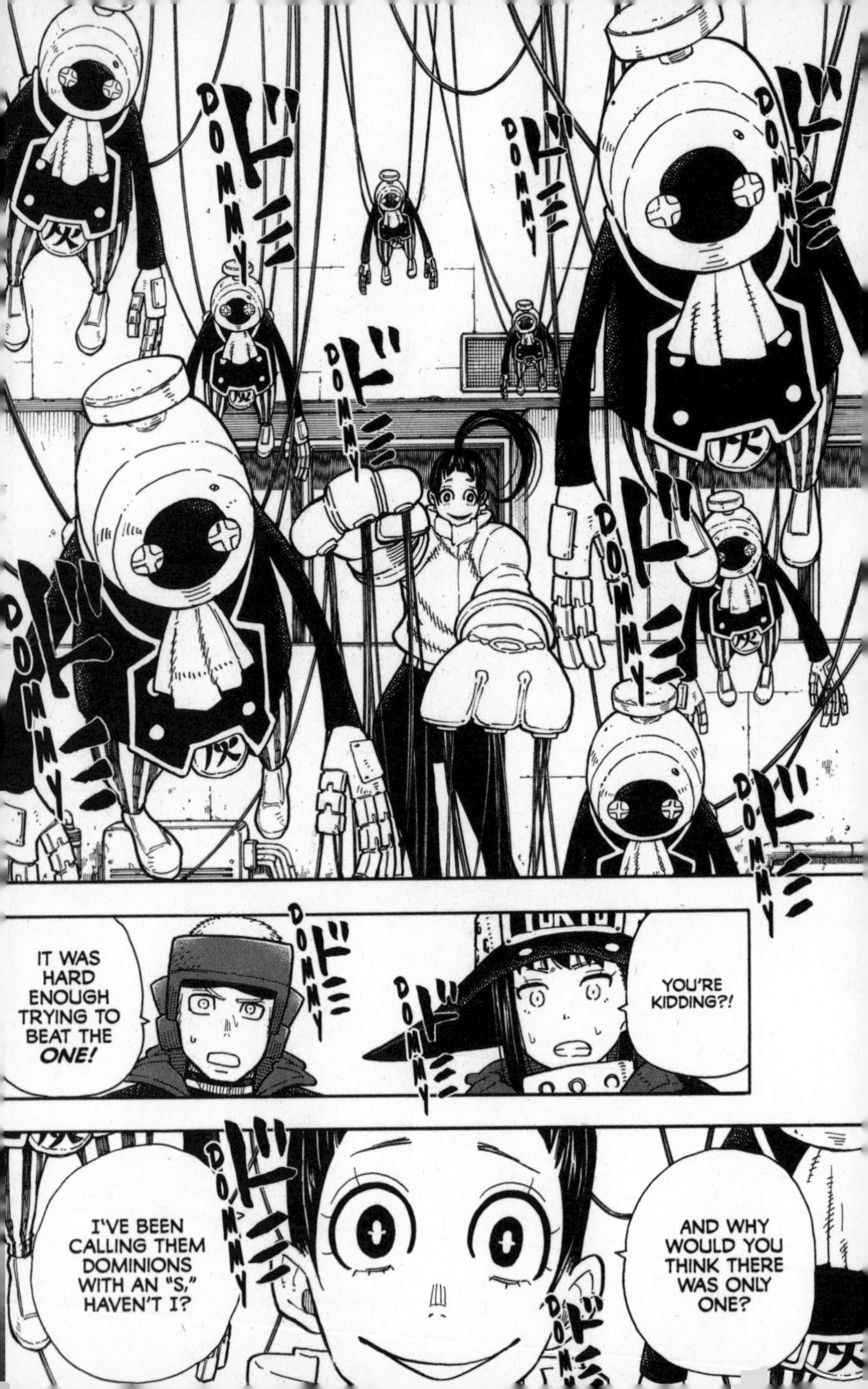
DOMMY
DOMMY
DOMMY
DOMMY
DOMMY
DOMMY
DOMMY
DOMMY
DOMMY
YOU'RE KIDDING?!
DOMMY
IT WAS HARD ENOUGH TRYING TO BEAT THE *ONE!*
AND WHY WOULD YOU THINK THERE WAS ONLY ONE?
DOMMY
I'VE BEEN CALLING THEM DOMINIONS WITH AN "S," HAVEN'T I?

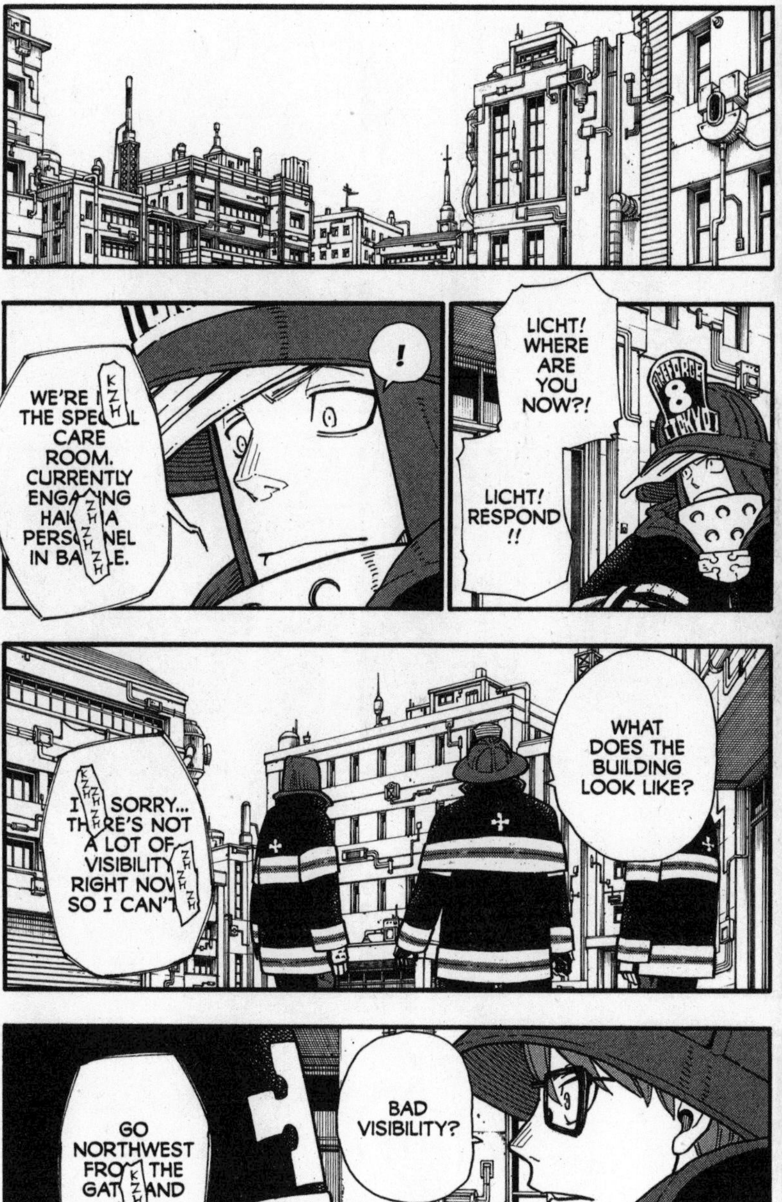
LICHT! WHERE ARE YOU NOW?!
LICHT! RESPOND!!
!
WE'RE I THE SPEC L CARE ROOM. CURRENTLY ENGA NG HAI A PERSO NEL IN BA LE.
KZH
ZH ZH ZH ZH
WHAT DOES THE BUILDING LOOK LIKE?
I SORRY... TH RE'S NOT A LOT OF VISIBILITY RIGHT NOW SO I CAN'T
KZH ZH ZH
ZH ZH ZH ZH
BAD VISIBILITY?
GO NORTHWEST FRO THE GAT AND I
KZH ZH

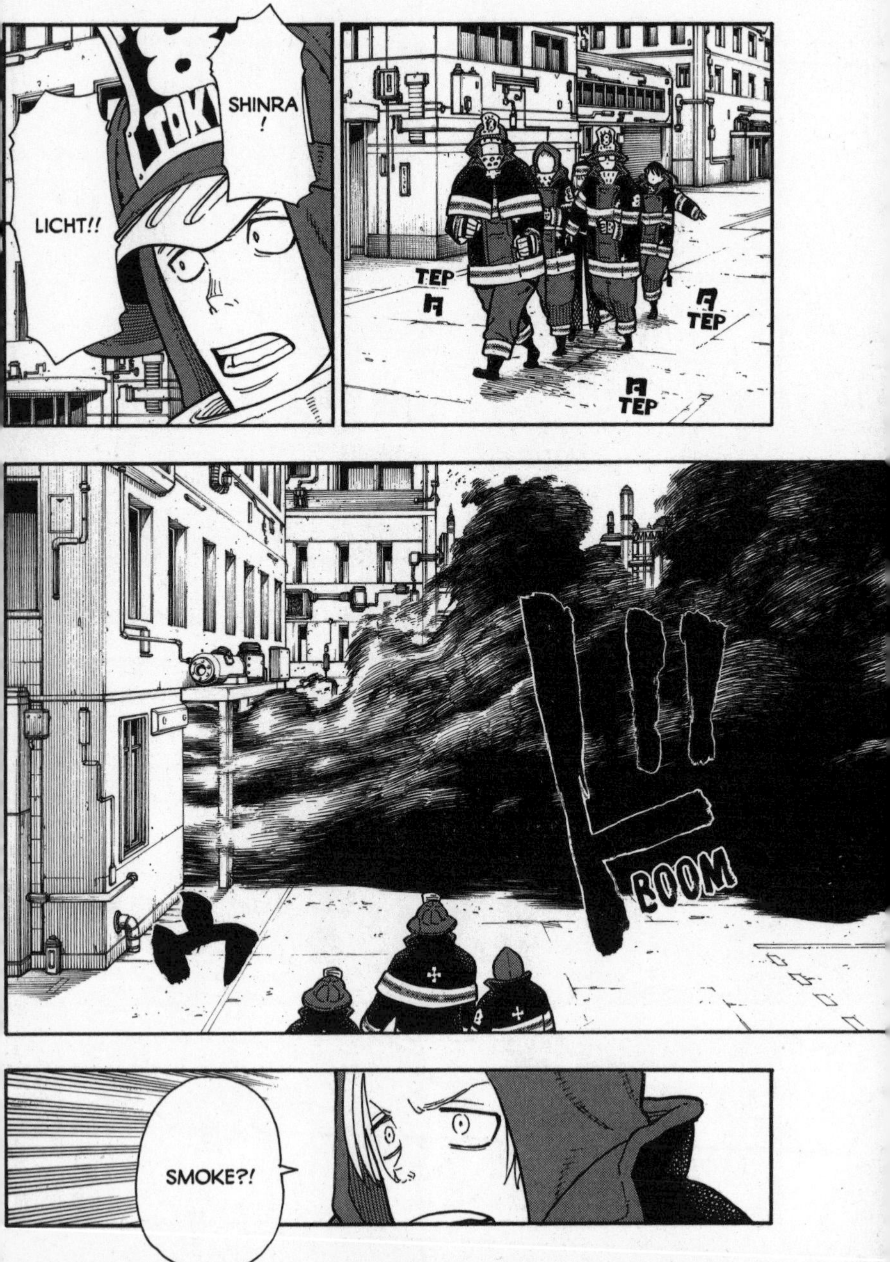
TEP
TEP
TEP
SHINRA!
LICHT!!
BOOM
SMOKE?!

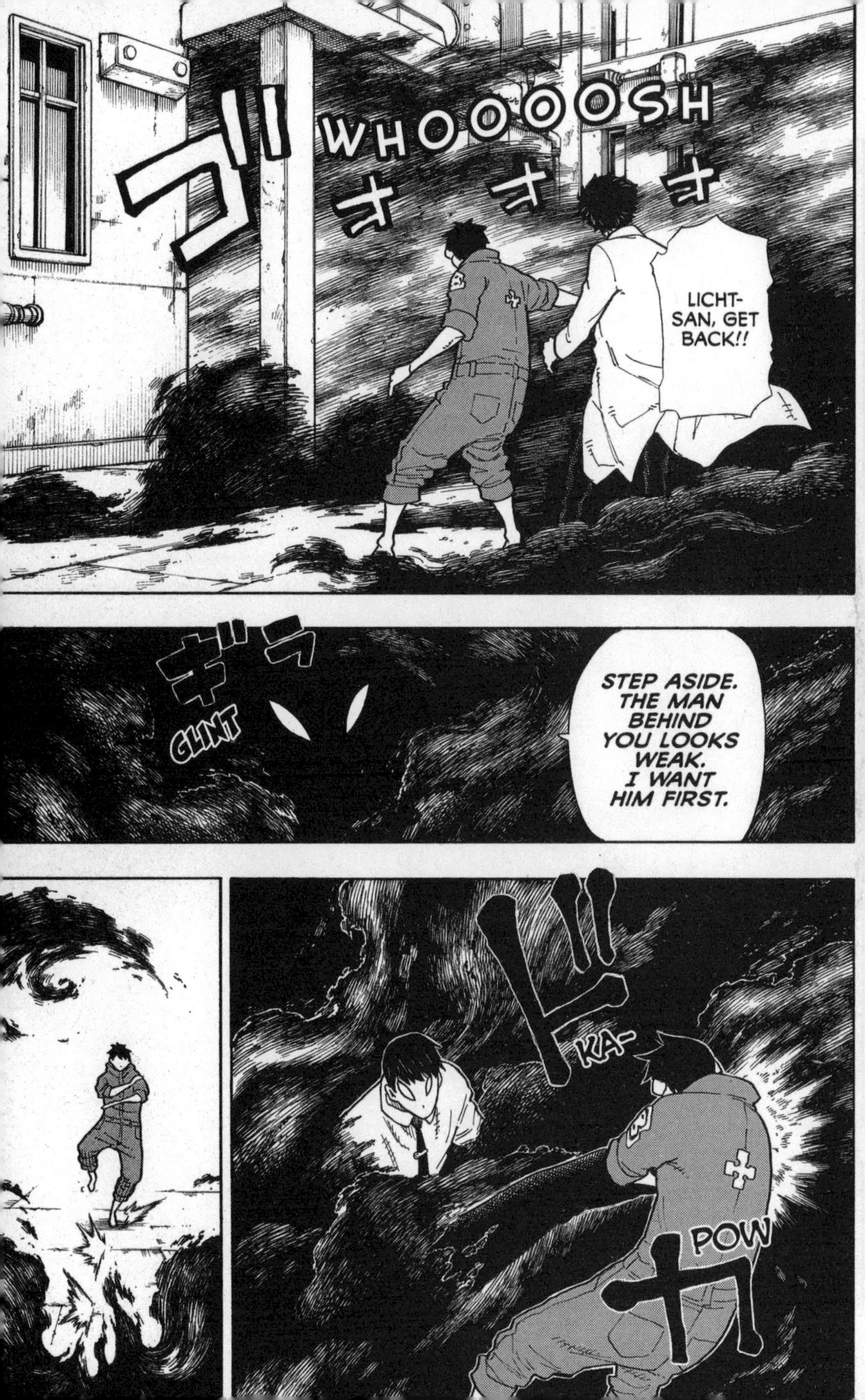
WHOOOOOSH
LICHT-SAN, GET BACK!!
STEP ASIDE. THE MAN BEHIND YOU LOOKS WEAK. I WANT HIM FIRST.
GLINT
KA-
POW

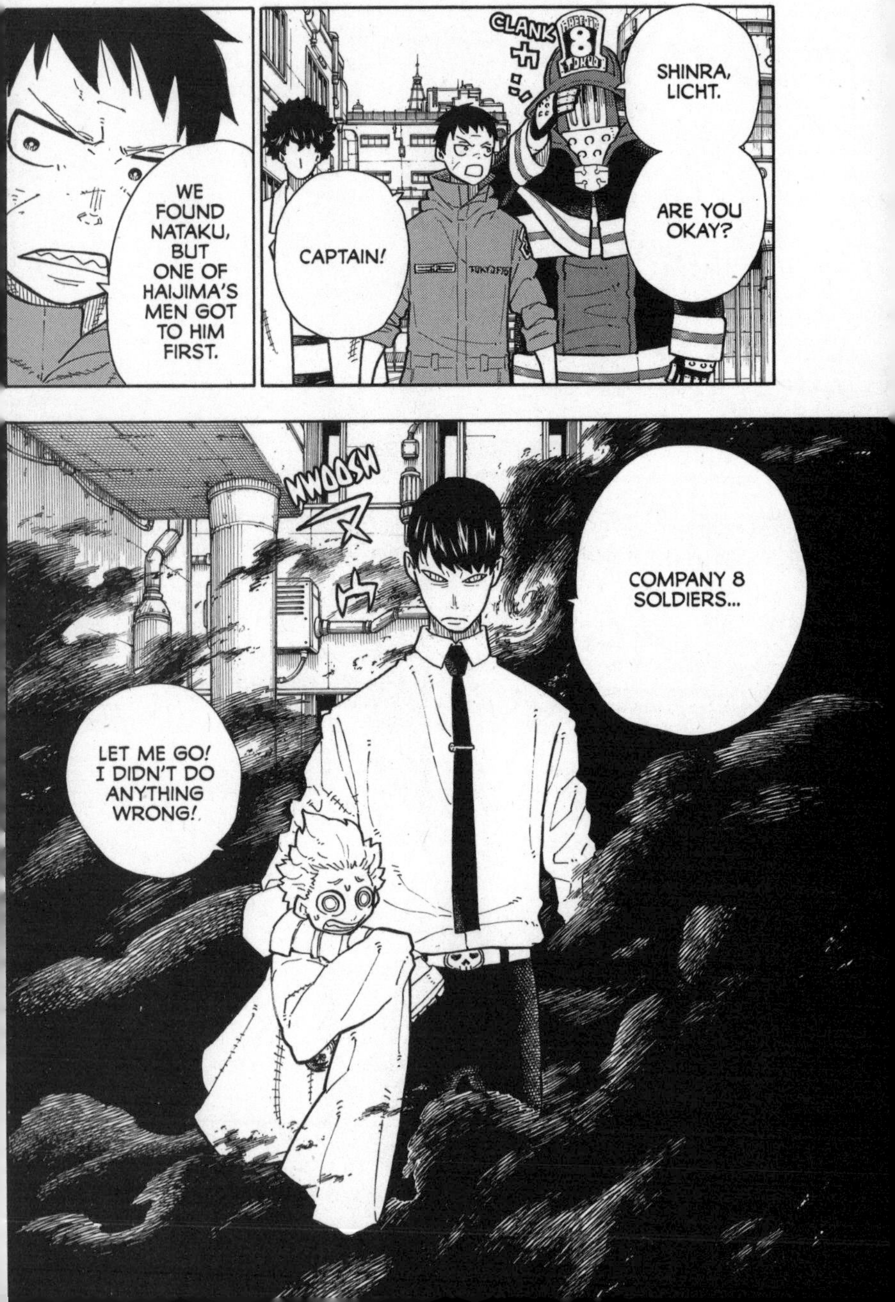
CLANK
SHINRA, LICHT.
ARE YOU OKAY?
CAPTAIN!
WE FOUND NATAKU, BUT ONE OF HAIJIMA'S MEN GOT TO HIM FIRST.
WHOOSH
COMPANY 8 SOLDIERS...
LET ME GO! I DIDN'T DO ANYTHING WRONG!

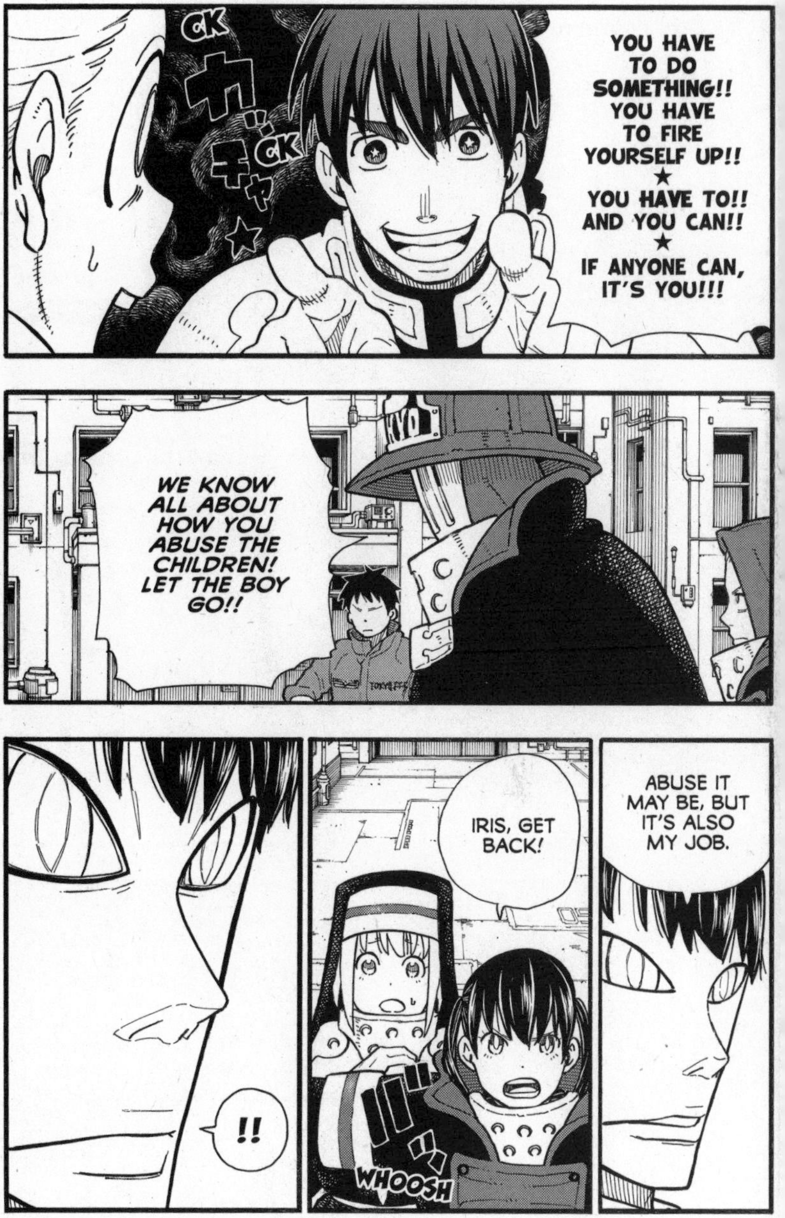
YOU HAVE TO DO SOMETHING!! YOU HAVE TO FIRE YOURSELF UP!! ★ YOU HAVE TO!! AND YOU CAN!! ★ IF ANYONE CAN, IT'S YOU!!!
CK
CK
WE KNOW ALL ABOUT HOW YOU ABUSE THE CHILDREN! LET THE BOY GO!!
ABUSE IT MAY BE, BUT IT'S ALSO MY JOB.
IRIS, GET BACK!
WHOOSH
!!

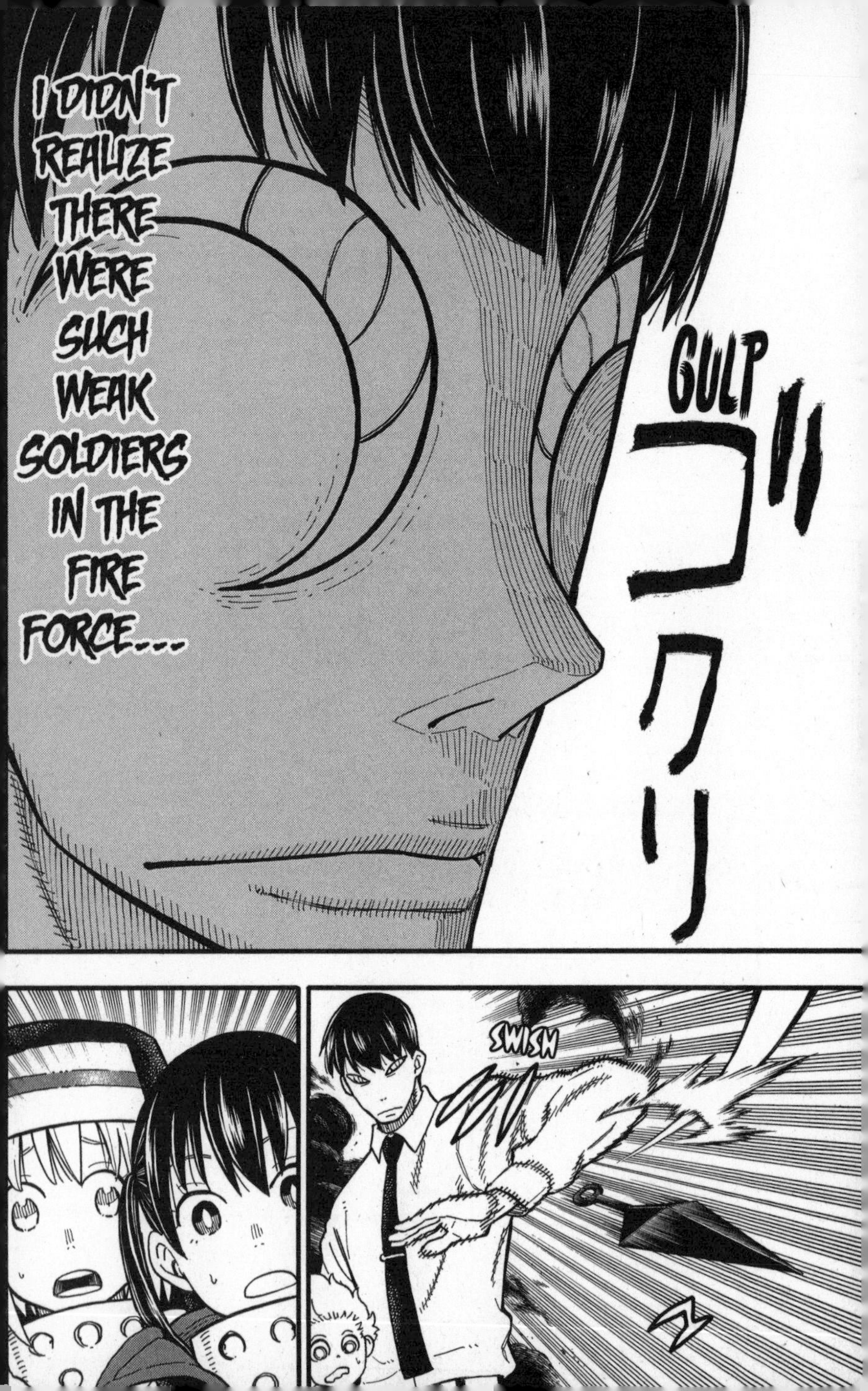
I DIDN'T REALIZE THERE WERE SUCH WEAK SOLDIERS IN THE FIRE FORCE....
GULP
ゴクリ
SWISH

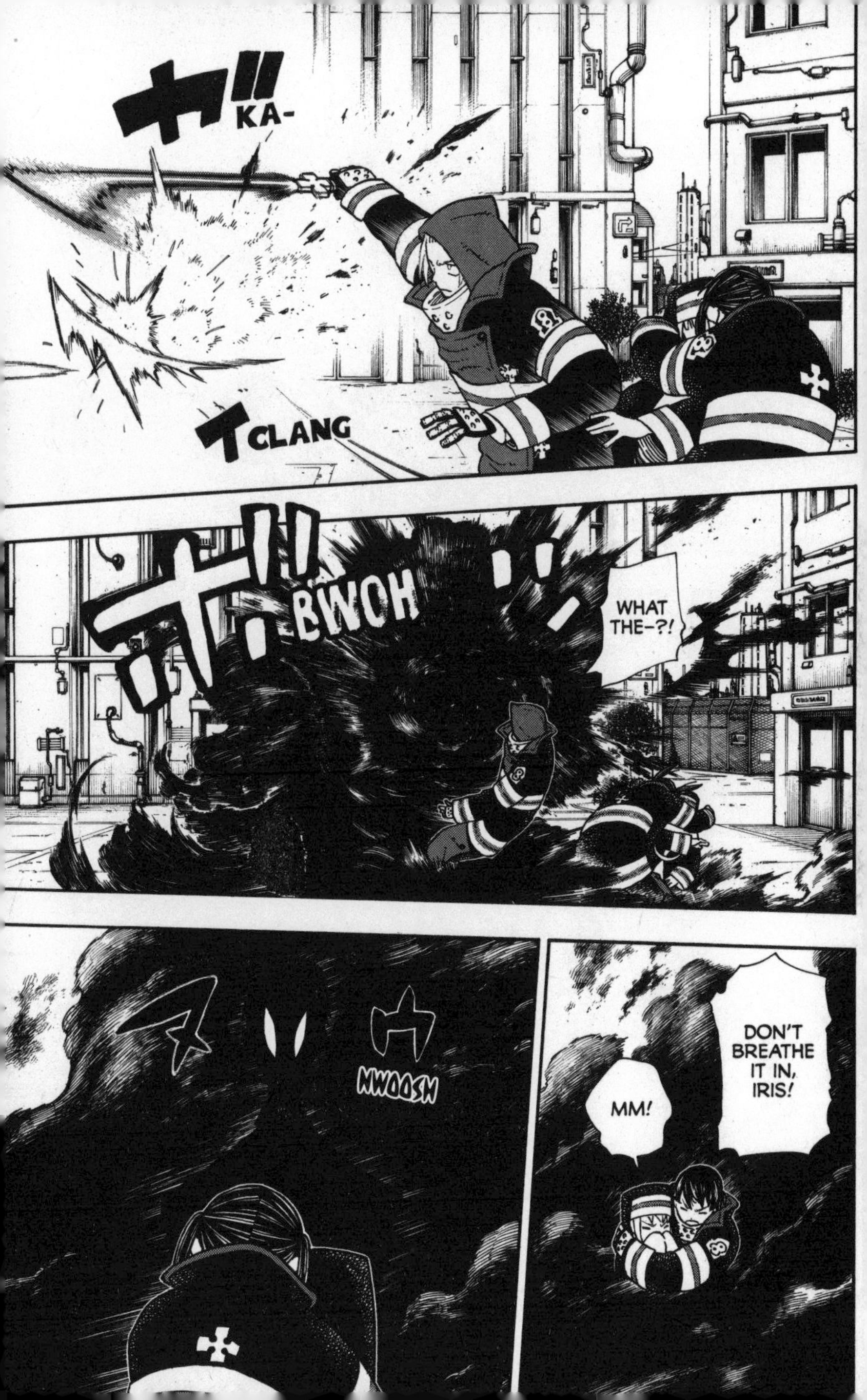
KA-
CLANG
BWOH
WHAT THE-?!
DON'T BREATHE IT IN, IRIS!
MM!
WHOOSH

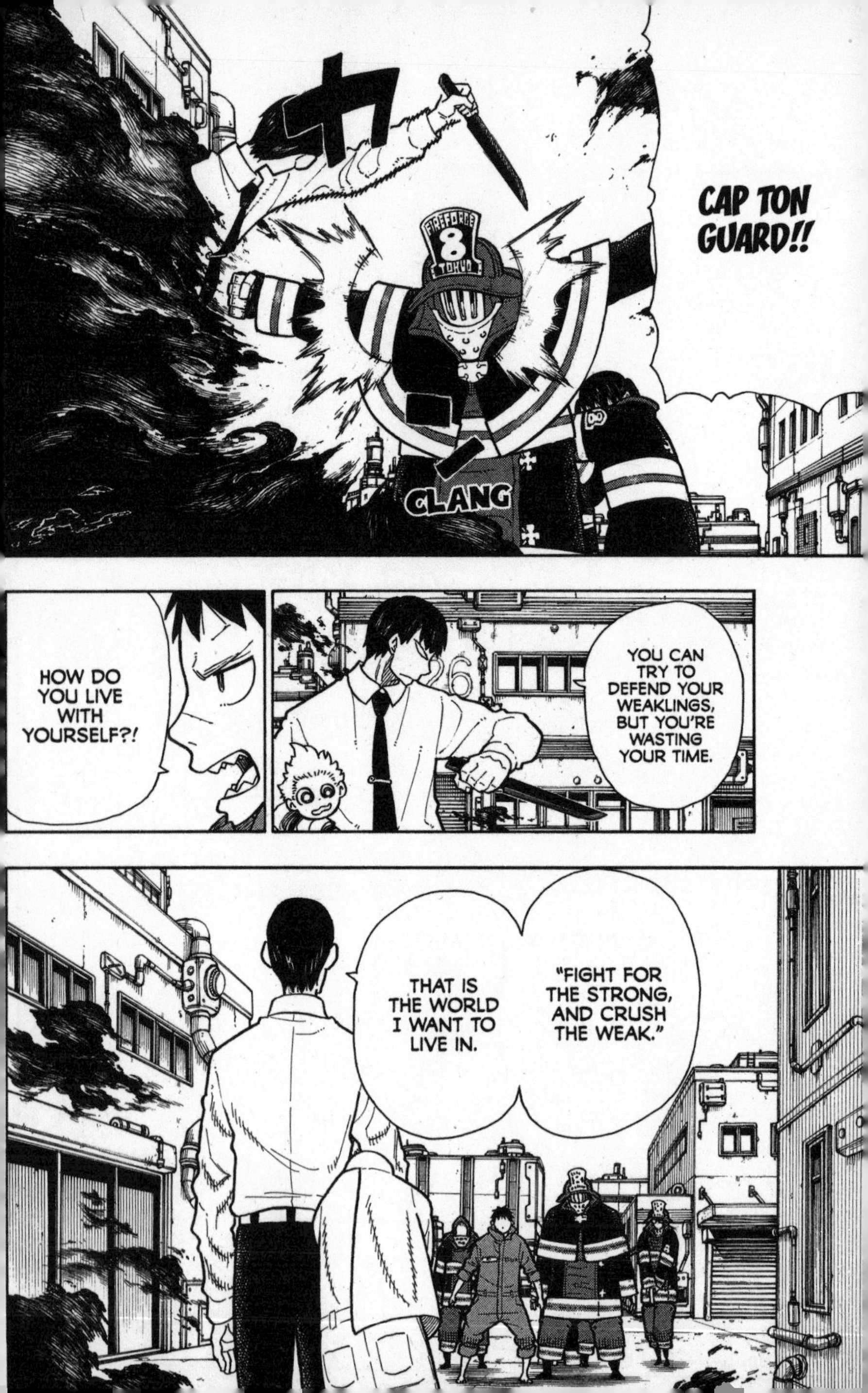
CAP TON GUARD!!
CLANG
YOU CAN TRY TO DEFEND YOUR WEAKLINGS, BUT YOU'RE WASTING YOUR TIME.
HOW DO YOU LIVE WITH YOURSELF?!
"FIGHT FOR THE STRONG, AND CRUSH THE WEAK."
THAT IS THE WORLD I WANT TO LIVE IN.

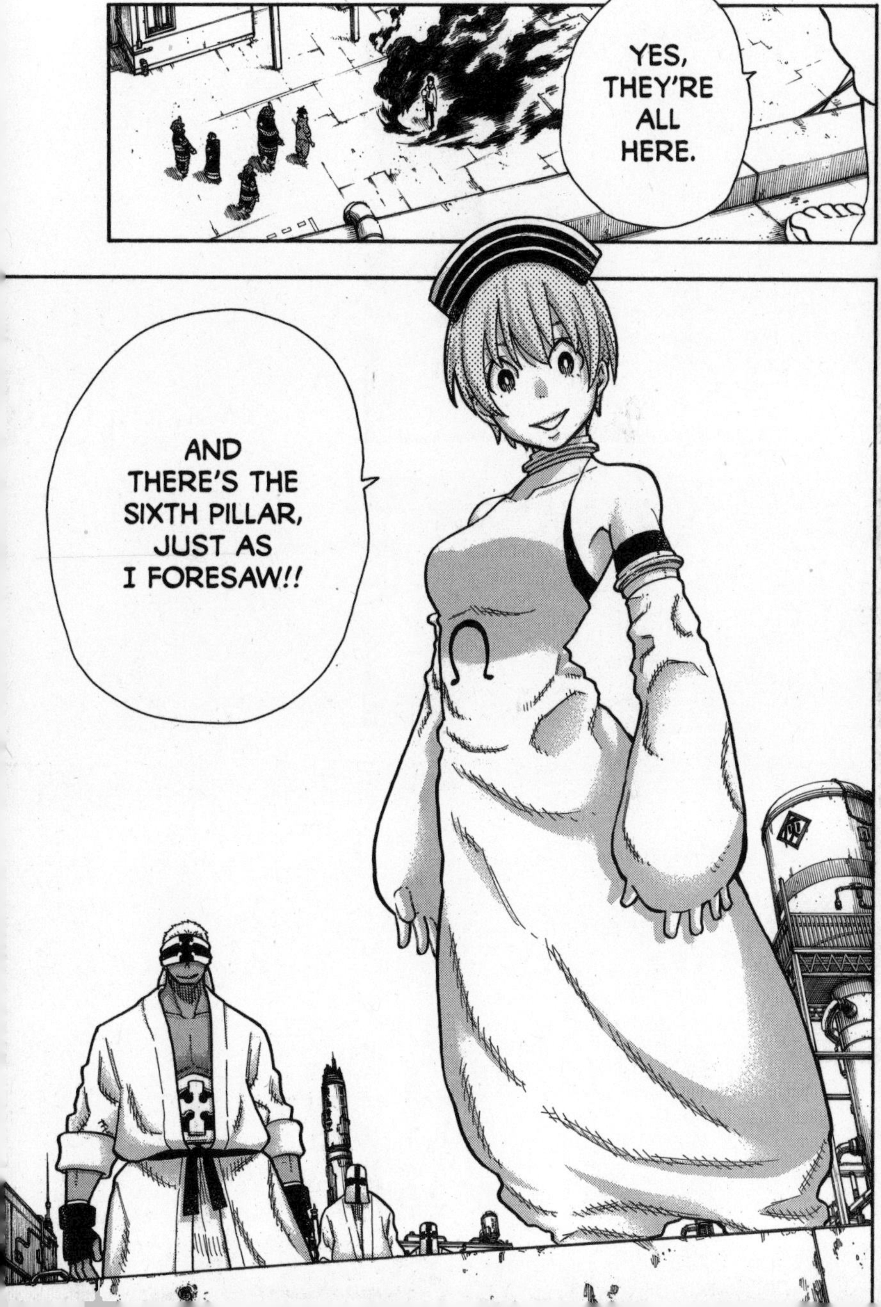
YES, THEY'RE ALL HERE.
AND THERE'S THE SIXTH PILLAR, JUST AS I FORESAW!!

FIRE FORCE

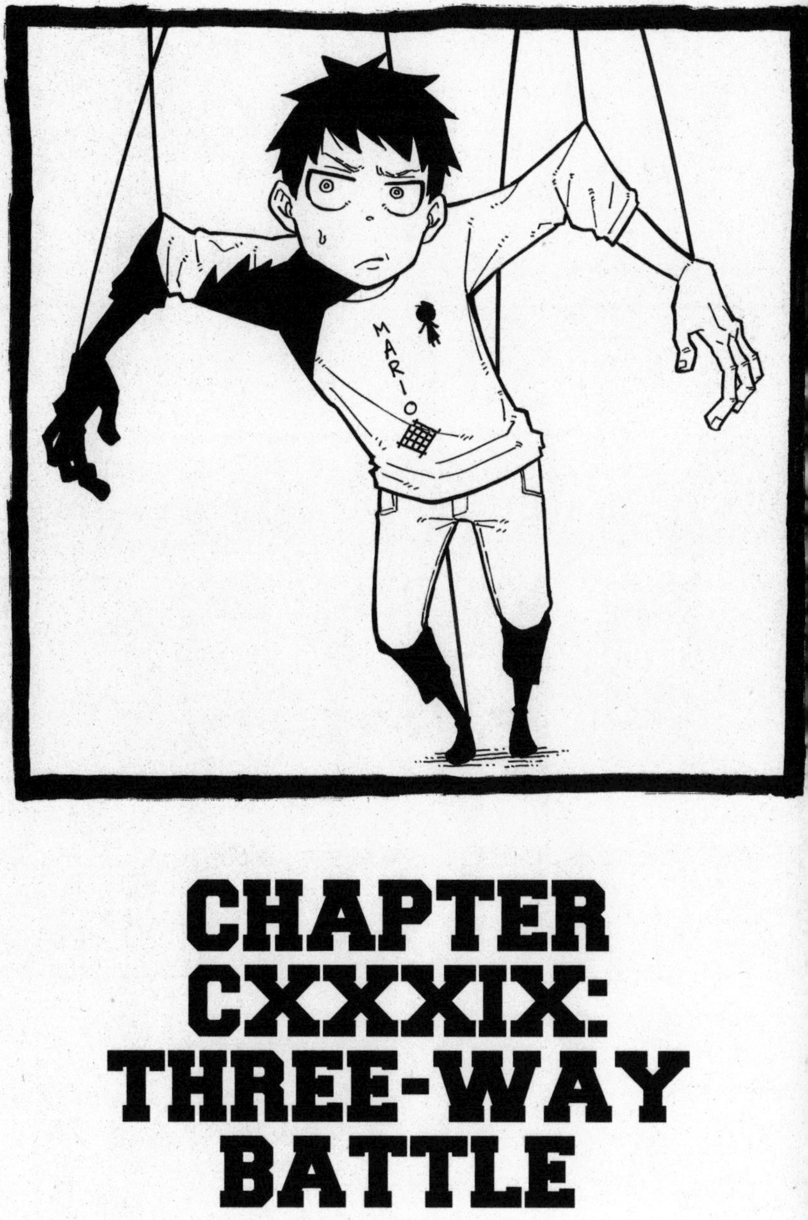
MARIO

CHAPTER CXXXIX: THREE-WAY BATTLE

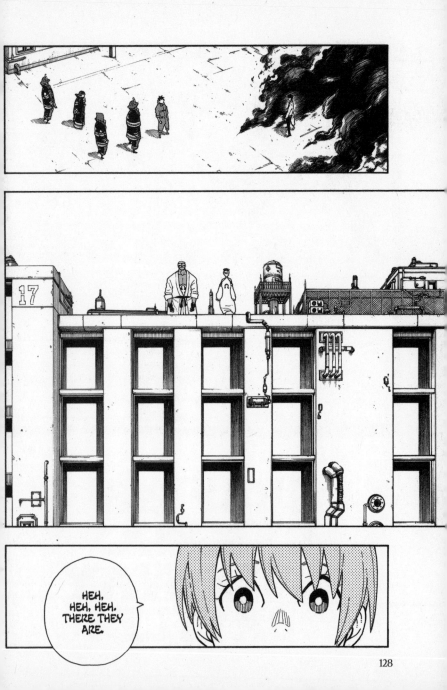

HEH,
HEH, HEH.
THERE THEY
ARE.

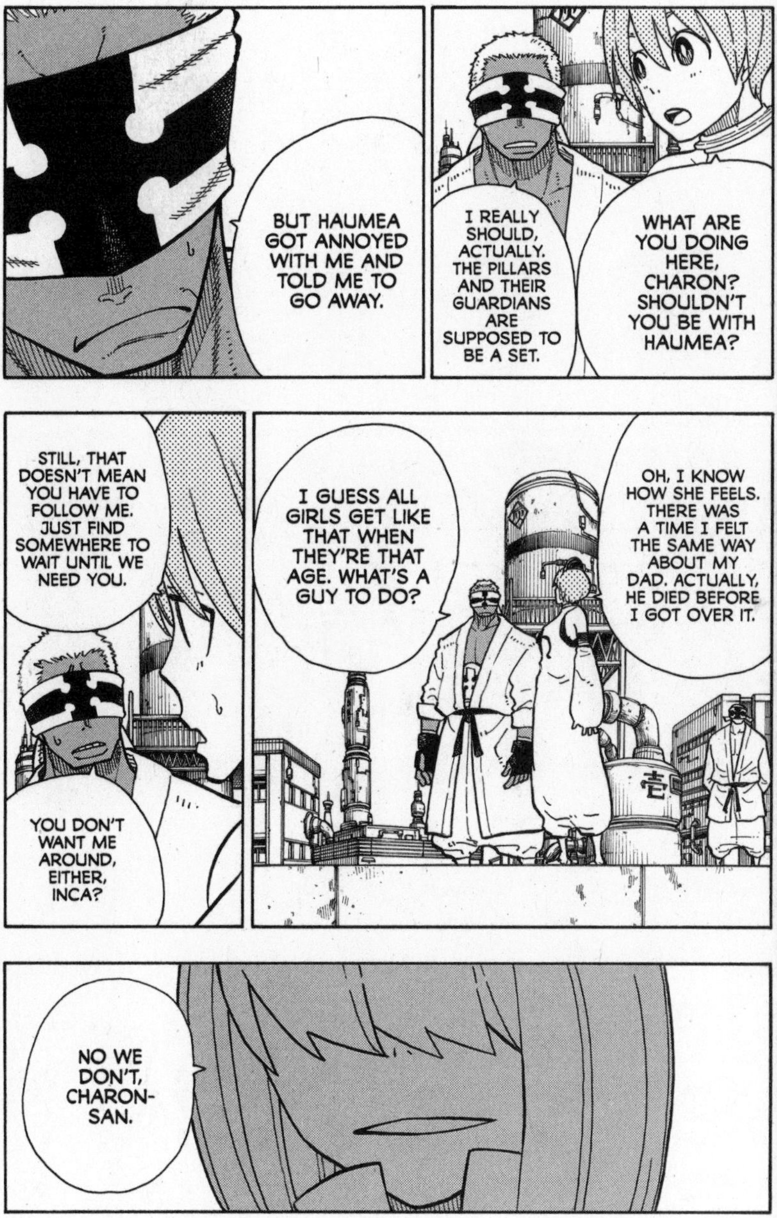
WHAT ARE YOU DOING HERE, CHARON? SHOULDN'T YOU BE WITH HAUMEA?
I REALLY SHOULD, ACTUALLY. THE PILLARS AND THEIR GUARDIANS ARE SUPPOSED TO BE A SET.
BUT HAUMEA GOT ANNOYED WITH ME AND TOLD ME TO GO AWAY.
OH, I KNOW HOW SHE FEELS. THERE WAS A TIME I FELT THE SAME WAY ABOUT MY DAD. ACTUALLY, HE DIED BEFORE I GOT OVER IT.
I GUESS ALL GIRLS GET LIKE THAT WHEN THEY'RE THAT AGE. WHAT'S A GUY TO DO?
STILL, THAT DOESN'T MEAN YOU HAVE TO FOLLOW ME. JUST FIND SOMEWHERE TO WAIT UNTIL WE NEED YOU.
YOU DON'T WANT ME AROUND, EITHER, INCA?
NO WE DON'T, CHARON-SAN.

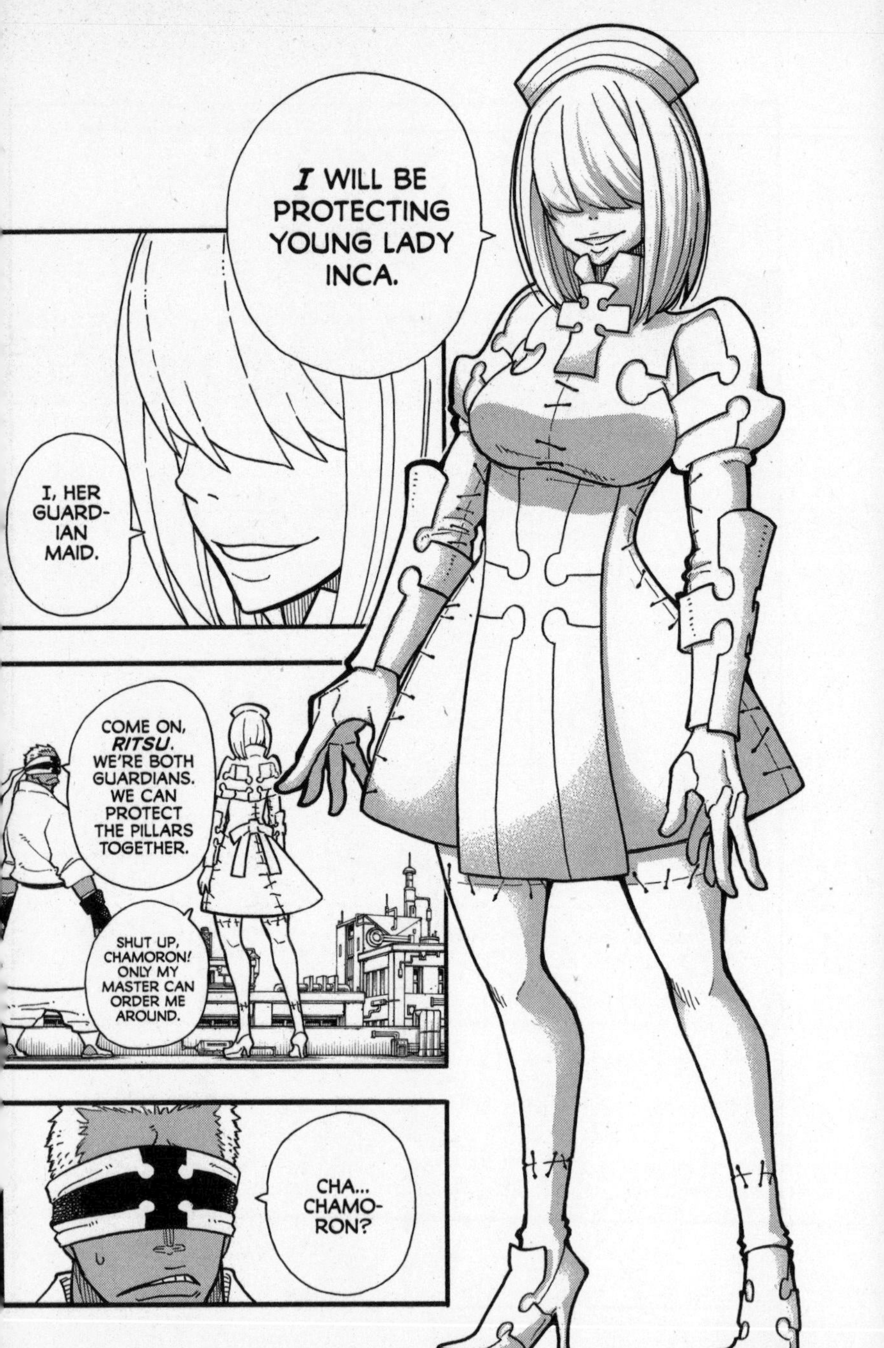
I WILL BE PROTECTING YOUNG LADY INCA.
I, HER GUARD-IAN MAID.
COME ON, *RITSU*. WE'RE BOTH GUARDIANS. WE CAN PROTECT THE PILLARS TOGETHER.
SHUT UP, CHAMORON! ONLY MY MASTER CAN ORDER ME AROUND.
CHA... CHAMO-RON?

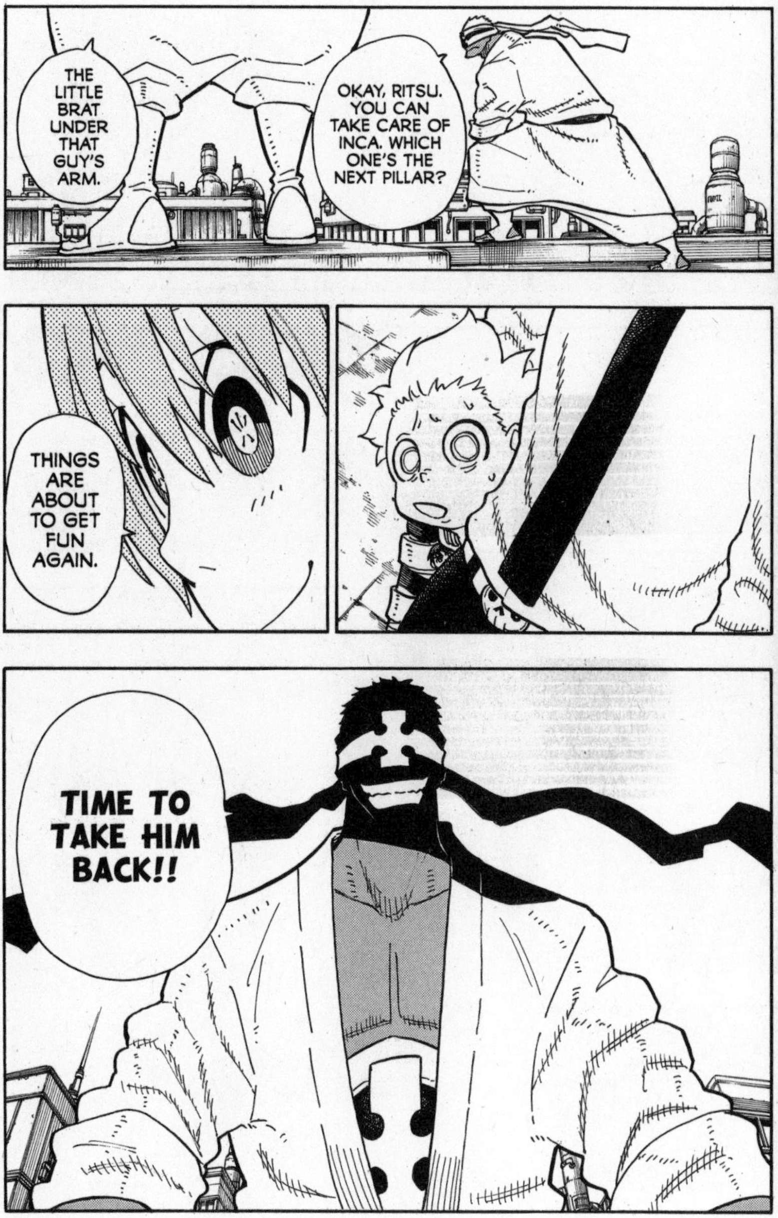
OKAY, RITSU. YOU CAN TAKE CARE OF INCA. WHICH ONE'S THE NEXT PILLAR?
THE LITTLE BRAT UNDER THAT GUY'S ARM.
THINGS ARE ABOUT TO GET FUN AGAIN.
TIME TO TAKE HIM BACK!!

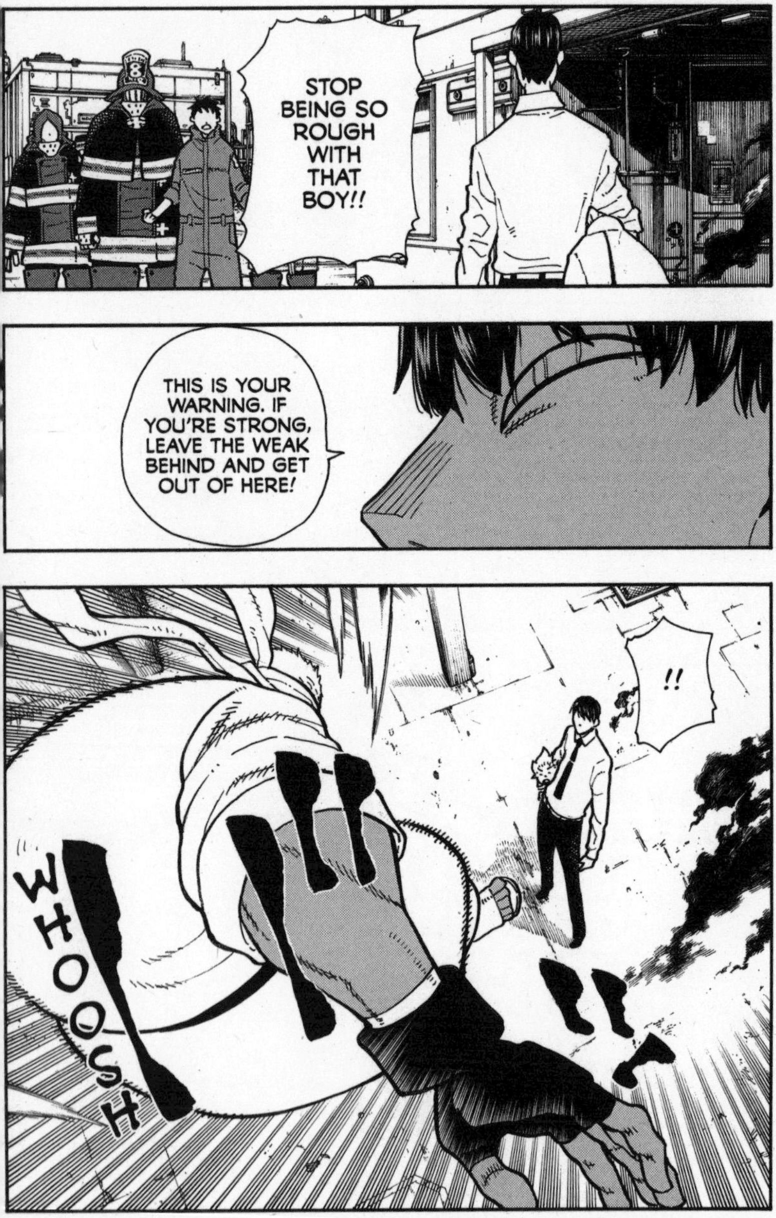
STOP BEING SO ROUGH WITH THAT BOY!!
THIS IS YOUR WARNING. IF YOU'RE STRONG, LEAVE THE WEAK BEHIND AND GET OUT OF HERE!
!!
WHOOSH
!!

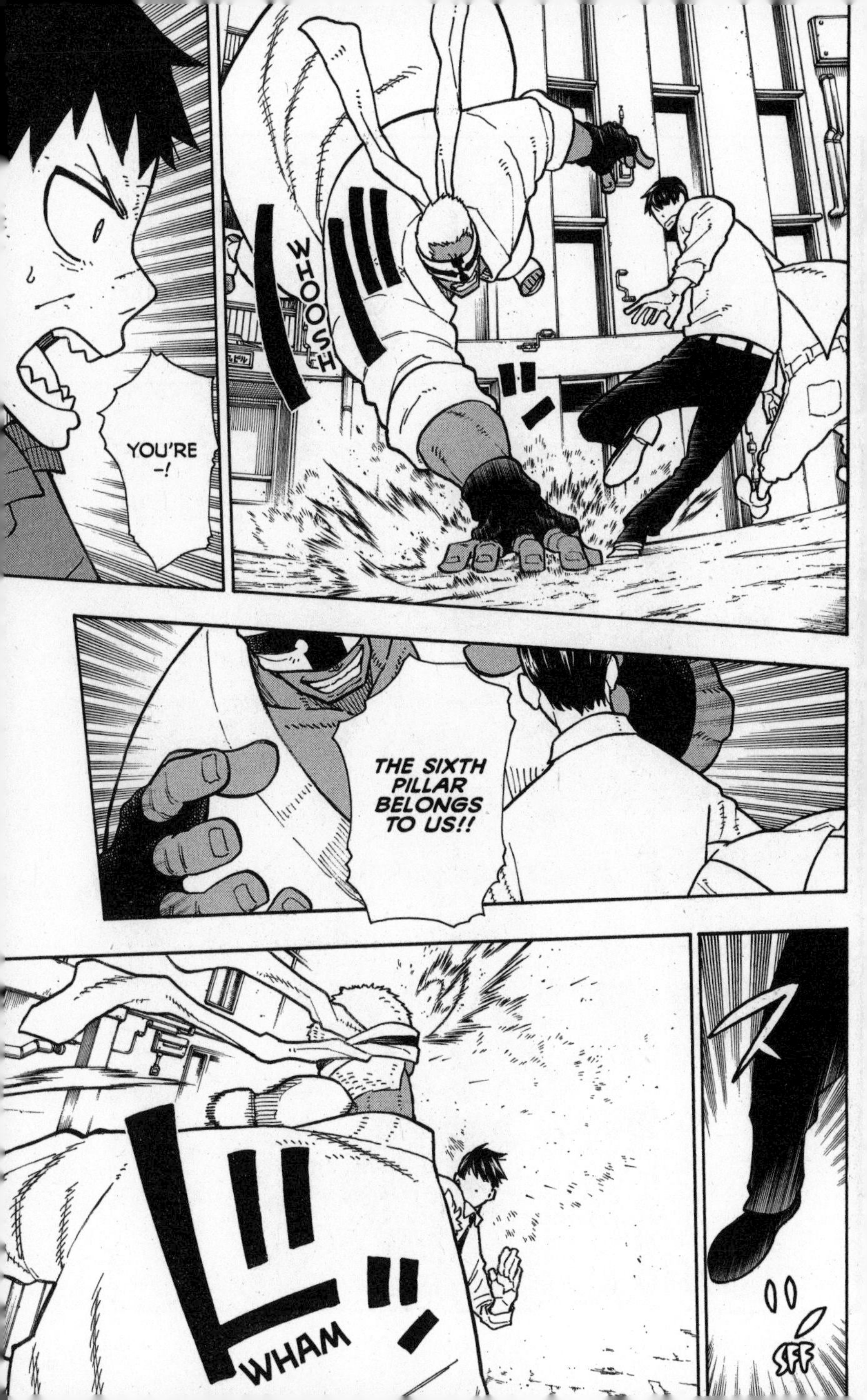
WHOOSH
YOU'RE –!
THE SIXTH PILLAR BELONGS TO US!!
SFF
WHAM

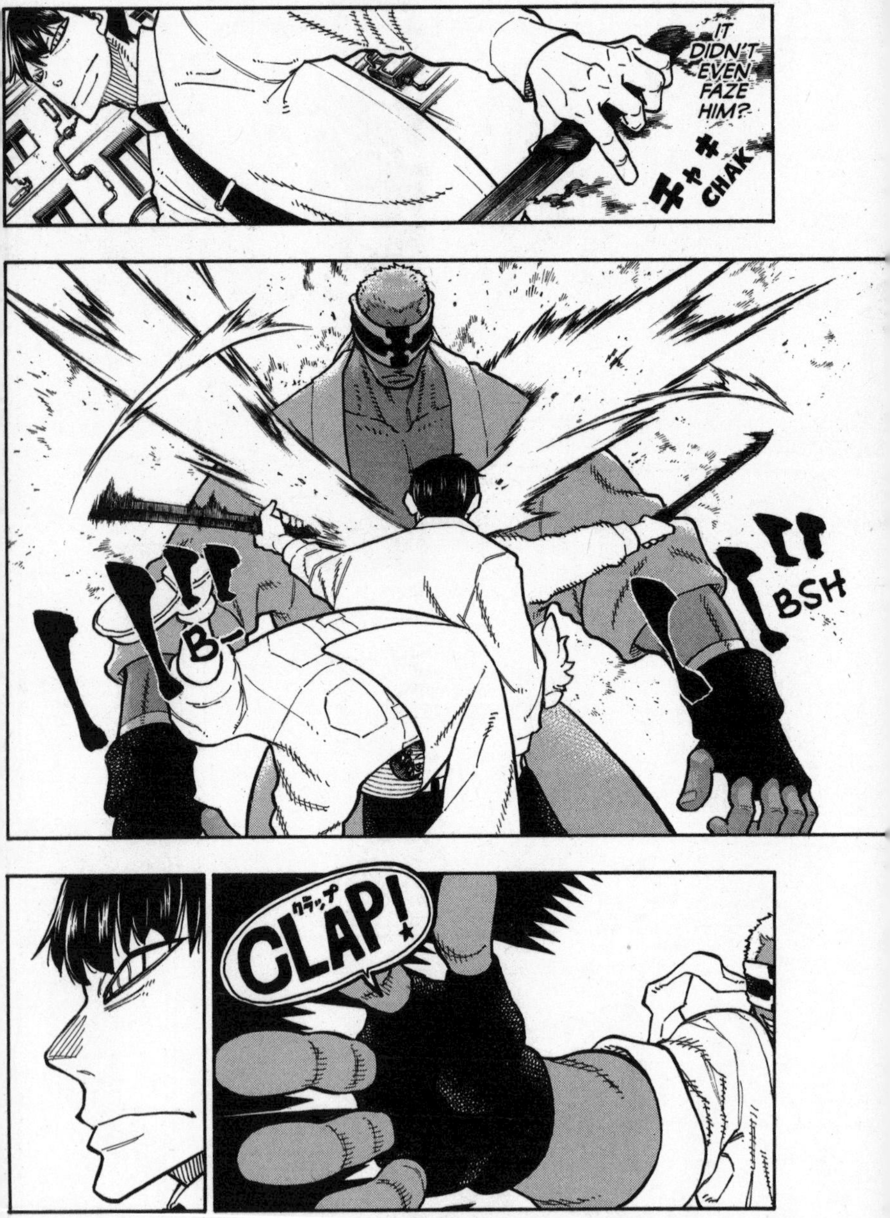
IT DIDN'T EVEN FAZE HIM?
チャキ
CHAK
BSH
B–
クラップ
CLAP!

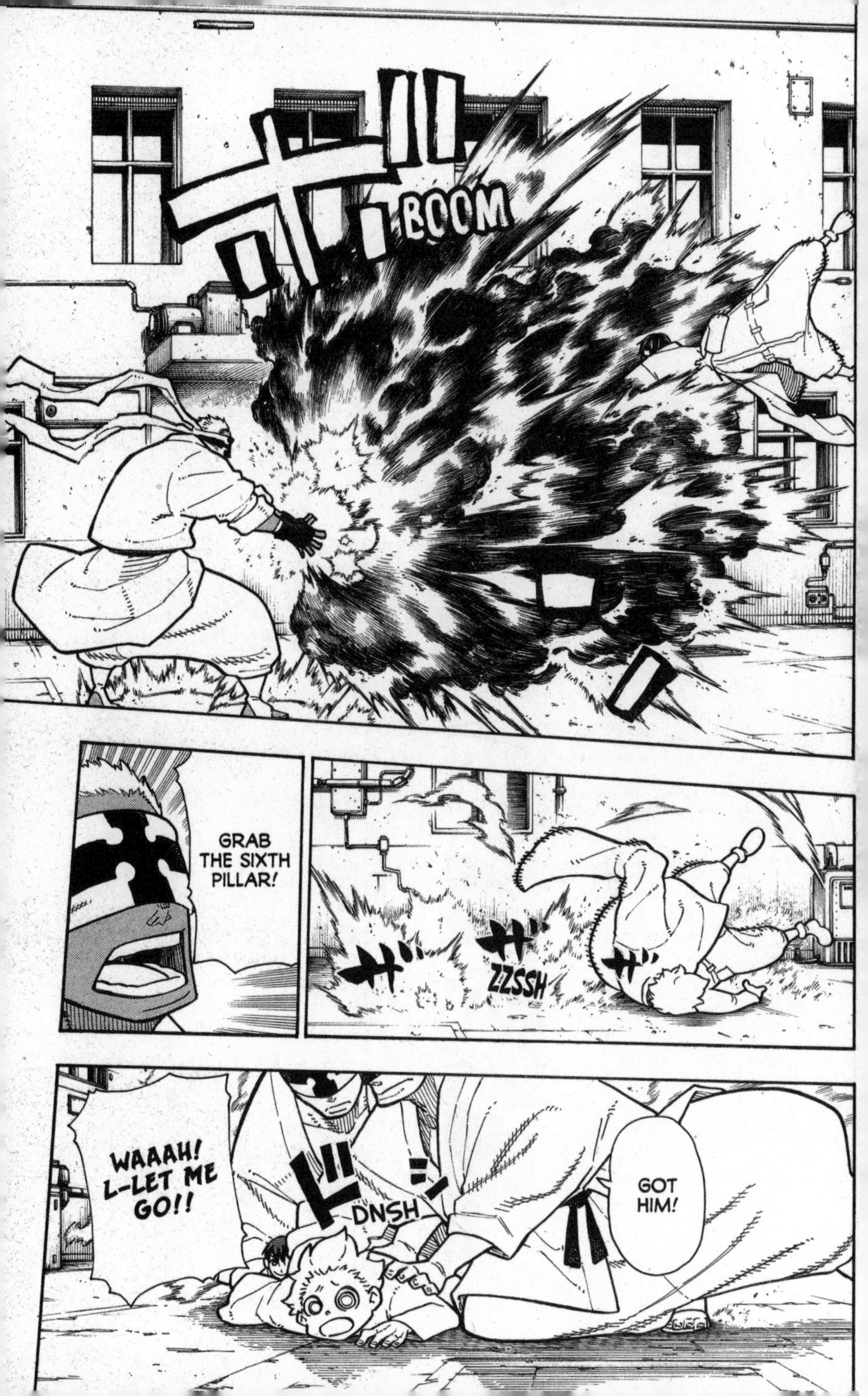
BOOM
ZZSSH
GRAB THE SIXTH PILLAR!
GOT HIM!
DNSH
WAAAH! L-LET ME GO!!

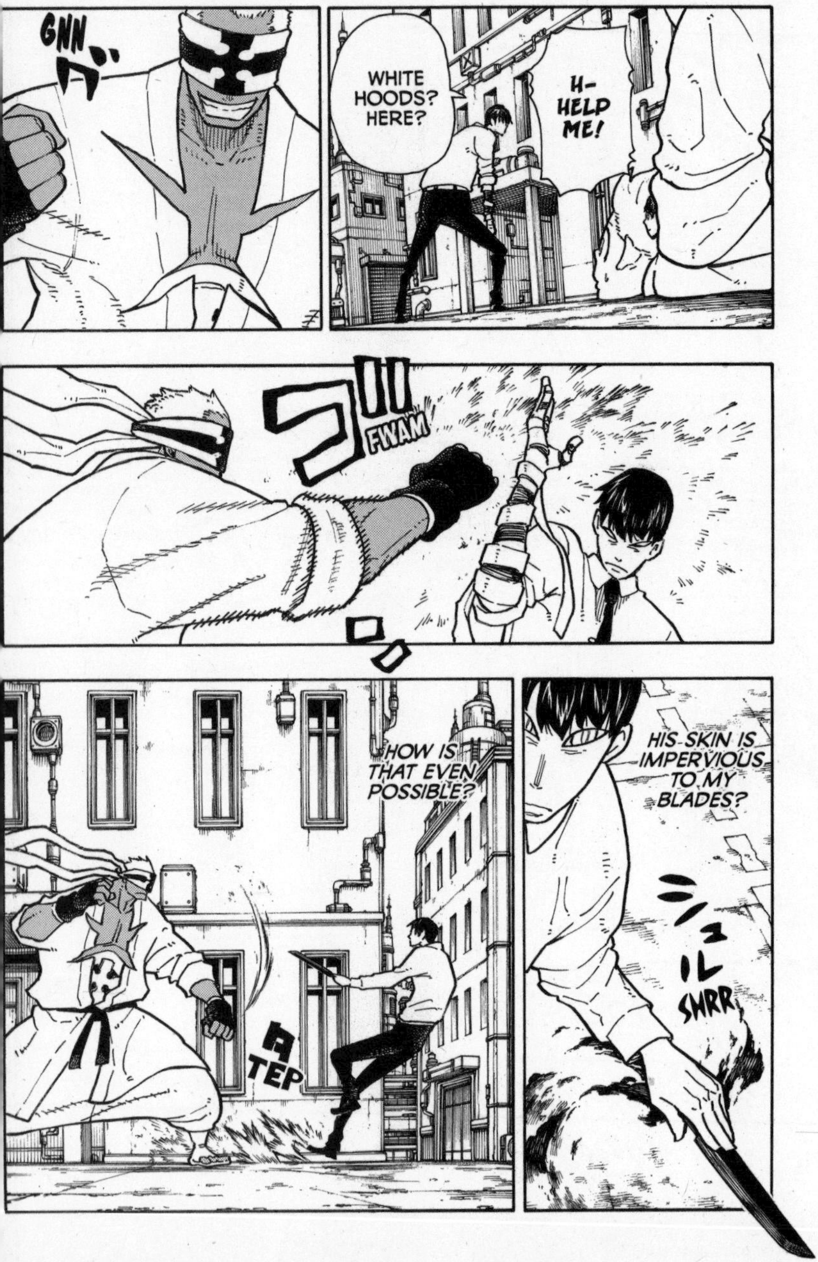
H- HELP ME!
WHITE HOODS? HERE?
GNN
FWAM
HIS SKIN IS IMPERVIOUS TO MY BLADES?
SHRR
HOW IS THAT EVEN POSSIBLE?
TEP

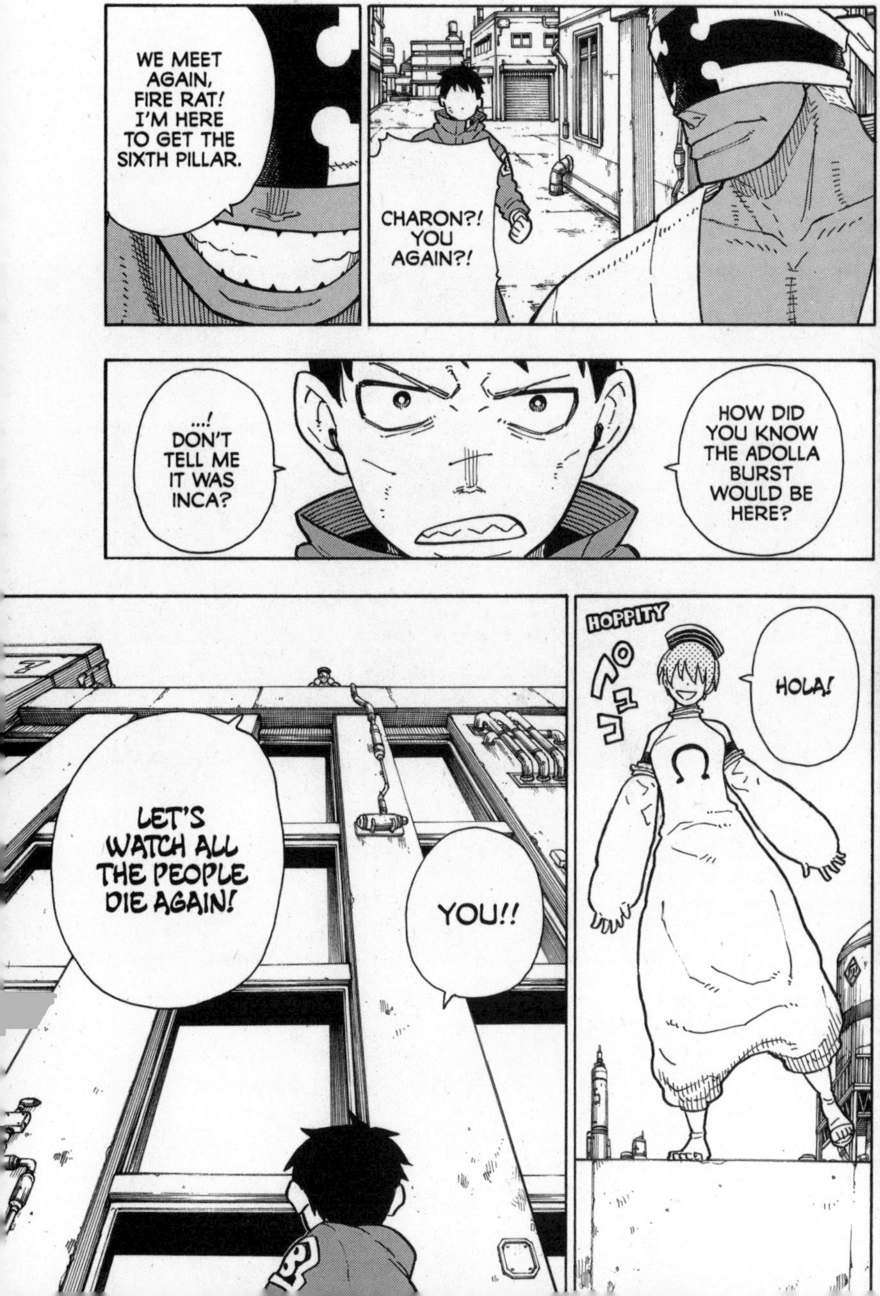
CHARON?! YOU AGAIN?!
WE MEET AGAIN, FIRE RAT! I'M HERE TO GET THE SIXTH PILLAR.
HOW DID YOU KNOW THE ADOLLA BURST WOULD BE HERE?
...! DON'T TELL ME IT WAS INCA?
HOPPITY
HOLA!
YOU!!
LET'S WATCH ALL THE PEOPLE DIE AGAIN!

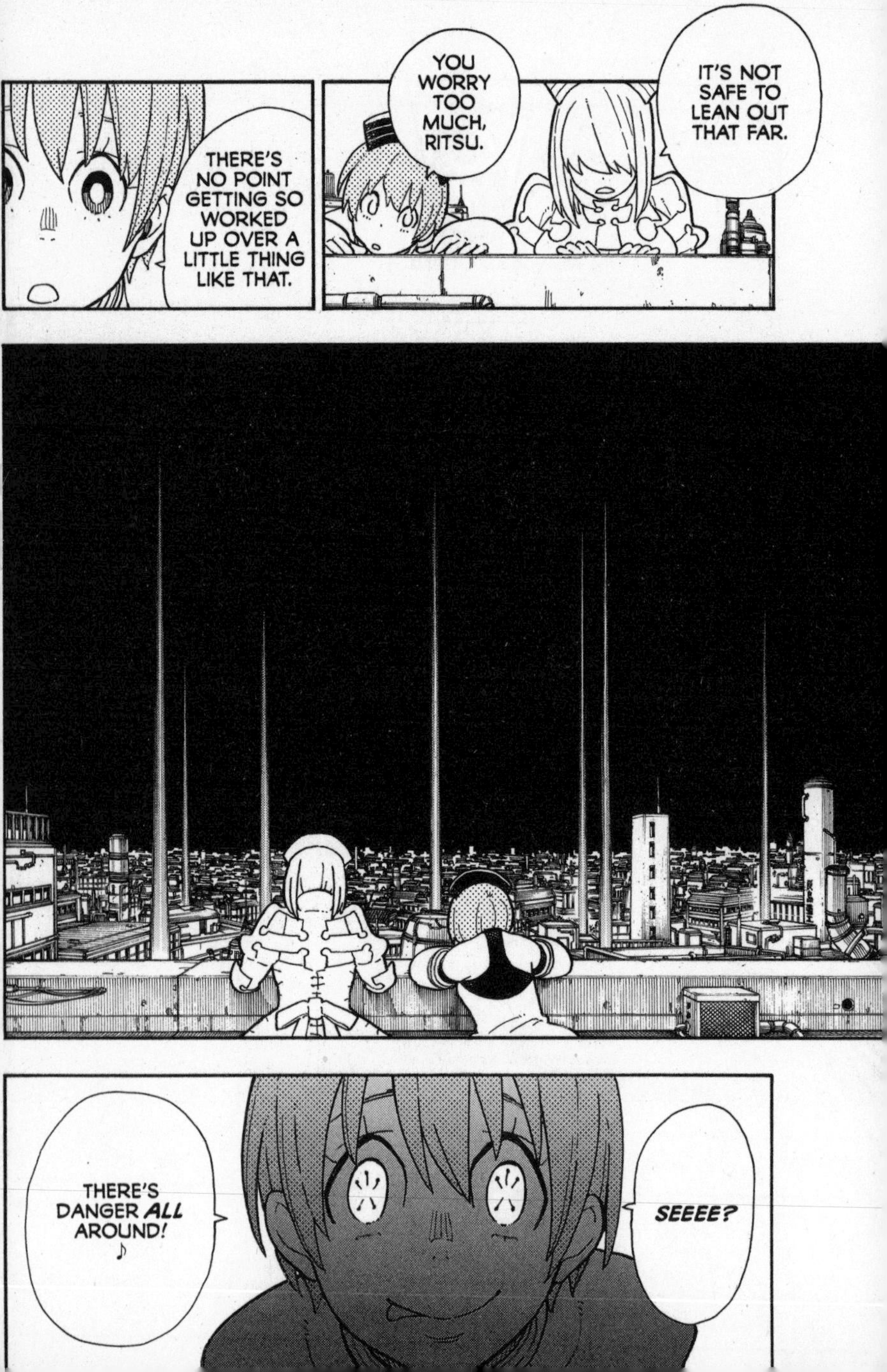
IT'S NOT SAFE TO LEAN OUT THAT FAR.
YOU WORRY TOO MUCH, RITSU.
THERE'S NO POINT GETTING SO WORKED UP OVER A LITTLE THING LIKE THAT.
SEEEE?
THERE'S DANGER ALL AROUND! ♪

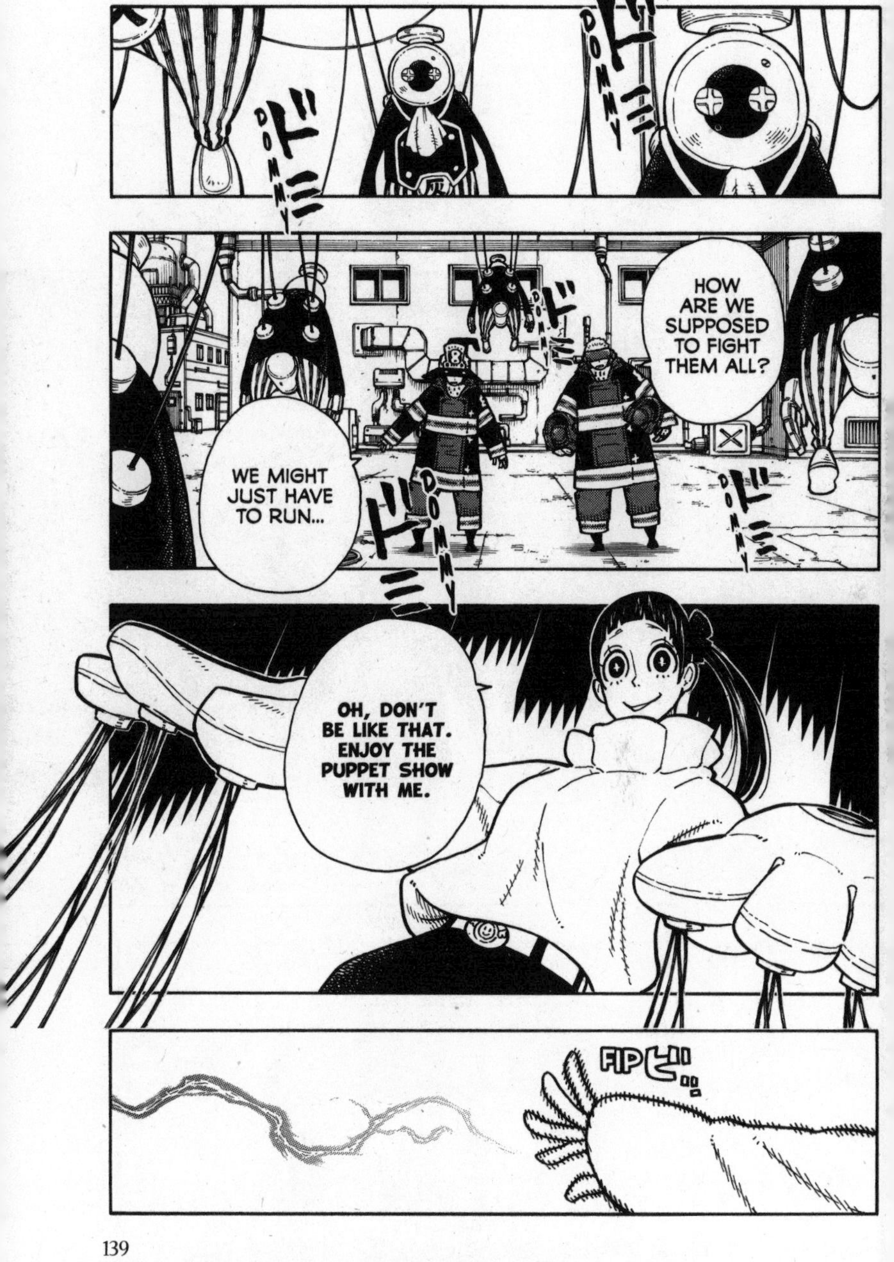
DOMMY
DOMMY
HOW ARE WE SUPPOSED TO FIGHT THEM ALL?
DOMMY
DOMMY
WE MIGHT JUST HAVE TO RUN...
DOMMY
OH, DON'T BE LIKE THAT. ENJOY THE PUPPET SHOW WITH ME.
FIP

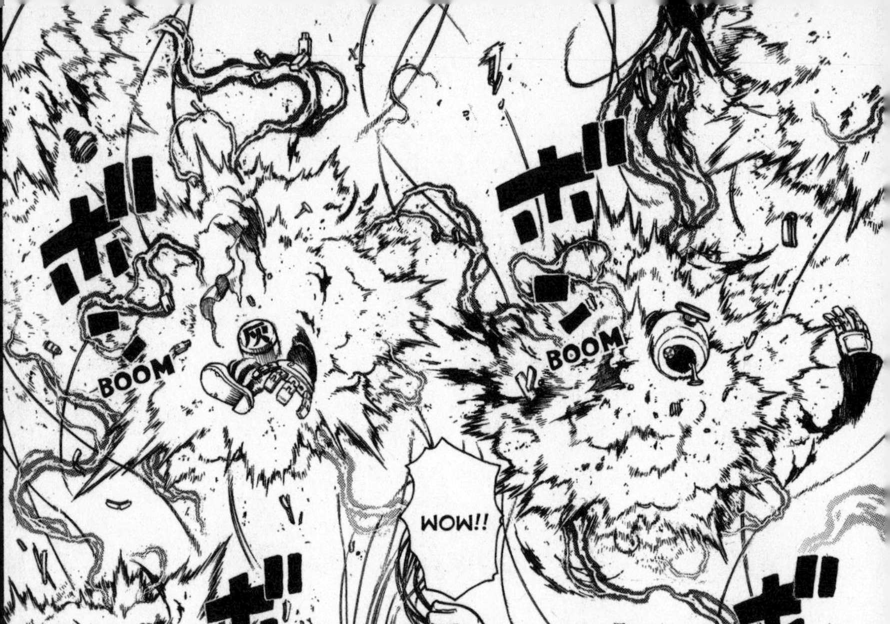
BOOM
BOOM
WOW!!
BOOM
BOOM
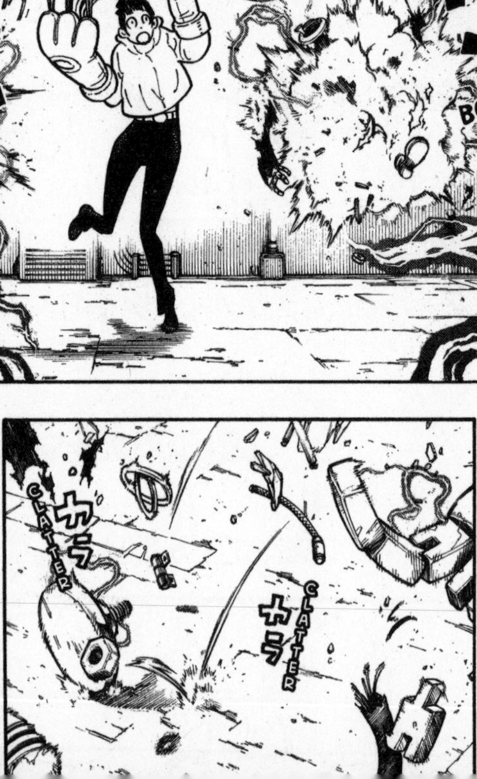
CLATTER
CLATTER
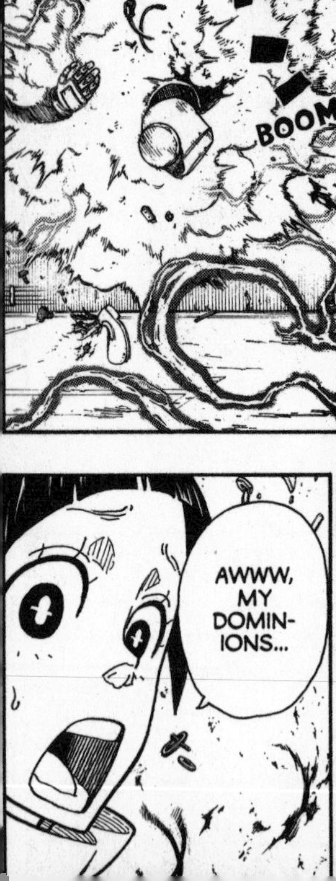
AWWW, MY DOMIN- IONS...

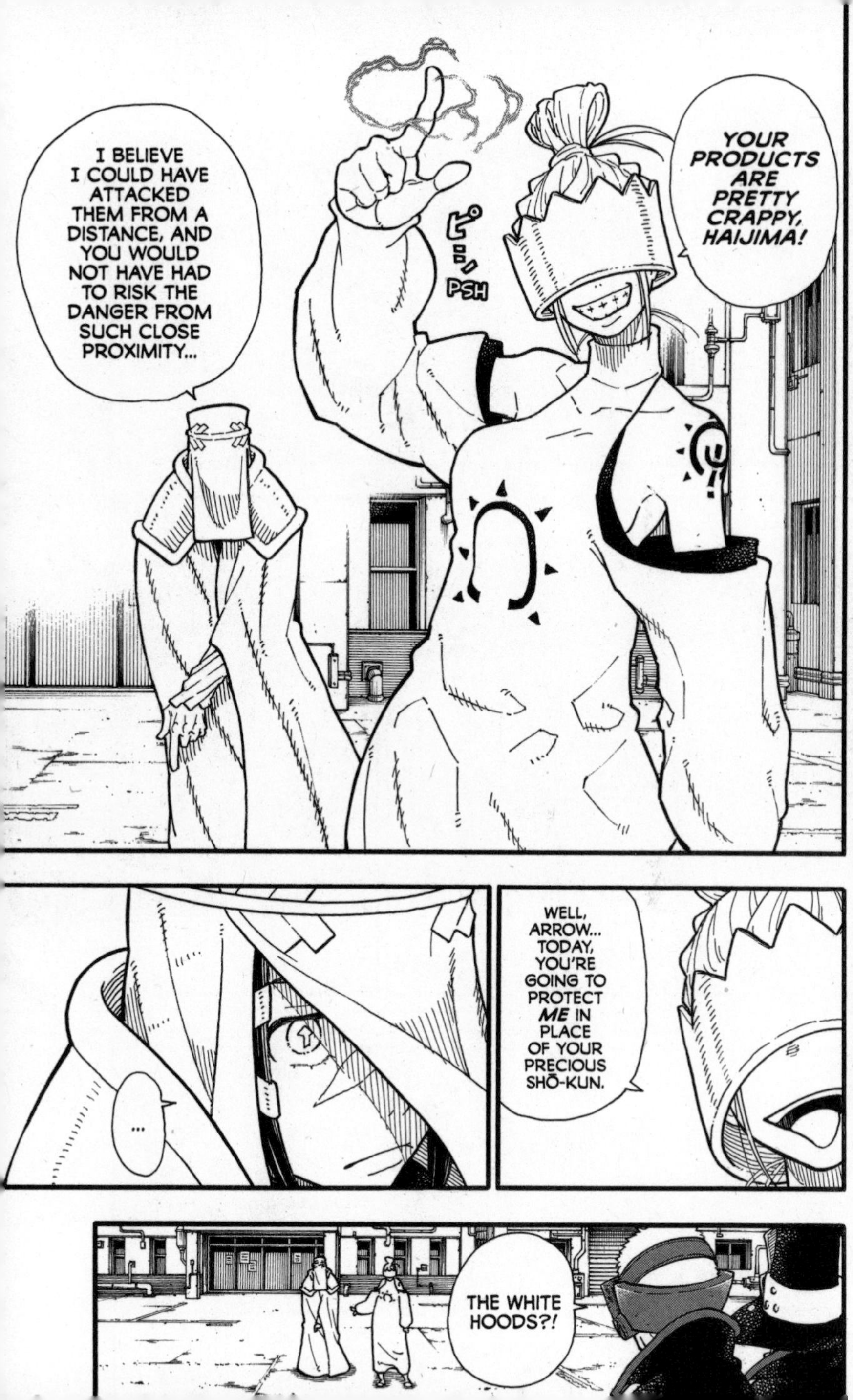
YOUR PRODUCTS ARE PRETTY CRAPPY, HAIJIMA!
PSH
I BELIEVE I COULD HAVE ATTACKED THEM FROM A DISTANCE, AND YOU WOULD NOT HAVE HAD TO RISK THE DANGER FROM SUCH CLOSE PROXIMITY...
WELL, ARROW... TODAY, YOU'RE GOING TO PROTECT ME IN PLACE OF YOUR PRECIOUS SHŌ-KUN.
...
THE WHITE HOODS?!

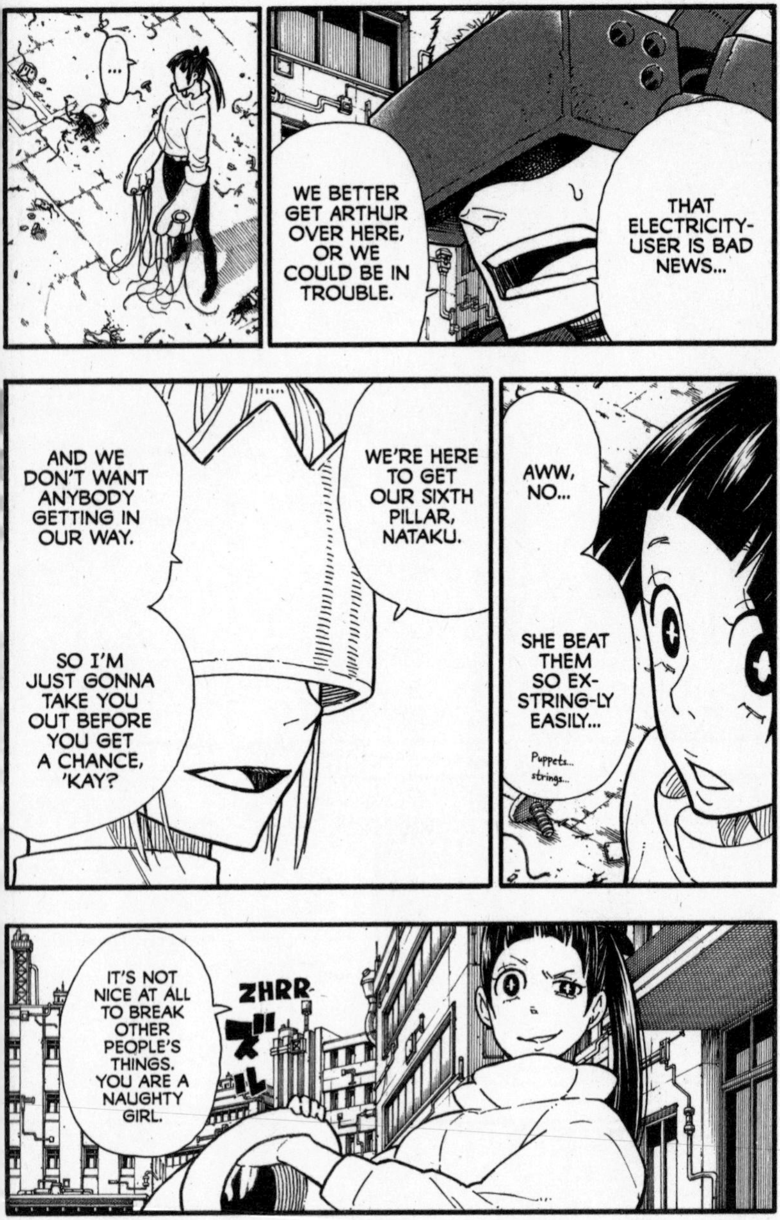
THAT ELECTRICITY-USER IS BAD NEWS...
WE BETTER GET ARTHUR OVER HERE, OR WE COULD BE IN TROUBLE.
...
AWW, NO...
SHE BEAT THEM SO EX-STRING-LY EASILY...
Puppets... strings...
WE'RE HERE TO GET OUR SIXTH PILLAR, NATAKU.
AND WE DON'T WANT ANYBODY GETTING IN OUR WAY.
SO I'M JUST GONNA TAKE YOU OUT BEFORE YOU GET A CHANCE, 'KAY?
ZHRR-
ズル
IT'S NOT NICE AT ALL TO BREAK OTHER PEOPLE'S THINGS. YOU ARE A NAUGHTY GIRL.

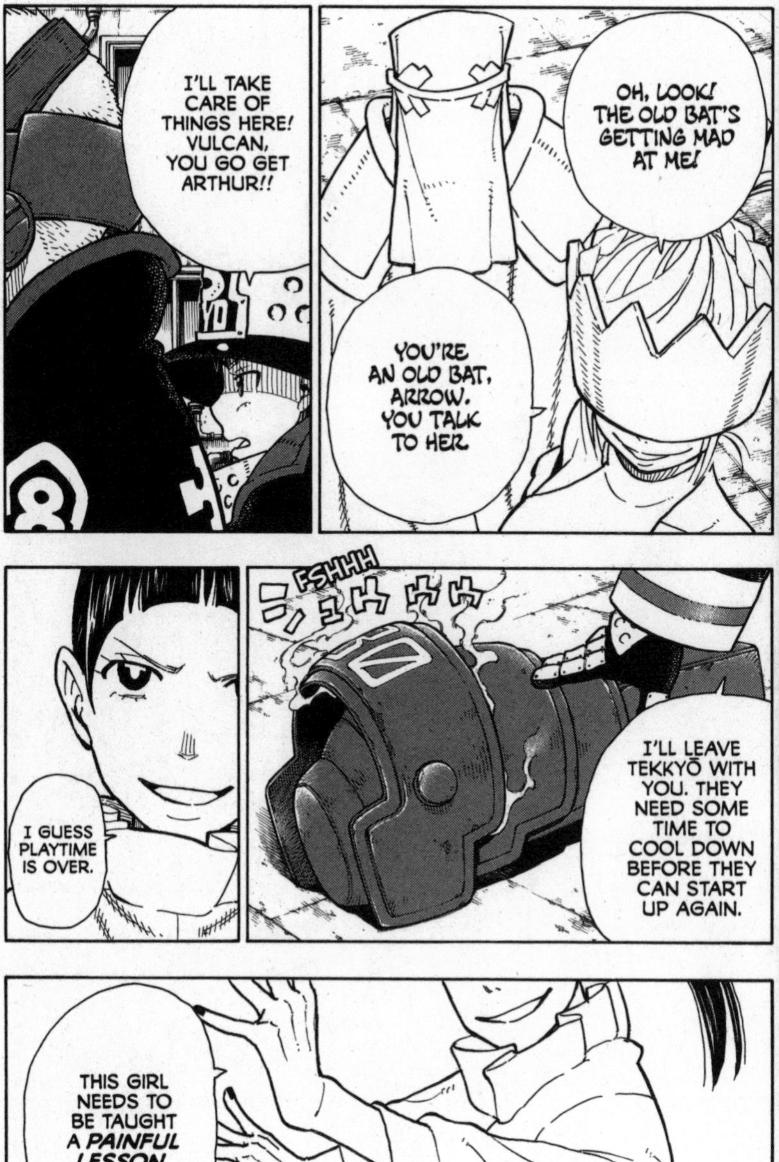
OH, LOOK! THE OLD BAT'S GETTING MAD AT ME!
YOU'RE AN OLD BAT, ARROW. YOU TALK TO HER.
I'LL TAKE CARE OF THINGS HERE! VULCAN, YOU GO GET ARTHUR!!
FSHHH
I'LL LEAVE TEKKYŌ WITH YOU. THEY NEED SOME TIME TO COOL DOWN BEFORE THEY CAN START UP AGAIN.
I GUESS PLAYTIME IS OVER.
THIS GIRL NEEDS TO BE TAUGHT A ***PAINFUL LESSON.***

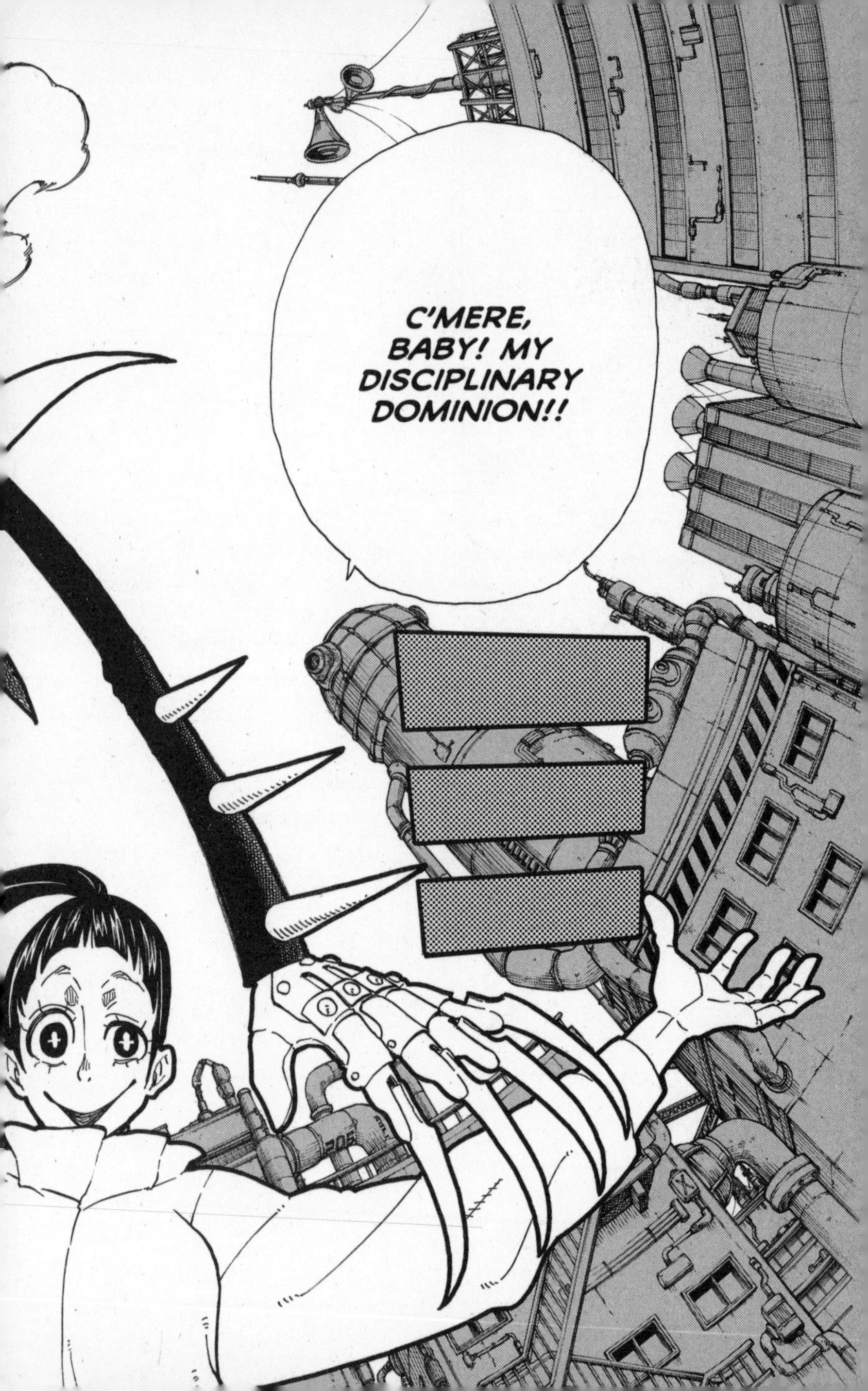
C'MERE, BABY! MY DISCIPLINARY DOMINION!!

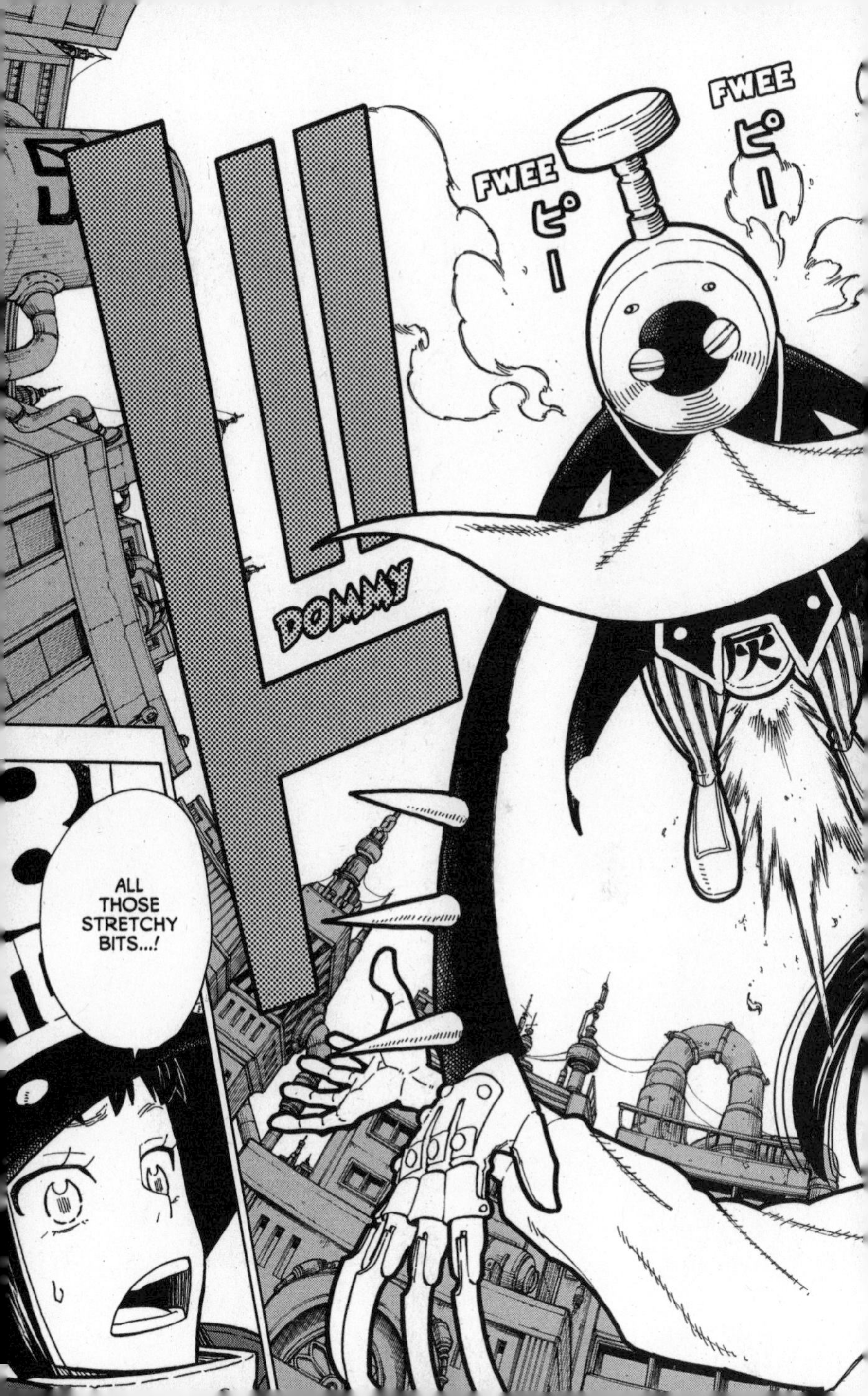
FWEE
ピー
FWEE
ピー
DOMMY
ALL THOSE STRETCHY BITS...!

FIRE FORCE

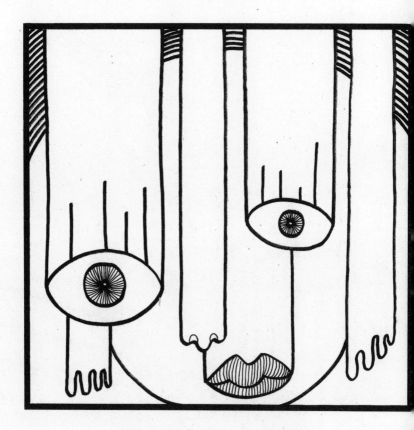

CHAPTER CXXXX: A WOMAN'S BATTLE

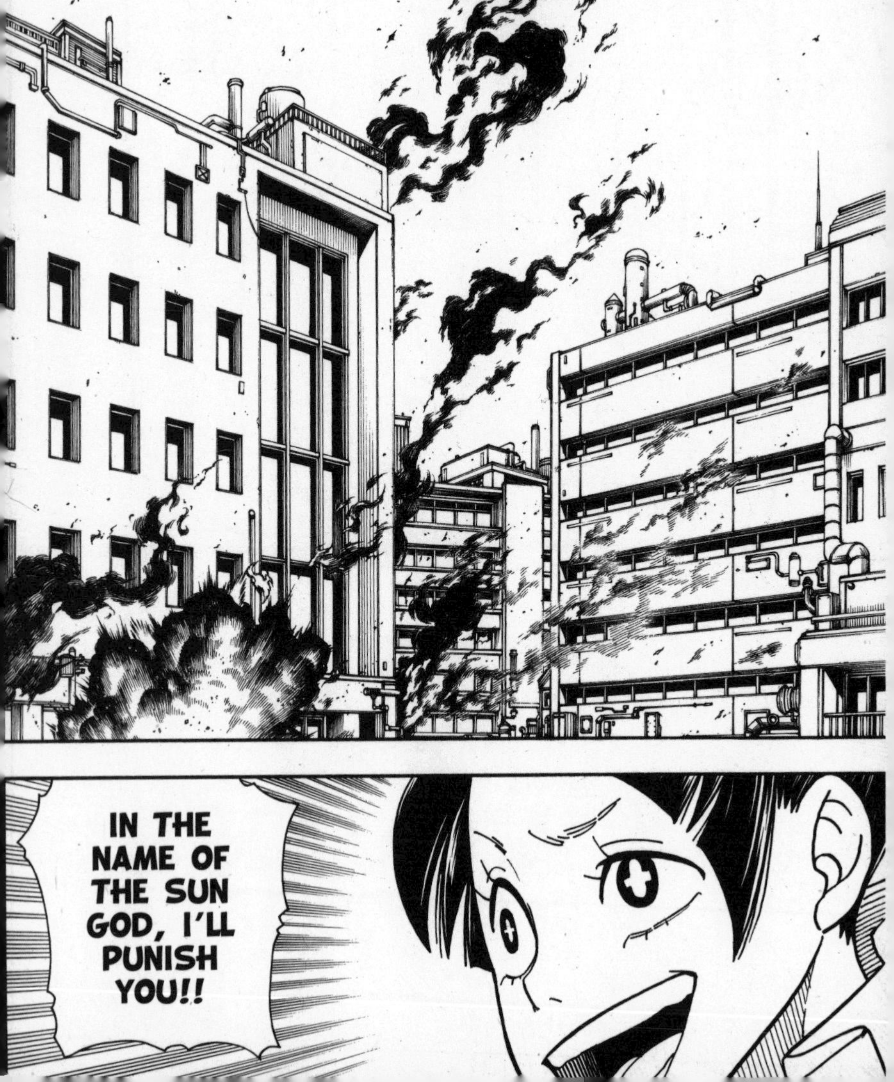
IN THE NAME OF THE SUN GOD, I'LL PUNISH YOU!!

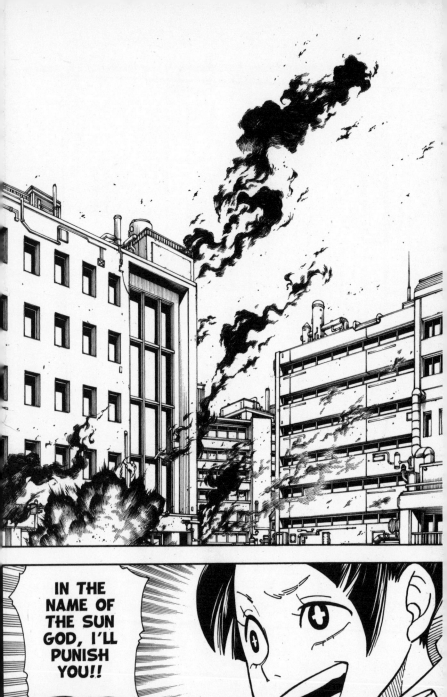

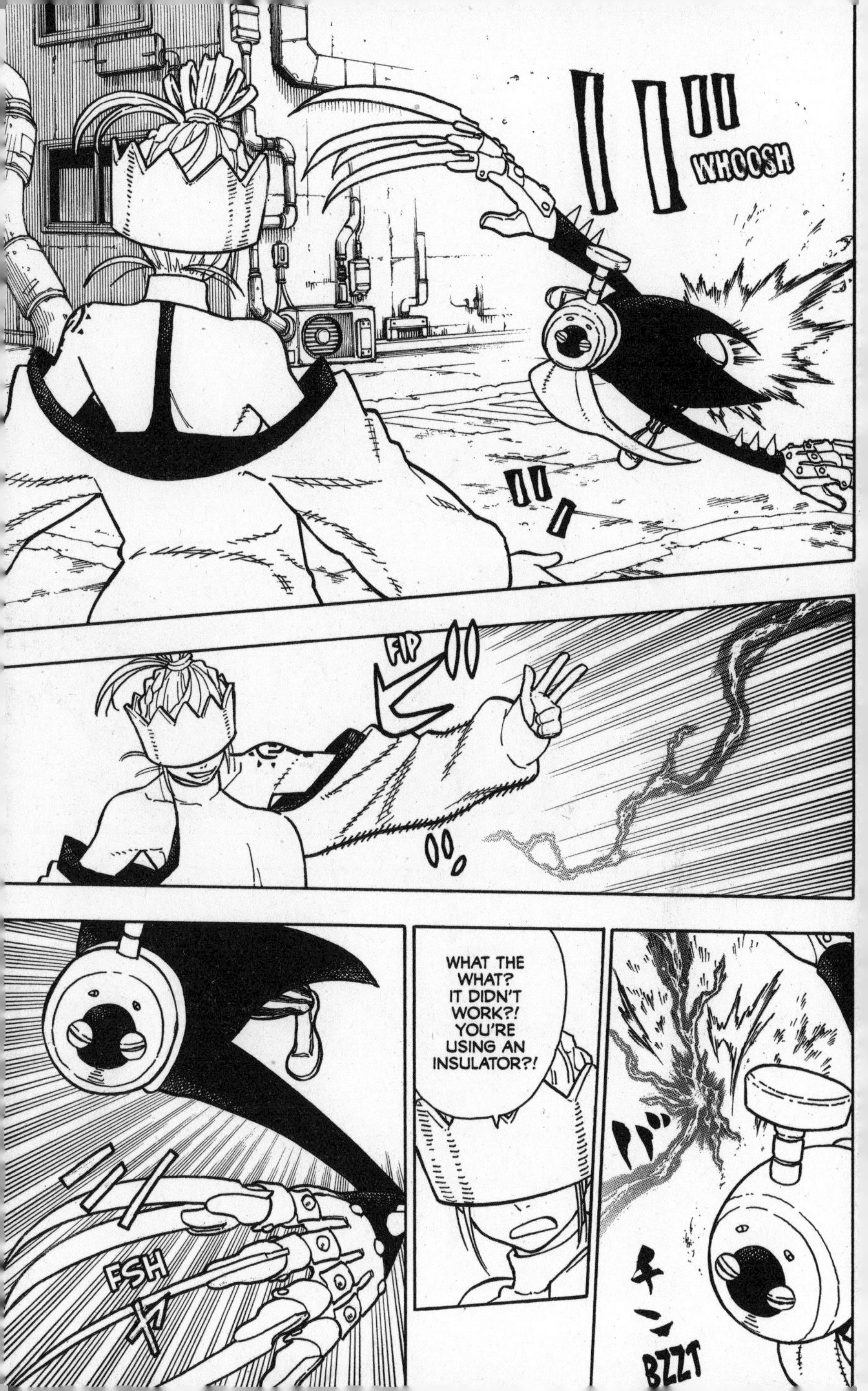
WHOOSH
FIP
BZZT
WHAT THE WHAT? IT DIDN'T WORK?! YOU'RE USING AN INSULATOR?!
FSH

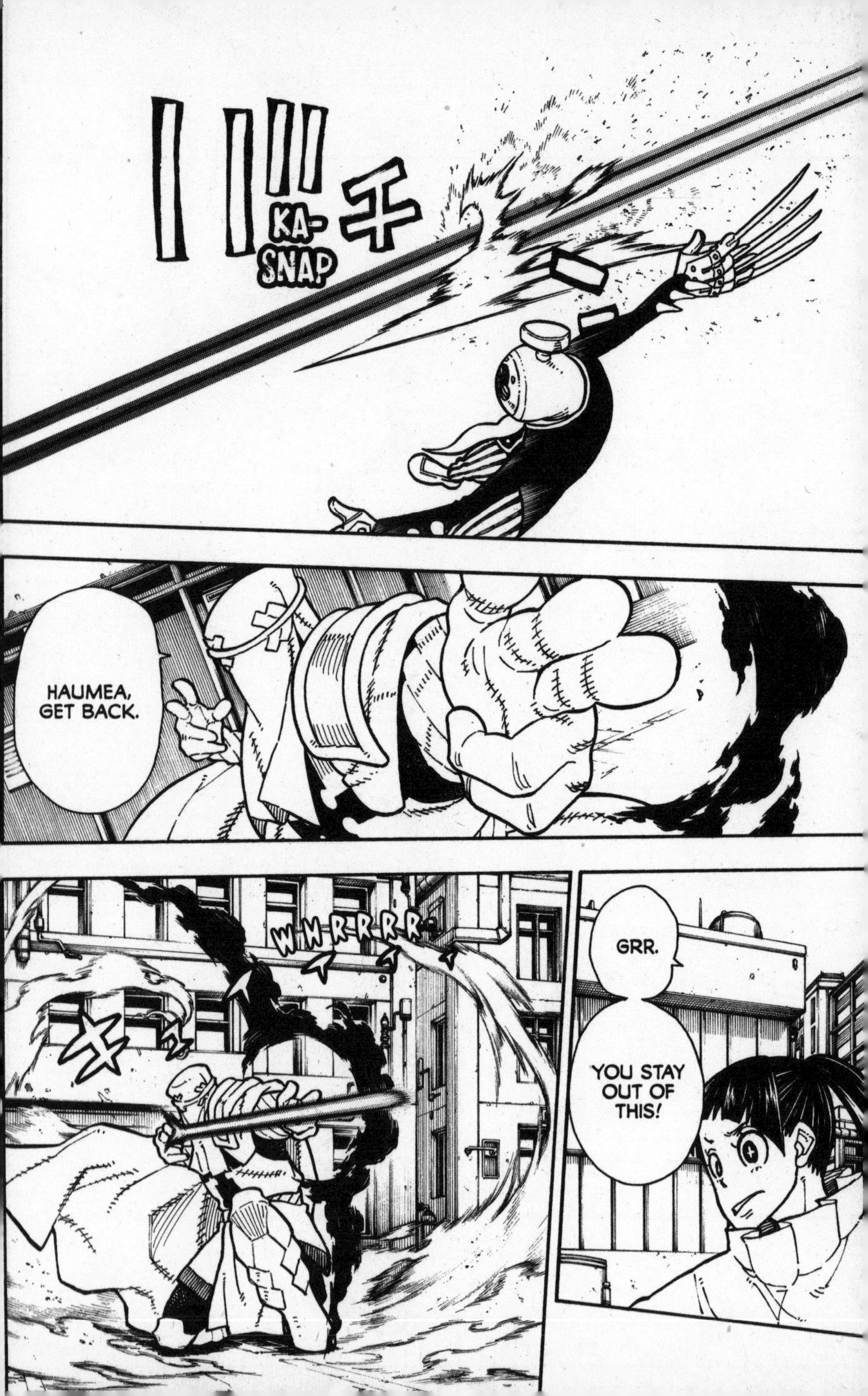
KA-SNAP
HAUMEA, GET BACK.
GRR.
YOU STAY OUT OF THIS!
WHRRRRR

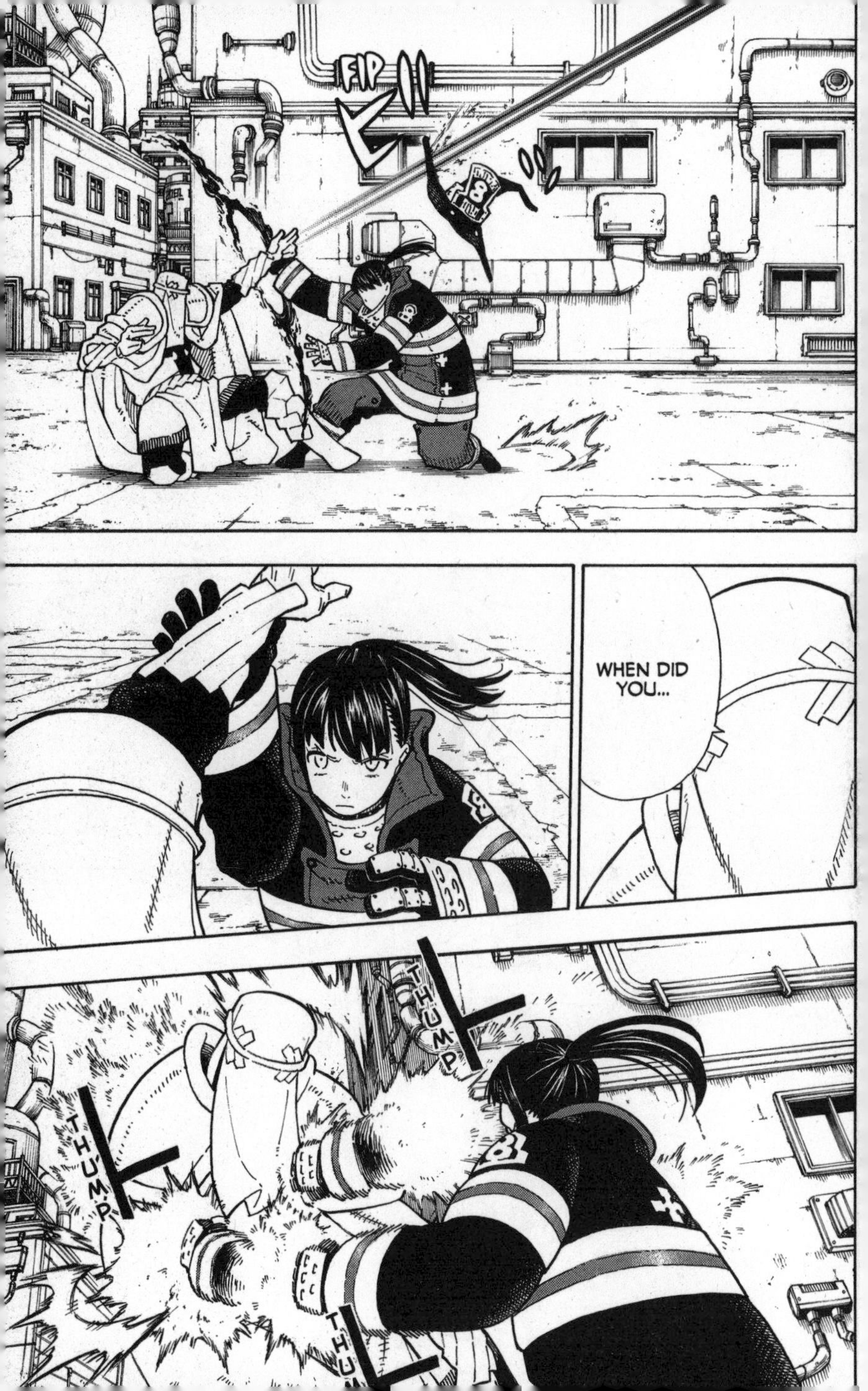
FIP
WHEN DID
YOU...
THUMP
THUMP
THU

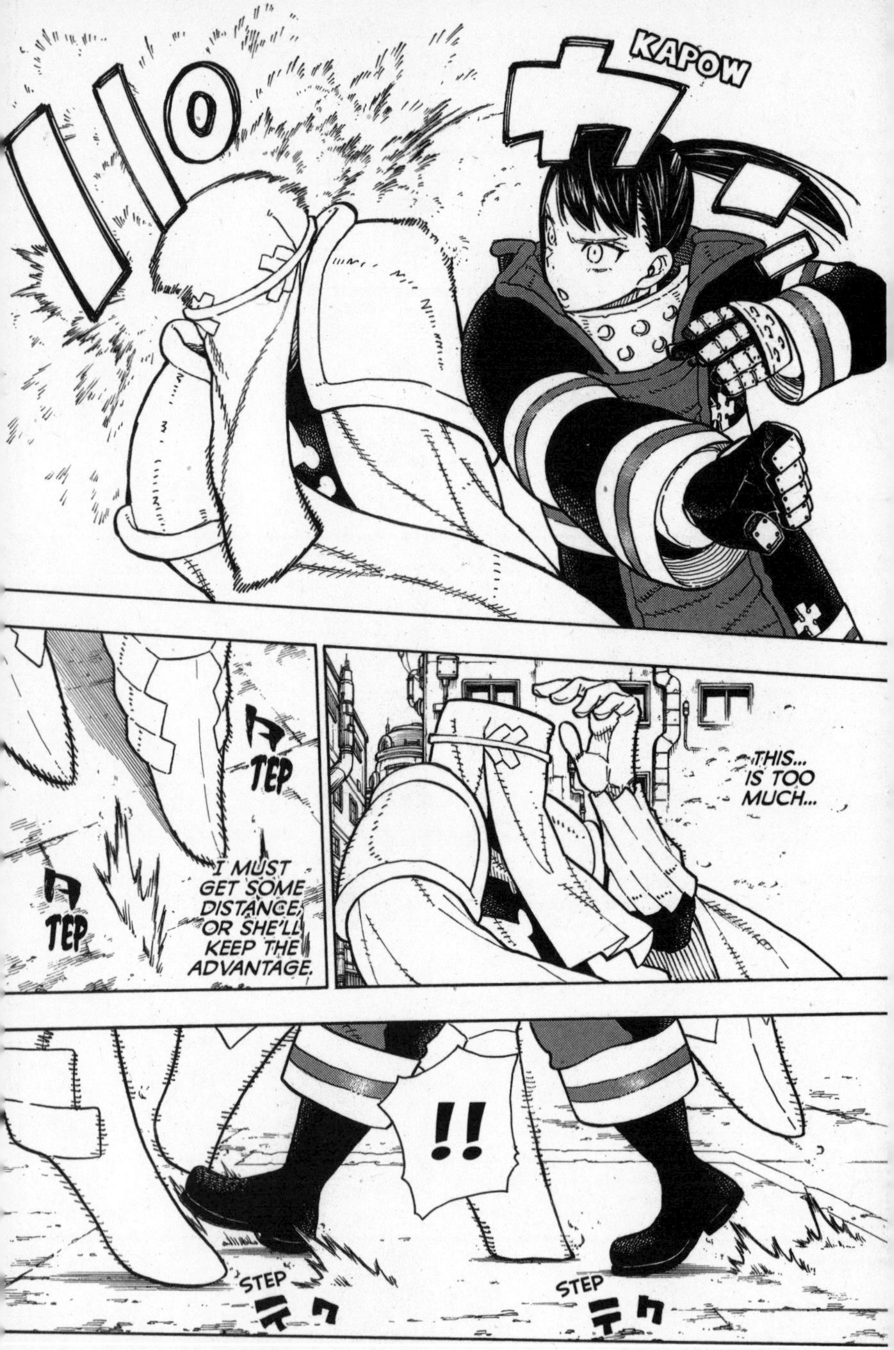
KAPOW
THIS... IS TOO MUCH...
TEP
I MUST GET SOME DISTANCE, OR SHE'LL KEEP THE ADVANTAGE.
TEP
!!
STEP
STEP

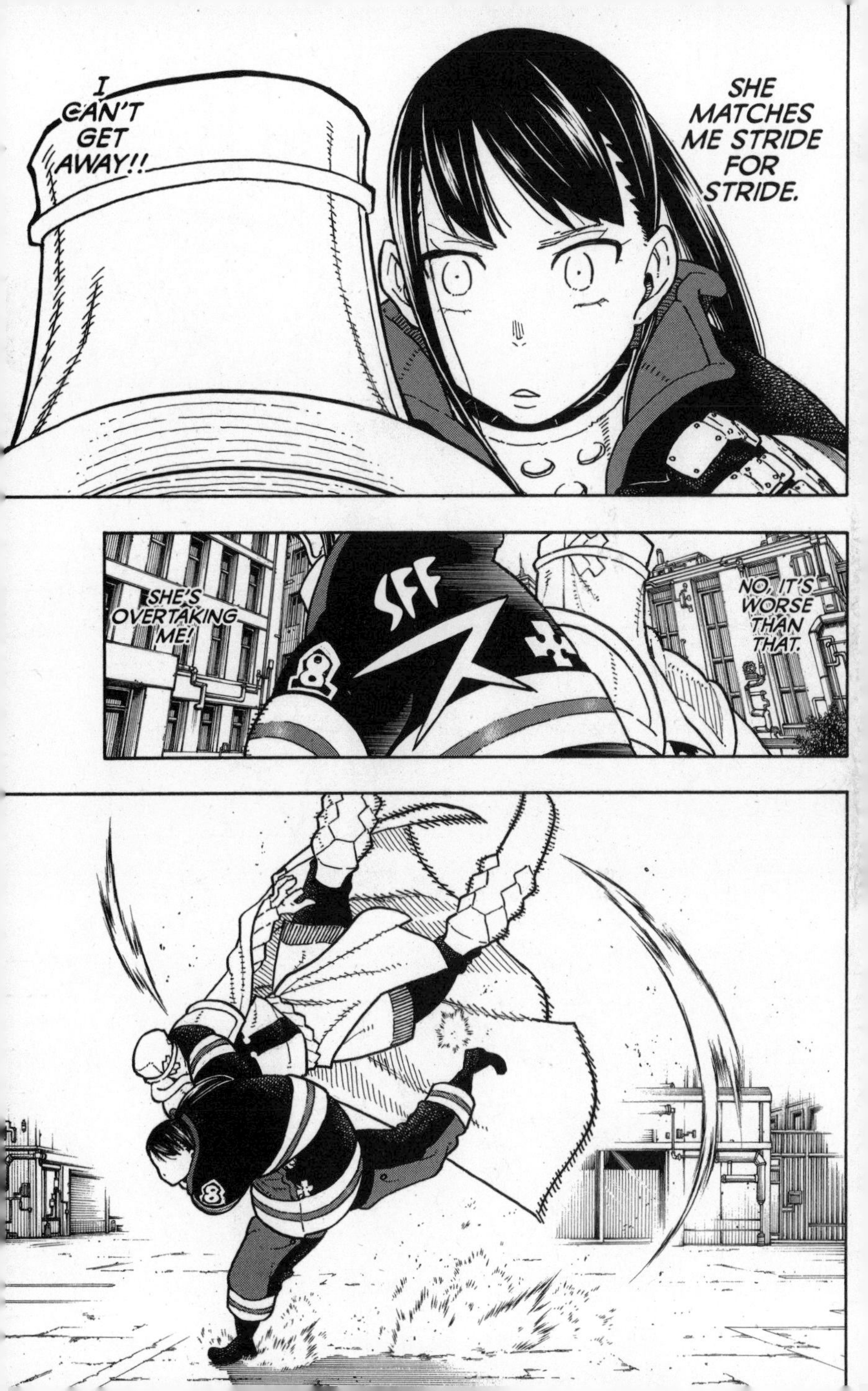
SHE MATCHES ME STRIDE FOR STRIDE.
I CAN'T GET AWAY!!
NO, IT'S WORSE THAN THAT.
SHE'S OVERTAKING ME!
SFF

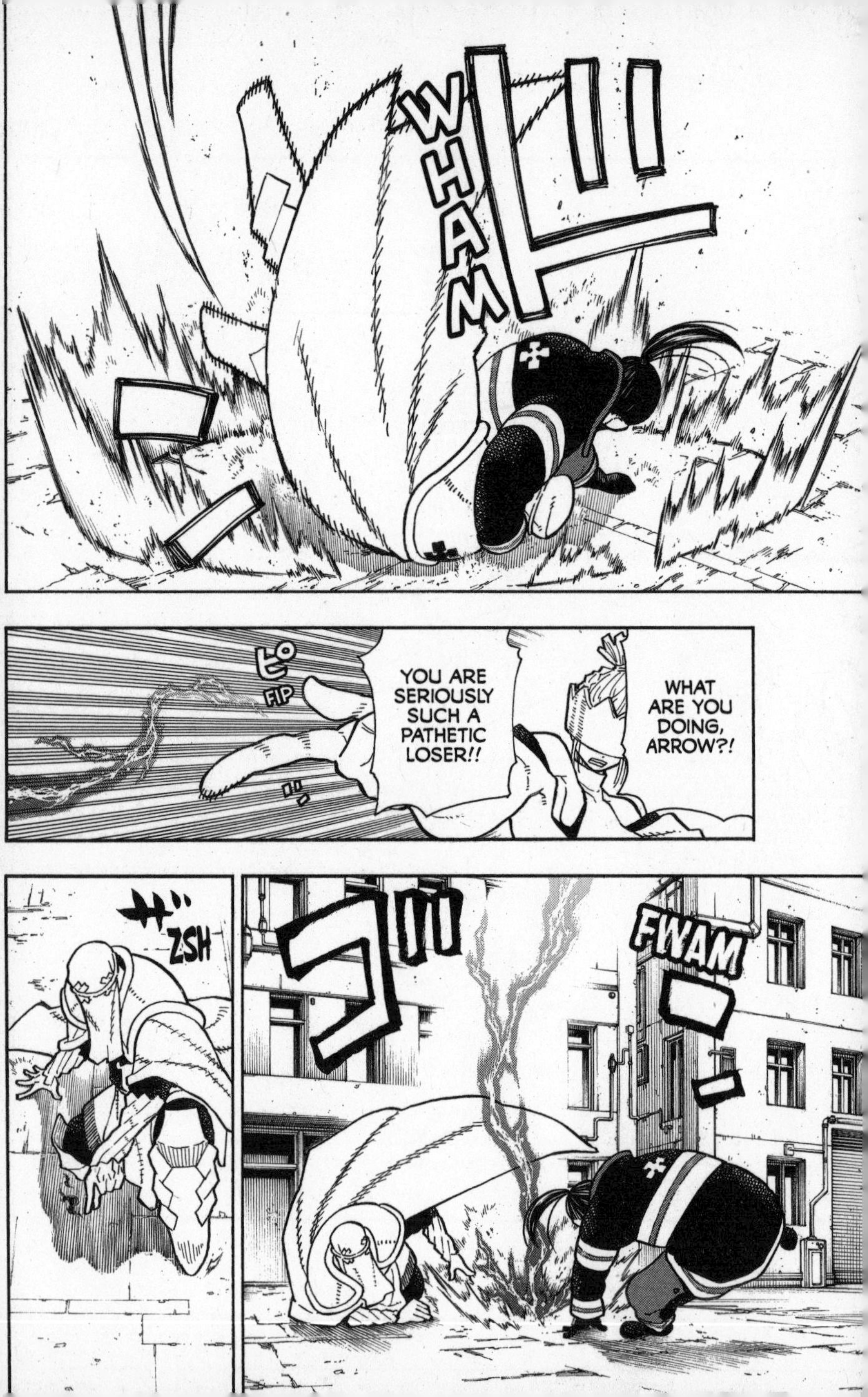
WHAM
WHAT ARE YOU DOING, ARROW?!
YOU ARE SERIOUSLY SUCH A PATHETIC LOSER!!
FIP
FWAM
ZSH

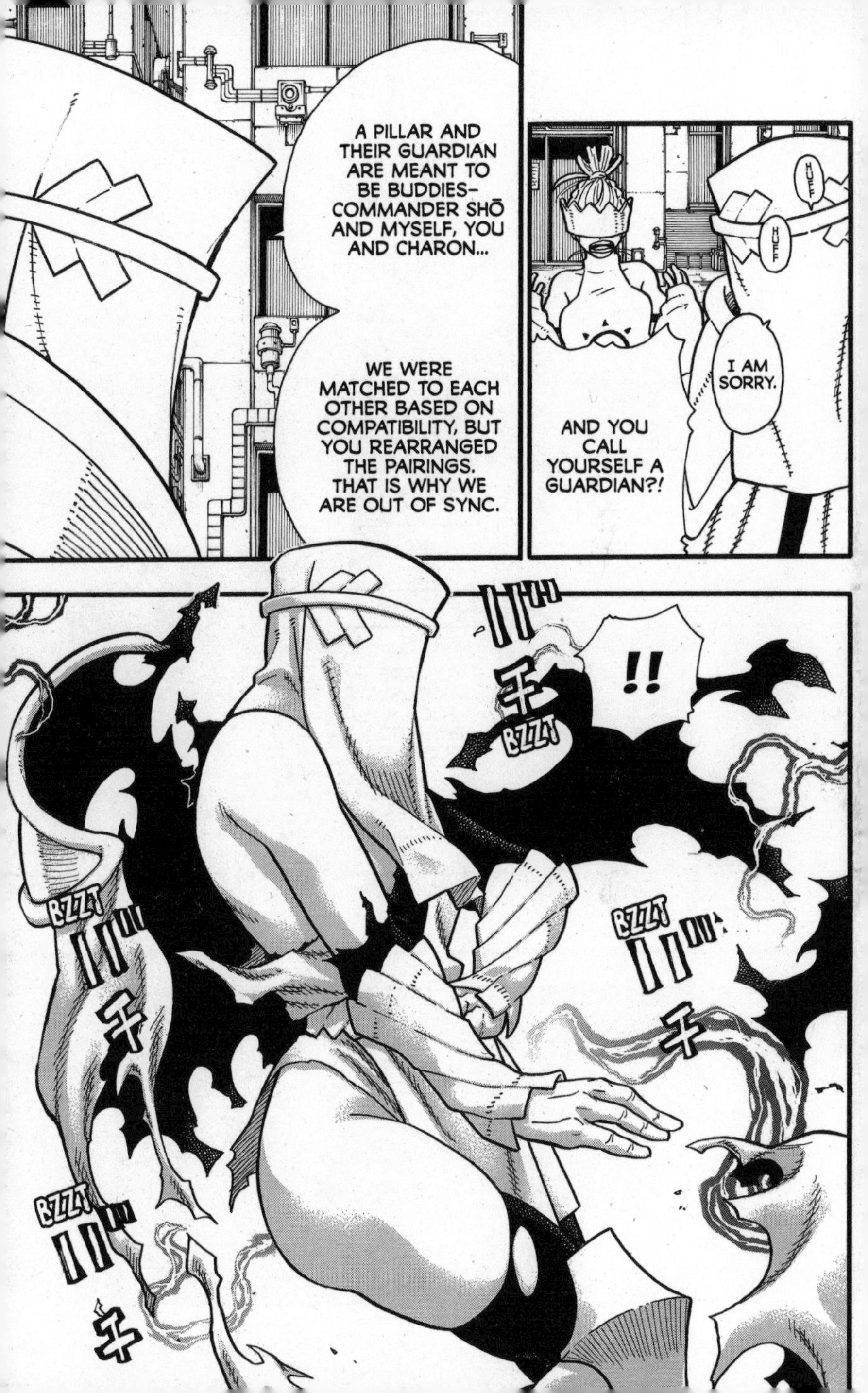
HUFF
HUFF
I AM SORRY.
AND YOU CALL YOURSELF A GUARDIAN?!
A PILLAR AND THEIR GUARDIAN ARE MEANT TO BE BUDDIES– COMMANDER SHŌ AND MYSELF, YOU AND CHARON...
WE WERE MATCHED TO EACH OTHER BASED ON COMPATIBILITY, BUT YOU REARRANGED THE PAIRINGS. THAT IS WHY WE ARE OUT OF SYNC.
!!
BZZZT
BZZZT
BZZZT
BZZZT

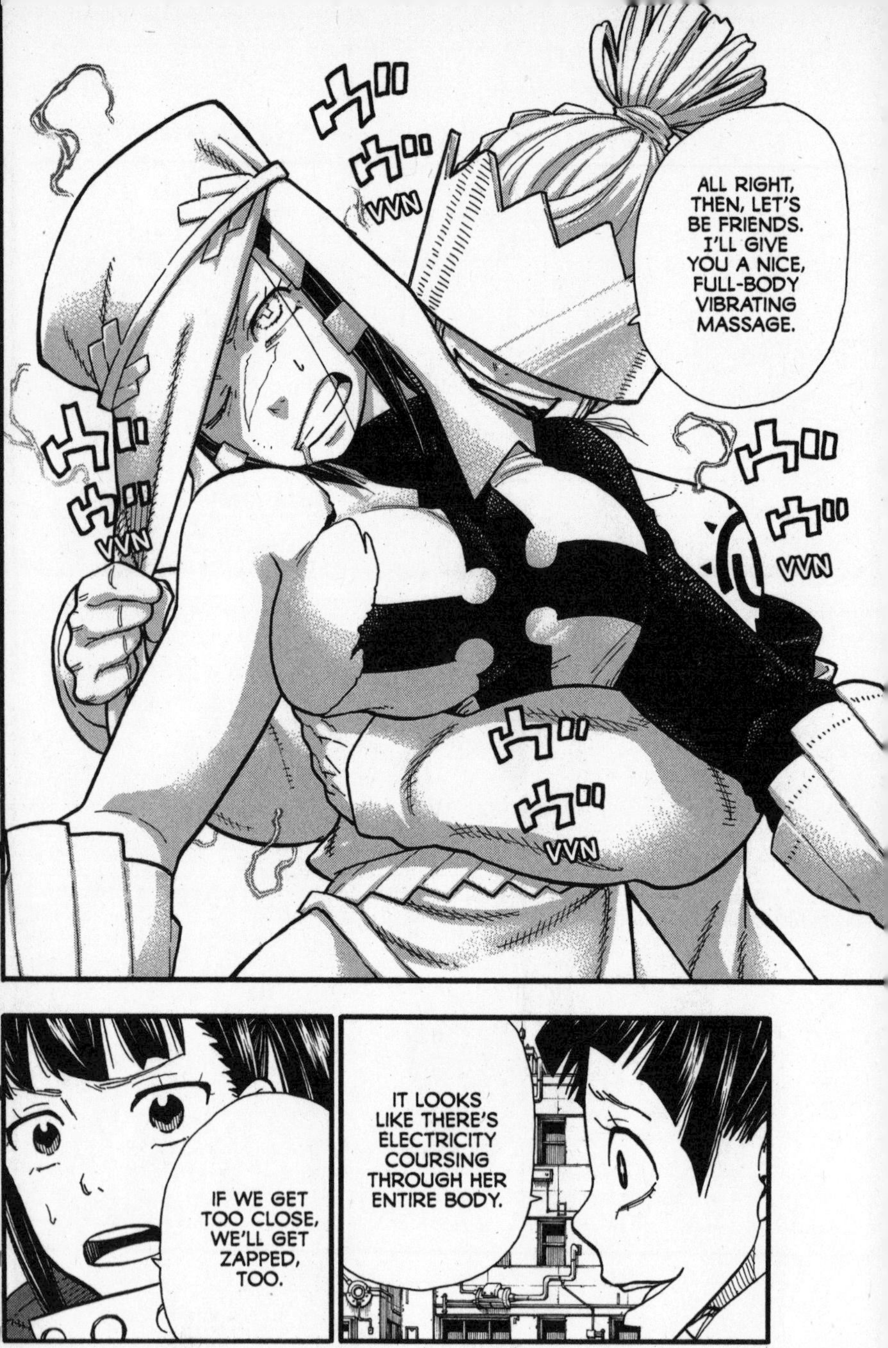
ALL RIGHT, THEN, LET'S BE FRIENDS. I'LL GIVE YOU A NICE, FULL-BODY VIBRATING MASSAGE.
VVN
VVN
VVN
VVN
IT LOOKS LIKE THERE'S ELECTRICITY COURSING THROUGH HER ENTIRE BODY.
IF WE GET TOO CLOSE, WE'LL GET ZAPPED, TOO.

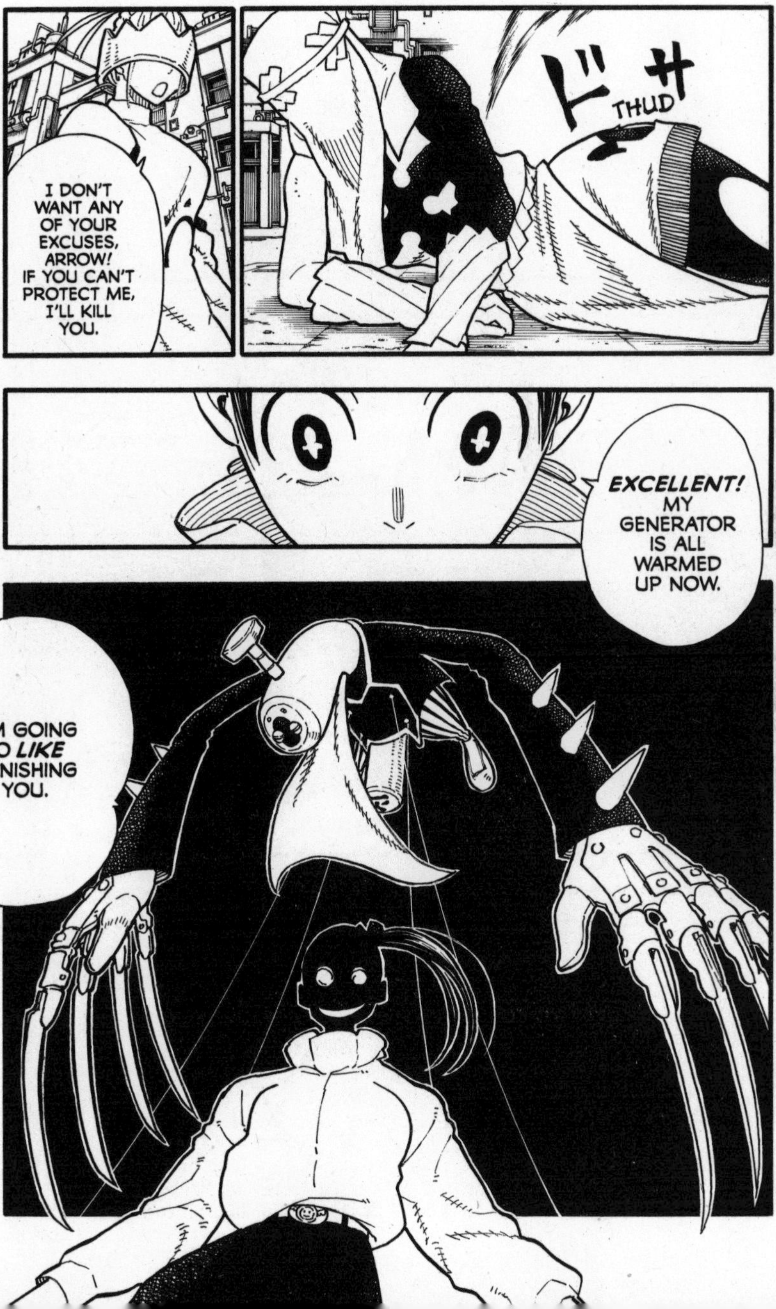
ドサ
THUD
I DON'T WANT ANY OF YOUR EXCUSES, ARROW! IF YOU CAN'T PROTECT ME, I'LL KILL YOU.
EXCELLENT! MY GENERATOR IS ALL WARMED UP NOW.
I'M GOING TO *LIKE* PUNISHING YOU.

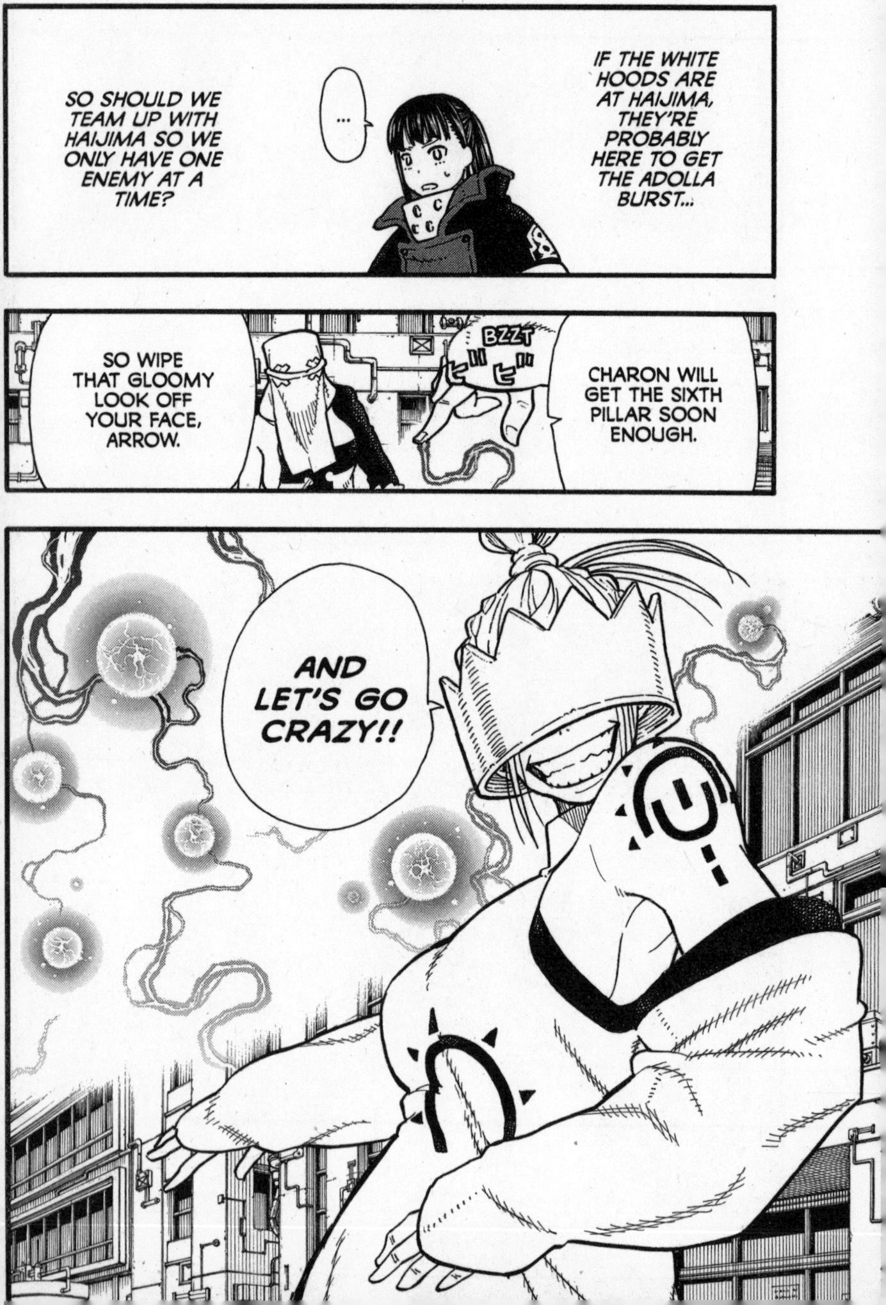
IF THE WHITE HOODS ARE AT HAIJIMA, THEY'RE PROBABLY HERE TO GET THE ADOLLA BURST...
...
SO SHOULD WE TEAM UP WITH HAIJIMA SO WE ONLY HAVE ONE ENEMY AT A TIME?
CHARON WILL GET THE SIXTH PILLAR SOON ENOUGH.
BZZT
SO WIPE THAT GLOOMY LOOK OFF YOUR FACE, ARROW.
AND LET'S GO CRAZY!!

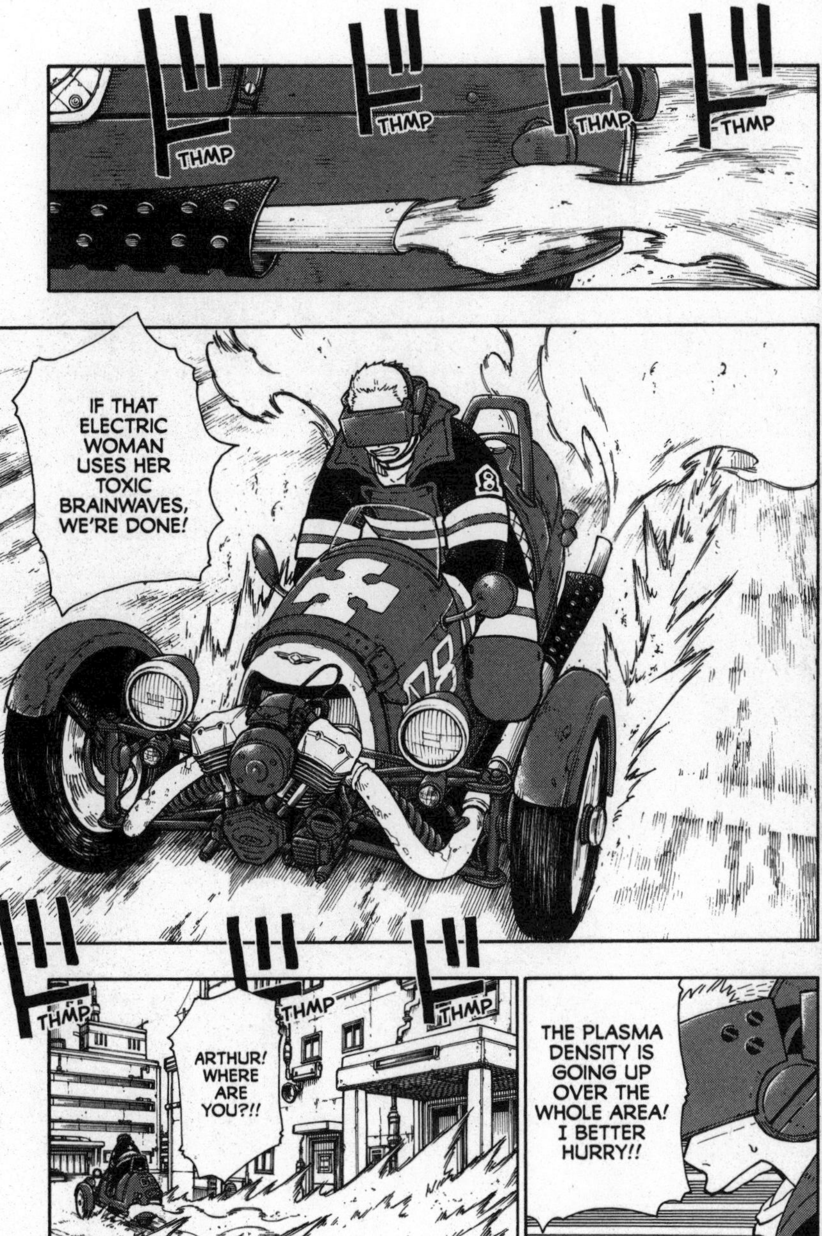
THMP
THMP
THMP
THMP
IF THAT ELECTRIC WOMAN USES HER TOXIC BRAINWAVES, WE'RE DONE!
THE PLASMA DENSITY IS GOING UP OVER THE WHOLE AREA! I BETTER HURRY!!
THMP
THMP
THMP
ARTHUR! WHERE ARE YOU?!!

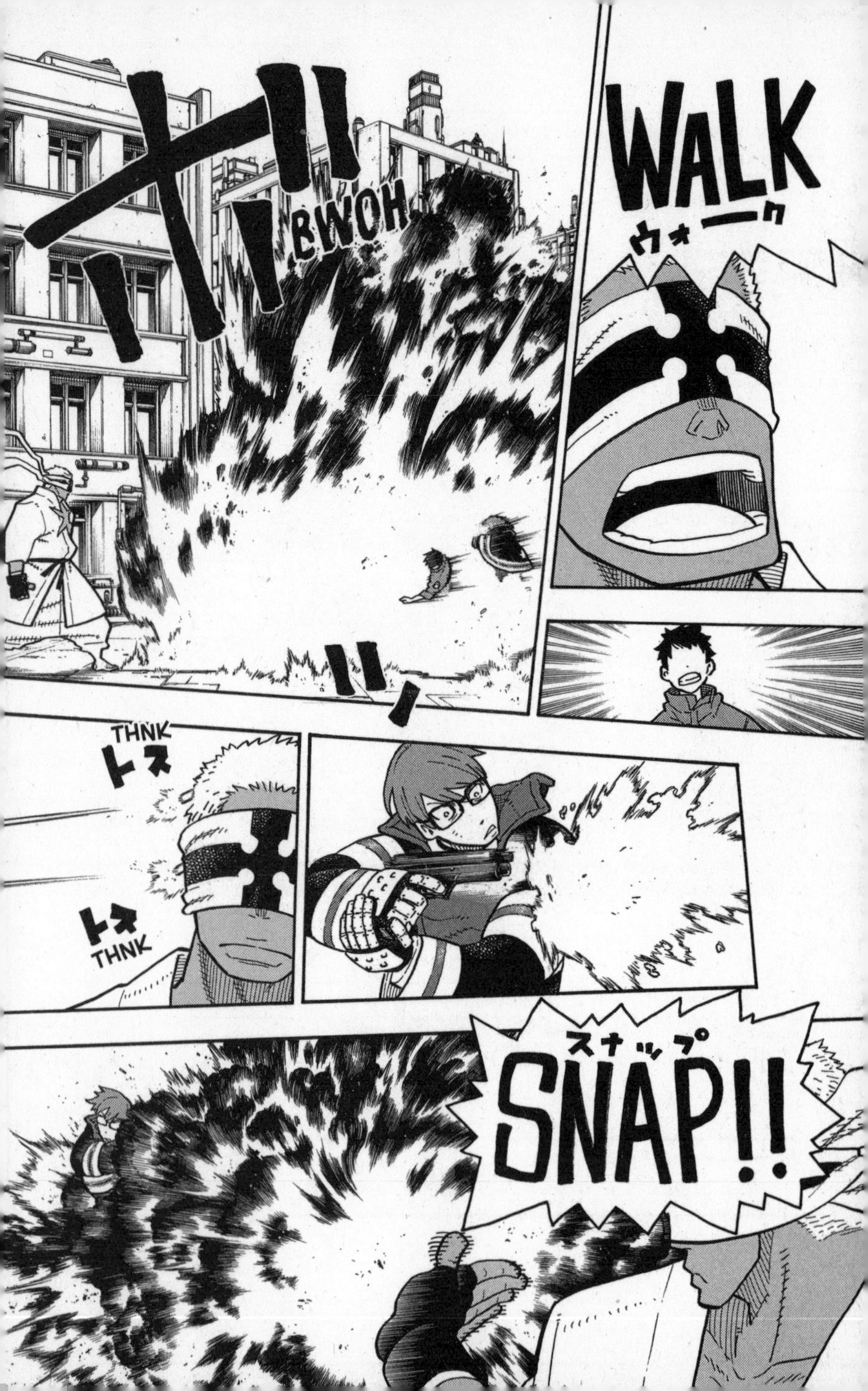
WALK
ウォーク
BWOH
THNK
トス
トス
THNK
スナップ
SNAP!!

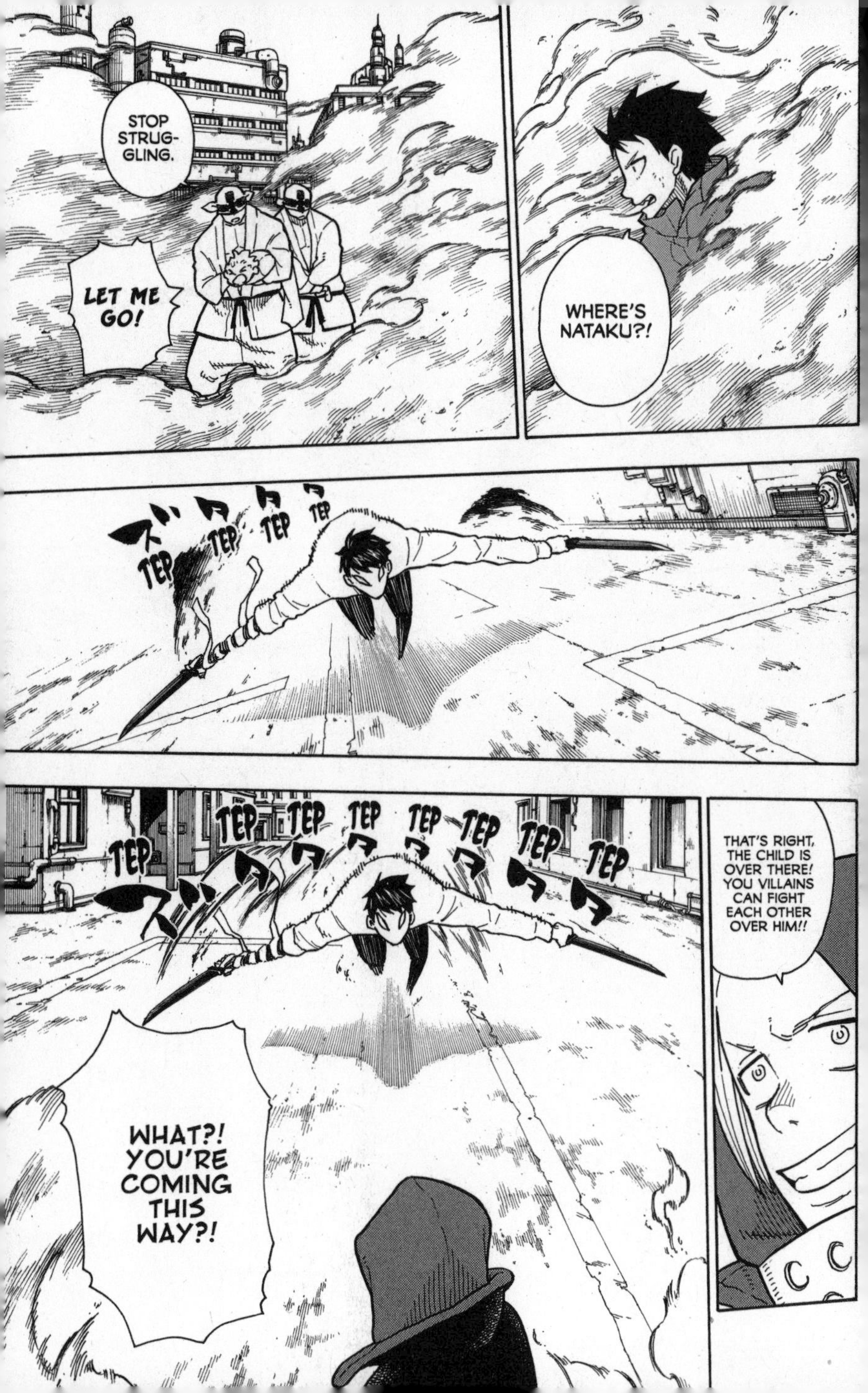
WHERE'S NATAKU?!
STOP STRUG-GLING.
LET ME GO!
TEP TEP TEP TEP
THAT'S RIGHT, THE CHILD IS OVER THERE! YOU VILLAINS CAN FIGHT EACH OTHER OVER HIM!!
TEP TEP TEP TEP TEP TEP TEP TEP
WHAT?! YOU'RE COMING THIS WAY?!

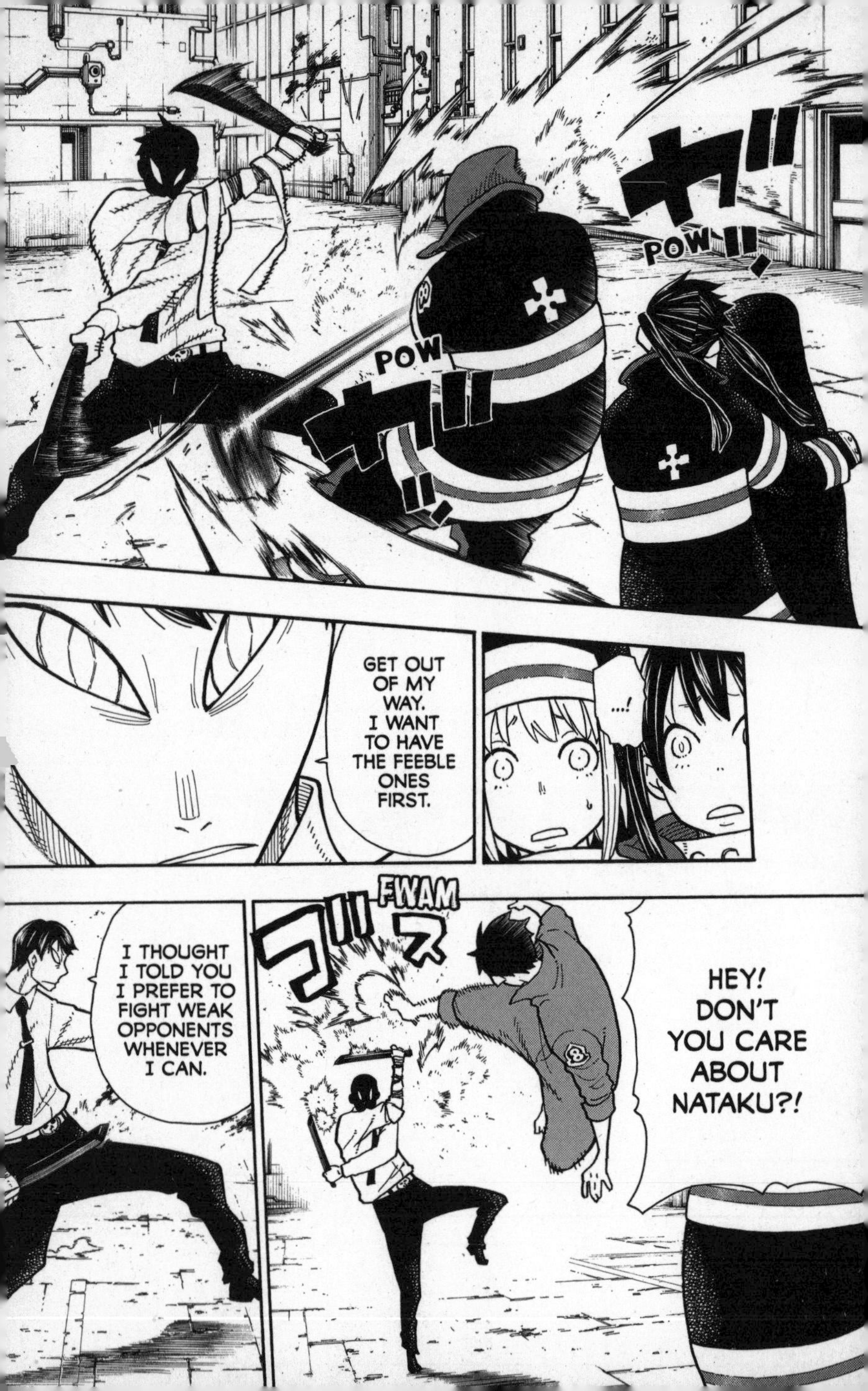
POW!!
POW
...!
GET OUT OF MY WAY. I WANT TO HAVE THE FEEBLE ONES FIRST.
FWAM
HEY! DON'T YOU CARE ABOUT NATAKU?!
I THOUGHT I TOLD YOU I PREFER TO FIGHT WEAK OPPONENTS WHENEVER I CAN.

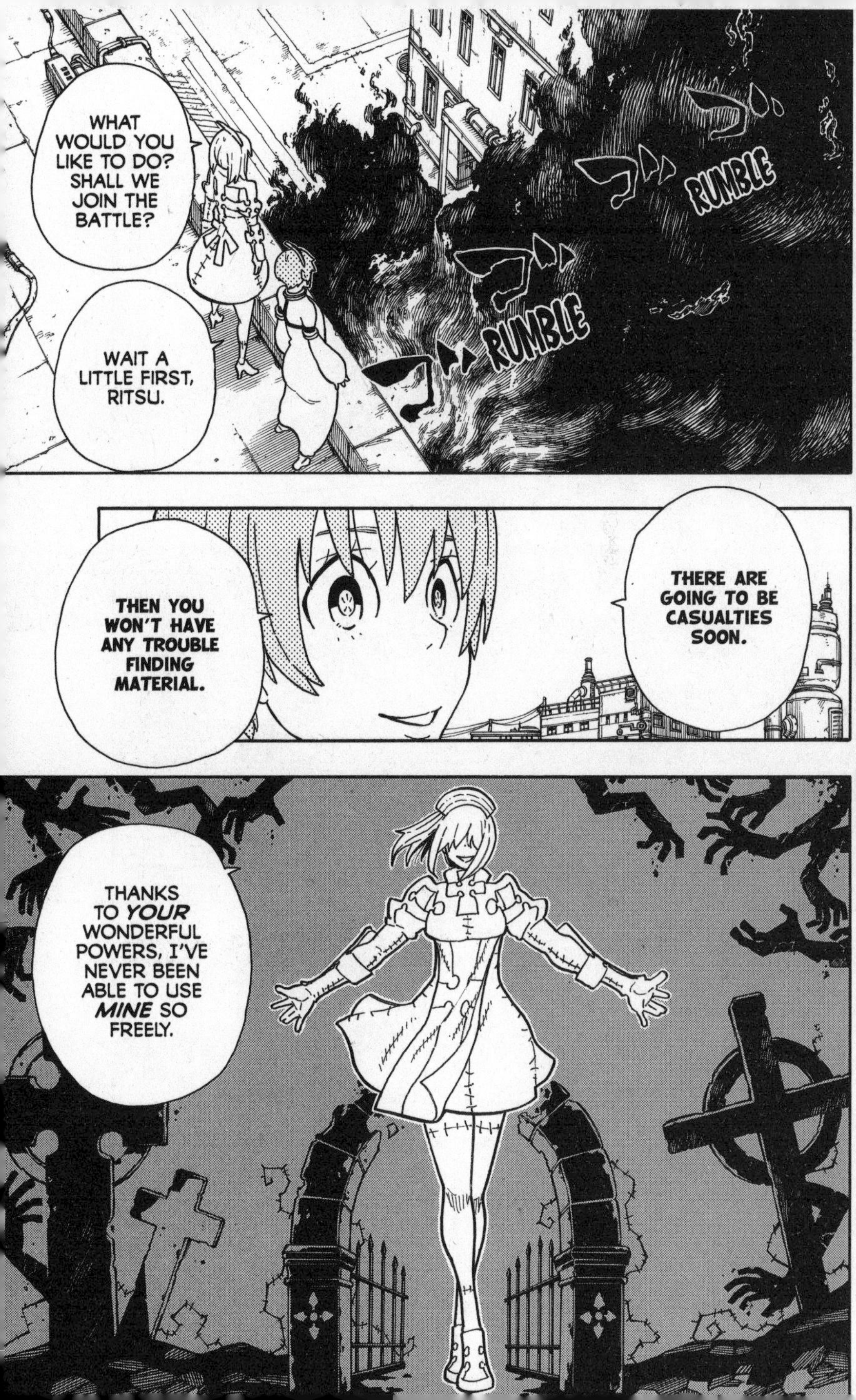
RUMBLE
RUMBLE
WHAT WOULD YOU LIKE TO DO? SHALL WE JOIN THE BATTLE?
WAIT A LITTLE FIRST, RITSU.
THERE ARE GOING TO BE CASUALTIES SOON.
THEN YOU WON'T HAVE ANY TROUBLE FINDING MATERIAL.
THANKS TO *YOUR* WONDERFUL POWERS, I'VE NEVER BEEN ABLE TO USE *MINE* SO FREELY.

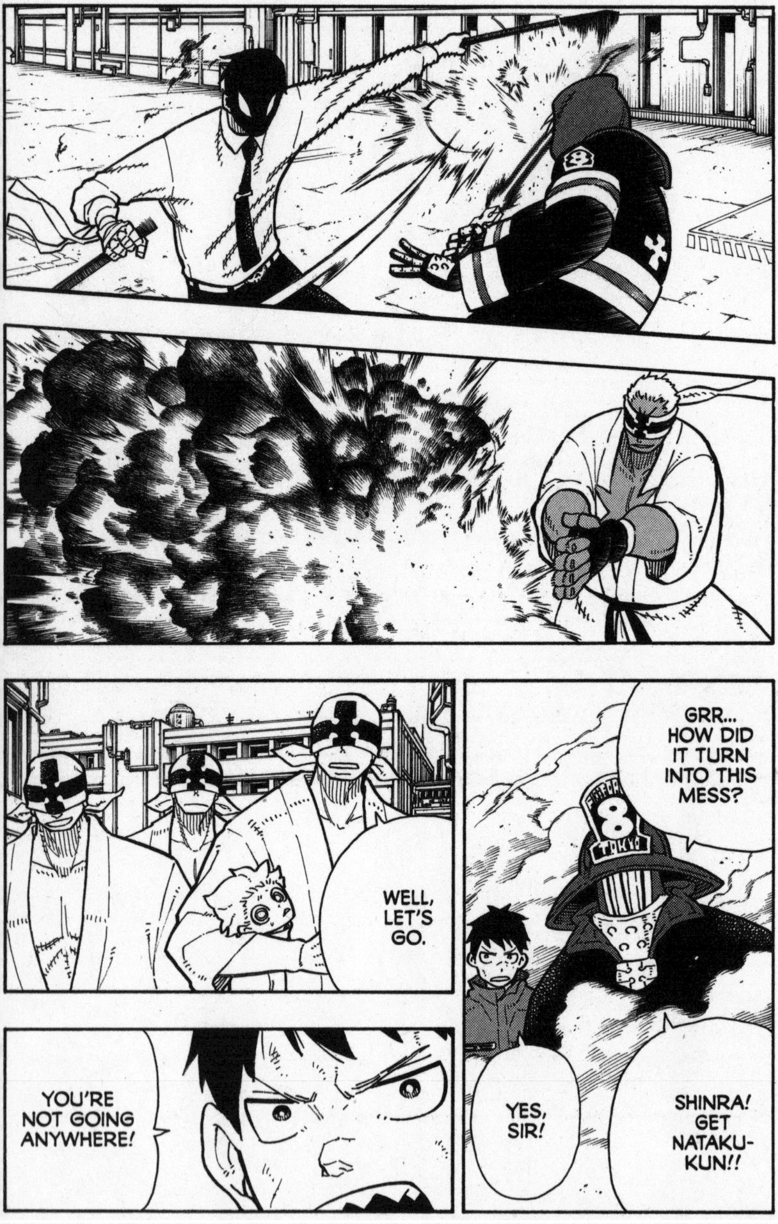
GRR... HOW DID IT TURN INTO THIS MESS?
SHINRA! GET NATAKU-KUN!!
YES, SIR!
WELL, LET'S GO.
YOU'RE NOT GOING ANYWHERE!

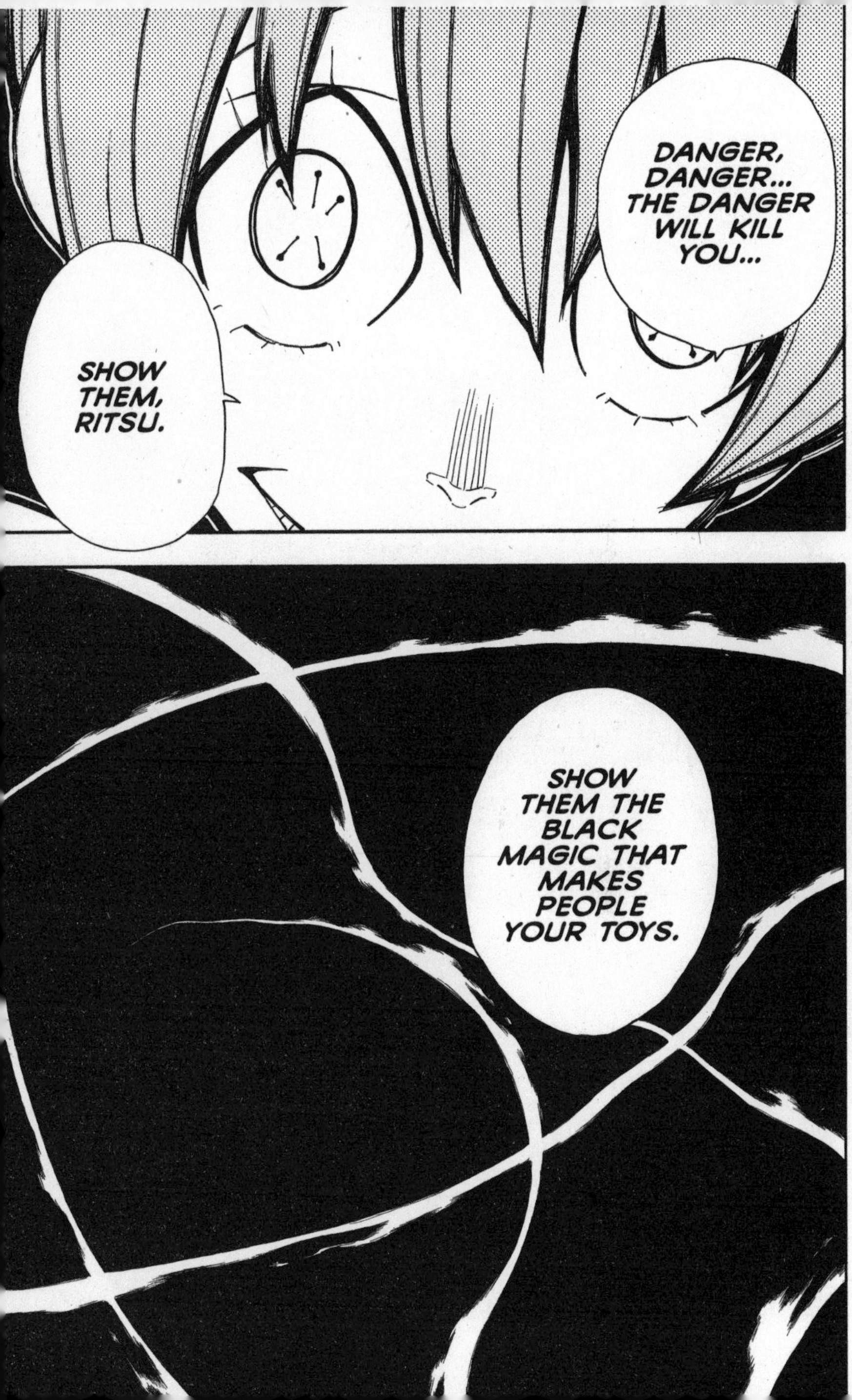
DANGER, DANGER... THE DANGER WILL KILL YOU...
SHOW THEM, RITSU.
SHOW THEM THE BLACK MAGIC THAT MAKES PEOPLE YOUR TOYS.

FIRE FORCE

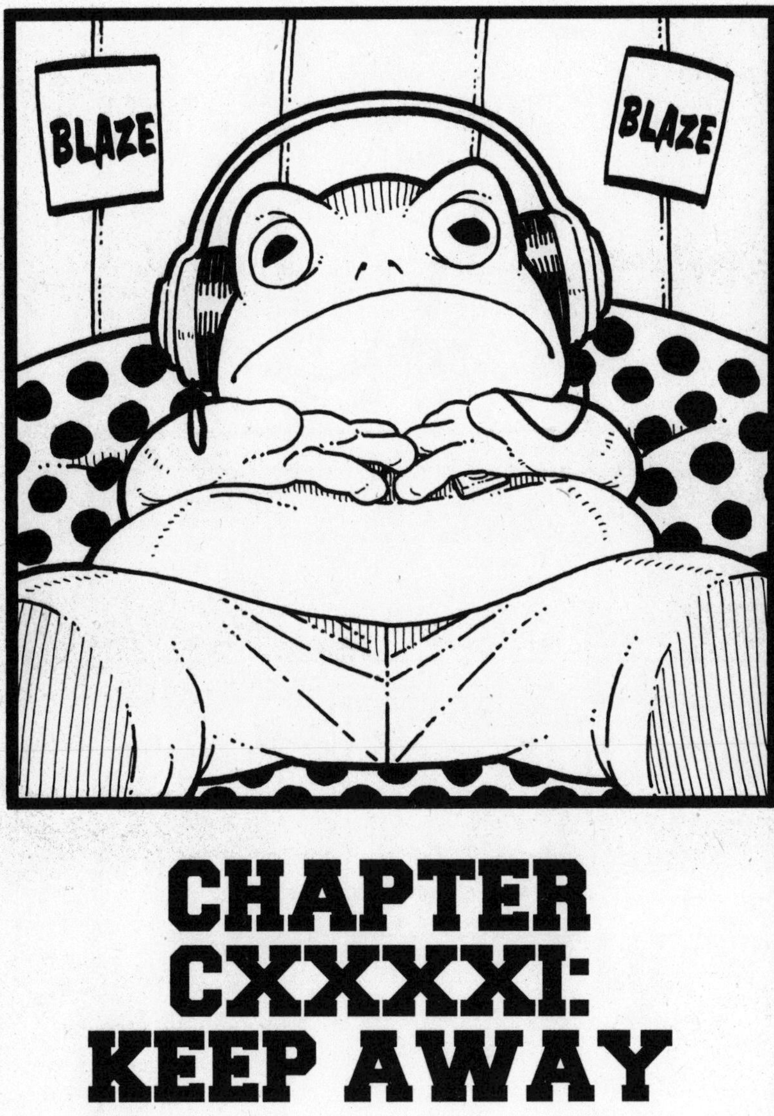
BLAZE
BLAZE

CHAPTER CXXXXI: KEEP AWAY

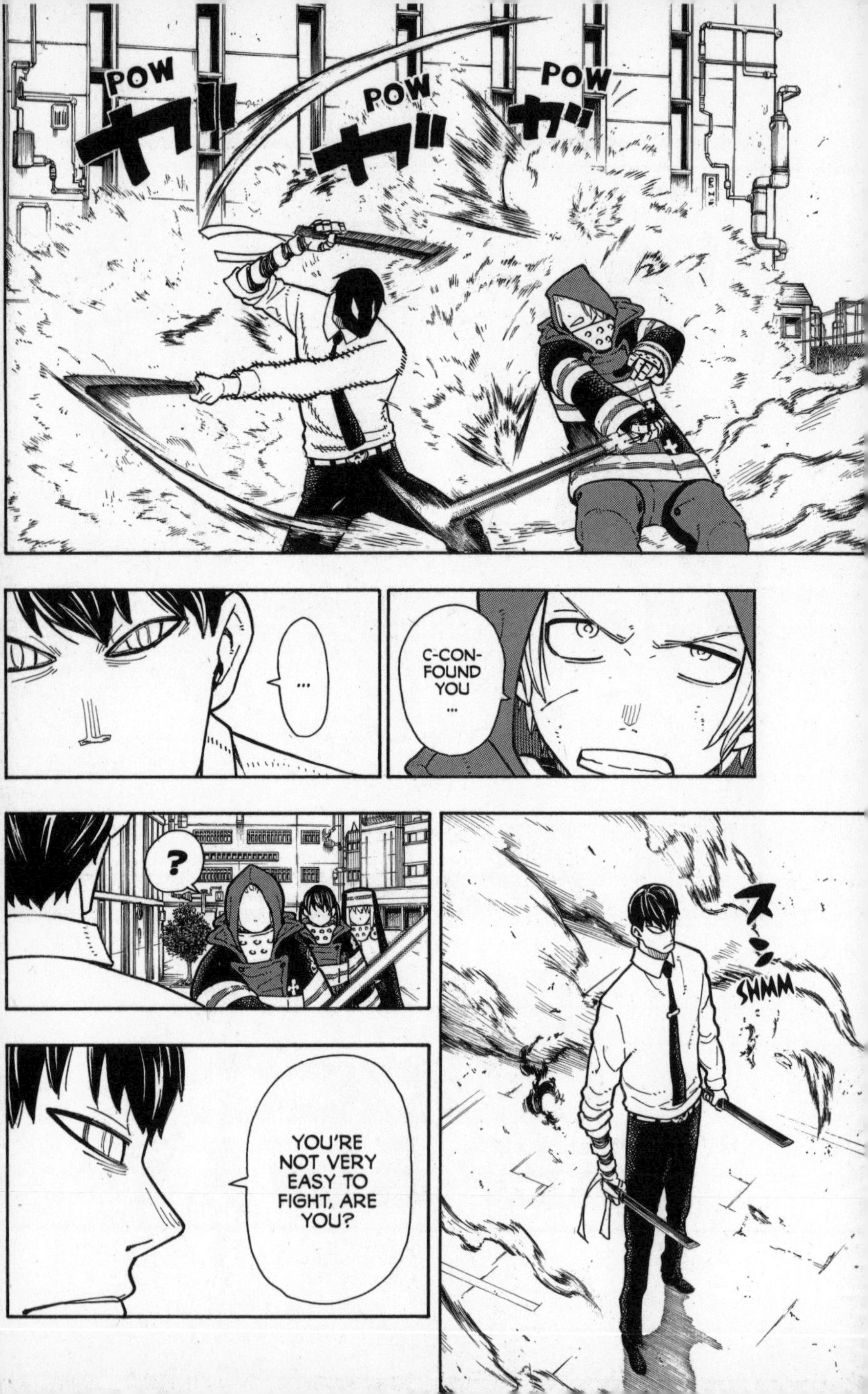
POW
POW
POW
C-CON-FOUND YOU ...
...
SHMM
?
YOU'RE NOT VERY EASY TO FIGHT, ARE YOU?

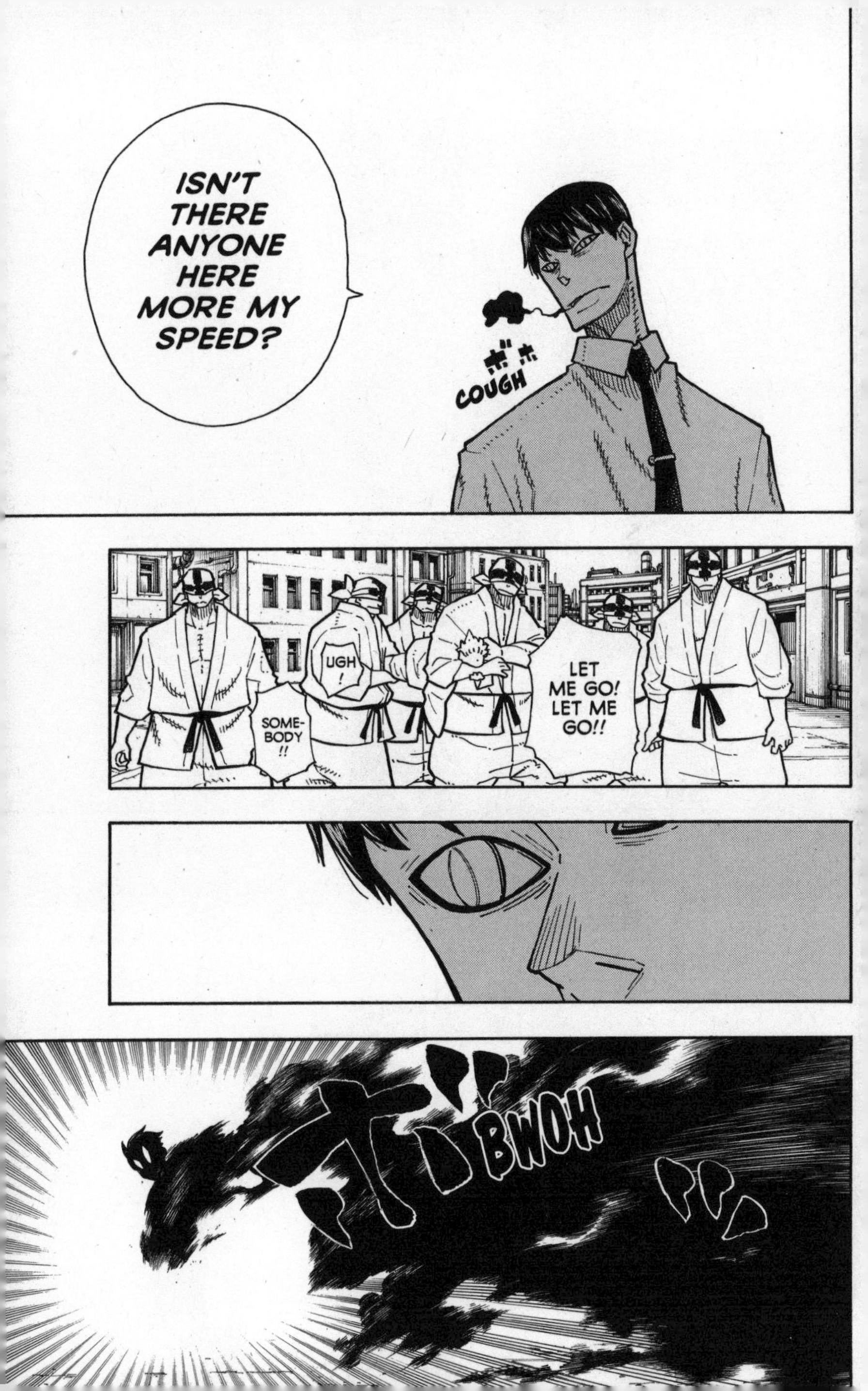
ISN'T THERE ANYONE HERE MORE MY SPEED?
ボホ
COUGH
LET ME GO! LET ME GO!!
UGH!
SOME-BODY!!
BWOH

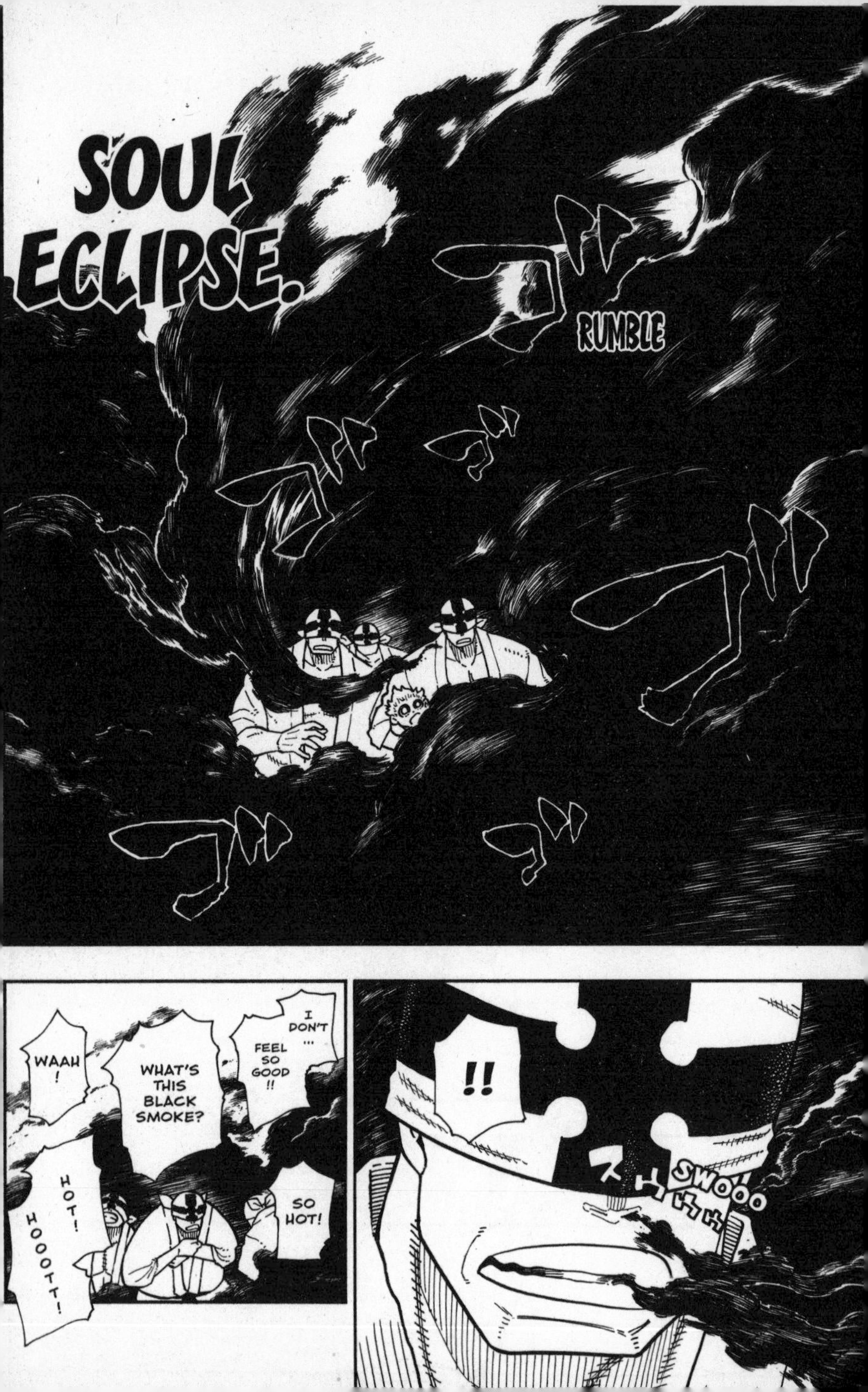
SOUL ECLIPSE.
RUMBLE
!!
SWOOO
I DON'T ... FEEL SO GOOD !!
WHAT'S THIS BLACK SMOKE?
WAAH!
SO HOT!
HOT! HOOOTT!

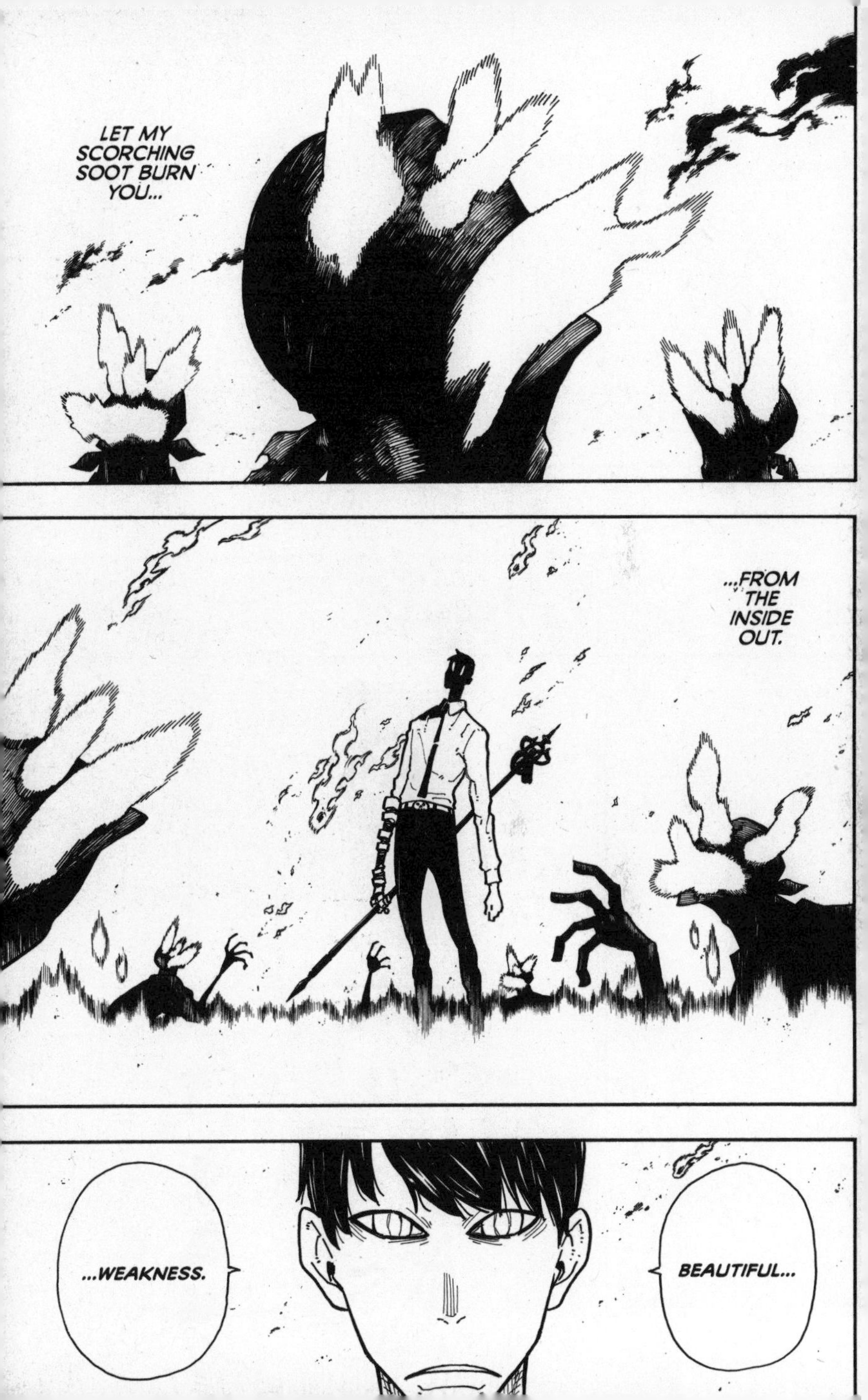
LET MY SCORCHING SOOT BURN YOU...
...FROM THE INSIDE OUT.
BEAUTIFUL...
...WEAKNESS.

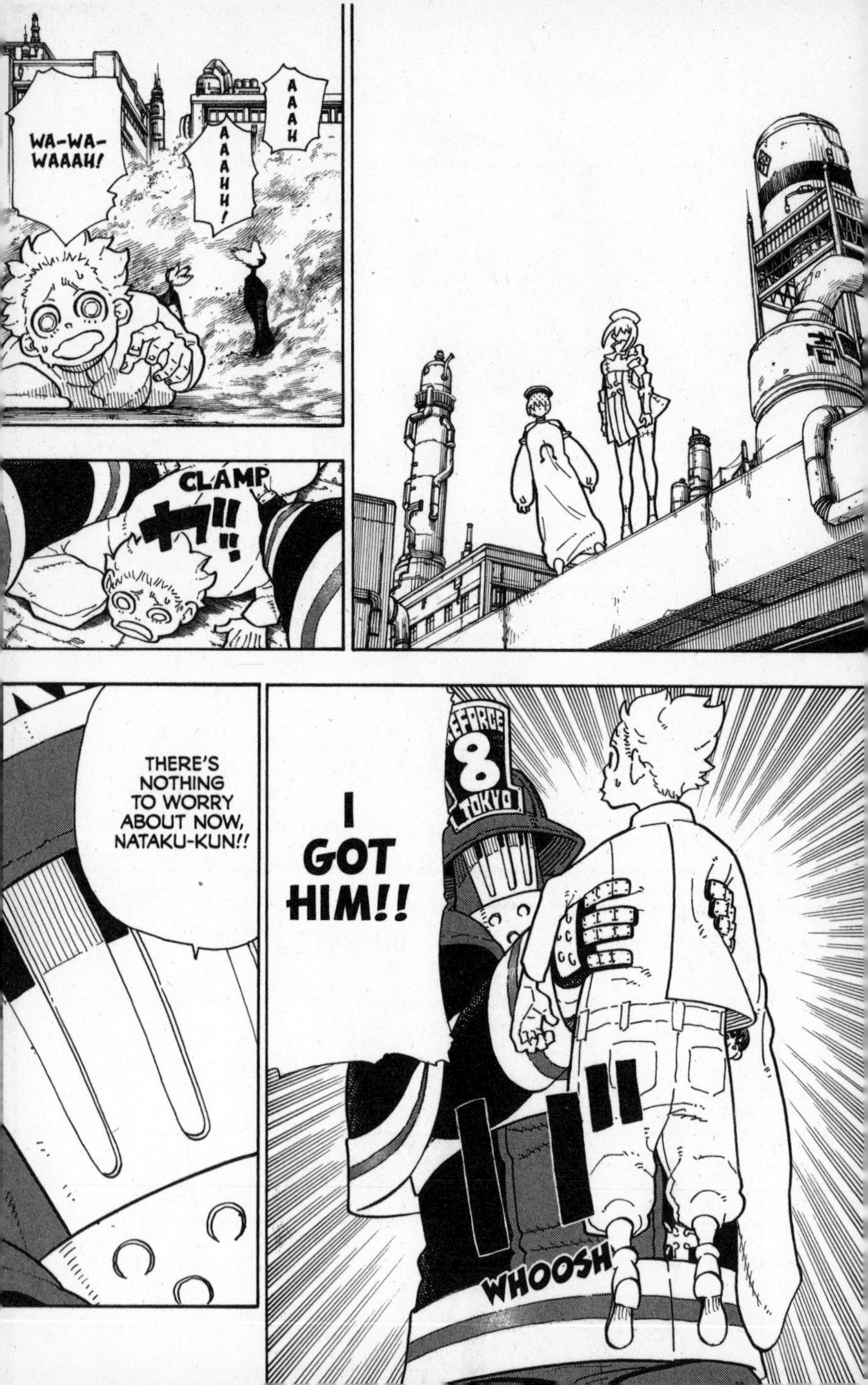
AAAH
AAAAHH!
WA-WA-WAAAH!
CLAMP
ガ!!
I GOT HIM!!
WHOOSH
THERE'S NOTHING TO WORRY ABOUT NOW, NATAKU-KUN!!

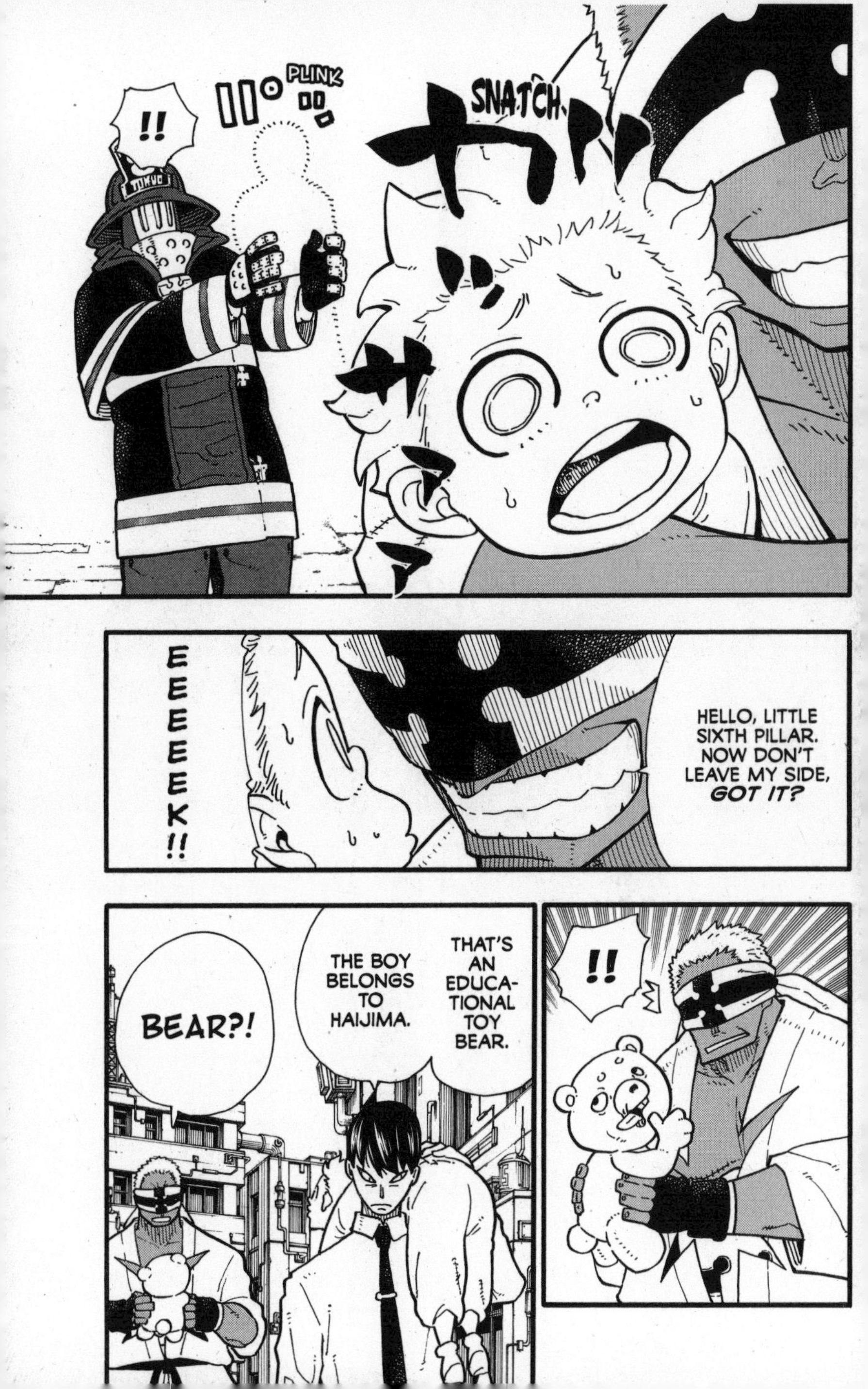
SNATCH
PLINK
!!
HELLO, LITTLE SIXTH PILLAR. NOW DON'T LEAVE MY SIDE, *GOT IT?*
EEEEEEK!!
!!
THAT'S AN EDUCA-TIONAL TOY BEAR.
THE BOY BELONGS TO HAIJIMA.
BEAR?!

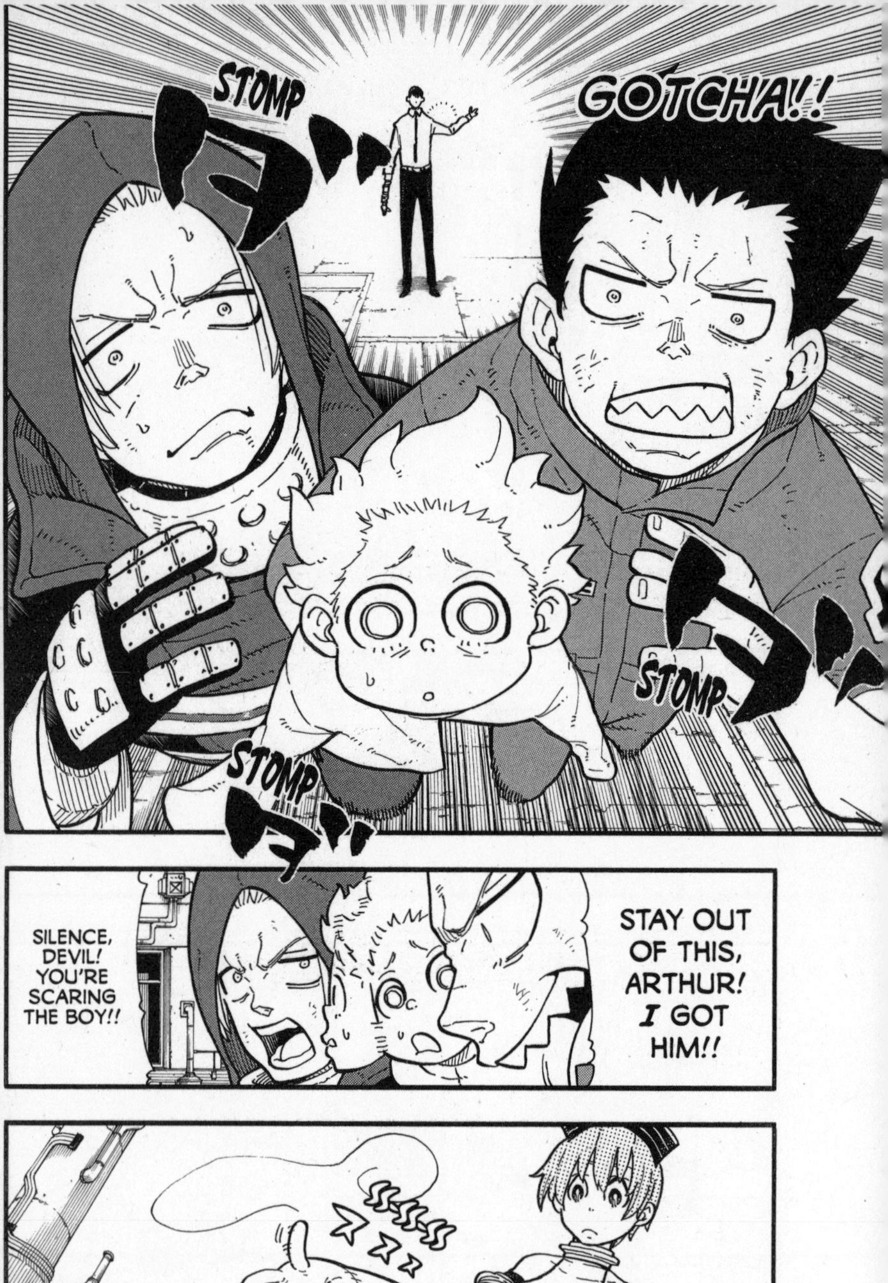
GOTCHA!!
STOMP
STOMP
STOMP
STAY OUT OF THIS, ARTHUR! I GOT HIM!!
SILENCE, DEVIL! YOU'RE SCARING THE BOY!!

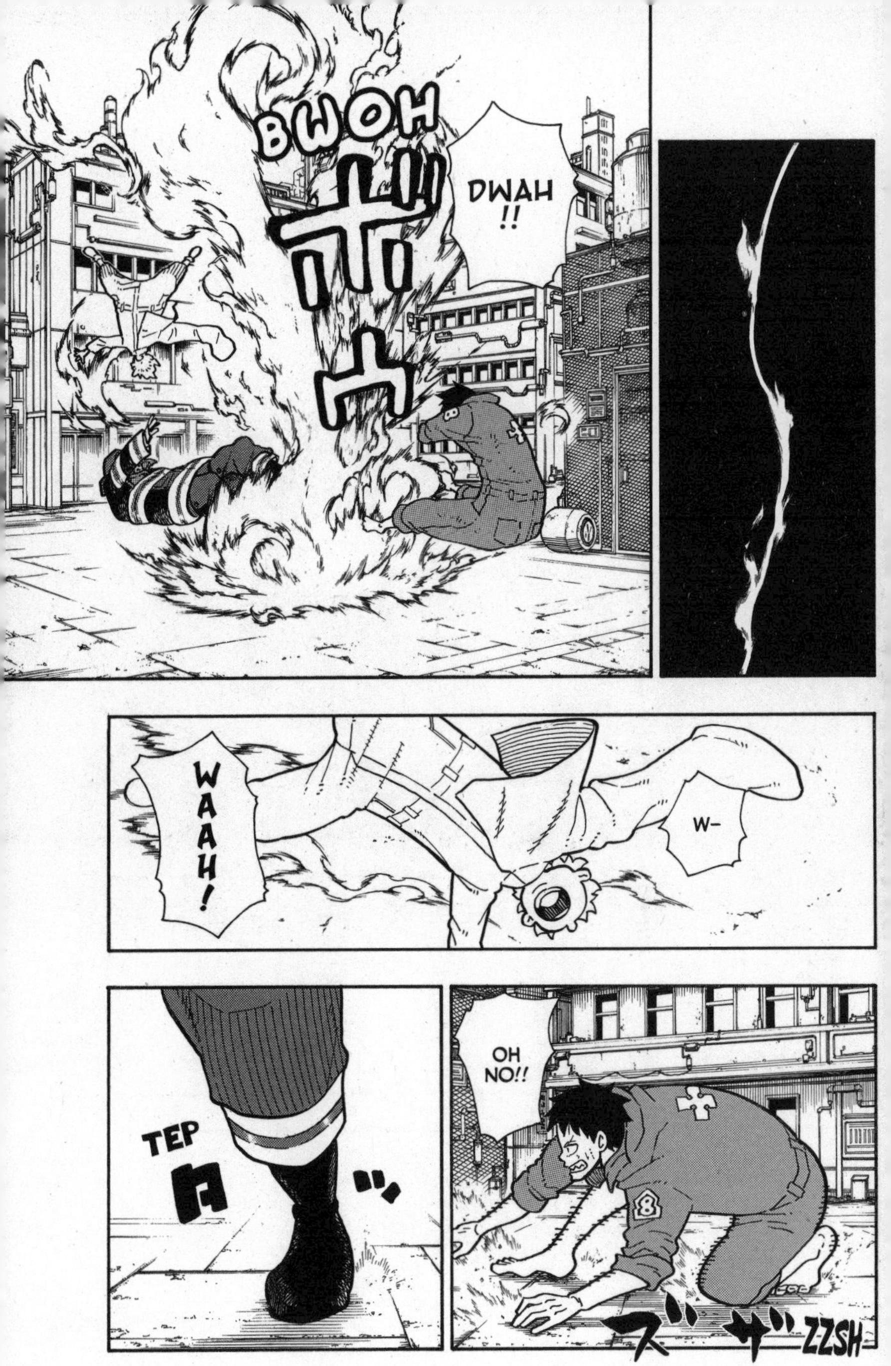
DWAH!!
BWOH
W-
WAAAH!
OH NO!!
ZZSH
TEP

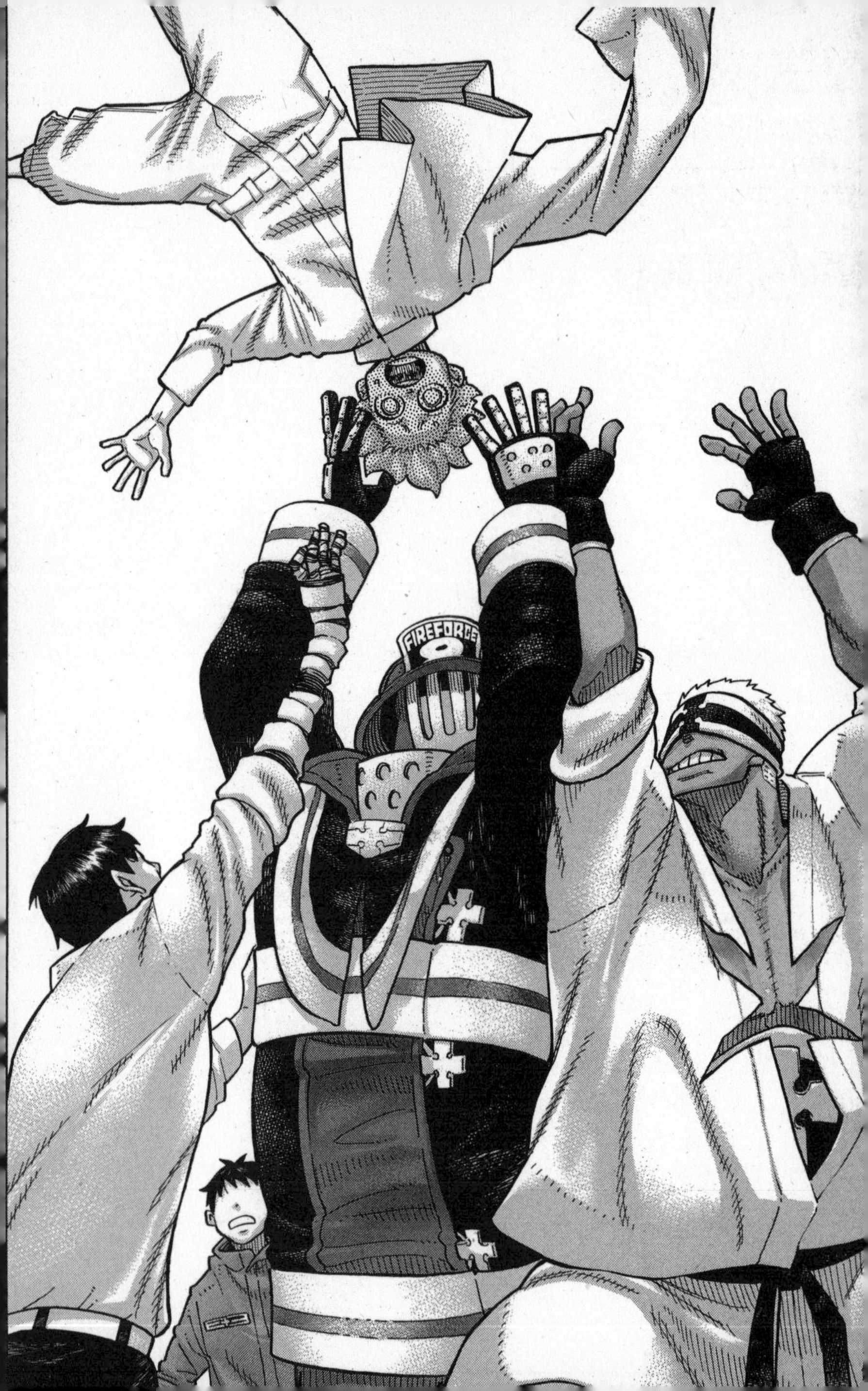
FIREFORCE

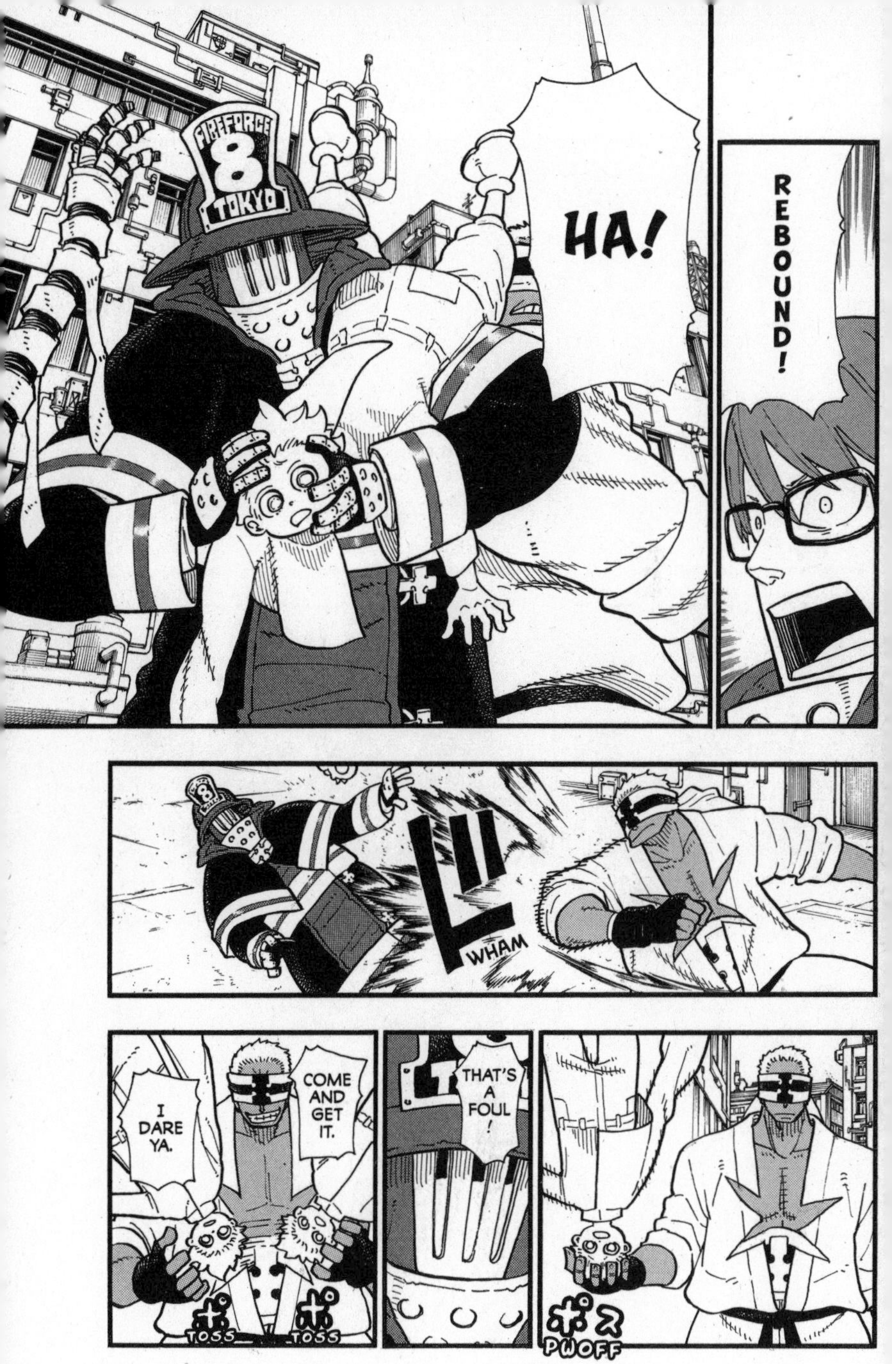
REBOUND!
HA!
WHAM
PWOFF
ポス
THAT'S A FOUL!
COME AND GET IT.
I DARE YA.
ポ
TOSS
ポ
TOSS

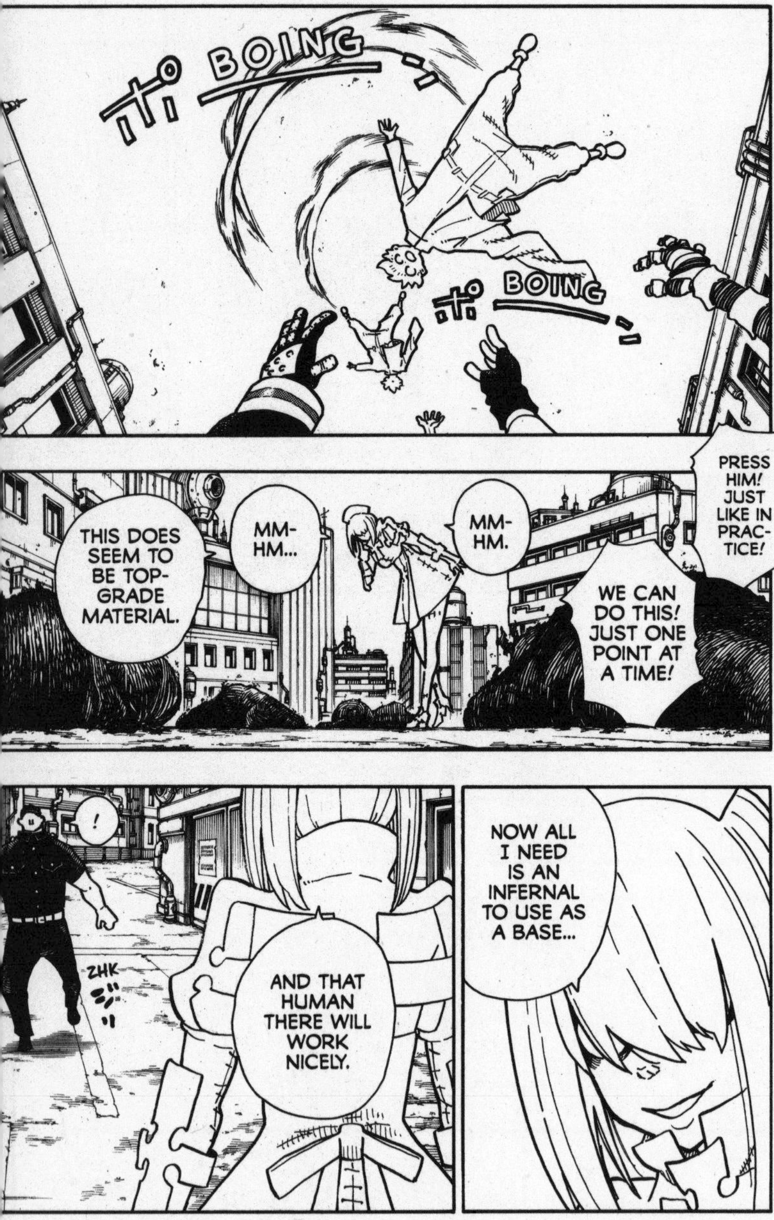
BOING
BOING
PRESS HIM! JUST LIKE IN PRACTICE!
WE CAN DO THIS! JUST ONE POINT AT A TIME!
MM-HM.
MM-HM...
THIS DOES SEEM TO BE TOP-GRADE MATERIAL.
NOW ALL I NEED IS AN INFERNAL TO USE AS A BASE...
AND THAT HUMAN THERE WILL WORK NICELY.
!
ZHK

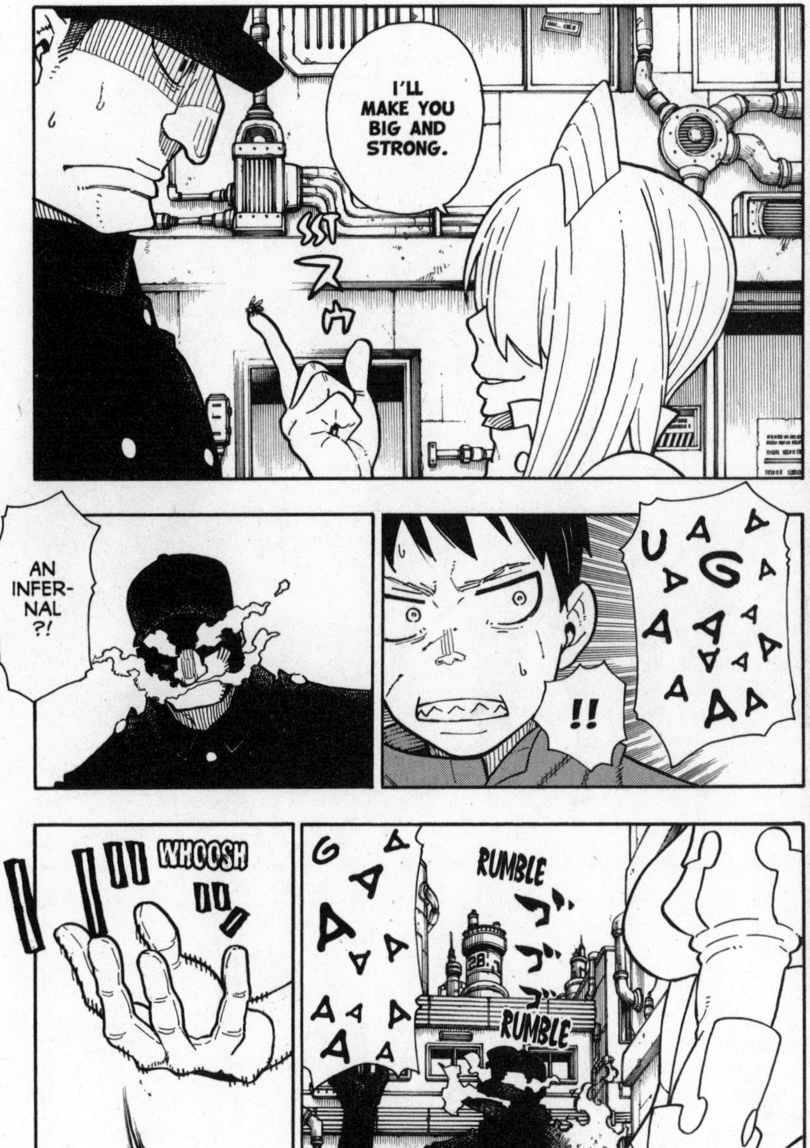
I'LL MAKE YOU BIG AND STRONG.
SST
スゥ
UAGAAAAAAAAAAAAAA
!!
AN INFERNAL?!
GAAAAAAAAAAA
RUMBLE
ゴゴゴ
RUMBLE
WHOOSH

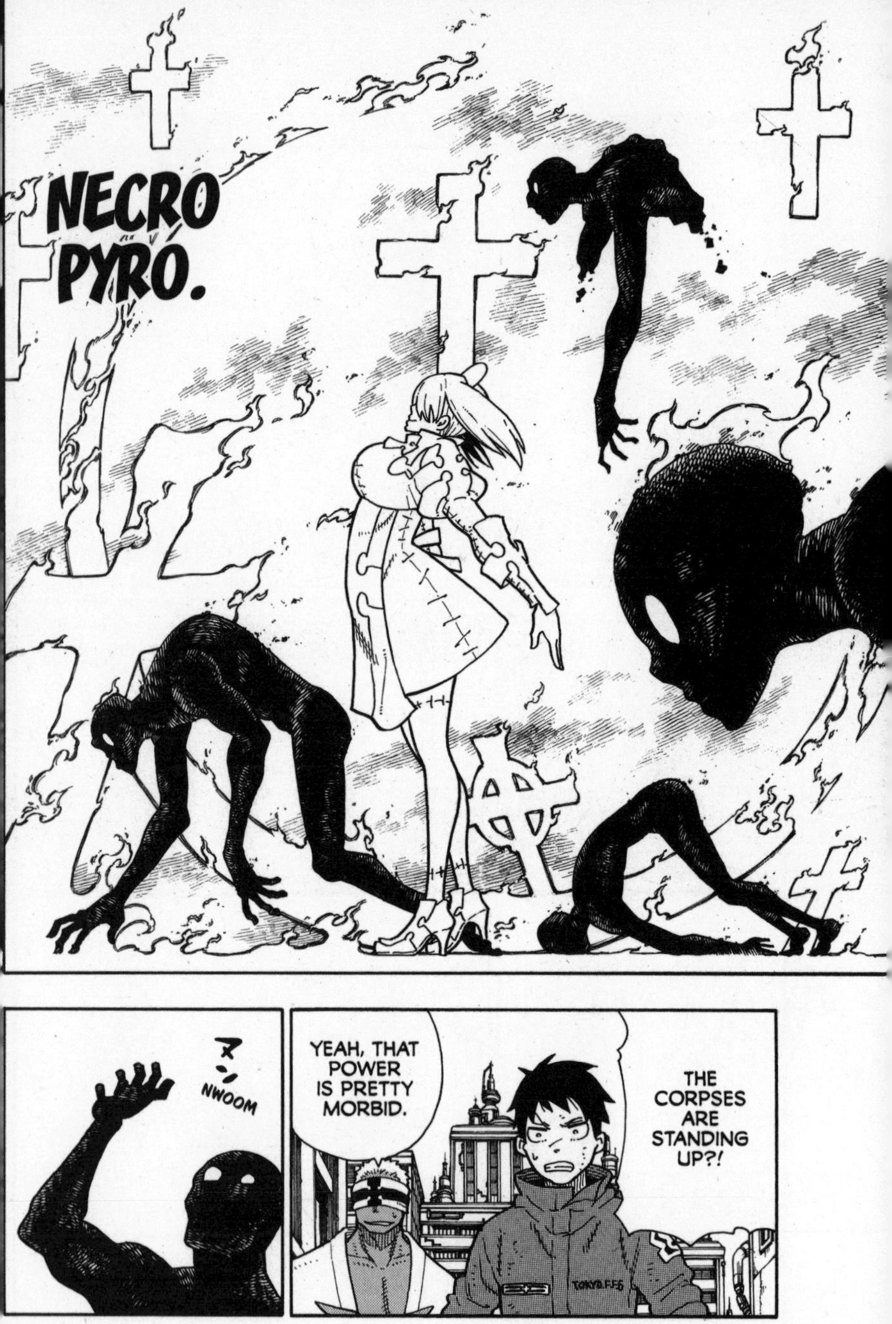
NECRO PYRO.
THE CORPSES ARE STANDING UP?!
YEAH, THAT POWER IS PRETTY MORBID.
NWOOM

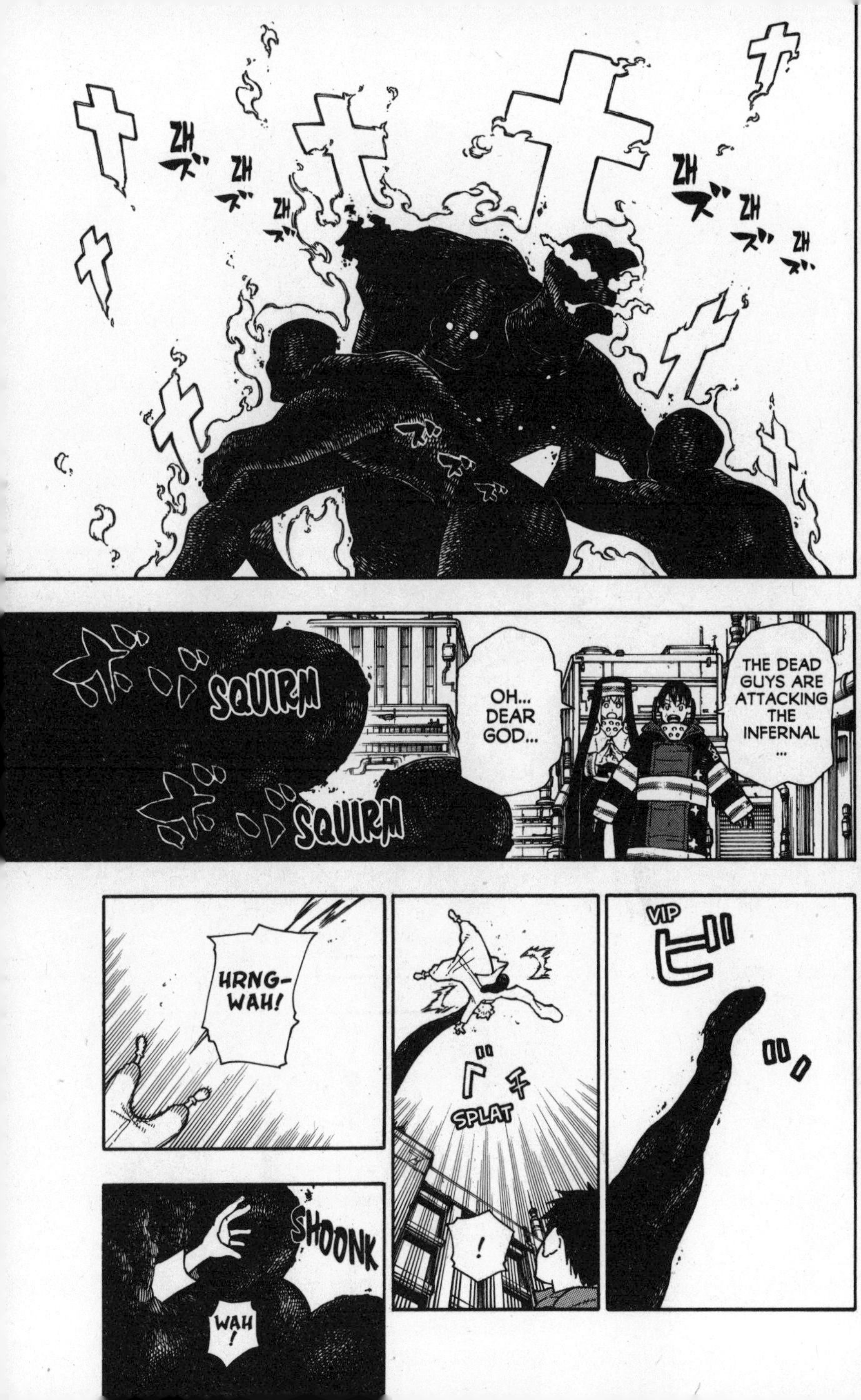
ZH
ZH
ZH
ZH
ZH
ZH
THE DEAD GUYS ARE ATTACKING THE INFERNAL ...
OH... DEAR GOD...
SQUIRM
SQUIRM
VIP
SPLAT
!
HRNG-WAH!
SHOONK
WAH!

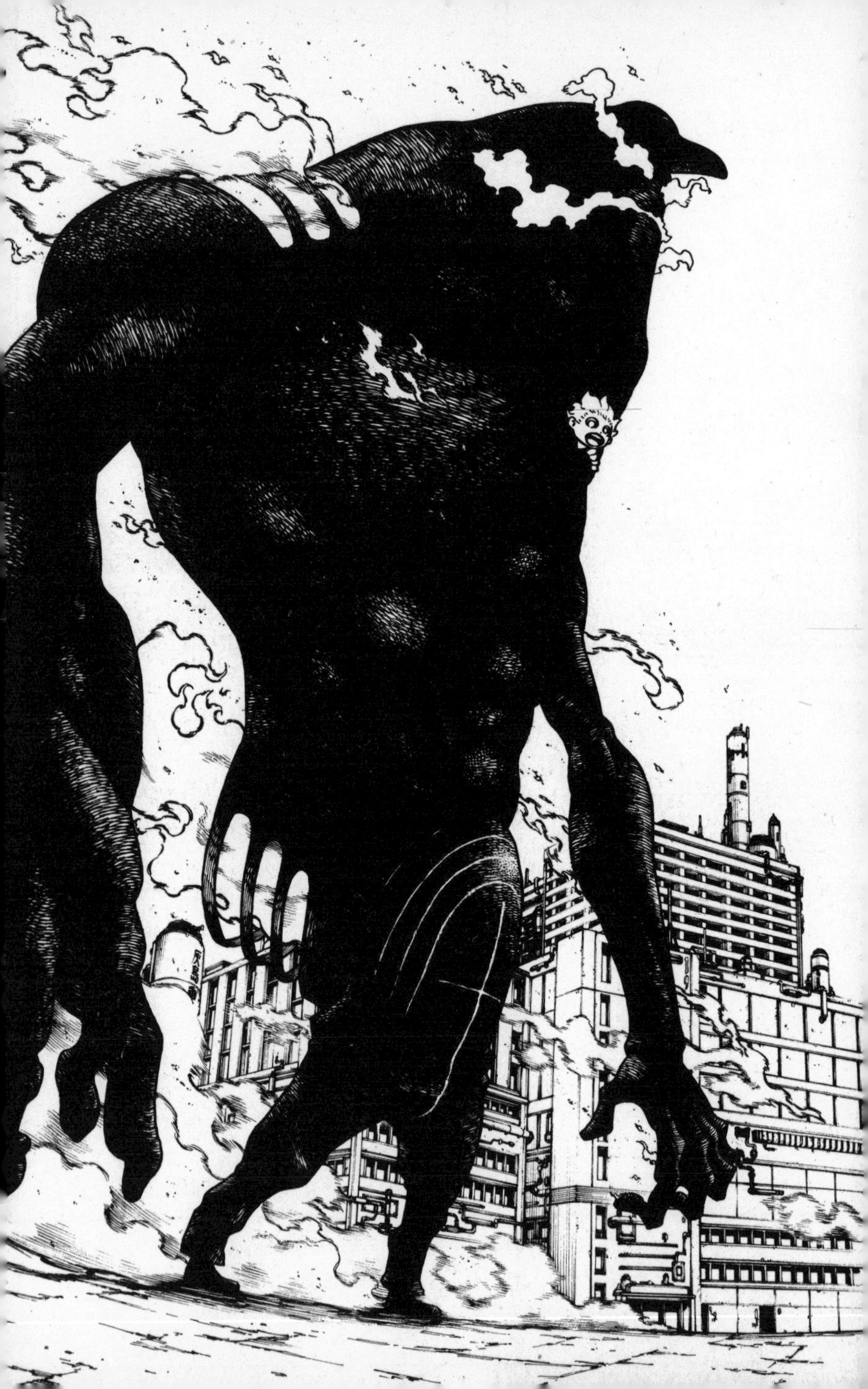

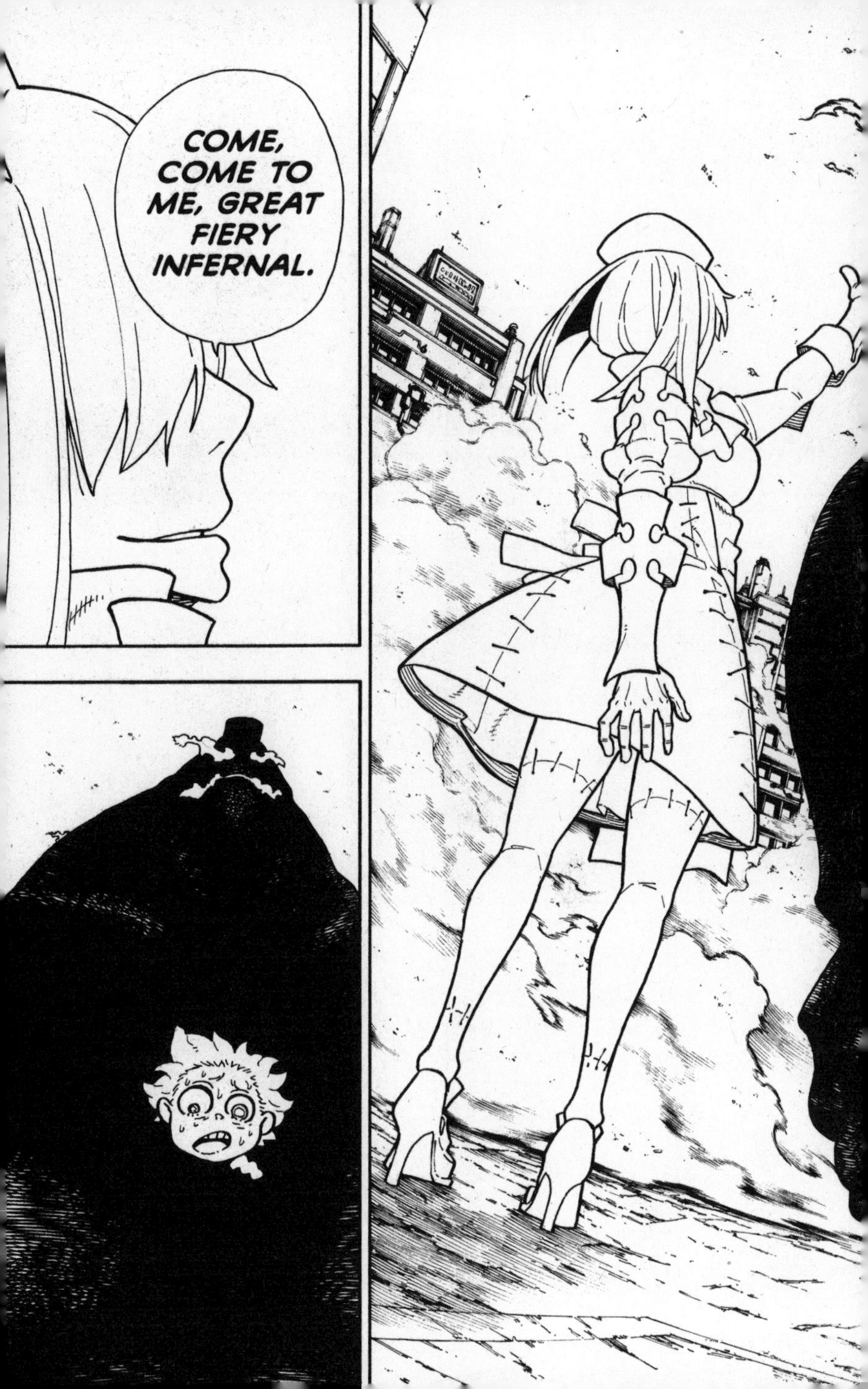
COME, COME TO ME, GREAT FIERY INFERNAL.

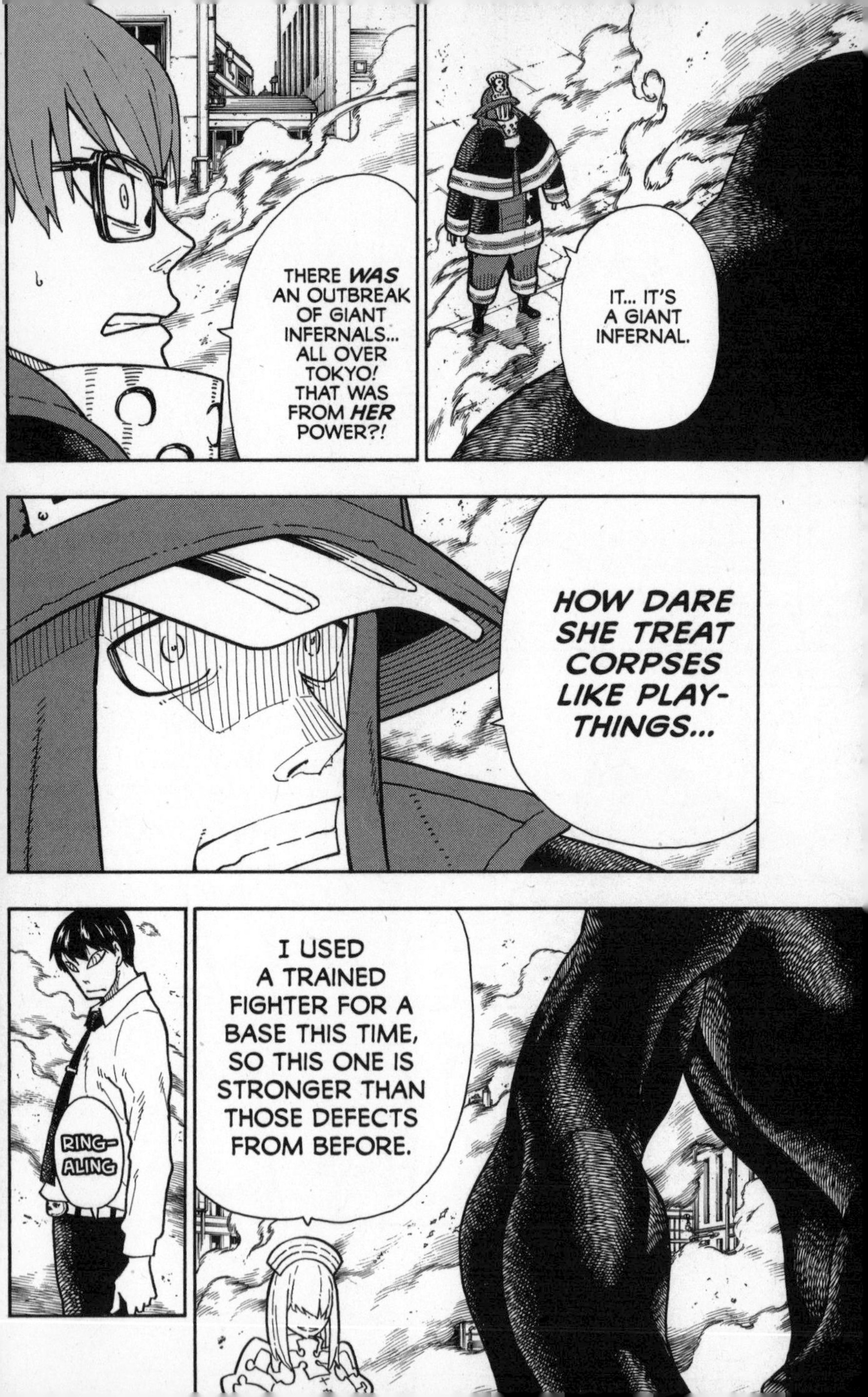
IT... IT'S A GIANT INFERNAL.
THERE WAS AN OUTBREAK OF GIANT INFERNALS... ALL OVER TOKYO! THAT WAS FROM HER POWER?!
HOW DARE SHE TREAT CORPSES LIKE PLAY-THINGS...
I USED A TRAINED FIGHTER FOR A BASE THIS TIME, SO THIS ONE IS STRONGER THAN THOSE DEFECTS FROM BEFORE.
RING-ALING

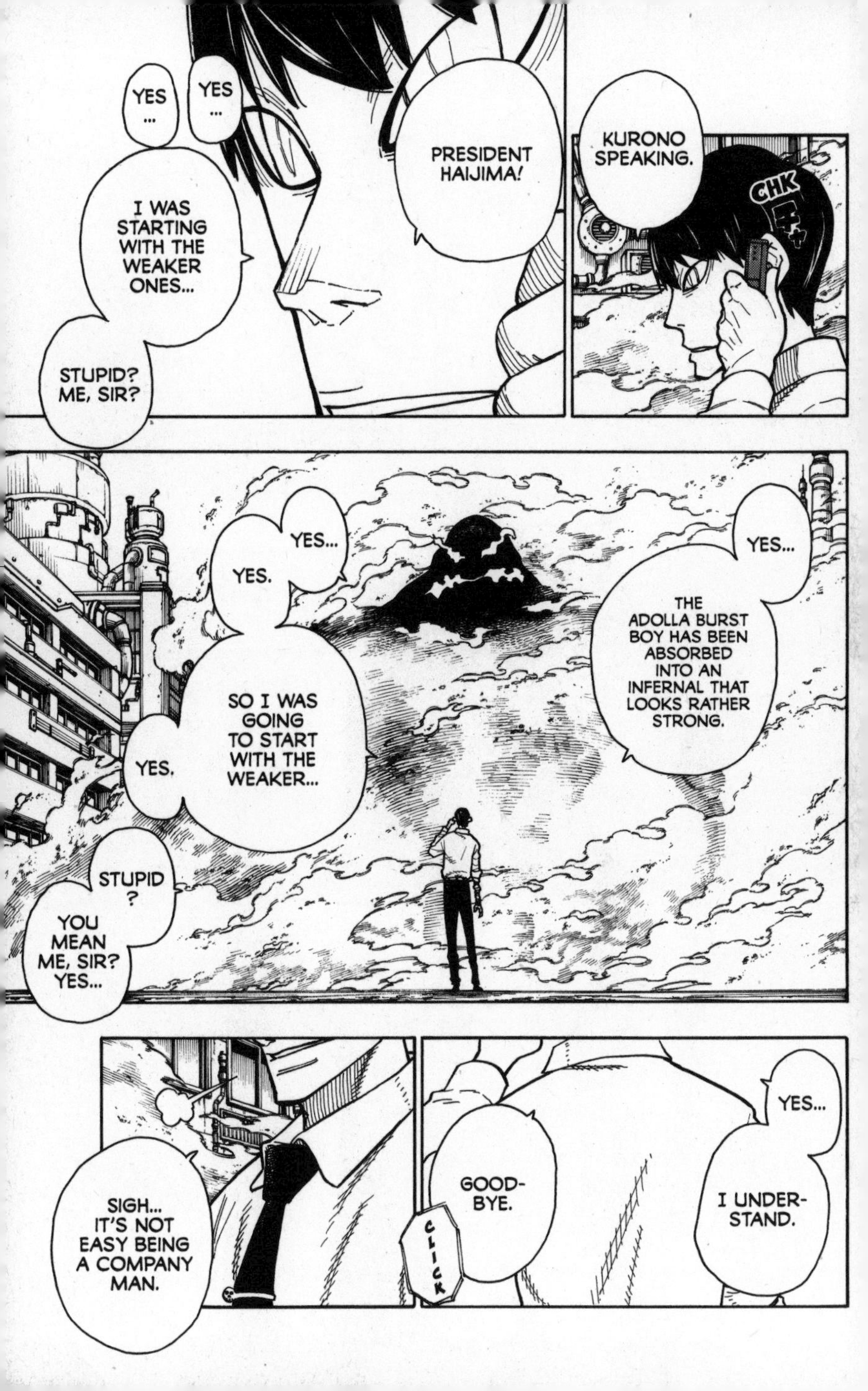
KURONO SPEAKING.
CHK
PRESIDENT HAIJIMA!
YES ...
YES ...
I WAS STARTING WITH THE WEAKER ONES...
STUPID? ME, SIR?
YES...
THE ADOLLA BURST BOY HAS BEEN ABSORBED INTO AN INFERNAL THAT LOOKS RATHER STRONG.
YES...
YES.
SO I WAS GOING TO START WITH THE WEAKER...
YES.
STUPID ? YOU MEAN ME, SIR? YES...
YES...
I UNDER-STAND.
GOOD-BYE.
CLICK
SIGH... IT'S NOT EASY BEING A COMPANY MAN.

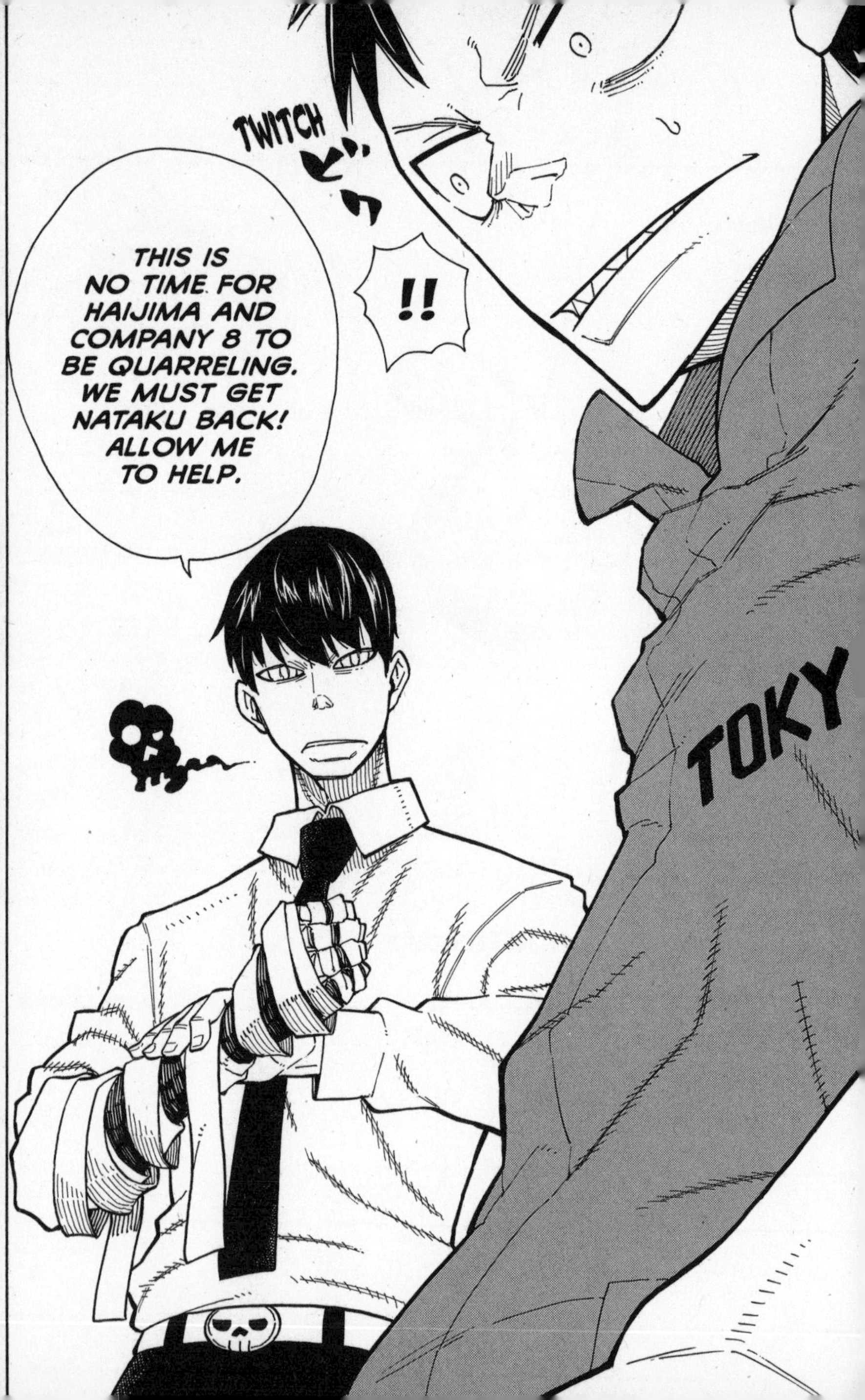
TWITCH
!!
THIS IS NO TIME FOR HAIJIMA AND COMPANY 8 TO BE QUARRELING. WE MUST GET NATAKU BACK! ALLOW ME TO HELP.
TOKY

TO BE CONTINUED IN VOLUME 17!!

Translation Notes:

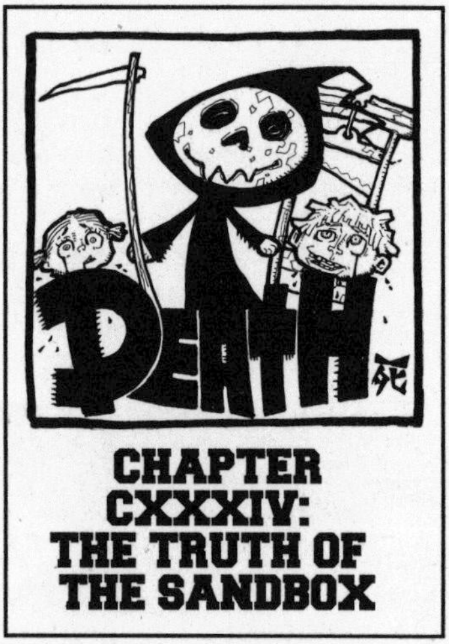
DEATH
死
CHAPTER CXXXIV: THE TRUTH OF THE SANDBOX

The Truth of the Sandbox, page 27

Here, the word "sandbox" is a reference to a box full of sand that children play in, as well as a translation of *hakoniwa*, which literally means "box garden" and refers to a miniature garden or diorama, usually kept in a box. The term *hakoniwa* is often used in fiction to describe an isolated community.

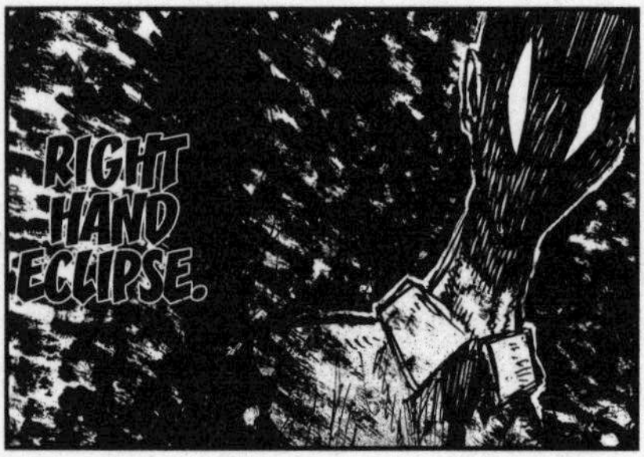
RIGHT HAND ECLIPSE.

Right Eclipse, page 46

In his attacks, Kurono uses the word *shoku*, which is the Japanese word for "eclipse." It is written with the same character as for *mushibamu*, a word that means "to eat away at."

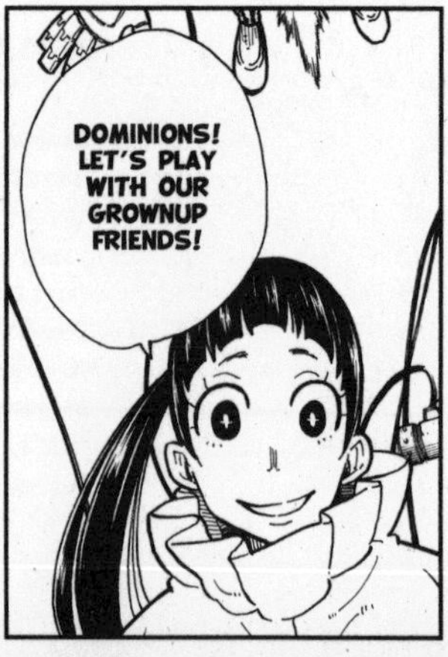
DOMINIONS! LET'S PLAY WITH OUR GROWNUP FRIENDS!

Dominions, page 83

True to her angel belt buckle, this Haijima employee prefers to name her minions after ranks of angels. According to *De Coelesti Hierarchia*, a book on the celestial hierarchy, Dominions are the highest rank of the second, or middle, sphere of angels.

Sanchin style launch stance, page 102

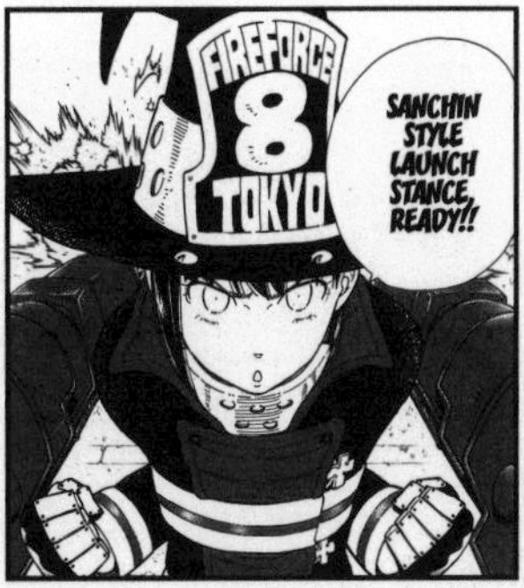
FIREFORCE
8
TOKYO
SANCHIN STYLE LAUNCH STANCE, READY!!

Sanchin, meaning "three battles" or "three conflicts," is a stance (or kata) in karate. It is the most basic stance in Okinawan-style karate and promotes stability and strength.

Jai, page 111

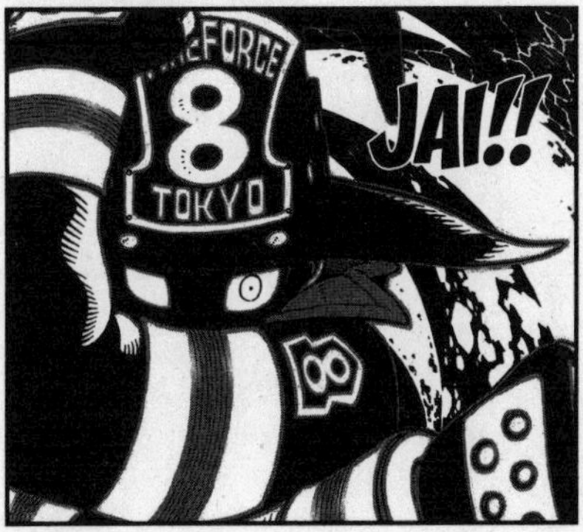
8
TOKYO
JAI!!

In this instance, Maki's choice of words for her *kiai* shout (see volume 4 notes: Sei) sounds remarkably like the Hindi word *jai*, meaning "victory." In India, "Jai Bhim" is used as a greeting, and it means roughly "victory to Bhim." The phrase is commemorative of Bhimrao Ramji Ambedkar, a social reformer who campaigned against discrimination and supported the rights of women and laborers. To someone unfamiliar with the spelling of the phrase, it may sound like the speaker is about to fire a beam of some sort.

Great Fiery Infernal, page 183

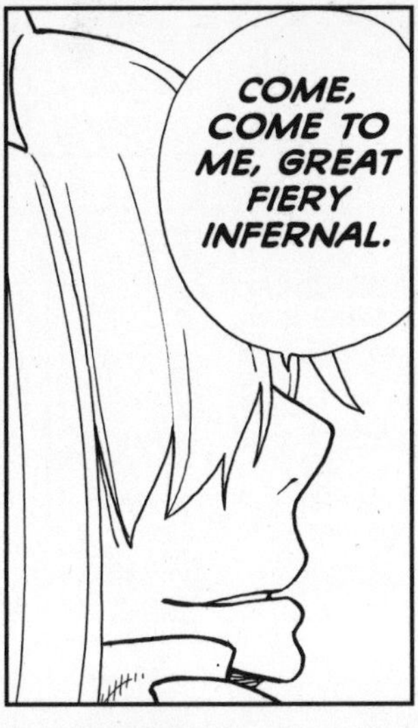
COME, COME TO ME, GREAT FIERY INFERNAL.

When summoning this massive creature, Ritsu uses an incantation similar to one used by Wataru Toki and Koyomi Himekuri in Yattodetaman, a classic anime from 1981. Wataru and Koyomi summon a robot named Dai Kyojin, which means "Great Giant God." As further evidence that Ritsu is a fan, instead the usual word for Infernal (*homurabito*), the incantation uses the alternate pronunciation of *enjin*, which more closely resembles *kyojin*.

AFTERWORD MANGA: ATSUSHIYA

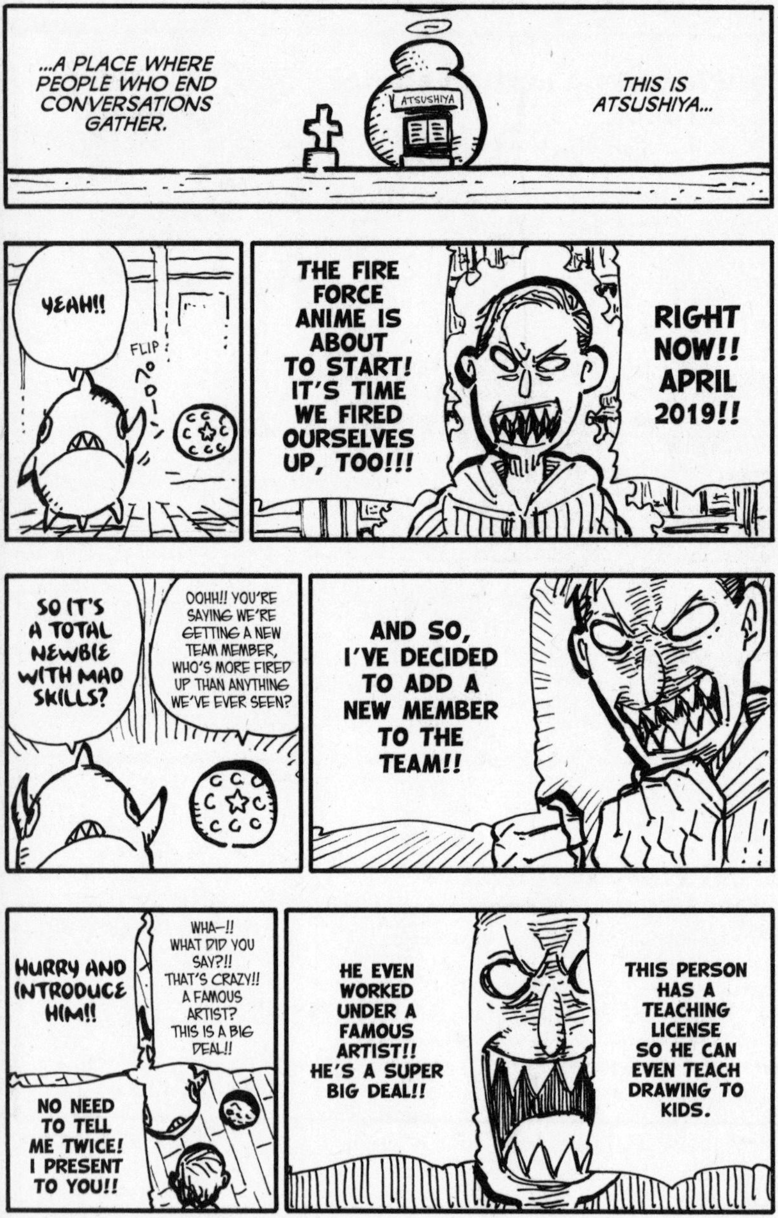
THIS IS ATSUSHIYA...
...A PLACE WHERE PEOPLE WHO END CONVERSATIONS GATHER.
ATSUSHIYA
RIGHT NOW!! APRIL 2019!!
THE FIRE FORCE ANIME IS ABOUT TO START! IT'S TIME WE FIRED OURSELVES UP, TOO!!!
YEAH!!
FLIP
AND SO, I'VE DECIDED TO ADD A NEW MEMBER TO THE TEAM!!
OOHH!! YOU'RE SAYING WE'RE GETTING A NEW TEAM MEMBER, WHO'S MORE FIRED UP THAN ANYTHING WE'VE EVER SEEN?
SO IT'S A TOTAL NEWBIE WITH MAD SKILLS?
THIS PERSON HAS A TEACHING LICENSE SO HE CAN EVEN TEACH DRAWING TO KIDS.
HE EVEN WORKED UNDER A FAMOUS ARTIST!! HE'S A SUPER BIG DEAL!!
WHA-!! WHAT DID YOU SAY?!! THAT'S CRAZY!! A FAMOUS ARTIST? THIS IS A BIG DEAL!!
HURRY AND INTRODUCE HIM!!
NO NEED TO TELL ME TWICE! I PRESENT TO YOU!!

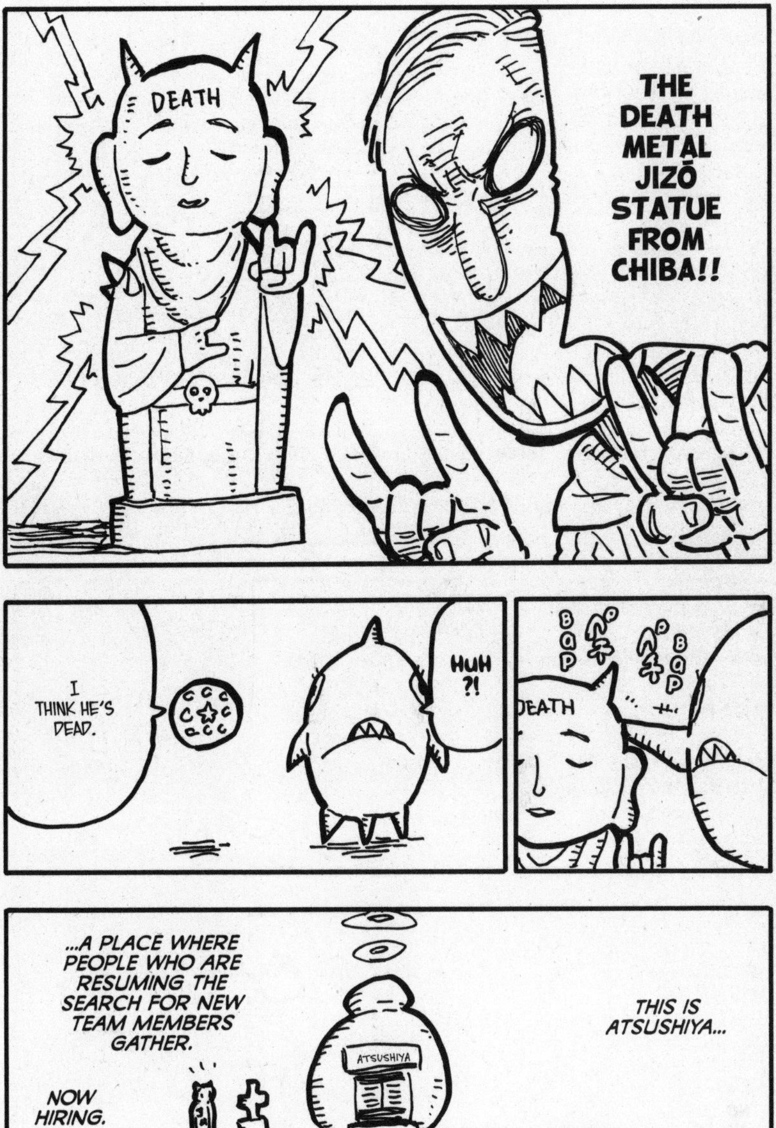
DEATH
THE DEATH METAL JIZŌ STATUE FROM CHIBA!!
BAP
ペチ
BAP
ペチ
DEATH
HUH ?!
I THINK HE'S DEAD.
THIS IS ATSUSHIYA...
...A PLACE WHERE PEOPLE WHO ARE RESUMING THE SEARCH FOR NEW TEAM MEMBERS GATHER.
ATSUSHIYA
NOW HIRING.

A Kodansha Comics Trade Paperback Original.

Published in the United States by Kodansha Comics, an imprint of Kodansha USA Publishing, LLC, New York.

Publication rights for this English edition arranged through Kodansha Ltd., Tokyo.

First published in Japan in 2019 by Kodansha Ltd., Tokyo.

ISBN 978-1-63236-789-1

Printed in the United States of America.

www.kodanshacomics.com

9 8 7 6 5 4 3 2 1

Translation: Alethea Nibley & Athena Nibley
Lettering: AndWorld Design
Editing: Haruko Hashimoto, Lauren Scanlan
Kodansha Comics edition cover design: Phil Balsman